$22.⁹⁵

FIRST EDITION

# 300 YEARS OF
# HOUSEKEEPING
## COLLECTIBLES

Tools & Fittings
of the
Laundry Room, Broom Closet, Dustbin,
Clothes Closet & Bathroom

by

## LINDA CAMPBELL FRANKLIN

Author of *300 Years of Kitchen Collectibles*

1,500 + Fully-described Price Listings
Hundreds of Items Pictured

Together with Pithy Advice for Collectors and Dealers,
Opinions in Polished Prose, and a
Fund of Fascinating Facts from Cookbooks, Trade Catalogs,
Encyclopedias of Arts & Manufactures
and Periodical Advertisements

BOOKS AMERICANA
INC.

ISBN 0-89689-093-7

Copyright © 1992 by Linda Campbell Franklin, exclusive marketing and publishing rights retained by Books Americana, Inc., P.O. Box 2326, Florence, Alabama 35630. All rights reserved. No part of the book may be used or reproduced in any manner whatsoever without permission, except in the case of brief quotations embodied in critical articles or reviews.

This book is dedicated to all my family and friends,
who have forgiven my poor housekeeping,
and who haven't forgotten the real me!
Thanks to my patient and creative parents,
Mary Mac and Robert Franklin; my ironing teacher,
Willie Lee Burton; and my brother, Robbie, who claims
I taught him to read, and who helped teach me to write.
Thanks also to all the readers who wrote
and sent me pictures, information and encouragement.
To all of you:
Remember that dust exists so that we can see the sunbeams!

*Adnil Nilknarf, sometime housekeeper and authoress, gets an assist from her busy beagle Darwin, whose specialties are D.W.A. (Dust Wagged Aloft), and a scoot 'n' lick method of kitchen floor polishing. A new cat, DuMonticello, is a Maine Dusting Cat, who was found eating popcorn at a gas station. His specialties are the unseen interiors of bookcases — behind the books where matter is often misplaced, and tchotchke-laden table and piano tops too. (Tchotchke, pronounced chahtz'key, means knicknack in Yiddish). DuMonticello also does really swift lateral dust-elephant elimination from under beds, but he needs considerable brushing afterward. Nilknarf wields some newly-developed de-dirting tools; strapped to her upper left arm — a ball-bearing two-ended broom that is twirled like a baton; a battery-operated reciprocating feather duster is strapped to her other arm, and, for easy gliding from room to room, she's wearing roller skates equipped with frontal whisks. They are also useful for stirring up dust whirlwinds which cut visibility to an inch or so, and create such magnificent solar flares that visitors are enraptured and forget to look around. NOTE: The spider is friendly but has no name as yet.*

# TABLE OF CONTENTS

\* \* \*

Picture is from ad in Century magazine, December 1888, for ''Albany Perforated Wrapping Paper Co., Albany, NY, toilet paper, and nickel-plated cast brass fixture. The 1888 price for two 1000-sheet rolls (wrapped in tin foil) and the fixture was $1.30. Today's price for the fixture alone would be about $40.00-$65.00. See the Bathroom Chapter for more on the subject.

\* \* \*

**Cover picture, with values**: Counterclockwise from upper left. Dimpled and bumped red rubber massage roller with wooden handles (about $45.00); aluminum spring clothespin from before or after WWII ($6.00); crocheted cotton potholder, 1940s ($3.00); handmade perforated metal soap saver ($25.00-$45.00); large wooden blanket pin ($12.00-$18.00); fancy wire hanger, c.1900 ($25.00-$55.00); common modern pins; wrought iron primitive snake-head sadiron, early 19th C ($85.00-$125.00); shoeshine kit, c.1930s, with polish & brush ($15.00-$20.00). Photograph by Bill LeFevor.

# INTRODUCTION
## TRENDS & THE FUTURE
## OF DOING HOUSEWORK

Electricity, gas, and now electronics have truly made cooking easier. Even such things as pressure cookers, or stainless pans with copper bottoms, or no-stick coatings, which we take for granted now, are indisputably labor-saving. Convenience foods, frozen foods, canned foods and the availability of take-out prepared meals have made of cooking a thing on which to spend discretionary time; some people still spend many hours preparing one meal, but others have fled the kitchen with glee. (Others have gone into retro-cooking and study old-fashioned hearth-cooking methods.) In the past, cooking wasn't given its own dedicated day — unlike washing (Monday), ironing (Tuesday), baking (Wednesday), sweeping and dusting (Thursday), housecleaning — scrubbing, polishing, scouring (Friday), and more baking plus cleaning the kitchen and all its equipment (Saturday).

Laundry is a housekeeping job which has definitely benefitted from modern, convenient labor-saving appliances and devices, and by certain not-necessarily preferred fabrics and fiber blends. The most time-consuming job is ironing, and even that can be obviated by ironing machines (mangles), and touch-up pressing rather than intensive ironing.

The housekeeper can cook in one place, and launder in one place. This is not the case with housecleaning.

In housecleaning, the whole house is that "one place", and the housekeeper must move around all over it, thinking and making repetitive motions for hours. No matter how much mechanical power, how much improved suction, how much cordless wattage, nor how much planning and organization there is, cleaning a house has always been and still is very labor intensive. In the 19th century, especially in the last half of it, after the mass-production of objects was widespread, houses started to fill up with a clutter unparalleled except in my basement. At the same time cleaning capabilities improved, germ- and bacteria-awareness rose, so that expectations (and guilt) escalated. Preachers, professional "homemakers", product advertisers, and children's fairy tale-tellers have laid it on thick: a clean house is the mirror of a (saved) soul. In 1867, an editor wrote in *The Englishwoman's Domestic Magazine* that "If with one part of his brain he [mankind] invents a labour-saving appliance, the other lobes immediately create as much new labour as the apparatus saves." Just when women were able to cope better with housecleaning because of all the newly-invented labor-serving devices, here came the designers and arbiters of fashion with frou-frous and furbelow up to (and including) the ceiling. Furniture, lighting fixtures, decorations and carpets were all just so many dust-catchers. And think of what those added ruffles did to the job of ironing.

It's arguable that housecleaning is as labor intensive in 1992 as it was a century ago, although lifting and carrying heavy loads (of wet clothes, parlor carpets, carved furniture) is not often a factor now. One problem today is that for close to 50 years, television commercials have been adding to housewives' psychological burdens by odious comparisons to an ideal, and by emphasizing, even exaggerating, all kinds of smellable, malefactory, unhealthful crevices and crannies we might have been able to ignore if so much light hadn't been turned on the subject!

Imagine what effect new video-telephones will have!

Is there hope in sight?

Maria Gay Humphries, author of a sort of how-to book called *House and Home*, published for housewives and housekeepers in 1896, wrote that "A busy woman is accustomed to say that her idea of the house of the future is one that can be cleaned with a hose." Not a bad idea!

Until there's a switch next to the front door that can be flipped as you leave the house, a switch that activates built-in, computer-directed laser microwaves or sonic vibrations that are capable of dust-sucking, decobwebbing, stain-removing, bed-making, toilet bowl-scouring, cushion-fluffing, sink-scrubbing, splatter-removing, rug-straightening, grease-dissolving, brass-polishing, vase-emptying, wood-waxing, catbox-changing, mildew-subduing, book-straightening, mirror-wiping, and lint-picking, housework will keep on being hard work.

# TRENDS & THE FUTURE
## OF COLLECTING
## HOUSEKEEPING TOOLS & APPLIANCES

It isn't a profound observation, but the general trend in collecting is for increasing numbers of people to collect more and more categories of things, including ordinary household objects. Now, if there's something not collected, I haven't heard of it. It used to be a minority of men and women who collected anything at all; and stamps, coins and dolls were the three most popular categories into the 1950s or so. About 1960, an art movement called Pop Art changed the way many people looked at things. They weren't necessarily willing to call a soup can "art", but they saw everything around them with new interest. While the Dada absurdist movement of 40 years before had emphasized, probably intentionally, the differences between Us [artists and the avante garde] and Them [the rube-cube public], Pop Art actually became very popular.

And maybe that's why people collect all the things in the book, or will soon if they don't now. Only a really profound change in attitude toward material objects, or some cataclysm of nature, or some new compelling pursuits will make people stop collecting. Or we could psychoanalyze it to death, I suppose. Maybe so many of us collect because we just can't stand to see things go to waste, and, hey!, we're saving landfill space!

This is particularly apropos when it comes to housecleaning artifacts. Since the early to mid-1980s, collectors have sought vacuum cleaners, dustpans, brushes and brooms. In the late 1980s, a symbolically important object — the wastebasket — was added. Not just any wastebaskets, but designer baskets. A pair of Art Deco plated mesh baskets designed by Emile-Jacques Ruhlmann (better known for his furniture) sold one at a time at an auction in 1989. $25,000.00 for the first, and $30,000.00 for the second. At a Savoia auction in South Cairo, NY, in January 1992, a marked Roycroft wastebasket in the Arts & Crafts style, with vertical slats of wood, sold for $1,250.00. Twisted wire or metal mesh office-type wastebaskets have been popular for a while, so much so that brand new ones are now being made and sold for upwards of $35.00, to people who want the look, but want neither the old grime, nor to spend time looking for an old one.

In the laundering field, sadirons and early gas-fueled irons, then early electric irons, are long-established collectibles. In the early 1980s, people began collecting ironing boards. In the fall of 1991, I saw a bulky 1870s folding ironing board, adjustable for standing and sitting at, for $175.00; that was the highest price I've seen to date (February 1992) for ironing boards. At a Mike Fallon (Copake, NY) auction on New Year's Day 1992, a handmade all-wood washboard, 30 inches long, sold at auction for $450.00. This followed by a few months an exhibit of utilitarian objects as art, at Aarne Anton's American Primitive Gallery in New York, which included some zoomorphic washing sticks, used to stir the roiling mass of clothes in the huge wash kettle. The sale also followed, by a couple of years, an exhibition of wooden and cast iron washboards at the prestigious O.K. Harris art gallery in New York City. In 1991, carpet beaters were given a show ("Rug Beaters 'r' Us") at O.K. Harris, by its proprietor, Ivan Karp. Most of the beaters were from the private collection of Denis Silva; those for sale were from dealer Bob "Primitive Man" Cahn (Carmel, NY), known up and down the Eastern Seaboard for his perceptive eye for old tools.

It seems a significant trend that art dealers are attending to objects used in cooking and housecleaning, objects that twenty years ago were derided as too mundane, too ubiquitous, for a serious antiques person, let alone an art dealer, to notice.

In the mid-1980s, I bought a coiled wire clothes hanger from one of my favorite dealers, Lenny Kislin, at a Pier Show in New York. I paid $25.00 for it, and recognized, as had Lenny, that much of its visual power comes from its abstract resemblance to an eagle. It is like a line drawing in three dimensions. I thought I was on the cutting edge of a new hot-ticket item, but I had company. For one thing, the famous Dada artist Man Ray had made a sculpture out of clothes hangers some 65 years before; and others were silently collecting them in the 1980s. Some four of five years before I bought my first hanger, dealer/collector Harris Diamant had bought his first — the same simple frame covered with a graduated coil of tinned steel spring that had attracted me.

In February of 1991, a folk art and antiques gallery, Ricco-Maresca of New York, exhibited ("Out of the Closet: American Hangers") over 150 hangers from Diamant's collection. The collection was for sale — $60,000.00 for all, or $15,000.00 for each of four parts. This exhibit took the fancy of many, and was written up in a number of trade and non-trade publications. In an article in *Maine Antique Digest* by Lita Solis-Cohen (herself a collector of clothespins), dealer Frank Maresca was quoted as saying he and his partner Roger Ricco hoped the show of clothes hangers "will wake people up and help them see."

If people will wake up and see, there'll be no end to this collecting of interesting utilitarian household objects.

---

## BEHIND THE BROOM

As you may have guessed, from reading my remarks on housecleaning, as well as the several quotations (in particular see "Unprincipled Neatness" on page three) I've chosen to put throughout the book, I have housecleaning on my mind. I have a file marked "Clean & Neat", with assorted clippings I've collected for the last ten years or so.

I would like to get letters from men, women and children who have any thoughts at all about the practice or philosophy of neatness and housecleaning as it relates to their lives. How might the pressure of housecleaning (or room-cleaning) have affected these aspects of your life: your hospitality, spontaneity, married state, sociability, response to advertising, private guilt feelings, leisure time, competitiveness, creativity, freedom, house-pride, education, etc. I am particularly interested in hearing from two or three generations of the same family. I am also interested in how your feelings and your practices might have changed over time.

I have prepared a questionnaire which might help to jog your thoughts, and would allow you to reply anonymously if you wish. There will be no coded marks to assist the Neat Squad!

Write me directly (and I'd love to get a #10 SASE to help with the postage):
Linda C. Franklin, 2716 Northfield Rd., Charlottesville, VA 22901.

# I. HOUSECLEANING:
## SWEEP, DUST, VACUUM & THROW OUT

I've got a nerve. I sit here doing this chapter in the most UN-thrown-out surroundings you can imagine. I started it in NYC, where taped to a shelf on the case behind my typing chair is a clipping about how people with messy desks are "more popular and generally more creative" than people with perfectly cleaned-off desks. (In January 1990, Ann Landers said "Mental Illness May Be Cause of Messiness." Thanks, Ann). I finished the chapter in our basement in Charlottesville — keeping dust elephants at bay with my feet and an occasional dampened Kleenex. Roughly, the number of pieces of paper within three feet of my chair is 10,000 (excluding 3300 sheets in the computer paper box); I'm proud that roughly three-quarters of them are filed, only one-quarter are piled.

My fascination with dustpans and brooms is easy: obviously I consider them art objects rather than useful objects. More and more people seem to find them appealing collectibles too, so competition is building. Some of the most unpredictable and astoundingly high prices since 1988 have been achieved for dustpans and wastebaskets. Well… ecological ramifications of waste disposal are big issues now. Might "Let It Be" become a rallying cry? Some futurists have suggested teaching Americans about the problems of dumps by making every American dump all their garbage and trash in their backyards (or fire escapes?) for just one week. Matter has to become either matter or energy, it won't just disappear. Me? I'm doing my part by storing *my* dustpans, fly swatters, brooms, etc., in their natural environment!

I don't know anybody who collects fly swatters except me, so I put a **Futurewatch** on them. There are few wastebasket collectors — so ditto for those. Brooms are somewhat more popular, as are vacuum cleaners. Fly traps are a well-established field; they're a sort of byway of bottle and glass collecting. I hope you find something appealing here.

---

Bed warmer, also called a warming pan. Copper pan with turned maple handle, pierced floral decoration in lid, English or American, early 19th C. • In the Oct. 11, 1890 *The Metal Worker. A Weekly Journal of the Stove, Roofing, Cornice, Tin, Plumbing & Heating Trades,* published in NYC, appeared the 16th installment of an occasional series of articles by John Fuller, entitled "Art of Coppersmithing". This one deals with making old fashioned warming pans. It forces collectors 100 years later to assume that a good number of copper warming pans were made by metal workers who were intrigued by the article. a good number of copper warming pans were made by metal workers who were intrigued by the article. Fuller introduced his subject by writing "Copper warming pans were once quite largely in demand, and kept men busy at work for a considerable time during the year, as almost every household, rich or poor, possessed a warming pan, and it is presumed it would be a difficult task to-day to find a house in the rural districts of England without its warming pan, many of them having been *handed down from father to son for generations.*" (Italics mine. Note that he is not saying the art of making them was passed down, but rather the pans themselves, leading one to suppose that perhaps warming the beds was a man's job?) Fuller states unequivocably "They were made in five sizes — namely, 10, 10 1/2, 11, 11 1/2 and 12 inch." Throughout, Fuller uses "was" and "is", without explaining the basis for the facts stated about the past. His information about sheets of copper may refer to a size that was standard in the 18th C as well as 1890. Fuller tells how to "make one to measure 11 inches, and from 10 pound plate (the plate or brazier's sheet, by which the strength was designated, measured 2 feet wide by 4 feet in length). …" Does he mean that a 2 x 4 foot sheet might weigh more or less than 10 pounds, and that it is the gauge not the "strength" that is told by "10 pound plate"? He goes on to tell how: to measure the discs cut from a sheet, that they be hammered up to form a slightly flared-sided pan

with brim to "receive cover"; and to make a perforated cover, and a tubular socket to be riveted to the pan for the handle, usually about 1 1/2 inches in diameter and 5 feet long, turned from some nice looking wood and oiled." • The hammered up and "razed" down pan body is made with ancient methods; if you found one with dovetailed seams along the sides, it wasn't made to Fuller's plan. A dovetailed seam around the outside bottom would probably be an indication of repair rather than original construction. *(Fuller's articles became a book, Art of Coppersmithing, 319 pp, pub'd in several early 1900s editions.)* **$275.00-$300.00**

Bed warmer, copper pan, ornate baluster-turned wooden long handle, with "traces of old spiral graining", the lid of the pan has only 12 small holes around perimeter, but is engraved with large design of flowers & bird, rather unusual for that, European or American, 45'L, poss. 2nd quarter 19th C. • It is said by some that the holes in the lid of warming pans was to allow the escape of "fumes and smoke", but actually they served as draft vents so that the hot coals inside wouldn't die before all the beds were warmed. • This reached $375.00 at the Garth Auction, May 26-27, 1989, Delaware, OH. **$350.00-$450.00**

Bed warmer, floral decorated pierced brass, turned wooden handle originally painted black, English or American, early 19th C. • The black on the handle should almost be like a fine polished ebony. **$275.00-$300.00**

Bed warmer, pieced & hammered brass, shallow pan with hinged perforated lid in pattern of stars and sort of tiny gothic arch cutouts, long turned wooden handle, English (?), 34"L, very early 19th C. **$275.00-$350.00**

• In William Hone's *The Table Book,* published in London about 1827, we find the following amusing story, **"The Thing to a T"**. "A young man, brought up in the city of London to the business of an undertaker, went to Jamaica to better his condition. Business flourished, and he wrote to his father in Bishopsgate-street to send him, with a quantity of black and grey cloth, twenty gross of black Tacks. Unfortunately he had omitted the top to his T, and the order stood twenty gross of black Jacks. His correspondent, on receiving the letter, recollected a man, near Fleet-market, who made quart and pint tin pots, ornamented with painting, and which were called black Jacks, and to him he gave the order for the twenty gross of black Jacks. The maker, surprised, said, he had not so many ready, but would endeavour to complete the order; this was done, and the articles were shipped. The undertaker received them with other consignments, and was astonished at the mistake. A friend, fond of speculation, offered consolation, by proposing to purchase the whole at the invoice price. The undertaker, glad to get rid of an article he considered useless in that part of the world, took the offer. His friend immediately advertised for sale a number of fashionable punch vases just arrived from England, and sold the jacks, gaining 200 per cent!

"The young undertaker afterwards discoursing upon his father's blunder, was told by his friend, in a jocose strain, to order a gross of warming-pans, and see whether the well-informed correspondents in London would have the sagacity to consider such articles necessary in the latitude of nine degrees north. The young man laughed at the suggestion, but really put in practice the joke. He desired his father in the next letter to send a gross of warming-pans, which actually, and to the great surprise of the son, reached the island of Jamaica. What to do with this cargo he knew not. His friend again became a purchaser at prime cost, and having knocked off the covers, informed the planters, that he had just imported a number of newly-constructed sugar ladles. The article under that name sold rapidly, and returned a large profit. The parties returned to England with fortunes, and often told the story of the black jacks and warming-pans over the bottle, adding, that "Nothing is lost in a good market.'"

Bed warmer, flower & scroll-decorated pierced lid, long turned wood handle, English or American, 33''L, late 18th or early 19th C. • "What — oh, whatever will future generations think of a warming-pan? already at the present day seen only in the hands of the clown in Christmas pantomimes, and by him employed as a weapon of offense. Let us trust that our descendants may be oblivious of any other purpose which the hideous article could serve, and that a fossil clown with an ancient warming-pan may be dug up somewhere or other for their edification.'' *The Metal Worker*, Dec. 9, 1882. **$275.00-$325.00**

Bottle brush—See Upholstery brush.
Broom, birch splint, for brushing out brick oven, 12''L, early 19th C. **$45.00-$60.00**
Broom, birch splint with wood handle, for small jobs, Otsego Co., NY, 7''L, 1859. **$50.00-$60.00**
Broom, push type, possibly for scrubbing floors, 45 cornshucks still attached to woody ends and stalk tips, set 5 rows x 9 into holes in plank, long broomstick handle set at angle, American, 5 feet long, 19th C. **$300.00-$450.00**
Broom, splint, for hearths, American, 54''L, early 19th C. **$85.00-$100.00**
Broom, wood splinters, early 19th C. **$45.00-$55.00**

Brush cleaner, metal, looks like cross between a rake & a fork, ''The Rapid Brush Cleaner'', American, early 20th C. **$18.00-$22.00**
Brush cleaner, nickeled metal, sort of a comb with a handle, cutout, flat crooked teeth, Fuller Brush Co., early 20th C. **$12.00-$15.00**
Candle snuffer — a misnomer commonly used for this tool, which is not meant for putting out the candle. They should really be called candle shears or wick trimmers. They have a small receptacle for catching the carbonized wick that is trimmed off. Small size scissor style, wrought iron, marked ''I K.'', American (?), 18th C or early 19th. • A true candle snuffer puts out the flame. One type, called a candle douse or a candle cone, is a small cone of metal attached to long handle; another is shaped like a thimble with a long handle, and is called a candle thimble. A candle d'outer is a device that works like scissors, but the ends have little broad pieces of metal that pinch out the flame. Alice Morse Earle, in *Customs and Fashions in Old New England* (Scribner's, 1893, page 127), says that ''snuffers' were called by various names, the word snit or snite being the most curious. It is from the old English snyten, to blow, and was originally a verb — to snite the candle, or put it out. In the inventory of property of John Gager, of Norwich, in 1703, appears 'One Snit.' '' **$60.00-$75.00**
Carpet beater, 6 spring steel wires twisted into 3 overlapped shapes — including a heart, though that was possibly inadvertent. Turned wooden handle. Holt-Lyon Co., Tarrytown, NY, pat'd March 3, 1908. **$25.00-$35.00**
Carpet beater, braided wire, American, 30''L, late 19th C. **$25.00-$35.00**
Carpet beater, looks almost like an old catcher's mitt mounted to a handle, head is padded doughnut shape of black imitation leather or oilcloth, bound with tan leather, handle is rattan wrapped in black & white cotton tape, very chic, American, 28''L x 6⅛''W, late 19th or early 20th C. **$45.00-$65.00**
Carpet beater, looped wire looks like flower, wooden handle grip, American, 26¼''L with 7⅞''L handle grip, late 19th C. **$25.00-$45.00**
Carpet beater, or rug beater, wicker or rattan in fancy basketweave., painted orange & green — a popular color combination of the time, American (?), 35''L, c.1900 to 1920s. **$25.00-$35.00**
Carpet beater, turned wooden handle, long twisted 4 ply wire shaft opening out to bulbous onion shape, 3l''L, early 20th C. **$15.00-$25.00**
Carpet beater, wicker in intricate ''lover's knot'' design, American (?), 35''L, 19th C. • Recycled hose. — ''A piece of garden hose makes an excellent carpet beater. While stout, its flexibility prevents the wear and tear of the stick or rattan beater.'' Signed L. M. *The Good Housekeeping Discovery Book No. 1, Compiled from the ''Discovery'' Pages of Good Housekeeping Magazine*, 1905. **$25.00-$45.00**
Carpet beater, wire loops like rabbit ears, tiller handle with wooden grip, American, 28¾''L, late 19th C. • Reproduction alert. — You can't really call them repros, because they don't look like anything old: the carpet & pillow beaters with turned wooden handles, and wire twisted in dozens of shapes and designs including cows, horses, people, ducks, socks, hearts, tulips, teddies, and sheep (all designs incorporating hearts, inside or outside). The

manufacturer, Mathews Wire & Wood, Frankfort, IN, say in their 1988 press release, "Each one is truly distinctive and ... add that extra touch of country class." The company also makes wall racks & hooks in similar shapes. They appear to be well made, but I doubt they will ever become collectible, because they are — in spirit, if not in fact — fakes. **$25.00-$45.00**

Carpet beater, wires twisted like a whisk, turned wood handle, 30"L, TOC. **$22.00-$45.00**

Carpet beater, wooden handle grip, then heavy wire shank and 3 forked beater part wound with spring wire, round and round, American, 23¼"L overall, 7"L wooden grip, 8" diameter beater, early 20th C. **$22.00-$40.00**

Carpet or rug beater, pretzel-like twisted wire, green wooden handle, "Bat Wing", Johnson Novelty, Danville PA, pat'd Oct. 4, 1927. **$22.00-$30.00**

Carpet stretcher, cast iron, plier lever action, lower part has rake-like teeth to grab carpet, top part stretches the carpet into place for tacking; these were used when people actually took the time and trouble to take up winter carpets and put down summer duggets, and then reverse the process at the end of the summer. Argghhhhhhh. Mfd by George S. Knapp, Bridgeport, CT, c.1908. **$15.00-$18.00**

Carpet stretcher, wood, cast iron, rope. Boy, am I glad I don't have to add carpet beating & stretching to my chores, "The Star", American, 15½"L, pat'd Oct. 28, 1890. **$10.00-$20.00**

Carpet sweeper, "Clipper Tidy Sweep", early 20th C. •
**1930s Carpet Sweepers.** — In the 1932-33 *Thomas' Register of American Manufacturers*, a list of makers of carpet sweepers is surprisingly short: S. Ward Hamilton Co., Harvey, IL; Metal Stamping Corp., Streator, IL; Porter Steel Specialties, Inc., Shelbyville, IN; Adler Mfg. Co., Louisville, KY; Bissell Carpet Sweeper Co., Grand Rapids, MI; and Vital Mfg. Co., Cleveland, OH. **$25.00-$35.00**

Carpet sweeper, Bissell "Silver Streak", Grand Rapids, MI, early 20th C. **$25.00-$35.00**

Carpet sweeper, boxy wooden housing, thumb screw at both ends of top to adjust brush inside, lever to pull on top to empty it without turning it over, "Crown", mfd by Heinz & Munschauer, Buffalo, NY, 1880s. **$35.00-$45.00**

• **"Unprincipled Neatness.** — "Cleanliness is akin to godliness," a good man says; but let us never forget that godliness is the first thing to be sought, and after that cleanliness to any extent. If any body supposes that I mean that you are to "get converted" in the ordinary sense of that phrase, and then go on scrubbing and scouring with all your might without any application of christianity to these wash-board and dish-pan affairs, that person has not made my acquaintance. The 'fruit of the spirit is love, joy, peace, etc.,' and beyond all price; neatness is only a secondary matter.

"We are putting cleanliness above godliness if we brush and scour until our nerves are so wearied that good temper becomes almost a physical impossibility; or if we keep our friends in constant dread of making a speck of dirt upon our premises; or if we allow ourselves to be greatly put out by any disasters that happen to our carpets or tablecloths. It is hard to bear these things, if we have not abundant means and plenty of assistance; and I don't know of anything but a true philosophy, believed in by the heart as well as by the intellect, that will help us through. Do we really desire to lead true lives, and to do our duty by our families? Then we must settle in our minds what are the essentials to this end, and resolutely make other matters subordinate.

"It is neatness without principle that insists upon clean aprons and polished faces for the children more than upon gentle words and patient sympathy with their plans and pleasures, or which concerns itself more about flies and dust than about the family health and happiness. Bright windows and spotless paint and well-scoured floors are excellent things in their way; but if you can only secure them by a loss of all time and relish for reading and out-of-door recreation, have the nobleness to bear with some dirt and rags, rather than sacrifice the life for meat or the body for raiment. For the sake of all about you, as well as for your own sake, save your nerves from over-strain and your intellectual life from starvation." F. E. R., *Agricultural Digest*, May 1871.

Carpet sweeper, lithographed wood case, metal working parts, "Eubank", English (?), 1909. • **German vocabulary** — Teppich-Kehrmaschine: carpet sweeping machine. Also spelled as one word. **$25.00-$35.00**

Carpet sweeper, oak box, dustbag inside, long pivoting handle, pneumatic suction action plus brush that revolves, "Duntley Special", mfd by Duntley Pneumatic Sweeper Co., Chicago, IL, c.1910s. **$35.00-$65.00**

Carpet sweeper, oak with original label, 2 sets of ball bearing wheels, long handle, ad states "The Bissell is the original, genuine machine that has been thirty-four years on the market, and while imitated, has always maintained the foremost position. ... Will outlast fifty corn brooms." This "Cyco" Bearing sweeper design was advertised at least as early as 1901 and as late as 1929, as a "sturdy broom and dustpan-on-wheels". This ad urged "Use your old sweeper as an extra — get the better improved Bissell for daily use." Bissell Carpet Sweeper Co., 1910 (but made before and long after with little change). • An ad in an April 1894 *Ladies Home Journal* said the wood used for the Bissell was "Vermilion Wood — a wine colored, durable wood from India." • A trade magazine editorial stated in 1905 that Bissell had factories in Toronto, Canada, and Paris, France. Furthermore, "The company makes carpet sweepers exclusively, in many styles, ranging from the **tiny toy machine** to the large hall sweeper with brush 25 inches long. ... The capacity of the factory (in Grand Rapids) is 3,000 regular domestic size sweepers per day, and 4,000 toy sweepers — or five regulars and six and a half toys per minute, for ten hours a day." Whew! **$25.00-$35.00**

Carpet sweeper brush cleaner, stamped metal, looks like little toy rake with 6 teeth, fattish handle stamped with name, "Bissells Sweepers", c.1934. **$8.00-$12.00**

Carpet sweeper display stand, oak & metal, for a housewares store, Bissell Carpet Sweeper Co., 41"H, early 20th C. • Added value. — Probably worth more to many collectors than an early Bissell sweeper itself, because it's a nice advertising piece. **$100.00-$250.00**

Crumb sweeper, celluloid, "Fuller Brush Co.", 20th C. **$15.00-$18.00**

Curtain tiebacks, cast iron in form of daisy with lots of detail, painted in shades of yellow, American, 2½" diameter, late 19th C. • Also saw a pair in shades of blue. Both with original paint. Pair: **$22.00-$28.00**

Curtain tiebacks, cast iron in form of lily and leaf, no paint (possibly stripped, or possibly once was bronzed-japanned), American, 3½''L, 19th C. **$25.00-$30.00**

Curtain tiebacks, cast iron, set of 6, brightly painted in various colors, bouquet of flowers, American, 3'' diameter, late 19th C. **$45.00-$60.00**

Curtain tiebacks, press-molded glass, rich medium blue with slight hint of opalescence, knurled knobs, American, 2''H x 2'' diameter, 19th C. • **Reproduction alert.** — The glass and cast iron ones were being made in the 1980s. Pair: **$125.00-$150.00**

Door knocker, cast iron, eagle with wings down, looking over right shoulder, shield across breast, standing on a scallop shell, no mark, American, 8⅛''H x 5¼''W, prob. 1870s-80s. **$65.00-$90.00**

Door knocker, cast iron, neo-classical woman's head, finely detailed with bellflower garland or swag, headdress with fruits & leaves, crested backplate, large horizontal oblong plate with narrow gadrooned border is for engraving name above head, marked on back "Wilson's Patent", Wilson Foundry, New London, CT, 8½''H x 4½''W, pat'd by I. Wilson, March 11, 1831. • This is the only door knocker patent in the *Subject Index to Patents 1790-1873*. Wilson got his patent on a cast-iron door-knocker, but this one was also made in cast brass. **$375.00-$500.00**

Door knocker, painted cast iron, rooster, unmarked, but probably Hubley, Lancaster, PA, 4¾''L x 3''W, 1930s-40s. **$155.00-$170.00**

Dust beater, looks like a very strange paintbrush, with black painted wood paintbrush handle with brass plate bearing legend, & inset into it, like bristles in a brush, are 14 round 9'' lengths of leather or rawhide, "Planet Dust Beater", Planet Mfg. Co., Holyoke, MA, 16''L overall, leather strips 9''L, pat'd Apr. 30, 1895. **$65.00-$75.00**

Dust bellows, all wood cylindrical shape, decorated with eagle & shield, flowers and scrolls, "Universal Dust-Bellows", August Kraushaar, American, 23''L, 1902 U.S. Trade Mark No. 39301. • **"Dusting Ornaments.** — The best way to remove dust from delicate articles, the parts of which can not be readily reached by an ordinary duster, is by blowing. The city furnishing stores keep small and exceedingly neat bellows, which, when we first saw them, we supposed were some child's toy, but learned that they were made expressly for dusting mantel ornaments and similar articles; they give a small but strong stream of air which, reaching every minute crevice, very cleverly dislodges the dust." *American Agriculturist*, July 1875. **$60.00-$100.00**

Dust mop container, round tin, "Ward's", English (?), **$5.00-$8.00**

Duster for insects, painted tin cylinder with metal and wooden-handled plunger, "Black Flag", c. 1930s (?). **$7.00-$12.00**

Dusting brush, horsehair with wooden handle, Shaker, 9''L, 19th C. **$70.00-$100.00**

Dusting brush, variegated colors of wood, turned handle, Shaker style, 20''L, 19th C. **$85.00-$125.00**

Dusting brush, white & black horsehair with wooden handle with leather hanging strap, marked only "No. 14", poss. Shaker, American, 14½''L, 19th C. **$55.00-$85.00**

Dustpan, at first glance, looks like simple pan with tubular handle, but rounded back wall of pan "has a concealed chamber ... which receives the dust, ... entrance to this chamber is ... through the cylindrical head at the rear. Inside this head is a slotted tube, ... rotated by grasping the handle of the removable cap which closes the end, ... the handle (is) a reservoir for ... liquid disinfectant. The dust is taken up in the usual manner and the pan is tilted until the dirt falls through the slot into the cylinder, which is closed previous to subjecting the germs to. .. the liquid." Imagine a plain dustpan, the back wall being a cylinder the width of the pan, with a twisting cap at one end, for opening or closing the slot. The tubular handle holds the disinfectant. Yech! This was written up in *House Furnishing Review*, and apparently was really made, by Thomas Clover, Philadelphia, PA, April 1903. • A similar looking one, worth about $85.00-$100.00 in good condition, has wide flared sides & short tubular braced handle, has a back wall with a difference — a sort of "gutter" made from a nearly cylindrical length of tin, with a permanent cap on one end and a hinged one on other, for emptying neatly from small opening rather than off the whole front edge. Wish they made these now. **$20.00-$30.00**

Dustpan, baked enameled steel, buttocks corrugations on pan floor, capped conical tubular handle, back wall is rounded, and has long heel plate to tilt pan slightly up so the lip (sweeping edge) was flat along floor, "Brown's Patent", mfd by Brown Oil Can Co., Toledo, OH, c.1905. • This could be ordered in several colors, and if a company ordered 72 or more they could get their name stenciled on the top plate of the pan. Wish I could place an order; my stencil would be "300 Years of Dust". **$20.00-$30.00**

Dustpan, beautiful rich greenish blue paint enameled color with midnight blue lettering & red brand name in oval, twisted wire handle, when you set it down it automatically opens. Assembly directions read "First insert end of handle with double bend into hole in side of pan marked A, next insert the end with single bend into hole marked B. Then close the cover and spring both sides of handle into loops in cover wire." "Androck Sanitary Dust Pan", Androck, pat'd Aug. 24, 1909. **$65.00-$80.00**

Dustpan, black painted tin, large, well braced, high wall in back, sold as a spinning room piece, Shaker, Canterbury, NH, 12'' across, 1864. **$95.00-$120.00**

Dustpan, black-painted tin, silver painted trim, step-through looped strap handle to hold it firm while you swept, a candle holder sticks up from top of handle, for lighting those hidden recesses, Monroe, CT, 12¾''W, pat'd Nov. 7, 1882. • **DUSTPAN PARTS.** A dustpan is best described when you know the names of the parts. The dust receptacle is the pan, I have used floor of pan to describe what design or embossing might be found on the large flat part; the front sweeping edge is the lip; the raised sides are the wall, and I have used back wall frequently because most old dustpans have three raised sides; there is a handle, which may be a tapered tube, sometimes with a boss (a brace or support at the shoulder or the neck where the handle joins the back wall, or the handle may be at right angles to the floor of the pan and be long; a hanging loop or a hole may be at the end of the handle, or the handle may be a loop of strap metal, meant sometimes to hold toe of foot, or the handle may be pivoting; there may be feet or a heel plate under the back wall or heel to hold the pan at a slight angle; a cover or lid, fixed or hinged, may enclose the open top of the pan forming an enclosed chamber. Candle-pan:**$200.00-$225.00**

Dustpan, "brass finished" tin pan with deep hood over back, long vertical handle with knob end, has wire clips for holding broom when not in use, "The Upright", Craighead & Kintz Co., Ballardvale, MA, introduced c.1891. **$30.00-$45.00**

Dustpan, & brush, pieced tin, japanned & decorated with floral stencils, curved out side walls, tapered tubular handle, back wall is a large cylinder with one end capped, the other end open for inserting the brush to be used with the pan. This type is called a brush pan. Possibly made by Benhams & Stoutenborough, Glen Cove, NY, 1870s. • I bought a billhead from 1876, showing a decorated water can from a toilet set, which is a bill sent to the NYC Board of Education for six dozen "japanned dust pans" at about 14ᶜ each, for a total bill of $9.99. This invoice was examined and signed by five Bd. of Ed. bureaucrats checking delivery and correctness as well as justness and reasonability of price. Wish those guys could be installed at the Pentagon. **$125.00-$145.00**

Dustpan, crimped tin, painted salmon with design of gilded flowers & leaves, 7½"L x 5"W, 19th C. • **Toys or Crumb Pans?** — This could be a toy dustpan, but is also so highly decorated that it might be simply a genteel little parlor dustpan for the tea table crumbs. • A "mini crumb pan" was recently advertised as being Shaker. Had the flared pan side walls and a triangular braced handle, which was rather stubby and ungraceful. It was 5"L x 4½"W, and I believe it was a Shaker-type toy dustpan. **$45.00-$55.00**

Dustpan, deftly made by tinsmith, probably from a pattern book, American (?), 12"W, 19th C. • **Don't Excuse My Dust.** — An article in *Pinnock's Guide to Knowledge*, London, Sept. 22, 1832, tells about the **Dustman** (in the U.S. called a ragpicker), who took his cart around London, ringing his bell and calling out "Dust ho!" ... "If we did not know his trade and his purpose, we should think that the dustman came to raise dust rather than to remove it. What then do they make of the dust? There is a good deal of coal-dust and cinders in it; and these form what is called "breeze," and is one of the materials of bricks; so that new houses are in part made out of the very sweepings of old ones. Then there are old tin pans and kettles, and bits of pewter, and brass, and iron, in the dust; and there are also pieces of broken crockery and glass. The tin, copper, brass, and all the metals that can be made new again by melting, more cheaply than they can be originally smelted out of the ore, are collected and sold to the founder. Old iron in moderate pieces goes back to the smith's forge, and is made into new articles....If it be too thin for bearing the proper degree of heat without burning away, but still be whole and tough, it is sent to workmen who cut it into shapes, japan it, and sell it to the trunk-makers, who, to appearance at least, strengthen the corners of their boxes with it; and if it be too bad for that purpose, it is dissolved in acids and forms black ink, black stain, and black dye. Sometimes the tinman's chips, and the old pans and kettles, are laid down as a bottom for roads, or for the street pavement; but that is a very foolish plan, it is a waste of the materials; and ... they ... bend under carriages, and also retain water. ... The broken crockery, however, is excellent for this, if it be beat firmly together; for it is dry, and as it does not hold moisture, it acts as a sort of drain. When pounded small too, and mixed with other materials, it very much improves the hardness and

quality of bricks. Glass is collected and sold to glass-blowers....The bones which are in the dust, are useful in making ammonia, or hartshorn, in furnishing oil for soap, or burnt for ivory black. ... Rags can be made into coarse paper; and woollen rags become ammonia or soap. The rest makes no bad brick earth." Dustpan: **$35.00-$45.00**

Dustpan, gray graniteware, quite dinged, late 19th C. **$35.00-$45.00**

Dustpan, green japanned tin, slightly hooded, flared shape with tapered side walls, strap handle suitable for "hand or foot", according to 1892 ad, which also stated it came in "attractive colors" (probably red, blue, and amber), "Perfection", J. Hall Rohrman & Son, Philadelphia, 1890s. **$12.00-$18.00**

Dustpan, hammered sheet iron, with a handle fitted to it made of metal pipe, 20th C. • These homemade or one-of-a-kind dustpans are the most fun to me. **$25.00-$35.00**

Dustpan, heavy sheet metal pan, enameled & pinstriped, triangular with domed partial hood or cover, strap handle, "when not in use it hangs on the wall, making it valuable as a scrap-pan" (wastebasket). "The Lightning", mfd by D. B. Smith & Co., Utica, NY, c.1903. **$12.00-$15.00**

Dustpan, homemade, heavy weight sheet iron, tinned, folded & riveted construction, high wall, wood handle, American, 9¾"W with 4¹/₁₆"L handle, late 19th C. **$20.00-$30.00**

Dustpan, homemade sheet copper, folded, bent & screwed to wooden handle, American, 14" x 12", late 19th C. **$28.00-$38.00**

Dustpan, japanned steel, with corrugations like buttocks on floor of pan, step-through strap handle meant for toe of foot, although eventually you'd have to lean over to pick it up, "Foot-Hold", mfd by Lawrence Mfg. Co., Toledo, OH, c.1905. **$10.00-$13.00**

Dustpan, japanned (with dark brown asphaltum) tin, in the "Shaker style" with distinctive tapered & capped tubular handle with ring at end for hanging, 8"W with deep pan, 19th C. • **"Shaker Style".** — I've seen some, especially in larger sizes, for as much as $350.00, but until someone writes a definitive book on Shaker, it'll be hard to identify this type of dustpan accurately and price accordingly. *Shaker Smalls*, by David Serette, pictures a number of "Shaker" dustpans, without measurements or closeups of construction details. So it is hard to say. One is marked with initials, stamped in the back near the handle. **$55.00-$75.00**

Dustpan, large hammered sheet iron pan with deep side walls, japanned, long attentuated, slender turned vertical wooden handle with small knobbed tip, very rare form, Shaker manufacture, pan approx. 7" deep x 14" W with 4"H sides, handle approximately 26"L, 19th C. • Two of these (not identical) showed up at the auction of the Roberta & George Sieber Collection, Litchfield Gallery Auctions, July 30, 1988. Price realized: **$880.00; $1760.00**

Dustpan, large, sheet tin, ring on tubular handle, stamped "ERIE R R", used on the railroad, 14¾"L x 13"W, early 20th C. • A very nice railroad piece, and I was a dope not to have bought it. **$35.00-$45.00**

Dustpan, long handle attached with pivot, like a carpet sweeper handle, to the deep rounded-back hooded or chambered pan. When you pick it up to move to new sweeping location, the pan pivots to hanging position so nothing falls out, mfd by Delphos Mfg. Co., Delphos, OH, c.1908. **$12.00-$15.00**

Dustpan, molded swirly colored rubber, short handle, curved-up wall, little feet in heel, came in 5 colors at first, including green, red, blue & white, first product of now enormous company, "Rubbermaid", later made by Wooster Rubber Co., Wooster, OH, (which became Rubbermaid, Inc. in 1957), Norton, MA, 12"W, 1st made 1932; pat'd 1933 by James & Madeleine Caldwell. • By 1934, there was a family of kitchen accessories to match: drain board mat in corrugated rubber, plate scraper, triangular sink strainer, and sink scraper. They were advertised as "noise-proof". **$35.00-$45.00**

Dustpan, paint-enameled tin, deep hood, polished metal lip curves from floor to interior of dustpan, long upright handle with hanging ring, finished in pastel blue (also came in pastel green & black), "Polly Prim", mfd by Patent Novelty Co., Fulton, IL, c.1930. **$12.00-$15.00**

Dustpan, pieced sheet iron, tinned, with nice tubular handle & triangular attachment of handle to body, in style usually called "Shaker", American, 14"W, 19th C. • **Express Elevator ... Getting Off, Please.** — "Excellence in housekeeping has come to be considered as incompatible with superior intellectual culture. But it is not so. The most elevated minds fulfil best the every-day duties of life." Mrs. Cornelius, *The Young Housekeepers Friend, or, A guide to Domestic Economy & Comfort*, Boston & NY: 1846. **$55.00-$75.00**

Dustpan, shapely tin pan, low walls, side walls curved out to make lip wider than back wall, triangular brace, well-turned short rosewood handle, Shaker, 10 1/2"W, 19th C. • Sold at the Karl Mendel auction, Sept. 25, 1988, at Willis Henry in Albany, NY. The price below is the final bid after, as it was put in the *Maine Antique Digest*, the "lady from Pennsylvania battled a redhaired lady from New York City". The NYC bidder won. It's a great piece, but to pay so much? Price without 10% buyer's premium: **$3800.00**

Dustpan, stamped & japanned steel pan with corrugations in buttocks shape, long twisted wire handle at right angles to pan, hinged at back with clip, "The Twentieth Century", mfd by Case Mfg Co., Fenton, MI, pan is 12"W x 9" deep, handle 26"L, c.1903. **$10.00-$16.00**

Dustpan, stamped steel pan with extra steel strip along lip or sweeping edge, pan has squared folded corners, with straight back wall, short tapered tubular handle with ring handle, triangular support to handle, japanned black (or assorted colors), "The Steel Edge Dust Pan Co.", mfd by Central Stamping Co., Boston, MA, various sizes, c.1906. **$15.00-$20.00**

Dustpan, tin, short handle, adv'g "S. H. Curtis & Sons Hardware", Waverly, IA, TOC. **$20.00-$30.00**

Dustpan, triangular steel pan, flat top, pivoting twisted wire handle, japanned in green or blue or black, mfd by Geuder, Paeschke & Frey, Milwaukee, WI, pan 9" x 12" with handle 33¼"L, c.1930. **$10.00-$15.00**

Dustpan & brush combined, long pivoted handle with brush-broom on end, pivoting leg holds triangular tin pan, looks extremely unusable, called the "Hygenic Brushup Pan", c.1935. **$12.00-$15.00**

Fly cover, domed wire screening, with blue japanned tin rim, American, 10½"D, TOC. It's amazing how the price of these has gone up. I bought mine about 15 years ago for a couple of dollars; shall I sell 'em and buy a country place? • **Added value.** — Try for a "nesting" of these in 3 to 5 sizes. **$45.00-$55.00**

Fly fan, cast iron base, steel shaft & 2 wing struts, cotton scrim, clockwork windup motor runs 1¼ hours, "The Fowler", or "The Improved Keyless Fly Fan", mfd by Matthai-Ingram Co., Baltimore, MD, 29¼"H x 48" wingspread, pat'd May -?, 1885, June -?, 1885, March 1 & March 8, 1887. • Matthai-Ingram's instructions read: "It drives all flies away by the shadow and movement of the wings while revolving, .. can be rewound at any time by simply turning cross-piece at the top of base. ... The improvements of our Keyless Fans over all others consist of patent adjustable wing-holder (which admits of wings revolving at any angle — an important advantage where space is limited). The patent automatic stop-catch prevents unwinding when wings are taken off. Interior machinery, strengthened and simplified, and specially adapted for easy motion and long wear .... We are the patentees & sole manufacturers." • **Accurate patent dates always fall on Tuesday.** The May and June dates given by Matthai-Ingram, or its successor company — NESCO (National Enameling & Stamping Co.) of Baltimore — don't fall on Tuesday, neither May 20, nor June 20, 1885. On an object, a marked "patented" date may simply mean the date the patent was applied for. • Motors for these fly fans alone have sold for $100.00; a complete fan, even if scrim is a bit weak, or even holey, is worth much more. • There is some crossover interest from clock collectors. **$400.00-$470.00**

Fly fan, slender obelisk-like cast metal base (brass? iron?), high vertical shaft with 2 wings, keywound with automatic stop if "it is desirable to detach the wings" (?). Vertical key on base, you'd get 90 minutes on one winding — long enough to get through a Victorian meal. "National", Bridgeport Brass Co., "improvement on the one heretofore made by" Bridgeport — 1892 ad. **$400.00-$470.00**

Fly fan, or punkah, decorated & painted cast iron, with accordian-pleated fan (paper? cloth?), clockwork action inside cylindrical housing on ornate scrolled wood & cast iron base, "The Indian Zephyrion", mfd. under Bennett's patent, sold by jobbers F.A. Walker, Boston, MA, 1870s. Poss. 1874. • Nonagenerian Alice Steele, writing about **"Spring Cleaning In Great Grandmother's Day"** in the Early American Industries Association *Chronicle*, Sept. 1989, describes a homemade sort of fly fan. "Most effective in those days (prior to Civil War) was the swatter, but every kitchen had its paper fly drivers which were strips of paper cut about an inch wide and 12 to 15 inches long, bound and tacked on to a wooden handle long enough to reach the ceiling. Then with a driver in each hand a housewife could drive the flies out the open door, but it was only a short time before they were all back again." She describes another method, to use in the cold early morning before the stove was fired up and heated the air. This was to hold "a tin can of warm soapy water up to them (on the ceiling) and they would drop into it." **$400.00-$450.00**

Fly killer, insecticide, dome top can, depicts traffic cop stopping giant fly, "Flystop", Hits-It Mfg. Co., Camden, NJ, c.1920s-30s. **$18.00-$22.00**

Fly killer, insecticide, wick type, "Seibert Magic Fly Killer", H. E. Seibert, St. Paul, MN, 1913 at least to early 1930s.
$12.00-$15.00

Fly swatter, also called a fly killer, black turned wood handle, flexible steel shaft, folded wire screen head, cloth bound, only legible marks are "—ATTUC—", and the place: "Decatur" (IL?), head 6"L x 4½"W, overall length 14", pat'd April 1916. $10.00-$15.00

### Swat the Fly

Oh every fly that skips our swatters,
Will have five million sons and daughters,
And countless first and second cousins;
Of aunts and uncles, scores and dozens,
And fifty-seven million nieces;
So knock the blamed thing all to pieces.
—Walt Mason, from "Fight the Fly",
International Harvester Co., 1915

Fly swatter, fan-shaped splints on long wooden handle, possibly Shaker, late 19th or early 20th C. $85.00-$100.00

Fly swatter, folded screen & wood, American, late 19th, early 20th C. • **Futurewatch:** Fly swatters are an upcoming (albeit slowly) collectible, because there's lots of variety. My specialty is homemade ones, of everything from inner tube rubber & coat hangers, to screening bound with calico. $12.00-$20.00

Fly swatter, homemade, blued steel wire screening with crudely cutout shoulder of folded leather, shows stamped design indicating it was made from an old sports glove or something else unidentifiable, black, red, yellow and white calico hemming all around edge, string-wrapped wire handle, American, 16"L, c.1910s. $7.00-$10.00

Fly swatter, homemade, rubber (probably an old inner tube), coat hanger wire & string, holes punched through rubber, one of 3 from caboose from New Jersey Seashore Lines, 1920s or 1930s. I have not seen one from a railroad with holes punched with a ticket punch — but that would be a treasure to find! This one: $5.00-$7.00

Fly swatter, homemade, wood and leather, the handle made of a ¾" x ¾" length of wood, the corners rounded, one end carved to a truncated point to fit into sewn sheath in the floppy leather head. Holes punched in different directions into the leather spell out a name, not easily or possibly correctly readable; apparently the letters are "S A M M E N E K" or "S A M M K E N E", so possibly Sam Menek (?) or -?-, found in PA, 20½"L overall, with leather part 7¾"L x 3½"W, prob. 1910s-1930s. $7.00-$15.00

Fly swatter, homemade, wooden dowel handle, small leather blade with pattern of regular holes punched cleanly through. The leather blade has perfect flexibility, like rubber or wire screening — the key to a successful fly swatter. American, 16"L x 3"W, prob. 1920s-30s. • **Lookalike alarm.** – Being made in Ohio right now is a leather and wire fly swatter, that is about 18"L. The leather head is perforated, the end is folded over the wire and riveted. $10.00-$12.00

Fly swatter, long turned wooden handle, fine wire screen head, folded at shoulder, attached with small metal plate. Ad copy for this one reads "Flies are the worst in the Fall; Buy the King Fly Killer, saves trouble, that's all. The "King" Fly Killer is made of a specially prepared light steel wire netting; it kills without crushing, and you can clean your entire house of all flies in a few minutes." "King", mfd by R. R. Montgomery & Co., Decatur, IL, 5"W x 18"L overall, pat'd Jan. 9, 1900. • This is almost like the other Decatur-made swatter, or "fly killer" as they called them then, and you wonder if one manufacturer copied the other. In 1932-33 *Thomas' Register*, only the United States Mfg. Corp. is given as a maker of fly swatters, in Decatur. $10.00-$15.00

Fly swatter, long turned wooden handle, with spring steel plated wire head made almost like broom, "does not crush the fly" — a big selling point. J. F. Bigelow, Worcester, MA, about 12"L, pat'd Jan. 8, 1895, still being sold 1905. • **Save Wear & Tear on Your Fly Swatter:** "To Prevent Flies from Settling upon Picture Frames. — Brush them over with water in which onions have been boiled." Mrs. A. P. Hill, *Mrs. Hill's New Family Receipt Book*, NY: 1870. $10.00-$13.00

Fly swatter, thin wood dowel handle, very flexible fringed black rubber head, "Corner Clipper", Seiberling Latex Products, Akron, OH, 18"L, Oct. 1932. • In the 1932-33 *Thomas' Register of American Manufacturers*, the only fly swatter maker in Ohio, was in Ashland — The Faultless Rubber Co. $12.00-$15.00

Fly swatter, wire mesh, flat wooden handle, adv'g "Coca-Cola", 1942. $5.00-$10.00

Fly trap, 3 part, wooden plate base where you put bait, wire interior cone of wire screening with small hole in top, then a tall wire screen upper compartment with tin top, from which there is no escape, ring handle on plate & large part, is this the Harper's Patent (?) or the Globe (?), American, 9¼"H overall x 5½" diameter, inner cone 4"H, last quarter 19th C. • When you try to figure this one out, you get confused. Do you put it out with the plate & inner cone first? Wait for the inner cone to be filled with buzzing flies, unable to discover the small hole in the top? Then why do you need the outer cover? $55.00-$75.00

Fly trap, blown glass vessel, clear glass — so fun to see the flies buzz around, eh? shaped something like a ship's decanter, applied feet, corked bottle top, upside down like funnel opening in bottom, flange around neck near top to anchor a cord for hanging from ceiling if wanted, American, 6"H, 2nd to 3rd quarter 19th C. • **October 13, 1837, Lake Simcoe, Canada.** — "But the great annoyance of this country is the plague of mosquitoes, of which there is a larger and a smaller sort, together with that of black flies and of sand-flies. Such is the misery these insects occasion, that the settlers generally, in summer, regardless of the heat, fill their houses almost to suffocation with smoke, in order to get rid of these tormentors." Charles Giles Bridle Daubeny, *Journal of a Tour through the United States and Canada, made during the years 1837-38.* Oxford, England, 1843. $100.00-$150.00

Fly trap, blown pale green glass in pear shape, flange near top for cord to hang from beam or ceiling, American or European, about 5"H, early to mid 19th C (?). • **Early Patents.** — A Fly-killing Machine patented by A. Glendening, of Loudoun County, VA on Sept. 9, 1824, is the earliest patented fly killer. I don't know what it looked like. And although biting flies were an awful problem, I don't think another patent in this field was granted until W. Shreve's Fly-trap was awarded one on Aug. 22, 1848. Shreve lived in Elkton, KY. $45.00-$60.00

Fly trap, clockwork mechanism housed in wooden base, with revolving baited drum, wire screening dome exactly like the wire screen plate covers. offered in catalog of jobber F.A. Walker, of Boston, MA, c.1870s. Possibly this is Charles Kallmann's (Newburg, NY) April 6, 1869 patent. • **Time Flies** — As Described by Kallmann: "The nature of my invention consists in combining two useful instruments into one, the clock and the fly trap. … the power to revolve a small cylinder which is covered with cloth, which is saturated with a solution of sugar or molasses in water, to invite flies and mosquitoes to sit down on the drum, is so very small that, if it is attached to a clock, its effect would hardly be felt by the spring of the clock." In other words, it sounds as if Kallmann meant it to be run off an existing household clock.
$250.00-$300.00

Fly trap, domed wire screening, tin base, "Shur Katch Bug & Fly Trap", mfd by NESCO Co. (National Enameling & Stamping Co.), 4" x 5½", early 20th C.    $35.00-$45.00

Fly trap, glass, 2 parts, sort of like a baking dish or casserole (ugh), bottom part has large convex part in center, lid has funnel top, marked "FLY TRAP" on lid, late 19th C.    $100.00-$150.00

Fly trap, high double dome wire mesh, 2 part, interior wire is conical; exterior is tall & shaped like a lighthouse, with knobbed, close-fitting tin lid, "Dover Stamping Co.", Boston, MA, 1870s-80s. • Dover describes it thus: "The trap here is the invention of a lady, and is a perfect success. … The flies are attracted inside the cage by bait and can't get out, and are easily killed and trap set for more." It is baited with dish of sweet treacle or sugar water.
$55.00-$75.00

Fly trap, round turned stepped wooden base plate for bait, 2 part demi-spherical wire screen dome like an aeronaut's balloon, joined around widest part with tin rims that fit together, inner screen cone, the top part of dome could be taken off for packing, "Harper's Patent 1875 Balloon Fly Trap", mfd by Peabody & Parks, sold by many famous hardware companies, Lansingburg, NY, 7"H, pat'd June 22, 1875 and Sept. 9, 1879. • **A different kind of fly trap.** — "Kitchens are the favourite resort of the common fly. In these a fly trap , as it is called, may be used to attract the fly to settle upon it rather than upon the walls or ceiling. Flies seem to incline to settle more on suspended objects than on any other; and thence the use of "the fly trap," which is usually formed of papers of various colours cut out fancifully, in order to render them somewhat ornamental as well as useful." Mrs. Parkes, in *An Encyclopedia of Domestic Economy*, 1848 NY edition of English book of 1845. A far sight better than those spiraled gummy twists of fly paper with a hundred flies mummifying on them. • Washburn Wire Goods made this one in the 1920s & called them "Balloon Fly Traps". Another, that was taller and had slanting sides (bigger at bottom), a tin top with ring loop, and a tin bottom, as well as a large cone of wire inside, was what they called the "Harper Fly Trap". It was 9½"H. They sold them by the gross, and the catalog illustration is just that, with maybe 50 dead & dying flies. Yuck. • Wire fly traps, not delineated in *Thomas' Register*, were made in the early 1930s by Hamblin & Russell Mfg. Co., Worcester, MA; Bromwell Wire Goods, Cincinnati, OH; and Fred J. Meyers Mfg. Co., Hamilton, OH.    $85.00-$110.00

Fly trap, stepped molded glass base that gets baited, with 4 feet, and scalloped out places between the feet for entrances, to be used with any inverted glass container "from milk bottle to 3 gallon globe", the flies trapped within to be drowned by holding the 2 parts upside down under faucet, directions say "Don't swat 'em — Pot 'em". Molded on 3 of 6 steps are "Pat Appld For" & "FLY-RY-CYDE PYR-Y-MYD", mfd by Evan L. Reed Mfg. Co., Sterling, IL, c.1919.    $50.00-$75.00

Fly trap, tin & wire screeening, a nifty modernistic thing that looks like a cracker or popcorn server from the 1950s (oh, dear, did I really say that?). Low square base with openings underneath the blue japanned tin pan with flared sides, decorated with bronze pin striping, stepped rim to receive demi-spherical wire screen dome, inner chimney like part has wooden bottom and is open at top. This is where bait is placed, while the surrounding pan is filled with soapsuds. The directions state that the flies crawl up from bottom, "then soar upward, being misled by the wire cover through which the light has free access. In the course of time they become wearied by their futile efforts to escape and drop back into the soapsuds where they drowned." • **Dangerous Sap** — The writing of this and many other ads & instruction sheets of the late 19th C is typical in that it incorporates drama and anthropomorphic emotions. It is a crueler deed to allow a fly to "soar upwards" (toward enlightenment? heaven?), become weary after realizing the hopelessness of escape, and then drown. **Disgusting Jokes** — It is hard to respect the people of the 19th C who would desire the death of any living thing to be accompanied by awareness and hopelessness, and who would write reams of editorials and jokes in serious publications about filthy foreigners and lazy overbreeding immigrants, and denigrate on every hand the black people who were slaves for almost two thirds of that century. To top it off, magazines for children and women were full of sentimental stories and sappy poems about roosters, pigs, bunnies, cats, and dogs, that appeared in columns next to recipes for poultry, pork, and rabbit.    $75.00-$90.00

Fly trap, turned wooden base with 2 wire screen domes, one small, has hole in top, then much larger tall round topped one with tin rim at base so it fits well into wooden plate part, paper label reads "GLO— FLY TRAP" (probably "GLOBE"), with information that "soup bone is the best bait to use". c.1870s.    $35.00-$50.00

Fly trap, wire & wood, with original instructions, "Sur Katchem Fly Trap", mfd by Olsen & Thompson, TOC to 1930s. • At some point, either Shur Katch or Sur Katchem probably got sued by the other for infringement of trade name. Once a company seemed to find a nifty name (Gnifty Gname), everyone else jumped aboard. P.S. I've also seen this spelled "Sur Ketchum" in ads, but don't know if it is another company entirely.    $20.00-$30.00

Fly trap, wood frame with mesh, looks like tiny pup tent, "Curry Fly Trap", Tulsa, OK, pat'd Jan. 4, 1916.
$25.00-$35.00

Fly trap, wooden base, screen quonset hut-shaped top, inner dome has small hole at top, end of trap has a bung hole & plug for inserting bait, quite primitive, although probably a manufactory product. 11'L, 1870s.
$50.00-$60.00

Hearth brush, red painted turned wood handle, decorated with painted black leaves & yellow pinstripes, most of natural fiber bristles still in place, American, 24"L, from look of decoration, c.1830s to 1850. **$75.00-$90.00**

Hurricane lamp snuffer, forged iron, scissor-like device with long vertical shaft that fits down inside the glass hurricane lamp shade, when part above the shade is worked, the reciprocal action is transferred down to the snuffer, which has a wick-cutter & box to catch the snipped-off charred wick, American, 1870s. • "Let us start with the most **commonplace object, a tallow candle** — so useful and yet so vulgar, compared with the sperm, ozokerit, stearine, composite and other beautiful varieties of our own day. Where are the farthing dips and the 'long sixteens' of our youth? Well, we shall breathe no sigh of regret for them; peace be to their ashes, or rather their 'snuffs,' which were malodorous, productive of conflagrations and exigent of constant trimming. And this last item brings us to the point — where are all the snuffers gone? It is only a few years since the snuffers-tray appeared regularly with the candles at nightfall. Now they are never seen, and 10 years hence will be as rare and as valuable as Queen Anne's farthings, unless some specimens are preserved in our museums. As modern candles consume their own wicks, snuffers have become things of the past...." *The Metal Worker*, Dec. 9, 1882. Snuffer: **$85.00-$100.00**

Pillow beater, varnished wicker, handle wrapped with cane, American (?), 26"L, 1890s to 1920s. **$15.00-$20.00**

Pillow beater, varnished wicker, simple love knot design, short handle wrapped with wire, American (?), 27½"L, 1890s to 1920s. **$15.00-$20.00**

Scouring powder can, with cone top, lithographed <u>Black Americana</u> tin with great depiction of man gazing at his reflection, "Grady's Liquid Scouree Polish", American. TOC picture style, but has to be much later — at least, cone-tops for beer didn't come in until 1939.

**$85.00-$100.00**

Scrub brush, wooden, heavy fiber "bristles", for floors, adv'g "Mrs. Jones Homemade Catsup", 19th C. •
**"Brushing Up On Brushes. —** When you buy a brush, if you don't know a fiber from a bristle, ask the dealer. He may say: "No this is not Bristle, it is made of Bass" (or Bassine, Kitool, Palmyra or Palmetto or Rice Root, or mixed fibers, or union or union marble). ... Of all the fibers, Tampico (from Mexico and Central America), the product of a species of cactus, is probably the best fiber. Palmyra too is excellent." Ethel R. Peyser, *House & Garden*, April 1921. Everything is plastic now, except for a particular kind of very durable fiber & wood dish-washing brush. Perhaps it's made of tampico, I don't know. Bristle is mainly from hogs. You can examine it under a loupe or good magnifying glass and see that it is a type of hair. If it's not too weatherworn and dirty, it should appear to the naked eye to have a sort of sheen, whether it is white, black, or dark brown. **$25.00-$30.00**

Scrub bucket & wringer, wood, "Eagle Mop-wringer & Bucket Combined", Eagle Woodenware Co., Hamilton, OH, early 20th C. **$20.00-$25.00**

Soap dishes—See Bathroom chapter, though used elsewhere.

Spring brush, long-handled, for cleaning bed springs, fiber bristles, 19th C. **$12.00-$18.00**

Squeegee, pieced tin, composed mainly of tubes, felt & rubber strips, reservoir in tube for water, brass ID plate reads "O. K. Cleaner, Extra felt or rubber 50 cents each", O. K. Mfg. Co., no place, 6"W x 5⅛"L, pat'd Sept.-?, and Dec. 22, 1908. **$15.00-$18.00**

Umbrella stand, painted cast iron, heron holding a very realistic snake, coiled to form 2 horizontal open loops on each end & a closed loop in center, mounted to smallish drip pan, American, 19th C, or poss. 20th C reproduction. • **Reproduction alert.** — In the 1920s, all forms of cast and wrought iron decorative pieces, from the 18th and 19th Cs, were reproduced to satisfy the Colonial Craze that swept the nation. They continued to be made, in fewer numbers, from then on, but the late 20s and early 30s were the heyday. **$2000.00-$2500.00**

Umbrella stand, painted cast iron, intricate design comprising a pyramidal assemblage of crossed anchors, tied packages or bales, belaying pins & chains formed around a vertical pier post, on top of which stands a beautifully-detailed American sailor holding a thick line arranged in simple knotted double loops that form the holder for the umbrellas and/or canes. American, 27"H, original poss. 2nd to 3rd quarter 19th C, this one? • **German vocabulary** — <u>Schirmstander</u>: umbrella stand. • **Reproduction alert.** — Ahoy! No sooner had I seen this at an antique show in York, PA, and thought how fine it looked, than I found an ad in the June 1930 *House Beautiful*. The very same design, which the advertiser claimed was 18th C. (Hah.) The ad also says "Design Patented" — presumably by Valda, Inc. who sold the reproduction. It was "made of cast iron. ... Painted in colors. .... Base black, figure in red, white and black ... 27" high, 21" wide at base, 9½" deep." Price was $25.00 in 1930. Price for an old one from 19th C: **$550.00-$750.00**

Umbrella stand, very Deco moderne or even Directoire style from 100 years before that. Black lacquered tin, bottom tray is elongated octagon, connected by crosswise & vertical metal rods to the top rim which echoes octagon shape, small "gold" medallions at point where pieces cross, American, 21¼"H x 19¼"L x 6⅛"W, c.1930. **$85.00-$115.00**

Umbrella vase, stamped & pieced brass bound with copper bands, embossed interior home scene with dog & family, not marked, prob. American, 29"H x 14¼" diameter, early 20th C. **$175.00-$225.00**

Upholstery brush, natural black-colored fiber, turned wooden handle, nickeled-iron crank handle with wooden knob. This was misidentified in last edition as a bottle brush, but it is actually a "rotary upholstery brush ... for cleaning button indentations" on carriage linings, mattresses, furniture, etc. Since I first misidentified it, the incorrect ID has been picked up by an author in England, and printed in his book (without credit, of course). Mfd by Horace E. Britton, Stoughton, MA, 10¾"L, c. late 1880s to 1900. **$12.00-$18.00**

Vacuum cleaner, "Old Victor", early 20th C.

**$100.00-$110.00**

Vacuum cleaner, "Winchester", early 20th C. **$65.00-$75.00**

Vacuum cleaner, bentwood veneered box, drive wheel on gears inside works 2 bellows that go up & down, pump PUMP pump PUMP poooof, "Sweeper-VAC", mfd by Pneuvac Co., Worcester, MA, 1912. **$55.00-$100.00**

Vacuum cleaner, electric, brown Bakelite® (or other molded phenolic resin) body or motor housing and brush cover, steel tubular long handle with built-in switch, red plastic tip on handle, air vents in body, height of brush regulated by foot switch in body, "Sweep-O-Matic, Catalog #1000", mfd by Davis Mfg. Co., Plano, IL, body 11" square, 1942, 1943 and 1946 patents numbers 2280077, 2316709, and 2406247. • It may be only 40 years old, but it's really trig and I was surprised that Second Chance Antique Appliances had it for only $28.00 in 1987. True value: **$70.00-$100.00**

Vacuum cleaner, electric, cast aluminum housing & hood, shiny metal handle, nifty boldly checkered bag that looks like something for Purina® dog food, streamlined in style of period, "Premier Duplex", mfd by Premier Vacuum Cleaner Co., division of the Electric Vacuum Cleaner Co., Cleveland, OH, late 1920s, early 1930s. • Premier also made at least two hand held electric models: (1) the "Pic-up", with fat little bag, suitcase-style handle attached to motor housing, and (2) the "Spic-Span", with checked bag. Also a "Junior" size for apartments, with much narrower hood and nozzle, and smaller bag. **$65.00-$100.00**

Vacuum cleaner, electric cylinder type on slides, vertical, carrying handle on top, a long hose with many attachments, looks just like the Electrolux, "Cadillac Cylinder Vacuum Cleaner", mfd by Clements Mfg Co., Chicago, IL, 1908. **$55.00-$65.00**

> She swept the dusty carpets,
> The hallways and the rugs;
> She hunted up the cobwebs
> With all their flies and bugs.
> She was so very, very good,
> That mother had to keep her.
> I s'pose by now you know that she
> Was just a vacuum sweeper.

T.M. Bray, in *There is More Leisure for the Housekeeper in Electrical Housekeeping*, NY Edison Co., 1924

Vacuum cleaner, electric, hand held, A. C. Gilbert, New Haven, CT, 1920s-30s. **$25.00-$35.00**

Vacuum cleaner, electric, hand held, well balanced cast & plated nozzle and motor, black cloth bag suspended from long rod, suitcase handle on top, "Beating-Brush Cleaner", Hamilton Beach, subsidiary of Scoville, Mfg. Co., c.1930. **$18.00-$30.00**

Vacuum cleaner, electric, metal motor housing, hood and nozzle, wheels, long handle with cloth bag, could be use with or without revolving brush, this one is a big step forward from their 1912 version, "The Electric Sweeper-Vac", mfd by Pneuvac Co., Worcester, MA, c.1920. **$55.00-$100.00**

Vacuum cleaner, electric, streamlined cast & plated motor housing and wide nozzle, long curved handle with black cloth bag, "Beating-Brush Cleaner", Hamilton Beach, subsidiary of Scoville, Mfg. Co., Racine, WI, c.1930. **$30.00-$65.00**

Vacuum cleaner, electric upright, cast aluminum motor housing with red rubber bumper on 3 sides of hood & red plastic top, very streamlined design like a car of the period, long pivoting handle with cloth bag, "Premier Duplex" (for thick or thin rugs), mfd by Premier Vacuum Cleaners, Cleveland, OH, c.1947. **$35.00-$75.00**

Vacuum cleaner, electric upright, cast metal, probably aluminum, body & hood, with bullet-shaped motor housing with wheels in back, long pivot handle, bag inlet at side of back of the domed sucker part, "Cadillac Revolving Brush Cleaner", mfd by Clements Mfg. Co., Chicago, IL, c.late 1940s, early 1950s. • Clements also made an upright, just a little bit more old-fashioned looking in style of body, as long ago as mid 1930s. **$35.00-$60.00**

Vacuum cleaner, electric upright, large tin canister motor housing, painted black with decorative pin striping, carpet sweeper type brush roller in front, tin hood, long pivot handle with large red sateen dust bag hung from it, "Model 0", Hoover Electric Suction Sweeper Co., New Berlin, OH, 1908. • **Hoover has a museum** now, The Hoover Historical Center, featuring antique housecleaning implements including sweepers and vacuum cleaners. It is at 2225 Easton N. W., North Canton, OH 44720. • They're not the same folks, but I thought it was interesting that a Joseph H. Hoover, along with Jerry E. Harvey, of Hubbard, IA, patented an "Apparatus for maintaining and regulating vacuums in cow-milking machines" on Oct. 1, 1895 — a whole new Hoovering sideline. **$200.00-$250.00**

Vacuum cleaner, hand pumped, tin cylinder, decal marked "Evans", American, TOC. **$15.00-$18.00**

Vacuum cleaner, hand pumped type, tin canister at bottom, long cylindrical body, slightly flexible vacuuming tube at bottom (missing brush?), "Superior Vacuum Cleaner", mfd by -?- Sales Co., American, pat'd Dec. 26, 1911. **$65.00-$80.00**

Vacuum cleaner, handpump type, metal, wood and cloth, "Regina Model A", 1903. • **German vocabulary** — Staubsauger: dust sucker. An electric one is elektrisch. **$145.00-$165.00**

Vacuum cleaner, long copper tube with vacuuming tip, wooden platform with wheels, wooden lever to pump it up, rubber tube, canvas bag inside with rubber gasket or seal, filter or seal in front, "Everybody's Vacuum Cleaner", TOC. **$150.00-$175.00**

Vacuum cleaner, long tin cylinder that screws together in center, turned vertical wooden handle worked up and down like a bike pump, cast aluminum nozzle with slit to pick up dust, neat checked plaid bag inside to catch dust, "The Reeves Suction Sweeper", mfd by Reeves Vacuum Cleaner Co., Milford, CT, about 40'L, pat'd Jan. 20, 1914 & Apr. 14, 1914, • Electric ones were available at the time, but not everyone had electricity. What I never understood is why these didn't just blow the dirt out again each time you pumped down on the pump, and how anyone with only two arms and hands could operate such a thing! **$40.00-$75.00**

Vacuum cleaner, oak box, looks like locomotive from side, with 2 front pairs of wheels and back wheel, electric suction machine (without brush). • They also offered an electric vacuum sweeper with brush. mfd by Bissell Carpet Sweeper Co., Grand Rapids, MI, 1915. **$75.00-$95.00**

Vacuum cleaner, or suction cleaner, wooden body is sort of a treadle or see-saw box with bellows inside, upon which the lucky housewife balanced herself, whilst maneuvering the very very long hose & nozzle. (Richard Simmons would love this one.) "Kotten Suction Cleaner", H. G. Kotten, Brooklyn, NY, c.1910. • **Original instructions.** — "The simple act of swaying the body back and forth will draw all the dust out of rugs, draperies or carpets, making sweeping no longer a hardship. This suction is created by the motion of the body in moving the nozzle back and forth, which naturally throws the weight from one foot to the other, thereby developing a strong suction at each stroke of the nozzle. The dust passes through the nozzle into the bag located under the machine, which can readily be removed and cleaned. The knack of easy and successful operation is in moving the nozzle in unison with the pumping of the bellows.'' Well, sure! And who needs exercise videos, or Bonnie Pruden exercise records (remember those from the 1950s?), with a suction cleaner like this! **$100.00-$150.00**

Vacuum cleaner, pieced tin, pump type with wooden handles, painted dark green with shield, has original manual, words ''National Eagle'' in gold, 1911. **$65.00-$100.00**

Vacuum cleaner, pump type, metal canister with 2 handles to ''row'' in & out to create suction, ''New Home Vacuum Cleaner'', mfd by R. Armstrong Mfg. Co., Cincinnati, OH, late 19th C, patent pending. **$85.00-$100.00**

Vacuum cleaner, sheet metal, pump action ''like a reversed bicycle pump'' wrote one editorial writer of the day, roller so it glides over carpet, very narrow hinged nozzle or sucking mouth, (ooh, yuck), Dusto Mfg. Co., NYC, NY, c.1909. • A **1909** article on vacuum cleaners says, ''The broom, and the ordinary sweeping appliances scatter dust, and after sweeping the furniture must be gone over with a dust rag. Until the new dustless dusters came on the market even this operation was of only momentary value to the housewife, so that even after the sweeping was all done, dirt and germ-laden dust remained in the carpets, only the surface dirt having been removed, necessitating taking up the rugs and carpets twice a year, and sending them to the steam cleaner to be cleaned, or taking them out of the house and giving them a thorough beating. The vacuum cleaner enters at this point as the salvation of the housewife, and particularly the head of the house whose knuckles often become sore, and whose back is wrenched while applying the carpet beater.'' *House Furnishing Review*, July 1909. • **1910 Vacuuming.** — An article in *House & Garden*, suggested the installation of ''vacuum-cleaning plants'' with holes in the walls of every room to connect tubes from the cleaner — all emptying into a bag in the cellar. Of course, now we know what a recycling headache that would be. **$35.00-$50.00**

Vacuum cleaner, small cast aluminum body which houses motor, rubber back and front wheels, long tubular handle painted black, probably aluminum or steel, hollow at top, screws into the body, woven bag with airplane on it, jacquard weaving in black & gray like those old-fashioned shoe bags, electric switch is mounted to the black tubular handle, plastic disc on body says ''Remove plug from socket before taking out indicator. The Air-Way Sanitary System Replogle Patents'', ''Air-Way'', Air-Way Electrical Appliance Co., Toledo, OH, about waist high, electric cord is about 10 feet L, c.1928-30. • Fully restored & working, with new wire in motor. This was for sale by J. Allen Barber, Second Chance Antique Appliances, of Hawley, PA at a show in 1987. Really spectacular. Hey! Let's go for a ride on our Air-Way! Vroooom. **$195.00-$250.00**

Warming pan—See Bed warmer.

Waste can, step-on type, enameled sheet metal, simple round cylinder with domed lid, rubber gasket, inner pail, ''Sanette'', Master Metal Products, Inc., Buffalo, NY, early 1940s. **$5.00-$8.00**

Wastebasket, expanded metal giving effect of woven wire, but actually slit & pulled or stretched to create interstices (like those foil or paper Christmas garland decorations), stamped sheet metal bottom, flared flowerpot shape, mfd by The Northwestern Expanded Metal Co., Chicago, IL, 12''H x 12'' diameter, c.1920s (?). **$12.00-$18.00**

Wastebasket, flared bucket shaped, openwork twisted wire, another office wastebasket of the type most widely admired & collected, American, 13''H x 10'' diameter at top, TOC. **$22.00-$35.00**

Wastebasket, high square wooden box with slightly slanted sides, the 4 sides held together ¼ of the way down with beautifully proportioned wide leather straps that are bound around corner and disappear inside slots. Wood painted medium greenish blue, signed ''C. A. Brown'', Shaker made, 19th C. **$350.00-$475.00**

Wastebasket, lightweight ''vulcanized fibre'' round cylinder (also came in oval) with slightly flared sides, rolled rim, pastel green finish (came in other pastels, and probably the natural rich brown), ''Vul-Cot — the national wastebasket'', by National Vulcanized Fibre Co., Wilmington, DE, about 12''H, late 1920s. • **That man ... he's so clean;** or, A Chicken In Every Pot, etc. — ''Make it easy for him. Give him a convenient place to throw his ''trash'' and you won't have to be picking up after him all the time ... A wastebasket for every room. See the dainty new home Vul-Cot, the dainty little sister of the famous business Vul-Cot. Light as a feather, yet super-strong. Solid at sides and bottom so dust or ashes cannot sift through onto your floors.'' August 1928 ad in *Good Housekeeping*. • To be a desirable collectible, this one would have to be in very good condition. **$10.00-$15.00**

Wastebasket, lithographed metal, licensed product using ''Return of the Jedi'' images, 1980s. **$18.00-$20.00**

Wastebasket, nickel plated copper wire mesh, solid bottom, straight sides, only the narrow lip flares slightly & has two curved projections to lip forming handles, designed by Emile-Jacques Ruhlmann (highly desirable Art Deco designer), for the Maharaja of Indore, French, 12¾''H, c.1930. • According to Sam Pennington, editor/publisher of *Maine Antique Digest*, in his editorial write-up of the sale of this wastebasket, **''The peak (of the 1980's art and antiques market)** occurred on ... May 6 (1989), with lot #84 of Sotheby's sale of the very spiffy contents of...the Philip Johnson town house ... (NYC).'' This peak happened when the first example of this wastebasket sold for $27,500.00, and the second of the set for $33,000 (including 10% buyer's premium). Dirt, where is thy sting? **$25,000.00-$30,000.00**

Wastebasket, oval, galvanized sheet metal, covered with green fake leather, painted with landscape & flowers, & even tooled like Italian leather, Venezian Art Screen Co., NYC, NY, 11¼''H, early 1930s. **$6.00-$12.00**

Wastebasket, pieced tin, basically an oval having both ends extended with much smaller rounded pieces — giving the effect of columns or anterooms, these each having a ring handle of a stamped gilded lion's head with ring through mouth. Grayish dark green paint finish with flowers painted in freeform ''tole''-like style, 4 small gold painted ball feet. *House Beautiful* editorial note says they are "decorated to match the room." Maker not marked, nor mentioned in magazine ad of time. 12¼"H x 12"W the long axis, Oct. 1922 magazine. **$25.00-$35.00**

Wastebasket, square base, mirrored glass sides cant out & fit together with small glass-headed bolts, at each corner, top and bottom. One ad said "it's a great idea to have a mirror near the floor so you can check up on the appearance of your feet." American, 12½"H x 12" square at top, early 1930s. • This would be close to impossible to find in perfect condition. Crossover interest from Deco collectors of mirrored furniture & accessories. **$45.00-$65.00**

Wastebasket, square with slightly canted sides, plywood painted a sort of gray medium green, triangular cutout hand holes on 2 sides, assembled with 4 slide-on corner posts, mfd by Spaulding-Moss Co., Boston, MA, early 1920s. **$8.00-$12.00**

Wastebasket, stamped & slit sheet metal, the slits allow silhouette or shape to go in at the "neck', copper plated steel with green paint, "DANDEE", mfd by Erie Art Metal Co., Erie, PA, 16"H, pat'd Jan. 5, 1909. **$50.00-$65.00**

Wastebasket, typical modern oval cylinder, painted heavy tin, with a band of stamped-out square perforations around the top, plus the best feature for people interested in metal-working: ingeniously stamped out & applied 3-D flowers with petals & leaves sticking out. The devil to clean, especially when dust bunnies run rampant in your house. American, 14"H, c.1950s. **$6.00-$10.00**

Wastebasket, wire mesh, openwork basketweave, sheet iron bottom, rather tall & skinny, actually an office wastebasket, American, 22"H x 9" diameter, early 20th C. • This is the most widely-admired & coveted "collectible" wastebasket, especially sought by wirework collectors. It was made with slight variations by several wirework manufacturers. **$22.00-$35.00**

Wastebasket, wire, woven in a square mesh, very flared at top, tin bottom with slightly raised sides, looped swags around top rim, rather flimsy — or you could say delicate & pretty. The Wire Goods Co., Worchester, MA, 11¼"H x 15¼" diameter at top (9¾" at bottom), 1910s. **$15.00-$25.00**

Whisk broom, in original leather holster with image of the Steel Pier & boardwalk, a useful souvenir, 20th C. **$15.00-$20.00**

Whisk broom, very old turned wooden handle with hanging hole, wire bound, natural bristles, American (?), 13"L, late 19th C. **$20.00-$28.00**

Whisk broom, with Black Americana "Mammy" is the handle, 4½"L, 20th C. **$12.00-$22.00**

Whisk broom doll, natural bristles, glazed porcelain doll head and bust, American (?), 8"L, early 20th C. One of many such whisk brooms, and related to other period doll-top forms including powder puffs, vanity boxes, etc. **$55.00-$70.00**

Whisk broom doll, zingy Flapper with pink dress, not for the serious broom collector, but fun, 1920s. **$20.00-$22.00**

**I-1.**
**"This is (a) House Cleaning Time—**
*and it's a time of trouble and much work for unbelieving women."*
*Ad for Pearline house-cleaning soap, mfd. by James Pyle, NYC, in* Century, *5/1892. "Peddlers and some unscrupulous grocers will tell you (something else) is as good as or the same as Pearline. It's false—Pearline is never peddled."*

# THE HAVEN AIR PURIFIER.

Destroys foul odors, sewer-gas and disease germs. Recommended by Physicians. Cost to maintain, about five cents a month. No objectionable features. Other styles for Refrigerators, Factories, Hotels, etc.

No. 5. For Sleeping-rooms, Nurseries, etc. In Japanned Case, Decorated. Price $4.00.

*Write for special offer where* we pay expressage.

**The Haven Air Purifier Company,**

**38 PLYMOUTH PLACE,**

**CHICAGO, ILL.**

**I-2.**
**Air purifier.**
*Japanned decorated sheet metal cabinet, with (presumably) some kind of filtering system inside. Non-electric, of course. The Haven Air Purifier Co., Chicago. Ad in* Century, *5/1883.* **$25.00-$35.00**

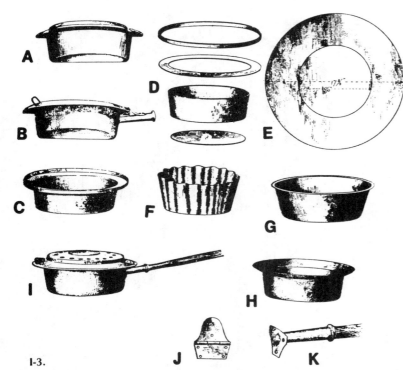

**I-3.**

**Steps in making copper bed warming pan.**

*As described, and drawn, by John Fuller, Sr., in a series called "Coppersmithing," whcih appeared in 1890 issues of* The Metal Worker, *and was also an 1889 book. (A)Wiring of pan and cover; (B) Edge turned on pan to receive cover; (C) Body of pan; (D) Parts of warming pan body; (E) Disk marked for bottom; (F) Disk wrinkled for razing; (G) Wrinkles worked out of pan; (H) Brim worked out on pan; (I) The finished warming pan; (J) Cover joint (hinge); (K) Socket for handle. Fuller explains here, and in other of his coppersmithing articles, that he is showing the modern metal worker how to make something as it was made a half century or more before—both in America and England. This is modeled on English pans.*

**I-4.**

**Bed warmer**

*Copper with brass cap. Simple, undecorated, round pan with socket handle (missing long wooden handle). Marked on top "P.P. Emory & Co., Springfield, MA." 14 11/16" diameter. Probably 2nd quarter 19th C. Picture courtesy of the National Museum of American History, Smithsonian Instution. John Paul Remensnyder estate.*

**I-5.**

**Broom holder with broom.**

*Blued steel spring mounted to round hardwood block, in turn screwed to wall. Spring grips broom handle. Mfd. by Slaymaker, Barry & Co., Lancaster, PA; 1892 ad. About the broom I have no information, but it is easy to see how well-made it is. The holder:*
**$3.00-$6.00**

**DON'T SWEEP THE OLD WAY!**

**THE NEW Woman**

**Sweeps Hard and Soft Carpets, Bare Floors, WITH A SWEEPERETTE**

**ALL DEALERS**

**SWEEPERETTE CO.,** *Grand Rapids, Mich.*

**I-6.**

**Ad of old besom.**

*"Besom" is the old English word for broom, as well as for broom-wielding hag — in other words, a witch. Ad is for a carpet sweeper; from* Century, *12/1895.*

# SAVE MONEY AND TIME
### By using the improved
## SILVER'S PATENT BROOM,
### WARRANTED the CHEAPEST, BEST, and MOST BEAUTIFUL BROOM IN AMERICA.

It is adapted to City or Country use. The Brush is so elastic that it wears twice as long as the old-fashioned tied Broom, sweeps with half the effort, and does not wear the Carpet one fourth as fast, thus saving *money* and *time*. Hon. Horace Greeley says; "I PREDICT ITS SUCCESS."

The Patent Brass Metallic parts, *which last a lifetime*, sent to Farmers (where we have no Agents), with full instructions for making their own Brooms, by mail, prepaid, for $1 25.

**AGENTS WANTED** in every County. Last year 350 Agents were selling it, making from $5 to $10 per day. With the Improved SEAMLESS BRASS CAP and WROUGHT-IRON LOOP it is perfect, and at OUR REDUCED PRICE 1000 active, energetic men can do as well this year.

The Agent's complete outfit sent by Express on receipt of $2.

Full particulars sent free. Address, naming your first, second, and third choice of Counties, C. A. CLEGG & Co., 207 Fulton St. (P. O. Box 5985), N.Y.

### I-7.
### Broom.

Silver's Patent, mfd. by C.A.Clegg & Co., NYC. Barkley distinguishable in the ad, shown enlarged here, is a pattern of upside-down hearts just below where the handle joins the neck and shoulder. Horace Greeley, whose recommendation was apparently elicited, was an extremely influential publisher, editor, and anti-slavery writer, who died in 1872. This ad appeared in Harper's Weekly, 4/11/1868. The hearts and the brass cap would add to value, if this broom could be found. **$35.00-$50.00**

### I-8.
### Feather duster.

Shown in two parts, as it was shipped. 10"L turkey feathers. "100 feathers, no pointers." Painted, turned wood handle screws into neck of duster. From Butler Brothers mail order catalog, 1899. This would only have some market value if in very good condition. **$15.00-$20.00**

### I-9.
### Dusting brush.

Natural bristles & shaped wood handle. From Duparquet, Huot & Moneuse catalog, c.1904-1910. **$10.00-$20.00**

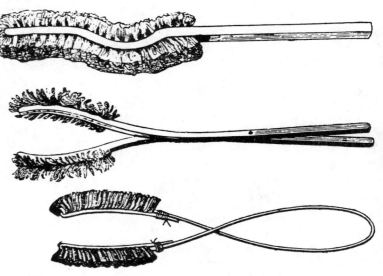

### I-10.
### Kerosene lamp brushes.

"A good kerosene lamp gives a light so fine and steady that those who live in the country need not regret the absence of gas. It is true that the care of lamps takes a little time. By a...few simple contrivances the labor...is reduced to a trifle. In trimming the wick, do not use scissors, but simply scrape off the charred crust with a knife. The metallic tube which encloses the wick, whether flat or circular, should be kept free of all incrustation...[And] the chinmeys must be kept clean." (L) and (M) which fit inside the chimney globe by compressing the handles. (R) is curved wood with lamp wick or "coarse worsted threads". Homemade, from American Agriculturist, 9/1867. **$5.00-$15.00**

"Charge of the Cleaning Brigade!"

YOU can clean your house best, easiest, and quickest with PYLE'S PEARLINE—besides, you'll spare your back, your temper, and the comfort of the entire household.

PEARLINE takes the hard work out of house-cleaning; surely, if this is true, it deserves a trial. It is sold everywhere.

**Beware of peddlers, imitations and prize schemes.** **Manufactured only by JAMES PYLE, New-York.**

**I-11.**
**Another Pearline ad.**

*This one plays on a phrase, still used today: "Charge of the Light Brigade." It refers to a tragic incident in the Crimean War, the Battle at Balaklava. A "light" (as opposed to a heavy) brigade of mounted English soldiers charged the defending Russians, against all common sense and apparently because of a mix-up in orders from headquarters. A third of the men, and many more of the horses, were killed in 20 minutes. Alfred Lord Tennyson wrote a poem, "The Charge of the Light Brigade," in 1854, which was widely read and admired. Here, a sort of pun — perhaps seen only in retrospect — comes from the common generic maid's name "Bridget", after all the Irish maids recently come to the U.S. At least to me, "Brigade" suggests "Bridget." Ad from Century magazine, 4/1888.*

THE "CLEANER" RUG and CARPET BEATER
IS MADE FROM THE BEST
FURNITURE SPRING STEEL,
is very Elastic.
The Handle is Guaranteed not to come off or Wire break off at the handle.

PATENT APPLIED FOR.

**I-12.**
**Carpet beater,**

*also called a **rug beater**. Mfd. by Holt-Lyon Co., Tarrytown, NY, known to many of you perhaps as the maker of a famous egg beater. Pat'd 3/3/1908, and formed of "six spring steel wires in the head where they are needed. Four wires only in the shank where more are worse than useless. The shanks are elastic. Guaranteed not to break off a handle." Picture of beater with now-valuable original tag is from ad claiming that this and the egg beater "beat but can't be beaten," which appeared two months before the patent was granted, in House Furnishing Reveiw. Other ads are found in Iron Age. This beater, the "blow" of which "is divided over a large space," was advertised early on as being made of wire" that can be formed in the shape required." The ads were for retailers — perhaps they were to shape the wires? Or did the ad mean the housekeeper herself could squash or bend them to suit herself? Another ad, in 1912, said that this beater was about the first one "sold for more than 10¢ each." By 1912, they were made in 6 sizes.*
**$25.00-$45.00**

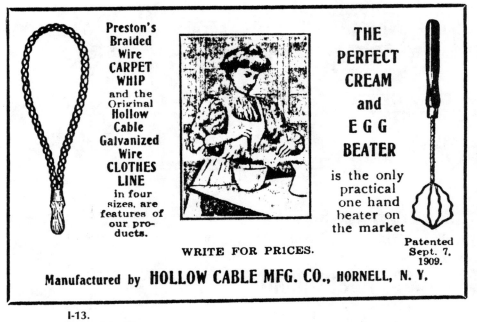

Preston's Braided Wire CARPET WHIP and the Original Hollow Cable Galvanized Wire CLOTHES LINE in four sizes, are features of our products.

THE PERFECT CREAM and EGG BEATER is the only practical one hand beater on the market

Patented Sept. 7, 1909.

WRITE FOR PRICES.

Manufactured by HOLLOW CABLE MFG. CO., HORNELL, N. Y.

**I-13.**
**Carpet beater.**
*Also an egg beater by another company making both. This one is "Preston's Braided Wire Carpet Whip." Hollow Cable Mfg. Co., Hornell, NY. Ad in* House Furnishing Review *(hereinafter shortened to* HFR*), 12/1910.* $25.00-$45.00

THE CYCLONE DUST BEATER
Is made of carefully coiled steel spring wire. Strong, light, durable and effective.

(Patent pending.)

SPRING BEATER MFG. CO.
BUFFALO, N. Y.

Manufacturers of Meritorious Articles

"It's the spring that's in the wire that does the work"

CATALOGUES AND PRICE LISTS ON APPLICATION

(Patented.)

THE PERFECT DUST BEATER
Is made of the best spring steel wire, tinned with interwoven coils

**I-14.**
**Carpet beaters.**
*The "Cyclone" and the "Perfect"—said later to be the "next to greatest" and the "greatest" dust beaters ever made. Mfd. by the Spring Beater Mfg. Co., Buffalo, NY. In 1903 ad, the "Cyclone" was not yet patented. The "Perfect" was pat'd 4/22/1902 in U.S., 1/21/1902 in Canada, and 6/3/1902 in Germany. Tinned steel spring wires, turned wooden handles.* HFR*ad.* $25.00-$45.00

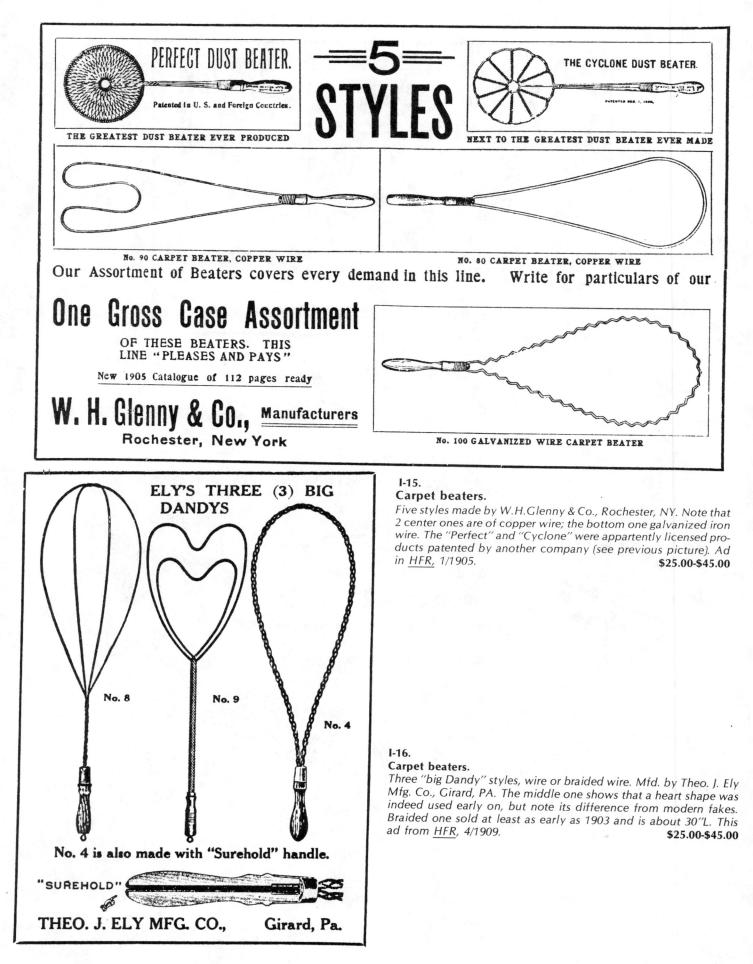

PERFECT DUST BEATER.

Patented in U. S. and Foreign Countries.

THE GREATEST DUST BEATER EVER PRODUCED

# 5 STYLES

THE CYCLONE DUST BEATER.

PATENTED DEC. 1, 1896.

NEXT TO THE GREATEST DUST BEATER EVER MADE

No. 90 CARPET BEATER, COPPER WIRE

No. 80 CARPET BEATER, COPPER WIRE

Our Assortment of Beaters covers every demand in this line.    Write for particulars of our

# One Gross Case Assortment

OF THESE BEATERS. THIS
LINE "PLEASES AND PAYS"

New 1905 Catalogue of 112 pages ready

# W. H. Glenny & Co., Manufacturers

Rochester, New York

No. 100 GALVANIZED WIRE CARPET BEATER

## ELY'S THREE (3) BIG DANDYS

No. 8

No. 9

No. 4

No. 4 is also made with "Surehold" handle.

"SUREHOLD"

THEO. J. ELY MFG. CO.,    Girard, Pa.

**I-15.**
**Carpet beaters.**
*Five styles made by W.H.Glenny & Co., Rochester, NY. Note that 2 center ones are of copper wire; the bottom one galvanized iron wire. The "Perfect" and "Cyclone" were apparently licensed products patented by another company (see previous picture). Ad in* HFR, *1/1905.* **$25.00-$45.00**

**I-16.**
**Carpet beaters.**
*Three "big Dandy" styles, wire or braided wire. Mfd. by Theo. J. Ely Mfg. Co., Girard, PA. The middle one shows that a heart shape was indeed used early on, but note its difference from modern fakes. Braided one sold at least as early as 1903 and is about 30"L. This ad from* HFR, *4/1909.* **$25.00-$45.00**

# THEO. J. ELY MFG. CO.

## GIRARD, PENN., U. S. A.

## The "DANDY" Line

. . OF . .

## Carpet, Rug, and Clothes Beaters

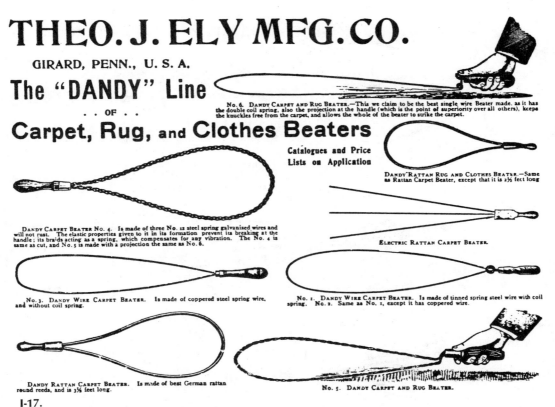

Catalogues and Price Lists on Application

No. 6. DANDY CARPET AND RUG BEATER.—This we claim to be the best single wire Beater made, as it has the double coil spring, also the projection at the handle (which is the point of superiority over all others), keeps the knuckles free from the carpet, and allows the whole of the beater to strike the carpet.

DANDY RATTAN RUG AND CLOTHES BEATER.—Same as Rattan Carpet Beater, except that it is 2½ feet long

DANDY CARPET BEATER NO. 4. Is made of three No. 12 steel spring galvanized wires and will not rust. The elastic properties given to it in its formation prevent its breaking at the handle; its braids acting as a spring, which compensates for any vibration. The No. 4 is same as cut, and No. 5 is made with a projection the same as No. 6.

ELECTRIC RATTAN CARPET BEATER.

No. 3. DANDY WIRE CARPET BEATER. Is made of coppered steel spring wire, and without coil spring.

No. 1. DANDY WIRE CARPET BEATER. Is made of tinned spring steel wire with coil spring. No. 2. Same as No. 1, except it has coppered wire.

DANDY RATTAN CARPET BEATER. Is made of best German rattan round reeds, and is 3½ feet long.

No. 5. DANDY CARPET AND RUG BEATER.

**I-17.**
**Carpet beaters.**
*More by Theo. J. Ely, in their "Dandy" line. All those shown here are carpet and/or rug beaters, except for small-appearing one upper right, which is a rattan rug and clothes beater that is 2-1/2 feet long. The rattan one lower left is a simple hoop, and is 3-1/2 feet long. Get out your magnifying glass to read details. HFR, 2/1903.* **$25.00-$45.00**

**I-18.**
**Carpet beater.** (above)
*The "Star Dust Beater," with heavy twisted shank and strengthening cross-pieces within the petals. Mfd. by A. Clausing & Co., Milwaukee, WI. HFR ad, 4/1915, "patent applied for."* **$25.00-$45.00**

**I-19.**
**Carpet beater.** (left)
*Similar, but obviously not so well made. Bent charmingly out of whack by use. 26 1/4"L simple wooden grip. Collection Mary Mac Franklin.* **$25.00-$40.00**

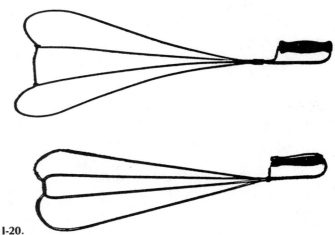

**I-20.**
**Carpet beaters.**
*Very similar beaters with what were called "guard" handles to protect the knuckles. (T) is photograph of one 28 3/4"L, turned wood handle painted black, collection Mary Mac Franklin. (B) is linecut from catalog, representing one of "hard drawn steel wire, No. 10 gauge, "30"L. From Sno-Cap catalog of the Wasburn Co.'s Androck line, Worcester, MA & Rockford, IL, 1927. These were originally sold for $12.00 per gross!* **$25.00-$45.00**

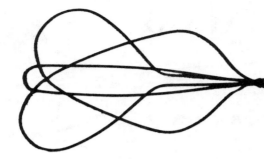

**I-21.**
**Carpet beater.**
*Bent wire resembling diagram for the molecules of some element. Black-Opainted turned wood handle. Note retaining ring at head end of shank. 32 3/4"L. Collection Mary Mac Franklin.*
**$25.00-$45.00**

**I-22.** (right)
**Carpet beater.**
*"Ideal 3-in-one" beater, with "lashes" of tinned spring steel wire, and flat wire frame at neck. Turned wood handles seems difficult to hold. 36"L. Sno-Cap catalog of Washburn Co., 1929.*
**$25.00-$45.00**

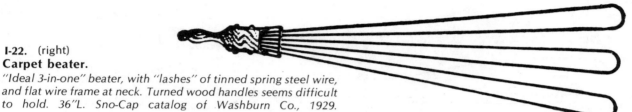

**I-23.** **Carpet beater.** (left)
*There's no way, from looking at it, that you would think this could be advertised as "a novel twist wire." The editorial write-up in HFR, 1/1904. explains that it is "composed of two wires twisted together at their centers and bent to form a loop which terminates in a stout handle through which the ends of the wires pass. It is practically two beaters in one." (I wonder why?) Mfd. by Cady Mfg. Co., Auburn, NY, pat'd 4/21/1903.*
**$20.00-$40.00**

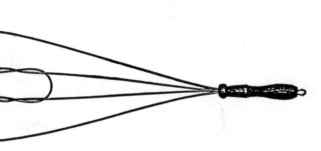

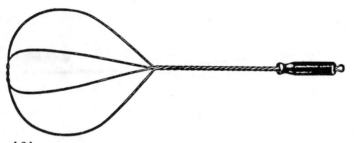

**I-25.**
**Carpet beater.**
*The "Androck", mfd. by Andrews Wire & Iron Works, Rockford, IL. Spring steel with "opposing coils near the handle (which) cause it to strike a heavy blow with only a slight movement of the wrist, while the extra weight at the end...adds to the force of the blow." 30"L x 12"W, riveted handle. I bet tennis players at the turn of the century were frequently called on to beat carpets for their mothers and wives. HFR ad, 1/1908.*
**$25.00-$45.00**

**I-24.**
**Carpet beaters or whips.**
*(T) 31"L. Both made of coppered iron wire in No.11 gauge, with black-enameled turned wood handles. Both "Sherwood" items, mfd. by Wire Goods Co., Worcester, MA, 1915 catalog.*
**$25.00-$50.00**

**I-26.**
**Carpet beater.**
*Substantial coiled wire one called the "Boss." Note the forked neck-ferrule, which looks as if it could tear holes in weak carpeting. From dealer's catalog, Joseph Breck & Sons, Boston, 1905.*
**$25.00-$45.00**

# ROYAL DUST BEATER.

PATENT PENDING.

The finest thing ever produced for beating dust from carpets, rugs, cushions, clothing, etc. It is flexible and covers the surface so fully as to do its work effectively and rapidly.

## MADE IN TWO SIZES.

No. 1. For light work,..............................................................$3.00 per doz.
No. 2. For heavy work,.............................................................4.00 per doz.

MANUFACTURED BY

# WARNER HARDWARE CO.,
### FREEPORT, ILL.

**I-27.**
**Carpet beater.**
*This "Royal" (called the "Arcade" in a supplier's catalog of c.1916) beater was mfd. by Warner Hardware Co., Freeport, IL, in 2 sizes—for "light" work and "heavy" work. The No. 2 was 30"L. This illustration from undated flyer which looks to be c.1900-1910.*
**$25.00-$50.00**

**I-28.**
**Carpet beater.**
*Rattan hoop, Called the "Dandy" in this 1905 Breck catalog, as well as by a manufacturer, Theo. Ely. See illustration I-17.*
**$20.00-$35.00**

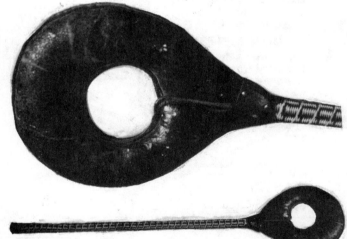

**I-30.**
**Carpet beater.**
*Padded black oilcloth or leatherette "catcher's mitt" type with cotton tape-wrapped rattan handle. 28"L x 6 1/8"W. Early 20th C. Courtesy of Dick Phelps, East Canaan, CT.* **$45.00-$65.00**

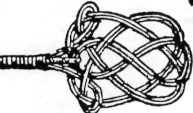

**I-29.**
**Carpet beaters.**
*These two twisted rattan & cane beaters are only slighlty different, but the original catalog pictures are difficult to see. Enlarged here, the picture at (T) is described in the Albert Pick jobber's catalog of 1909 as their "rattan, three strand 11" x 8" blade, twisted rattan handle, split cane wrapped in two places. 30"L. Picture (B) is from the 1905 Breck catalog, but they don't tell which one of six rattan ones offered this is. At any rate, the manufacturer is not known to me. Shorter pillow beaters were also made in this sort of lover's knot rattan twist.* **$30.00-$60.00**

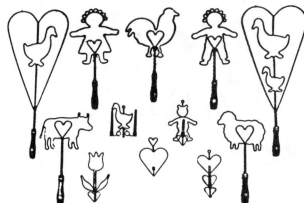

**I-31.**
**New pillow & carpet beaters in "country" style.**
*Assorted hearts, cows, ducks, tulips, etc., in painted twisted wire and turned wood. Meant to go with the "country look," and unfortunately have fooled some neophyte beater collectors. Mfd. by Mathews Wire & Wood, Frankfort, IN, c.1988. Photo courtesy Martin Mathews. Value range not because given these are subject to current retailing systems.*

**I-32.**
**Carpet stretcher & tack hammer combined.**
*"Excelsior," mfd. by Excelsior Mfg. Co., Chicago. Ad in Housewife, 1/29/1876. This is from the days when the carpet was taken up each spring, hung on a line and beaten to death, rolled and stored all summer, then put down again, tacks and all, in the fall. Argghhhh.* **$25.00-$45.00**

**I-33.**
**Carpet stretcher.**
*"Bullard's Improved," mfd. by George S. Knapp, Bridgeport, CT. "It is the cheapest on the market, showing large profits to dealers when retailed at 50¢." HFR, 1/1908.* **$25.00-$45.00**

**I-34.**
**Carpet stretcher & tack holder,**
*shown with a hammer being used. "Provides a third hand which holds the tack where desired." "Yankee", mfd. by Taylor Mfg. Co., Hartford, CT. HFR, 5/1190.* **$25.00-$45.00**

**I-35.**
**Early "sweeping box" carpet sweeper**
*An unidentified forerunner of the carpet sweeper as we know it. Note the belt and pulley arrangement on top of the large wooden case. The pulley passes through the box's top to turn the brush along the front of the box. The picture dates to the early 1850s; possibly it is A.C. Carey's "fan carpet sweeper" which was patented January 4, 1850. Certainly the box is large enough to house some kind of fan arrangement.*
*Note that there are no bumpers of any kind, so this would have been hell on wheels when it came to woodwork and furniture legs. Note also the handle, which closely resembles those of early (and later) lawn mowers.*

**I-36.**
**Carpet sweeper.**
*Closeup showing the button-lever pushed to dump the pans of their load of dust. Bissell's "XLCR" (Excelsior), showing the "hand decorated" cases. Bissell Carpet Sweeper Co., Grand Rapids, MI. Flyer from turn-of-century is worth at least $15.00 itself. The sweeper:* **$35.00-$65.00**

THE

# Boston Carpet Sweeper

**I**S superior to any other in the *Rapidity, Ease, and Perfection* of its operation. It is very simple in construction, consisting of a neat walnut case enclosing a rotary sweeping brush which is driven by cog-wheels that come in contact with the carpet as the Sweeper is moved across it. On each side of the brush, within the case, is a tin tray to receive the dirt and dust which the brush takes up by its revolution, so that *the annoyance of Dust is entirely overcome,* and the *Dirt is not sifted through the Carpet* by being driven across it, as in the old way.

### THE LONG PIVOTED HANDLE
#### PERMITS THE OPERATOR TO

## Sweep under Beds, Sofas, Tables and Pianos without moving them, or constant stopping.

A delicate lady, or a child, can thoroughly sweep a room without other exertion than is required to push the Sweeper before her across the carpet; and *Dusting is unnecessary.*

*Carpets wear much longer* when swept by a Sweeper than when the common broom is used, and as

## The Boston Carpet Sweeper

will last from five to ten years, doing its work perfectly all the time, it is really *cheaper than a corn broom.*

### PRICE, $3.50 EACH.

**I-38.**
**Another early "sweeping box".**
*Another unidentified box sweeper, of approximately the same age as one in I-35. This one has wheels in the back, off of which run pulleys which turn the brush inside. It's big enough that possibly it was used as a hall sweeper in large establishments, as also indicated by a male operator. Picture adapted from one in Bissell Collection, Public Museum of Grand Rapids.*

**I-37.**
**Carpet sweeper ad.**
*"Boston," mfd. by Haley, Morse & Co., NYC, c.1863. Walnut case, stenciled with name, pivoting handle so it would go either direction, 2 brushes and 2 tin trays to catch dust inside. The sweeper:*
**$35.00-$55.00**

**I-39.**

### Bissell booth at St. Louis World's Fair.

*In the manufacturer's Building, space 29, block 12A, was an attractive mahogany shop-like building, the canopy or roof of which was a gigantic sweeper "perfect in every detail, and measuring approximately 22 feet wide by 16 feet deep. It was "put into motion by electricity, and one of the first things that catches the eye of the visitor in the main aisle...is the revolving wheels." The wheels were 6 feet in diameter, the overall height of booth and sweeper was 28 feet, plus a 15 foot high flag mast. Inside was an automaton of a housemaid going through all motions of sweeping, even dumping the sweeper. Finally, "about 600 sweepers, of nearly fifty different varieties, ranging from the small toy six inches in length to the mammoth 'Hall' sweeper, and made in about as many finishes [i.e. 50], form the background of this exceedingly interesting booth." HFR, 7/1904.*

*When I examined the Bissell Collection at the Public Museum of Grand Rapids, Sally Bjork (who wrote an article for this book) showed me an old photograph in the archives. It depicts this booth in 1904, but shows more detail, including the company executive who manned the booth, Roy Shanahan.*

*I also found more information about the "automatic sweeping figure" in the May 1901 issue of Grand Rapids Furniture Record. It was apparently made in 1900 or 1901, to wit: "This year Bissell shows a wonderfully life-like automaton in the form of a pretty maid of the house, at work with one of Bissell's latest improved 'Cyco' Bearing Carpet Sweepers. She moves the valuable little household friend up and down the carpet just as easy as any child can do it; she lifts it up so that its self-working features can be shown, and then places it on the carpet again, and goes to work with the same ease that a master hand would use. This wonderful figure has been prepared for the Pan-American Exposition, at Buffalo this year." Where-oh-where is that automaton now! I suspect it would be worth $50,000.00 or more.*

**I-40.**
### Carpet sweeper.

*Although Bissell was the most famous name, still is, the first carpet sweeper, a rolling brush on a broomstick, was made in London about 1811. In 1858, another English sweeper, the Bigelow, came out, and a couple of years later, H.H. Herrick of Boston brought out a similar one in the U.S. According to HFR, 2/1926, "at first the New England metropolis had a monopoly on the patents,...(and) one New York merchant placed an order for 30,000," but the Civil War started and they were never delivered. Merville Bissell, of Grand Rapids, was granted a patent in 1876 for his carpet and bare floor sweeper. This illustration from Ladies' Home Journal ad for the "Cyco" Bearing sweeper, 5/1906.*

**I-41.**
### Carpet sweeper.

*The "Duntley Pneumatic Sweeper" which had a revolving brush and a pneumatic (vacuum) suction nozzle, and a dust bag instead of tin pans. Duntley Pneumatic Sweeper Co., Chicago, claimed to be the "originators of combination pneumatic sweepers," in this as from Modern Priscilla, about 1916. The Bissell company made a very similar-looking suction sweeper, but it had dust pans not a bag.* **$35.00-$60.00**

1. COVERS EYES AS CALLER'S DOG TOPPLES POLLY'S CAGE, SPILLING PARROT AND SAND TO FRESH-CLEANED RUGS

2. ORDER RESTORED—SKIPS TROUBLE OF SETTING UP VACUUM—DEPENDS ON HANDY BISSELL TO ERASE MESS

3. PLEASED BY CALLER'S ADMIRATION AS BISSELL'S HI-LO BRUSH AUTOMATICALLY ADJUSTS TO CLEAN HIGH AND LOW RUGS

4. EVEN DOG INTERESTED AS BISSELL CLEANS BENEATH CHAIRS—AND STAY-ON BUMPERS PREVENT SCRATCHING FURNITURE

5.

CHATS ABOUT NEW BISSELL...

"I use my new Bissell for all quick clean-ups and save my vacuum cleaner for periodic cleaning. Bissell's exclusive Hi-Lo brush automatically and *fully* adjusts to clean any rug nap. It's much better than the old sweeper."

*Models from $3.95 to $7.50*

MAINTAINS EVERY HOUSEWIFE SHOULD USE BISSELL FOR QUICK CLEAN-UPS AND SAVE VACUUM FOR GENERAL CLEANING

**BISSELL**
The really <u>better</u> sweeper
*Grand Rapids, Mich.*

$4.95

## I-42.
### Carpet sweeper ad.
*By the late 1930s, cartoons were widely used in advertising. This one, drawn by Lena Rue, shows a portly tiny-footed matron in a drawing style quite similar to at least two famous illustrators who did cartoons for* The New Yorker, *Gluyas Williams and Gardner Rea. This one from* American Home, *7/1937.*

Rufus stays home + makes dust bunnies to hide under the sofa

## I-44.
### Dust bunny drawing.
*I not only collect dustpans and dust, I also like drawings related to dusting, et. al. This is by Terry Ackerman, showing her cat Rufus making critters compounded of NYC dust and his own long hair. 1990.*

## I-43.
### Household oil ad.
*The product is the still-famed "3-in-One" oil. The old cans are collectible.* Good Housekeeping, *4/1934.*

GEE, MOM, YOUR CARPET SWEEPER RUNS EASY SINCE I OILED IT WITH **3-IN-ONE!**

IN **NEW** HANDY CANS AND BOTTLES

**3-in-One lightens housework—prolongs the life of household devices. As it lubricates it cleans and prevents rust. Get some today!**

## I-48.
## Dustpan.
*Another long-handled one, also from the American Agriculturist, of 1/1880. "A dust pan made of tin, with the sides and back higher than in the ordinary dust pan, and provided with a long, wooden handle, so that it can be used without stooping. The handle is fastened by a hinge at the bottom of the pan, and by a small hook at the upper eddge, so that when not in use the pan can be easily let down and the article hung up out of the way."*

## I-45.
## Dustpans.
*Both supposedly Shaker, with slender turned wooden handles, japanned tin pans. (L) From the Roberta & George Sieber Collection auctioned by Litchfield (CT) Gallery in July 1988 for $800.00*
**$800.00-$2000.00**

## I-46.
## Dust pan.
*Extremely similar to many of the long-handled so-called "Shaker" dustpans is this one, identified only as a "Patent Back-Saver" pan, "which consists of a dust-pan with high sides and a long handle. By resting the handle against a table or othjer piece of furniture, the dust may be swept into it, without the sweeper being obliged to stoop." It was part of the "new stock" in the household goods shop of W.H.Baldwin of NYC, where the editor of the magazine often went to "see new devices." The illustration and text are from American Agriculturist, 6/1872. There are several patents for dustpans in the Offical Gazette which might qualify (Ican't now check the patent drawings — you might want to).*

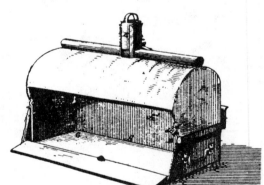

## I-49.
## Dustpan patent.
*Pat'd 4/20/1880 by N. Plyes, Westport,. MD. This one is sheet metal and mounted on rollers. Note that it has no handle at top, although it has a sort of drawer-pull handle at the side. This is because it is "pushed along by means of the broom to receive the dirt as it is swept up." It has a "hood to deflect the dust into the receptacle," but even better, a "water-sprinkler to lay the dust." The opening for emptying is "near one corner." Wow! but I bet it was never manufactured.*

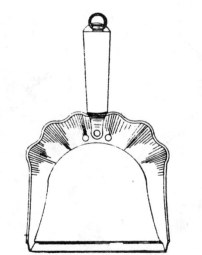

## I-47.
## Dustpan patent.
*Pat'd 5/8/1877 by Isaac S. Lauback, Chicago, IL, No. 190,499. "The back and sides are wired or hemmed when the metal is flat, and then corrugated, so as to turn them up to the desired angle.." Tubular handle with hanging ring in cap, riveted to pan. What appears to be a lip or sweeping edge may have been put on separately, or was ridged for strength. Offical Gazette.*
**$20.00-$30.00**

**I-50.**
**Dustpan patent.**
*Pat'd 7/12/1881 by Emma L. Dietz and Mary A. Dietz, Oakland, CA. Women's answer to women's need? The chamber or receptacle for the dust is "provided at the mouth thereof with double inclines forming a recess." It also has a weighted rod (1) which presumably keeps the lip down against the floor, and a "loop or shoe" (2) whcih is for foot.* <u>Offical Gazette.</u>

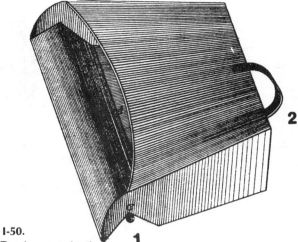

**I-51.**
**Illuminated Dustpan,**
*with a built-in candleholder and a springy foothold. Pat'd 11/7/1882. Made in Monroe, CT. Marked "A--OL-" (the last letter maybe another L or ann E). Japanned tin, 12 3/4"W x 12"D. Candle socket is 2"H. One sold at a Dick Withington auction in August 1985 for an astounding $425.00. I paid $12.00 for mine in 1984. Reasonable range:* **$45.00-$100.00**

**I-52.**
**Dustpan patent.**
*Pat'd 12/16/1884 by Lenonard B. Fletcher, Troy, NY, assignor of one-half to Cyrus S. Merrill, Albany, NY, who may have actually manufactured it. No. 309,215. This pan with tubular handle has an elliptical conical piece attached on the underside (the view seen here) which was for sliding onto the broom handle. The small foot, seen slightly to the left of the cone, is the support.* <u>Offical Gazette.</u>

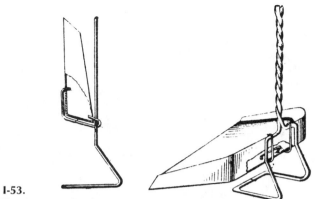

**I-53.**
**Dustpan patent.**
*Pat'd 12/23/1890 by William D. Martin, Warsaw, NY. No. 443,327. Twisted wire forms both the handle and the support for the pan, which can fold up flatter for hanging on the wall or in the broom closet.* <u>Offical Gazette.</u>

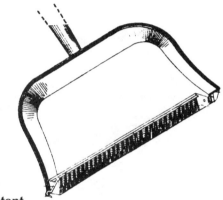

**I-54.**
**Dustpan patent.**
*Pat'd 11/4/1890 by James B. Dean, Lompoc, and Henry H. Earle, San Francisco, CA. No. 439,744. The patent is for a "swinging brush jointed to the pan at one corner of the front edge." Sounds totally unworkable to me, but that's par for a large percentage of 19th C. patents.* <u>Offical Gazette.</u>

**I-55.**
**Dustpans.**
*Both in "Greystonne" gray enameled sheet iron, mfd. by Matthai-Ingram, c.1890. (L) has an open pan and strength-giving ridges, and tubular handle with hanging hole; (R) is covered or hooded, otherwise substantially the same. Both measure 12 3/4"W x 8 3/4" deep.* **$35.00-$60.00**

**I-56.**
**Dustpan & broom holder combined.**
*"The Upright,"* mfd. by Craighead & Kintz Co., Ballard-vale, MA. The hook near the top of the handle can be raised up which drops the pan into emptying position. Sheet metal *"finished in brass,"* which probably means a sort of brassy japanned finish. <u>The Metal Worker</u>, *3/26/1892.*
**$35.00-$50.00**

**I-57.**
**Victor & Space Ship.**
*No, not really. This ill-favored little girl, who looks like Victor the Beast on TV, is having a close encounter with dirt, thanks to her "Only Perfect" dustpan, held securely against the floor with the foot. Stamped metal, 14" diameter. "You can sweep the dirt from all sides into it without turning it around." Detachable handle.* Ennis Specialty Co., Troy, NY <u>Hardware</u>, *2/25/1895.*
**$35.00-$50.00**

**I-58.**
**Dustpan.**
*The "West's", made by James R. West, Gas City, IN. Touted as "dainty, handsome, clean," but of course that depended on your dust. <u>Hardware</u>,2/25/1895.* **$35.00-$50.00**

**I-59.**
**Dustpan.**
*Another type often called and sold as "Shaker." Nicely painted tin, triangular boss braces the handle of turned wood. 10 1/2"W, and sold to a NYC woman for $4180.00 in 1988, at the Mendel Auction held by Willis Henry, Albany, NY. Let's just let that auction price stand here, although I don't believe that it is the value.*

**I-60.    Dustpan.**

*Hey! The same one! No, not quite, but scarily similar. This pieced tin English pan with triangular boss and black-painted turned wooden handle, was in the 1895 Harrod's Stores catalog, from the Ironmongery department. It could be had in bright tin or japanned finish, and also came in a hooded style. Sizes not given.*

**$65.00-$100.00**

**I-61.
Dustpan.**

*Here's a great one — a "germ-destroying gem." Mfd. by Thomas Clover, Philadelphia. Clover believes that after sweeping up the germs, the user should "be provided with some means of destroying" them. There is, therefore, a "concealed chamber beneath the flat surface, which receives the dust, and [the] entrance to this chamber is gained through the cylindrical head at the rear. Inside this head is a slotted tube, which can be rotated by grasping the handle of the removable cap (1) which closes the end, while the handle (2) serves as a reservoir for a liquid disinfectant." After sweeping in the dust, you tilted the pan so it fell into the slot, whereupon it was disinfected. HFR, 4/1903.*                **$65.00-$100.00**

## The **Lightning Dust Pan**

### Patent applied for

Admired by every one. Sells at sight. Made strong and durable. Enameled and striped, with gilded letters. No stooping to sweep. When not in use it hangs on the wall, making it valuable as a scrap-pan. This feature will be appreciated. Every household will have one when its value is known. Agents wanted. Send for catalogue and terms.

## D. B. Smith & Co.
### Utica, N. Y., U. S. A.
#### Sole Mfrs.

**New York Agents:**
White & Eisenmann,
124 Chambers Street.

**I-62.
Dustpan.**

*"Lightning," mfd. by D.B.Smith & Co., Utica, NY. Enameled & pinstriped sheet metal, gilt letters, wall hanging — where it serves as a form of wastebasket. When used by a little girl, as here, I guess there's no need to avoid stooping. HFR, 12/1903.*
**$40.00-$60.00**

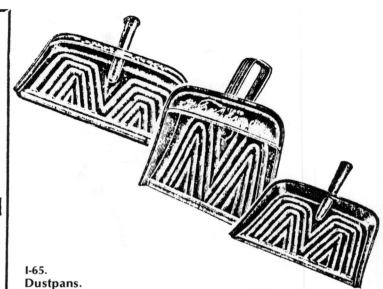

**I-63.**
**Dustpan.**
*Nice drawing, but the woman still has to bend over to pick it up, unless she's very acrobatic. Buttock-ribbing or corrugations in floor of pan gives strength, strap metal provides a foothold. Lawrence Mfg. Co., Toledo, OH. HFR 6/1905.* **$10.00-$20.00**

**I-65.**
**Dustpans.**
*All by Lawrence Mfg. of Toledo, including center hooded one shown in XIX-63.* Singly they may not look like much, but in good condition (at least as far as original japanning goes) and in multiples, they look great on wall. HFR, 7/1905.* **$10.00-$20.00**

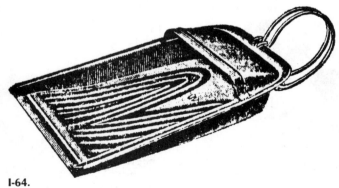

**I-64.**
**Dustpan & broom holder combined.**
*"The Gem," mfd. by Case Mfg. Co., Fenton, MI. What appears to be a strap handle is actually two lengths of heavy wire which slip tightly around broom handle for storage. Corrugated steel, japanned. HFR, 3/1904.* **$10.00-$20.00**

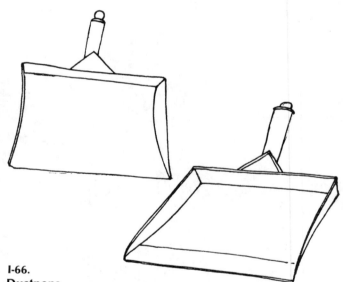

**I-66.**
**Dustpans.**
*Third type called "Shaker." Somewhat flared tapered side walls, triangular boss (brace) to tubular handle, hanging ring—all characteristic. In fact, this type was sold with name "Quaker" a bit later on (see I-68) as well as being "Puritan" brand. (Remember, cleanliness is next to godliness). Drawing (L) done from photograph of "Shaker" pan sold at auction for about $500.00 in 1988. At (R) is drawing done from very similar pan sold in 1907 by Central Stamping Co. (see I-67).* **$30.00-$80.00**

We make the BEST LINE of

# Extra Heavy Steel Edge Dust Pans

JAPANNED BLACK OR IN ASSORTED COLORS

Of special importance also is our **KORNERKLEAN DRIPPING PANS**

OUR CATALOGUE AND CIRCULARS TELL ALL

## The Central Stamping Co.

24 Cliff Street, New York City, and Newark, N. J.

KORNERKLEAN DRIPPING PAN

**I-67.**
**Dustpans.**
*Various styles of steel edge dustpans, mfd. by Central Stamping
Co., Newark, NJ & NYC.* HFR, *2/1907.*            **$10.00-$50.00**

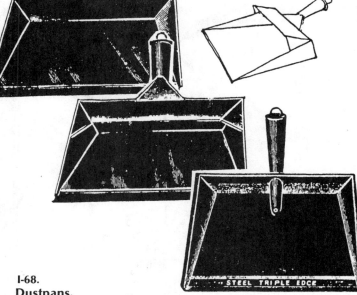

# The Delphos Dust Pan

## A USEFUL NOVELTY THAT SELLS ON SIGHT

1. Because it requires no stooping to operate it.
2. Because it does not easily upset.
3. Because the dirt can not be swept over the top of it.
4. Because it can be hung full of sweepings, if not convenient to empty at once.
5. Because it can be held close to the floor while the operator is standing in an upright position.
6. Because it is the best Dust Pan made.

**Write for Prices and Discount**

**Delphos Mfg. Co., Delphos, O.**

**I-68.**
**Dustpans.**
*All from Central Stamping Co. catalog of 1920. (T) is a "Puritan"
Quaker Dust Pan, japanned black, of 1XXX guage tin. 12 7/8" x
8 1/8". Note triangular boss an tubular handle. (M) is a hooded
or covered pan, otherwise of same description. I did a drawing
next to it to show the hood. (B) is an interesting variant — note
how the tapered tubular handle comes through the back wall and
is riveted to floor of pan. Also japanned black, triple steel edge,
and it says "handles bossed, riveted, capped and ringed," but the
boss must be hidden from our view here. They also made one
without the "Quaker" name, similar to this but with flared sides
and buttock-corrugated pan floor. Sold for many years.*
**$25.00-$80.00**

**I-69.**
**Dustpan.**
*"Delphos", by Delphos Mfg. Co., Delphos, OH. Note proportion
of pan used as dust receptacle — weight made it able to be "hung
full of sweepings."* HFR, *3/1909.*            **$10.00-$35.00**

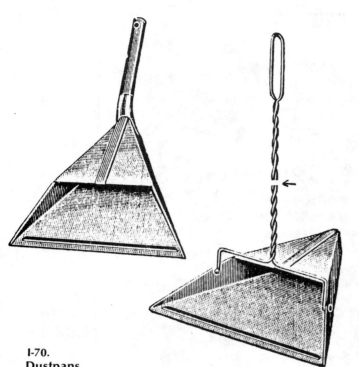

**I-70.**
**Dustpans.**

*Two styles of similar hooded pans, made of "double IXXXX 22 guage steel", one with stationary handle, one with free-swinging or pivoting twisted wire handle. The break in the handle at the arrow was frequently done for illustrations in old ads or catalogs to conserve space when a handle was very long. The pan (L) is 9"W x 12 5/8" deep by 16"L overall. One (R) is 9" x 12" with 33 1/4"L handle; both were available in "japanned green and blue with black handles or all black." Mfd. by Geuder, Paeschke & Frey Co., Milwaukee. HFR, 8/1930.* **$10.00-$25.00**

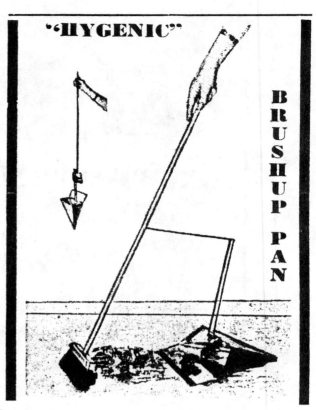

**I-72.**
**Dustpan.**

*"Hygenic Brushup Pan," maker not given. It appeared in an article on modern conveniences in HFR, 7/1935.* **$10.00-$25.00**

**I-71.**
**Dustpan.**

*"Polly Prim", mfd. by Patent Novelty Co., Inc., Fulton, IL, who made many household metal novelties. "Comes in beautiful pastel shades of blue and green, also black." Postpaid it was only $1.00. Good Housekeeping, 3/1931.* **$10.00-$25.00**

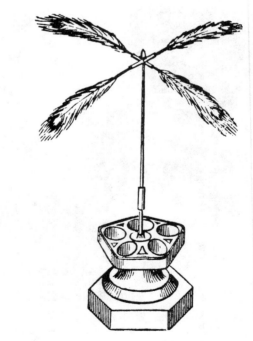

**I-73.**
**"Automatic Caster & Fan" patent.**

*Clockwork fly fan pat'd 10/20/1857 by E.A. Nordyke, Richmond, IN. No. 18,466. I love the peacock feathers. Official Gazette.*

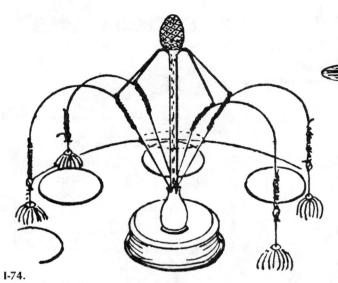

**I-74.**

**"Automatic Fly-bushes" patent.**

*"Imitates the casual and intermittent motion of fly-bush in the servant's hand." Apparently windup action causes the springy "fly-disturbers" to move around, bouncing slightly. Pat'd 9/22/1874 by Lyman D. Howard, Drury's Bluff, VA. No. 155,308. Official Gazette.*

**I-76.**

**Fly fan.**

*"The Improved Keyless Fly Fan," pat'd 1885 and 1887. Mfd. by Matthai-Ingram. 29 1/2"H x 48"W wingspread. "It drives all flies away by the shadow and movement of the wings while revolving." One of a number on the market up into early 20th C. The clockwork was wound by twisting the key-like "T" at top of the fluted cast iron base, and was supposed to run for 90 minutes — the length of a reasonable meal.* **$400.00-$500.00**

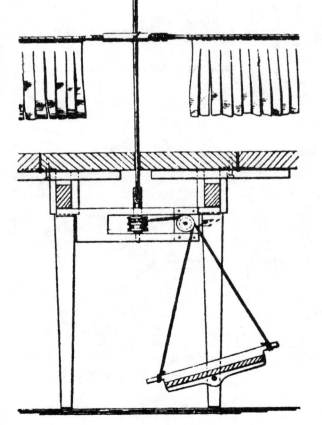

**I-75.**

**Fly fan patent.**

*Pat'd 1/2/1877 by S.W. Mills, Kingsville, MO. A table-mounted fan operated by a treadle underneath, which I guess was trod upon by whomever sat at that end of the table? Official Gazette.*

**I-77.**

**Fly fan.**

*"National," mfd. by Bridgeport Brass Co., CT. Makers referred to it as a "decided improvement on the one heretofore made by them. Among the many advantages alluded to are simplicity, elegance of design, superior workmanship, method of adjusting wings at any angle, and permanently attached key, which thus cannot be removed and lost. It can be rewound while in motion, started or stopped instantly by means of the stop pin in the base, and cannot run down when the wings are removed." Runs 90 minutes. The Metal Worker ad, 7/28/1892.* **$400.00-$500.00**

# DON'T LET THE FLIES REST | BUT SCARE THEM AWAY
## THE KEYLESS | FLY CHASER

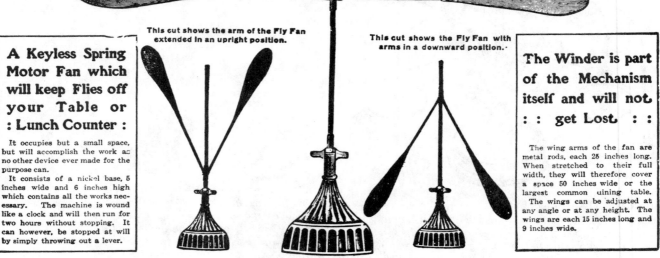

This cut shows the arm of the Fly Fan extended in an upright position.

This cut shows the Fly Fan with arms in a downward position.

**A Keyless Spring Motor Fan which will keep Flies off your Table or : Lunch Counter :**

It occupies but a small space, but will accomplish the work as no other device ever made for the purpose can.

It consists of a nickel base, 5 inches wide and 6 inches high which contains all the works necessary. The machine is wound like a clock and will then run for two hours without stopping. It can however, be stopped at will by simply throwing out a lever.

**The Winder is part of the Mechanism itself and will not : : get Lost : :**

The wing arms of the fan are metal rods, each 25 inches long. When stretched to their full width, they will therefore cover a space 50 inches wide or the largest common dining table. The wings can be adjusted at any angle or at any height. The wings are each 15 inches long and 9 inches wide.

### No. D 144 FLY FAN. Price, each, $1.75

**I-78.**
**Fly fan.**
*Another "keyless" one, very similar (possibly even the same but later) as the Matthai-Ingram one. Arms could be put in 3 positions, with total spread of 50". Cloth wings themselves were 15"L x 9"W (they're seen at angle here.) Nickeled iron base 6"H x 5" diameter. Wound to run 90 minutes, but could be stopped with a lever. Bakery supply catalog of Jaburg Brothers, NYC, 1908.*
**$400.00-$500.00**

**227,706. WIRE-CLOTH FAN FOR THE DESTRUCTION OF INSECTS.** Morse K. Taylor, (U. S. Army,) San Antonio, Tex. Filed Jan. 5, 1880.

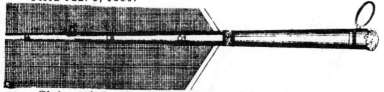

*Claim.*—A fan for the destruction of insects, consisting of a body entire of wire-gauze, having a binding of soft material, and provided with a flexible and elastic handle, as described.

**I-79.**
**Fly swatter patent.**
*Called a "wire-cloth fan for the destruction of insects" by inventor, Morse K. Taylor, U.S. Army, San Antonio, TX. Pat'd 5/18/1880. No. 227,706. "Body entire of wire-gauze, having a binding of soft material, and provided with a flexible and elastic handle." Official Gazette.*

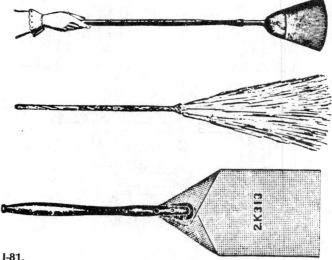

**I-81.**
**Fly swatters,**
*also optimistically called **fly killers**. (T) Folded wire screen riveted to turned wooden handle. From Sears' catalog, c.1895. (M) a **fly driver** — meant to discourage without killing. Two palm leaf versions — light or heavy. (B) Wire broom-like affair with long turned wood handle. Last 2 from Joseph Breck mail order catalog, 1905.*
**$10.00-$15.00**

**I-80.**
**Fly swatter.**
*With the object of its desiring. "The Bigelow," pat'd 1/8/1895, and mfd. by J.F. Bigelow, Worcester, MA. Made of fine spring steel plated wire set like a broom of sorts to a turned wooden handle. 18"L overall. "Kills, but does not crush the fly" — an admirable feat. HFR. 1/1903.* **$10.00-$15.00**

## I-82.
## Fly swatter.
*Simple wire "broom" with twisted wire handle. 15 3/4" overall. Another one was made with a maroon-finished wooden handle; it was an inch shorter. Wire Goods Co., Worcester, MA, 1915 catalog.* **$8.00-$15.00**

## I-86.
## Fly swatter.
*"Sanitary flexible rubber head, securely glued to varnished wood handle." Very handsome design, but did it crush the fly? Also Excelsior Stove, c.1916. I don't know if they made or just sold these various swatters.* **$12.00-$22.00**

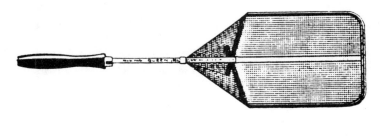

## I-83.
## Fly swatters.
*(T) "Queen" swatter with kinder, gentler corners. Black enameled wire cloth head, reinforced in center with six wires. Selvage felt bound. Securely fastened to flat steel handle with black enameled wood grip and nickeled ferrule. 17"L overall, striking surface 8 1/4" x 4 3/4". (B) "King", with similar description, but "triple wire selvage on each side and double folded, bound with imitation leather." 17"L; head 7 3/4" x 4 3/4". Both pat'd 1/9/1900, 12/22/1914 and 4/11/1916. From Excelsior Stove & Mfg. Co., Quincy, IL, catalog, c.1916.* **$8.00-$15.00**

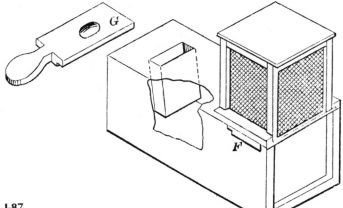

## I-87.
## Fly trap patent.
*Pat'd 1/22/1867 by M.M. Preble, Kokomo, IN. No. 61,358. "The flies enter a tube at the dark end of the box, and approaching the light end, pass to the box above. They are killed by a slide piece (G) containing a cup of burning sulphur which is introduced beneath the upper box (at F)." Official Gazette. When you read these descriptions sometimes, and their archaic language, you might easily think you're reading fiction of a rather theological kind. Umberto Eco, anyone?*

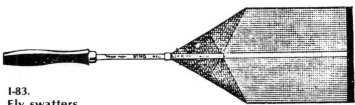

## I-84.
## Fly swatter.
*Another "King", this one mfd. by R.R. Montgomery & Co., Decatur, IL. 18"L overall x 5"W. The head is quite different, as is the handle. This one also "kills without crushing," and could be had for $1.00 ppd. for not one but a dozen of them! Ladies' Home Journal, 6/1902.* **$8.00-$15.00**

## I-88.
## Fly trap.
*Glass and wood. Upper rim under dome was baited with sugar water. Pat'd One of five traps patented in July 1872.*

## I-85.
## Fly swatter.
*"Kant-Mis" style, felt-bound wire screen head. Wire handle. 24"L; head 8"L x 4 3/4"W. Excelsior Stove & Mfg. Co., c.1916.* **$8.00-$15.00**

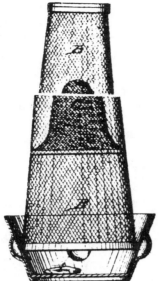

**I-89.**
**Fly trap reissue patent.**
*Pat'd 3/27/1877 by H.A. Farnam, South Bend, In. First pat'd 1/31/1871. Wire screening cones with metal bait cup.*

**I-91.**
**Fly traps.**
*(L) "Balloon" trap of wire screen and japanned tin. Mfd. by National Mfg. Co., Worcester, MA, and advertised by them as being theirs in HFR, 4/1904. Eleven years later, Wire Goods Co. of Worcester, which may have been the later incarnation of National, advertised them. (M) "American" trap, with large tin base with wooden bottom and tin truncated cone, and wire gauze dome, the whole japanned in blue with bronze striping. Mfd. by Geuder & Paeschke Mfg. Co., Milwaukee. Picture from The Metal Worker, 6/4/1890. (R) "Harper," with tin bottom, also made by Wire Goods Co., c.1915.* **$50.00-$100.00**

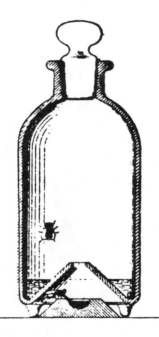

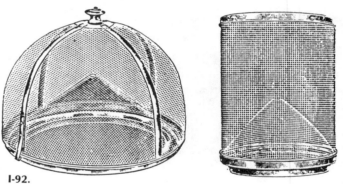

**I-92.**
**Fly traps.**
*(L) "Large Superior," of "rustless galvanoid wire cloth," heavy tin bottom and stays. 10"H x 11" diameter. (R) "Baby Superior," of same materials. 5"H x 4 1/4" diameter. From catalog of Excelsior Stove & Mfg. Co., c.1916.* **$40.00-$60.00**

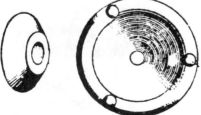

**I-90.**
**Fly trap patent.**
*Pat'd 10/21/1884 by Newton Chase, Fort Scott, KS. No. 307,016. Glass, with unidentified funnel-shaped base (probably made either of wood, glass or ceramic). Official Gazette.*

**I-93.**
**Fly killer.**
*Called "The Electric," though not actually galvanic. Mfd. by Syracuse Stamping Co., Syracuse, NY, of stamped metal. Unfortunately, I have no more info about how they work. HFR, 8/1908.*

# WAR ON FLIES
## They Must be Exterminated—They Carry Disease.

**No. D 150**
**OUR**
**NOVELTY**
**FLY AND**
**MOSQUITO**
**:: TRAP ::**

**Price, Complete**
**EACH**
**45 Cts.**
**Per Dozen,**
**$4.75**

Bottle of Glue,
Extra, 10 Cents.

It is a well known fact that Flies carry disease, they carry it from one house to another, and are otherwise a nuisance. Their presence affects the appetite. It is unnecessary to tolerate them.

**OUR NOVELTY FLY TRAP**
**IS THE EXTERMINATOR.**

**No. D 765 Catchie Fly Trap**
A clean, sure, simple fly attractor. Always ready for action and easy to clean. To operate, use a little stale beer or sugar water.
Price, each.................20c

Our Novelty Fly Catcher does away with the old time poison or sticky fly paper though it works on the sticky paper principle, it is more reliable and will last a lifetime. For catching mosquitoes, place the trap in the vicinity of a small light.

**No. D 393 Imperial Fly Trap.**
Made of fine strong wire and the surest fly catcher on the market, 9¾ in. high, 6 in. in diameter.
Price, each............$ .20
Per dozen in box......1.75

**No. D 150**
**OUR**
**NOVELTY**
**FLY AND**
**MOSQUITO**
**:: TRAP ::**

**Price, Complete**
**EACH,**
**45c**
**Per Dozen,**
**$4.75**

Bottle of Glue,
Extra, 10 Cents

The Novelty Fly Trap Ready for Action    The Novelty Fly Trap Showing a Fair Catch    The Novelty Fly Trap Showing Catch Being Removed

**I-94.  Fly & mosquito traps.**
*Large one shown in 3 views is the "Novelty," with a stick upright that is cleared of stuck-on insects by scraping up with inner cone. Note two ring handles. Smaller one at (L) is the "Catchie", baited with sugar water or stale beer. It appears to be surmounted by some kind of little figural finial. Small insect on at (R) is the "Imperial", described only as being made of "fine strong wire." Appears to be a truncated cone baited inside somehow. From hotel supply catalog of Albert Pick, 1909.*                                                          **$35.00-$100.00**

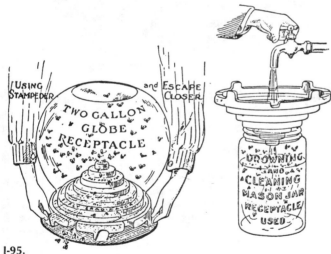

**I-95.**
**Fly trap.**
*"Pot the Fly", mfd. by Evan L. Reed Mfg. Co., Sterling, IL. Glass base with steps, with a glass globe (looks like fish bowl) inverted over it. It's baited at the top of the "Fly-ry-cide Pyr-y-myd" pyramid, then inverted and filled with water to kill. Sounds tedious and yucky, and what happens if you drop it? The base, when upside down, apparently fits a Mason canning jar exactly, but the thing was advertised as being useful with a receptacle from an "ink bottle to a 2 gallon globe." Editorial note in HFR, 7/1919.*
**$55.00-$100.00**

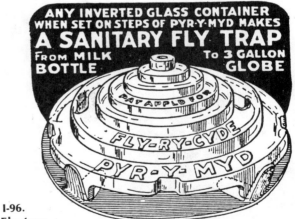

**I-96.**
**Fly trap.**
*Another depiction, this one from an ad, claiming a milk bottle to a 3-gallon globe would do the trick when inverted. HFR, 7/1919.*

**I-97.**
**Insect powder bellows.**
*You can tell this from a regular dust bellows or fireplace bellows by the canister on the nose. Wood with leather bellows; tin globular can holds about 3/8 lb. of insect powder. 19"L overall x 6"W. Advertised by Pick Barth, Chicago supply house, 1929. But they were made much earlier, for use in the garden and the house.*
**$20.00-$35.00**

**I-98.**
**Insect powder at work.**
*Great chromolithograph trade card, 2 7/8"H x 4 5/8"L, showing scene of here-invisible "Gilbert's Lightning Insect Powder" dropping them like flies. Back of card reads in part, "destroys..roaches, spiders, garden insects on plants, insects in bee hives, and every description of insect life. It contains nothing dangerous to human life. To be used with or without bellows, or can be sifted from the box...Will kill Mosquitos by burning a little of the Powder, at the same time closing the room. To kill Flies, sift the Powder on a fan and agitate in the air." Doesn't sound very safe to me! For the card, which is desirable for room view:* **$7.00-$15.00**

**I-100.**
**Umbrella stand.**
*There are two versions of the sailor & rope design. Both are cast iron, both 27"H, both with crossed oar and anchor, but the bases are different. This old one is decorated with the British Imperial lion, and is probably from mid 19th C. and has fine casting detail, and any remaining paint is darker, with a patina of age. The other version is a* **reproduction.** *It is marked: "Patented design. Copy of 18th [sic] Century Sailor cane and umbrella rack, made of cast iron... Painted in colors... Base black, figure in red, white and black...27"H, 21"W at base, 9-1/2" deep. Price prepaid $25.00 Valda Inc., Antiques & Decorations, NYC." Ad in* House & Gardens, *6/1930. Well? The repro is the one you see more frequently, with traces of what are always called "old paint." Details of the packing bales, anchor, chains, etc., are almost identical to old one, but the line (rope) is twisted differently. Also, the base is straight across in front, with set-back round ends. It's possible that for an American market, the base was redesigned. Value for the old one.* **$700.00-$1000.00**

**I-99.**
**Upholstery brush.**
*Rotary type, which I mistakenly called a bottle brush in last edition. Natural bristles, wooden handle, nickeled brass crank. Mfd. by Horace E. Britton, Stoughton, MA. 10 3/4"L.* The Metal Worker, *4/26/1890.* **$12.00-$22.00**

**I-101.**
**Housecleaning with Sapolio.**
*"Trained servants" cleaning an ornately carved mantle; scrubbing the bathtub; cleaning a coffee pot, a chance for a sit-down. Century, 4/1887.*

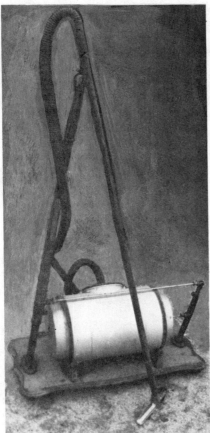

**I-102.**
**Vacuum cleaner,**
*of semi-stationary type on wooden platform which once had wheels. Long copper tube with vacuuming tip, wooden lever (leaning in from left) to pump it up, ribbed rubber tube, canvas bag inside with rubber gasket or seal, and a filter in front. No patent date, but marked "Everybody's Vacuum Cleaner." Courtesy of Coldwell's, showing at Farmington, CT.* **$150.00-$200.00**

**I-103.**   **Vacuum cleaner.**
*"Electric Renovator" from Skinner Mfg. Co., San Francisco, CA. According to the Hoover Co., North Canton, OH, who provided the photograph, this was made in 1905 and was the "first portable electric suction cleaner." It weighed close to 100 pounds!* **$200.00-$400.00**

**I-104.**
**Vacuum cleaner.**
*Truly portable, with large spoked wheels. Type T-4-50-61-3400, with 1/4 horsepower motor. Body of unidentified cast metal (probably aluminum), wooden lawnmower type handle. A sort of old-fashioned shop vac. Date unknown. Photo courtesy General Electric.* **$200.00-$400.00**

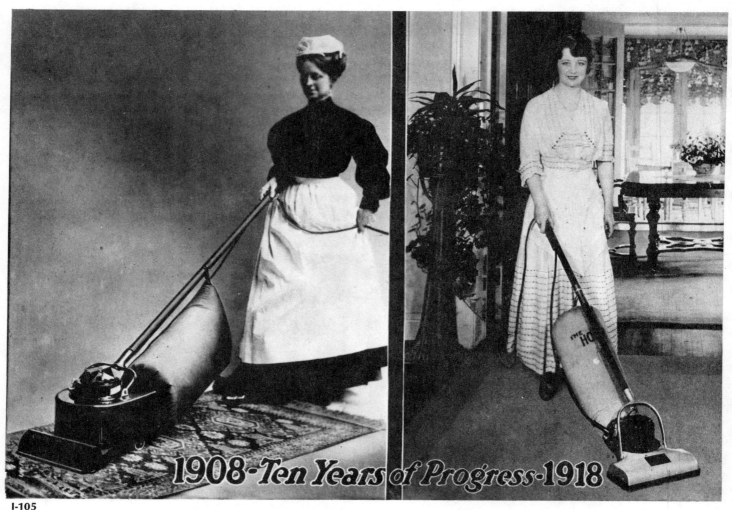

1908·Ten Years of Progress·1918

**I-105**
**Vacuum cleaners.**
*(L) Hoover's Model I, from 1908, pat'd by Murray Spangler. Usually called the "tin model" because it was made of tin and wood. I weighed only about 40 pounds. According to Hoover, "the main body was painted black on the first models, later gray, with lots of fancy striping. Two bags were provided, an inner one of coarse cheesecloth, and an outer one of gay red sateen." (R) The 1918 version. Photo courtesy The Hoover Co., North Canton, OH.*                      **$200.00-$400.00**

PRICE $25⁰⁰

PRICE $55 or $60

**I-106.**
**Vacuum cleaners.**
*"The Ideal," made by American Vacuum Cleaner Co., NYC. Ad from Harper's, 4/1909, said that since "tuberculosis is a floor disease, the greatest contribution you can make to the fight against tuberculosis is to establish vacuum cleaning in your own home." The only equipment capable of fighting TB germs was a vacuum cleaner, and "the absurdity of depending upon the broom to do successful battle should be evident to every thinking man." This one weighed only 20 pounds, and was not considered portable, though it could be lugged from room to room. At left, for $25.00, we see a girl apparently pumping up the vacuum; at right, for twice as much, one is shown hooked up to an electric motor, making it easy for the man.*                      **$200.00-$400.00**

## Pints of Dirt in Your Parlor

Awful, but true.  Prove it at our risk. Send for **"EASY" Vacuum Cleaner** on Ten Day's FREE Trial. Sweep any used room.  Then use the cleaner.  You will get from one to four pints of dirt out of that room. Write today for FREE Trial Order Form.

**DODGE & ZUILL** 221 J Dillaye Bldg., Syracuse, N.Y. or **Easy Washer Co.,** Bruce and Dundas Sts., Toronto.

**I-107.**

**Vacuum cleaner.**

*"Easy" lever pumped machine, being worked here by two housemaids. Mfd. by Dodge & Zuill, Syracuse, NY, and Easy Washer Co., Toronto, Canada. Ad greatly enlarged from Modern Pricilla, 10/1910.* **$150.00-$225.00**

**I-108.**

**Vacuum cleaner.**

*"Dusto", with tubular air pump in handle, a "hinged nozzle, held on a level with the floor by two springs, and their weight is sustained by a roller while traveling back and forth over the carpet, eliminating all friction." Dusto Mfg. Co., NYC. Can you imagine using this? Even at $5.00? HFR, 5/1909.* **$150.00-$225.00**

**I-109.**

**Vacuum cleaner.**

*The "Regina Model A," hand-operated with pump lever. It sold retail for $20.00 at the time, whereas Regina's electric one, the Model B, sold for $110.00. Regina Co., Rahway, NJ. From article in a trade publication of Buhl Sons Co., Detroit, called "Hardware News." 4/1912.* **$150.00-$225.00**

**I-110.**

**Vacuum cleaner.**

*The "P. & W.", tiresomely operated by moving the lever in the right hand up and down. Talk about carpal tunnel syndrome. Weighed about 4 lbs., cost about $5.00, and supposedly "takes the place of the costly electric machine, which in most cases is prohibitive to the average person on account of the excessive cost." P. & W. Vacuum Cleaner Co., NYC. HFR, 2/1910.* **$150.00-$225.00**

**I-112.**
**Vacuum cleaner.**
*"The Vortex" electric No. 1, early 20th C. Manufacturer not known.*
**$200.00-$300.00**

**I-111**

**"Auto vacuum" cleaner.**
*This automobile-size machine was driven to location, then used to "pull pail after pail of dirt from houses, from every crack and crevice of the floor..." and renovated "bedding, blankets, mattresses and pillows." It was advertised as doing the work in from one to four hours, and came with a vacuum condenser, water tank, vacuum gauge, two high pressure suction hoses, observation glass and cleaning tools. 12 hp motor with a carburetor, commutator, spark-coil and lots more. The Toledo Auto Vacuum House Cleaner Co., Toledo, OH. Ad in* Scientific American, *3/4/1911.*

**I-113.**
**Vacuum cleaner.**
*The British Vacuum Cleaner Co.'s semi-portable electric suction cleaner. (L) Boy using it to remove dust from the wall. Pictures from Maud Lancaster's* Electric Cooking, Heating & Cleaning, *1914.*
**$200.00-$300.00**

# The "PREMIER"
## ELECTRIC SUCTION SWEEPER

Here is a practical vacuum cleaner that WILL sell and STAY SOLD

Model C

### Price $30.00

Hose and Attachments Extra
$7.50

Total Outfit $37.50

Tools for Every Need

"The Suction Cleaner with the Brush."

Write for our "Selling Plan" and get full information regarding how to sell many cleaners at a big profit during the next four months. You will have to handle cleaners, begin right

## The Premier Vacuum Cleaner Co.
### Power Avenue and 12th Street, Cleveland, Ohio

Manufacturers of

## "PREMIER" and "EZEE" Vacuum Cleaners

# THE EZEE HAND CLEANER

## The Best Department Store Proposition Ever Offered

The only ONE-HAND cleaner the Housewife ever saw. SHE wants it, demands it, and you must supply her at a price which will move the machine in quantities.

Regular Price
$12.50

You can make 100 per cent. on every hand cleaner you sell, and the sale is a regular endless chain performance. Every sale meaning three more.

**I-114.**

**Vacuum cleaner.**

*"Premier" electric and "EZEE" hand vacuums, mfd. by Permier Vacuum Cleaner Co., Cleveland, OH. For collectors, the EZEE would probably be worth the most because of its unusal styling.HFR, 2/1912.* $150.00-$225.00

**I-116.**
**Vacuum cleaner.**
*An early Bissell electric suction cleaner, the "runabout" model on four small wheels. Picture from* Electric Cooking, *1914.*
**$175.00-$250.00**

**I-115.**
**Vacuum cleaners.**
*(L) "Magic" suction cleaner, mfd. by Magic Appliances, Ltd., Witton, England, near Birmingham. "Mounted on small rubber-covered wheels, therefore easy to use." It came with several attachments for cleaning linoleum, parquet floors, upholstery, curtains, etc. (R) The "Magic" shown with cap lying on floor and the flexible tube attached. Pictures from Lancaster's* Electric Cooking, *1914*
**$175.00-$250.00**

**I-117.**
**Vacuum cleaner.**
*The cylindrical upright "Wizard," mfd. by Westinghouse Co., Several attachments shown.* Electric Cooking, *1914.*
**$175.00-$300.00**

**I-118.**
**Vacuum cleaner.**
The "Sturtevant," mfd. by Western Electric Co. Cast aluminum body, three wheels, vent in front for tube and nozzle. Note that lawnmower handle again! *Electric Cooking,* 1914.**$175.00-$300.00**

**I-120.**
**Vacuum cleaner.**
Hand power, not electric. The "Household," mfd. by Shapleigh Hardware Co., St. Louis, c.1914. The triple bellows are connected to the drive shaft, as seen below, so that as the wheels turn, the pumping works continuously. 6"H x 18"L x 9"W, overall length with handle in place and upright is 60". **$150.00-$250.00**

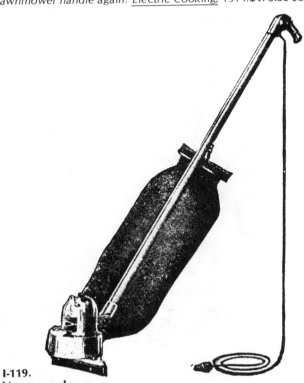

**I-119.**
**Vacuum cleaner.**
"Diamond" suction cleaner, made in America. The nozzle is diamond-shaped so that it could clean corners, and the angle of the handle was adjustable so that it could be pushed under sofas and beds. According to Lancaster's 1914 book, "a special adapter enables the device to be usded for blowing dust away from places impossible to reach with the suction nozzle, such as inside a paino action." **$150.00-$250.00**

**I-121.**
**Vacuum cleaner.**
"Frantz Premier," mfd. by The Frantz Premier Co., Cleveland, OH. Ad from *The Independent,* 1/3/1916. **$125.00-$200.00**

**I-122.**
**Vacuum cleaner.**
*"Bee" Model D, electric cleaner mfd. by Birtman Electric Co., Chicago, IL. Cast aluminum, weighs only 10 lbs. HFR 8/1918.*
**$125.00-$200.00**

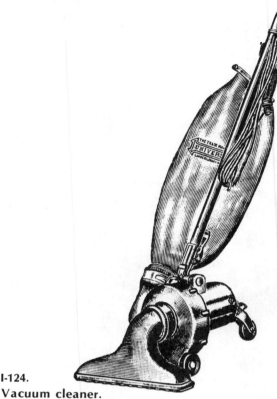

**I-124.**
**Vacuum cleaner.**
*This is the brushless "Universal," with "thread-picking self-cleaning nozle." Mfd. by Landers, Frary & Clark, in D.J. Barry catalog of 1924.*
**$100.00-$175.00**

**I-123.**
**Vacuum cleaner.**
*Electric "Sweeper-Vac" by Pneuvac Co., Worcester, MA. Combined suction power with motor-driven brush, and lever (shown being touched in circle) could be flipped to give suction power only. Pictorial Review, ad, 4/1920.* **$100.00-$175.00**

**I-125.**
**Vacuum cleaner.**
*General Electric's "Junior" model, for smaller homes. Attachments were available. GE Co., Bridgeport, CT. Woman's Home Companion, 12/1928.*
**$75.00-$125.00**

**I-126.**

**Vacuum cleaners.**

*"Premier Duplex," "Premier Pic-up," and "Premier Junior", mfd. by Electric Vacuum Cleaner Co., Inc., Cleveland. All of them are electric. The "pic-up" was made for use on stairways, autos and furniture upholstery, and was said to weigh "less than an electric iron." The Duplex combined suction and a powered brush, and came with a 20 foot cord. Woman's Home Companion, 12/1928.*

**$75.00-$175.00**

**I-127.**

**Vacuum cleaner.**

*"New Universal Model 58," mfd. by Landers, Frary & Clark. Motor driven brush, ball bearing cleaner, with attachments available such as hose and nozzle. Woman's Home Companion, 10/1929.*

**$75.00-$125.00**

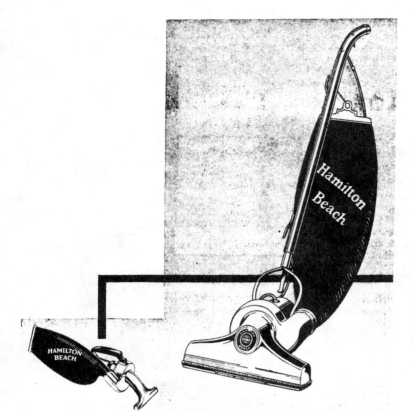

**I-130.**
**Vacuum cleaner.**
*Drawing showing Hoover "One Fifty Cleaning Ensemble," so-named because it cost $1.50 a month to buy on the installment plan. Cast of magnesium, supposed to be 1/3 the weight of aluminum, and finished in "Stratosphere Gray." Designed by famous industrial designer, Henry Dreyfuss, which alone makes it collectible. Came with automatic rug adjustor, a time-to-empty signal, adjustable handle positions, clip-on plug, etc. Good Housekeeping, 1/1937.*
**$85.00-$170.00**

**I-128.**
**Vacuum cleaners.**
*The hand vacuum on the left, with its own set of attachments, and the regular "beating-brush" model complete with Hamilton Beach's moth-destroyer, called "Expello." Hamilton Beach, division of Scovill, Racine, WI. Good Housekeeping ad 4/1931.*
**$65.00-$150.00**

**I-129.**
**Vacuum cleaners.**
*Two Hoover models—the "Dustette" hand cleaner for "above-floor" service; and a standard model with light to illuminate the floor as you worked. Cast aluminum bodies, cloth bags. Pictures from Lincoln's Electric Home, 1936.*
**$65.00-$150.00**

**I-131.**
**Vacuum cleaner.**
*"Universal Supreme Model No. E440,"* with the 8 foot long *"web
covered hose"* in place. It even has a *"streamlined headlight dirt
finder"* with a 15 watt bulb—better, and safer, than the candlestick
dustpan, eh? Information taken from a catalog of 1942. The
photograph was bought at a flea market, with no identification.
Dig that hairdo! The photo is worth $3.00 to $10.00 itself.
**$65.00-$130.00**

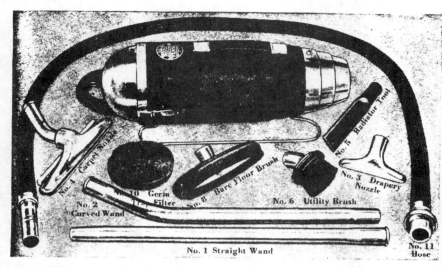

**I-132.**

**Vacuum cleaner & attachments.**
*A horizontal tank on chrome-plated wire runners, the "Roto-Verso" electric cleaner and purifier, manufacturer not know. 10"H x 22"L x 10"W. From a 1942 catalog of Ft. Dearborn Mercantile Co., Chicago, 1942.* **$65.00-$130.00**

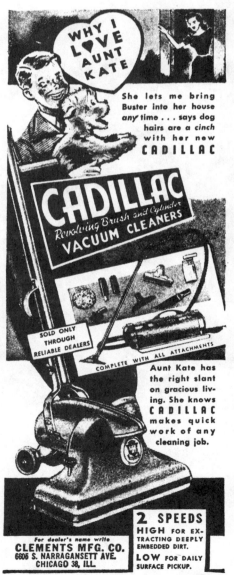

WHY I LOVE AUNT KATE

She lets me bring Buster into her house *any* time . . . says dog hairs are a *cinch* with her new CADILLAC

**CADILLAC**
*Revolving Brush and Cylinder*
**VACUUM CLEANERS**

SOLD ONLY THROUGH RELIABLE DEALERS

COMPLETE WITH ALL ATTACHMENTS

Aunt Kate has the right slant on gracious living. She knows CADILLAC makes quick work of any cleaning job.

**2 SPEEDS**
**HIGH** FOR EXTRACTING DEEPLY EMBEDDED DIRT.
**LOW** FOR DAILY SURFACE PICKUP.

For dealer's name write
**CLEMENTS MFG. CO.**
6605 S. NARRAGANSETT AVE.
CHICAGO 38, ILL.

**I-133.**

**Vacuum cleaner.**
*"Cadillac" revolving brush and cylinder vacuum cleaner, mfd. by Clements Mfg. Co., Chicago, IL.* Farm Journal, *10/1947.*
**$125.00-$200.00**

# HOOVER SERVICE

*has genuine parts for every Hoover Cleaner made in the last 25 years*

Hoover Cleaners today are giving their owners service far beyond anything ever asked or expected of them. The reason: the quality built into the Hoover Cleaner and service by Hoover. *The Hoover Company offers genuine Hoover parts for every Hoover Cleaner made in the last 25 years.* This authorized Hoover service is available at minimum cost to Hoover owners all over the United States and Canada.

THE HOOVER COMPANY, North Canton, Ohio; Hamilton, Ontario, Canada.

Model 105
1920

Model 700
1926

Model 750
1931

Model 150
1936

Model 60
1940

---

### Hoover Service Saves You Money

Take no chances! Give your cleaner genuine Hoover Company service and genuine replacement parts (available for all Hoovers made in the last 25 years). *Cost is low—for example:*

**MOTOR** cleaned, lubricated, new carbon brushes installed
**AGITATOR** or **BRUSH ROLL** cleaned and lubricated
**BELT** replaced
**BAG** completely renovated
**CORD, SWITCH,** all electrical connections checked
**APPEARANCE** improved
**CLEANING EFFICIENCY** restored

**TOTAL COST ONLY**
**$2.84**
**PLUS TAX**

*(25 cents higher in some areas)*

All work guaranteed. Estimates furnished. Prompt service.

You can get genuine Hoover service only at Hoover Factory Branch Service Stations, Authorized Hoover Dealers and Authorized Hoover Service Agencies (consult classified phone directory under "Vacuum Cleaners"). If there is no Hoover listing, write us. When the serviceman calls, insist that he show you his Hoover credentials.

*P.S. Never discard worn or broken parts. They must be turned in for replacements.*

 *The Army-Navy "E" award received three times for high achievement in the production of essential war equipment.*

*The*
# HOOVER
REG. U. S. PAT. OFF.

 IT BEATS ... AS IT SWEEPS ... AS IT CLEANS

**I-134.**

**Vacuum cleaners.**
*Hoover's service ad, put here to show pictures of five models from 1920 to 1940. Ad in* Better Homes & Gardens, *9/1944.*

**I-136**
**Vacuum cleaner.**
The "Lewyt," mfd. by Lewyt Corp., Vacuum Cleaner Division, Brooklyn, NY. Canister and attachments, with a disposable paper "Speed-Sak" instead of the common cloth bag which had to be emptied. *Saturday Evening Post*, 3/1951.     **$50.00-$100.00**

**I-135.**
**Vacuum cleaners.**
More Premier "Duplex" models, showing styling differences in models advertised in April 1947 (R) and Novemeber 1947 (L). Both ads touted the cleaner's ability to automatically adjust to the thickness of a rug, and were sprinkled with delightful phrases like "rug-meter," "Vibra-Sweep Action," and "Attach-a-Tools." Both ads from *Farm Journal.*

**I-137.**
**Wastebasket, and scroll saw.**
I was flipping through an old magazine and saw the wastebasket before I really noticed the "Prize Holly" scroll saw, with which it was possibly made. At the time, home projects such as the ornate wastebasket, were widely written about—many of them for boys and girls. This saw was for children's or ladies' use. Picture from *American Agriculturist Premium List,* 1882-83.

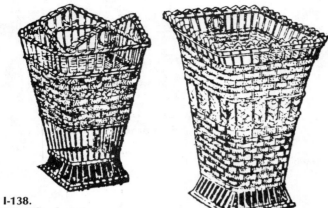

**I-138.**
**Wastebaskets.**
*Woven willow and colored straw braid, wooden bottoms, ring handles. One at left is 11 1/2"H, and came in other shapes too; (R) is 13"H. Unidentified mail order catalog, c.1895.* **$15.00-$40.00**

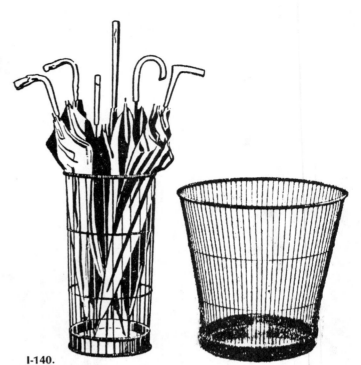

**I-140.**
**Umbrella holder & wastebasket.**
*Galvanized wire coated also with colored enamel paint. (L) has a "four pound glazed bottom which prevents it from being easily tipped over." (R) One of the "Daisy" waste paper baskets, which came in four sizes. All made by Massillon Wire Basket Co., Massillon, OH, and pat'd 7/21/1914. From HFR, 5/1915.* **$45.00-$65.00**

**I-139.**
**Soiled towel basket,**
*easily mistaken for wastebasket. Heavy nickeled brass wire, 18"H x 14" diameter. Mfd. by S.Sternau & Co., Brooklyn, NY, and in their 1900 catalog.* **$45.00-$60.00**

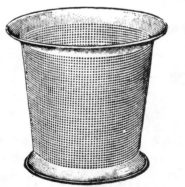

**I-141.**
**Wastebasket.**
*Stamped & perforated tin, finished in white, green, or oak graining. 11 5/8"H x 10 7/8" diameter at top. Central Stamping Co., 1920 catalog.* **$40.00-60.00**

**I-142.**
**Wastebaskets.**
*Both in the "cameo" shape—an oval with two "anterooms" at the ends. (L) Painted & at least partially hand-decorated tin, brass-finished stamped lion's heads ring handles, brass-finished ball feet. 12 1/4"H x 12"W. Maker not known, but shown in editorial in House Beautiful, 10/1922. (R) Similar one with flared sides, all-over printed pattern of flowers in gold and black, gold "brocade" pattern inside. No handles or feet, has false bottom of 3 7/8". Overall 12"H x 12 1/2"W. From Pick-Barth supply catalog, 1929.* **$25.00-$40.00**

### I-143.
### Wastebaskets.
*(L) Stamped steel with corrugated sides, raised bottoms "to conform with Southern Insurance Laws." 11 3/4"H x 113/4"W. Finished in green enamel, or "walnut" or "mahogany." (R) Sheet steel with baked-on enamel finish in white or green. 17 1/2"H x 16" diameter. Both are real heavy-duty institutional baskets. Also Pick-Barth 1929 catalog.* **$5.00-$8.00**

### I-146.
### Wastebasket.
*"Dan-Dee" steel in openwork pattern. "Mahogany" finish. Two sizes: "Guest Room," 12"H x 11" diameter; and "Writing Room," 14"H x 13" diameter. Pick-Barth, 1929.* **$15.00-$20.00**

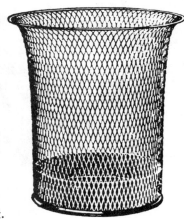

### I-144.
### Wastebasket.
*"Nemco" expanded steel with solid steel collar on inside to "catch and retain all pencil shavings, small scraps of paper, etc." White or "mahogany" finish. 12"H x 12"W at top. Pick-Barth 1929 catalog.* **$25.00-$40.00**

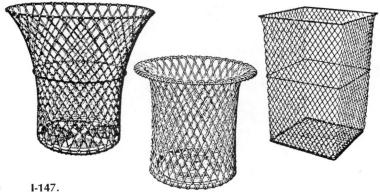

### I-147.
### Wastebaskets.
*All are "retinned" wire, all mfd. by the Andrews Division of the Washburn Co., Rockford, IL. (L) Large wastebasket, solid tin bottom, 1" mesh, 24"H x 18" diameter at top, or 18"H x 16-1/2" diameter at top. (M) Curved top basket, tin bottom, 1" mesh, 13"H x 14" diameter or 18"H x 16" diameter at top. (R) Janitor's basket, wire bottom, 1" mesh, in four sizes: 30"H x 22" square; 27"H x 20" square; 24"H x 18" square; 18"H x 14" square. Per dozen, these cost from $6.30 up to $55.00 (for the Janitor's biggest). Starting price for collectors now would surprise Pick-Barth! They are reproduced now.* **$45.00-$75.00**

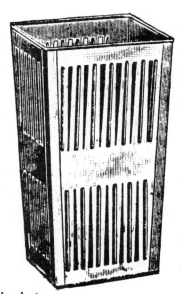

### I-145.
### Soiled towel basket.
*Enameled white steel, 26"H x 12" square. (Also came in a 30" x 14" size.) Maker not known, but in Pick-Barth catalog, 1929.* **$25.00-$40.00**

### I-148.
### Whisk brooms in display box.
*The "C" assortment, "fine natural color corn, 6 styles — 2 imitation celluloid, 1 genuine white bone, 1 full nickel and 2 regular "hurl" handles, all with hangers. The one fourth from left is "silk sewed." Note differences in the handles. I don't know what a "hurl" handle is, possibly a misprint for "burl." Butler Brothers Christmas catalog of 1899.* **$10.00-$25.00**

FRIDAY.

**I-149.**

**Friday**—*housecleaning day*—*tradecard.*

*One mopping maid, in a very pretty flowered dress, greets her plaid-suited, very spiffy suitor (note his brilliantined hair with the center part), while her friend looks on from her window-washing position. They're happy it's Friday. I'm happy I've finished this chapter, late Sunday night. I'm feeling limpsy—a new word I discovered while looking up "burl" for previous caption. The green monochrome lithograph card, 3 7/8" x 4 7/8", is part of a set of seven, with depictions of various housekeeping duties. the card:*

**$7.00-$12.00**

**I-150.**

**Doing windows — a "word of warning"**

*We hope those window frames are sound. This Ivory Soap ad from 1886 shows a maid doing a window which is at least two stories high. The ad reads: "The clearness of plate-glass windows is impaired by washing them with soap containing resin, which always leaves a thin, semi-transparent coating over the surface. Ivory Soap contains no resin, and if used with tepid water, a sponge to apply the soap and water with, and a chamois to rub the window-pane dry, your windows will prove the truth of the saying: 'Clear glass is to a house what beautiful eyes are to a woman.' " The "warning" in the headline was used by Ivory to caution against counterfeit Ivory soap. NOTE: In New York City, and probably in many big cities, a standard part of a rental lease prohibits washing windows above the ground floor; this is to save landlords from injury suits. Picture courtesy Ron Barlow.*

This article deals with carpet sweepers (and a few vacuum cleaners) produced from the beginning in 1858 to 1909. This significant period in the sweeper industry witnessed its birth, growth, and establishment in the housewares market, and is also the period that most interests collectors, especially those before 1900. Approximate value ranges are listed at end of article.

Research was primarily conducted with artifacts and archives in the vast Bissell Collection, a recent gift to the Public Museum of Grand Rapids, which contains over 1500 artifacts representing over 150 carpet sweeper and vacuum cleaner manufacturers.

*Photos of artifacts in the Bissell Collection courtesy of the Public Museum of Grand Rapids.*

HOME AS IT WAS.

HOME AS IT IS.

**II-1.**
**"Home as it was...Home as it is."**
*Product booklet cover, Bissell Carpet Sweeper Co., Grand Rapids, MI. About 1880.*
*Note the dust sheets thrown over everything, including the housewife herself, the hanging gasolier, the checker tilt-top table, the Rogers' statuary group in front of the mantle, the piano, and other things seen in the far room in the picture at right. In the before picture, Hubby is missing; note how oblivious he is to his wife, not even admiring her one-handed jockeying of the Bissell sweeper. As was proclaimed in an 1890's ad booklet, "Invention hath no nobler aim than to lighten the work of women".*

# II. Noble Inventions: CARPET SWEEPERS & EARLY VACUUMS

By Sally Bjork

### The Origins

Victorian women who took the maxim "Cleanliness is next to godliness" to heart when they did their housework, were considered paragons of virtue in the eyes of society. A messy house was seen as proof of amoral, if not downright immoral, character — on the part of the housewife and her family. Turn of the century ladies' magazines published innumerable articles on cleaning and the correct state of the home.

Daily broom-sweeping of carpets and rugs was recommended for all the high traffic areas and twice weekly in parlors, libraries and bedrooms. But, sweeping rugs seemed to cause more problems than solutions. Broom-swept dust billowed up, only to fall on other furnishings. Brooms also pushed the heavier gritty dirt down into the carpet, breaking the fibers and causing it to wear more quickly. Aside from these detrimental factors, sweeping carpets with a broom demanded extreme physical exertion, causing distress for the conscientious housekeeper, no matter how efficient she was.

But, not to fret, human ingenuity eased this problem with the invention of an important labor-saving device: the carpet sweeper. Finally! a device that would offer "cleaning pleasures" instead of "cleaning nightmares"! Women, after centuries of sweeping, beating, and dealing with dust and dirt, could rid their carpets of this nasty substance without covering the room in sheets and donning workclothes. For 19th century women, the carpet sweeper was awe-inspiring. Initially popular for its superior efficiency over the broom, its significance as a tool for daily sweeping did not die with the introduction of hand-operated or electrical vacuums, and hundreds of thousands of new ones are still sold now.

Conceptually, carpet sweepers are rooted in a horse-drawn street sweeper developed in England in 1699. The street sweeper did not meet with much success, because, like the broom, it raised dirt which would then settle elsewhere. The idea of mechanically sweeping dirt was abandoned until 1811, when Englishman James Hume patented a carpet sweeper with an encased brush rotated by a pulley system. The first American carpet sweeper of the type came in 1858. Manufactured by H.H. Herrick of Boston, Massachusetts, this crude-looking sweeper was the beginning of an industry in which hundreds of American manufacturers eventually participated. (A "fan carpet sweeper" was patented by A.C. Carey, Lynn, Massachusetts, January 4, 1850, and was possibly more like a "handvac" — see end of this article, figure **II-19.** Carey also got a patent in October 1858.)

**II-2.** — *"Herrick", by H.H. Herrick, East Boston, MA, pat'd Aug. 17, 1858. 4-1/4"H x 13-1/4"W x 10-3/4"D. The crude "Herrick" was the first sweeper designed and manufactured in the U.S. Its one brush, spanning the sweeper's width, is driven by iron cog wheels on the right side; a smooth wheel supports the left side. One of 2 tin dustpans slides out the side; other has hinged cover which can be opened for emptying. A wooden broom handle would have been screwed onto the screw of the toggle link. Herrick's next (1859) model had 2 separate brushes, each driven by a set of cog wheels located right and left.*

From 1858 until the mid to late 1870s, the United States carpet sweeper industry was small, and located mainly in the East. Carpet sweepers were relatively slow in overtaking brooms for household cleaning. But, by the 1870s, new developments kicked off a steady increase in the carpet sweeper's popularity, and substantial growth in the industry.

**II-3.** — *"Welcome", made by Henry Gardner, East Braintree, MA, 1877. 3-1/2"H x 13"W x 7-1/2"D. The "Welcome" — much more successful than Herrick's sweeper — was made 1874 to 1878. Gardner employed Herrick's basic concept, so the success might be attributed to the sweeper's aesthetics. Its popularity prompted other companies, such as Charles W. Bassett and Haley Morse & Co., both of Boston, to use the same model name & near-identical design. This model's rectangular wood frame & tin top house a single brush driven by iron cog wheels. Two stationary dustpans are emptied by opening the hinged top. Cases were japanned blue, green, red or black, with gold stenciling.*

**II-4.** — *"Bissell", mfd. by Melville Bissell, Grand Rapids, MI, 1876. 4"H x 14-1/4"W x 9-1/4"D. Melville Bissell's first sweeper, 1876, was based on Gardner's "Welcome" model which Bissell used in his crockery store in Grand Rapids. Bissell was able to cause a "positive rotation" of the brush by aligning the cog wheels along the short axis in the sweeper's center. After receiving a patent on his improvement — and several others — Bissell quickly moved to the forefront of the carpet sweeper industry. The Bissell Carpet Sweeper Co.'s 1878 model incorporated "Broom Action" that automatically adjusted brush to floor level by the user's pressure on the broom handle. At the turn of the century, the Bissell Co. patented another important improvement: "Cyco" Bearings, large wooden bearings connecting brush & wheels for easier rotation of the brush.*

*Although Bissell Co. created numerous improvements, most likely their product specialization, and innovative aggressive marketing were behind their success. In 1889, just 13 years after the company's beginning, Anna Bissell took over the presidency at her husband's death. It is not unlikely that Anna Bissell, one of the first women CEOs in American business, was the greatest influence in the marketing success of a company whose products were targeted mainly to women.*

# The Experiments Continue

Since 1858, only slight variations have been made to the carpet sweeper. However, during the early years, experiments with construction and design continued steadily.

Cases were given various shapes. Dustpans were treated differently; some, like Herrick's, would slide out; others were stationary and emptied by opening the top of the case, or a side panel. Most popular were mechanically operated dustpans opened with a lever on top of the case.

There were also variations in the setting of the bristles on the wooden "axle" of the brush; for example, instead of setting the bristles in straight rows, they were set diagonally or in scallops. Various motive powers for brush rotation were also tried. At first, cog wheels were used. These were noisy, and they tended to skid on smooth surfaces, and therefore couldn't turn the brushes. Pulley systems were partially successful, but they lost efficiency over a period of time. Best were rubber-covered wheels which rotated the brush by friction. Experimental features and gadgets developed early by trial and error eventually resulted in a standard design.

**II-5.** — "Hatlinger's Champion", J.C. Neal, Boston, MA, c.1874. 3-3/4"H x 12-3/4"W x 7-1/2"D. "Hatlinger's Champion" has a pulley system that was granted an award by the Massachusetts Charitable Mechanics Association in 1874. "Hyde & Eaton", as printed below the brand name, was, according to the New England Business Directory of 1877, a dealer of only carpet sweepers. There is one brush; stationary dustpans are emptied by opening the slanted, hinged front panel. A black & gold paper label is glued to the wooden top. Note the beautiful turning of the pulley top right.

**II-6.** — "Union", mfd. by Union Carpet Sweeper Co., Pawtucket, RI, 1877. 3-3/4"H x 17"W x 7-3/4"D. A new concept are side bristles for dusting baseboards & corners. Otherwise, the "Union" is very similar to the "Welcome", with rectangular wooden frame & hinged tin case top. It houses a single brush driven by friction rotation of rubber-covered wheels. The chromolithographed paper label on top, in green, red, & gold, has an anchor design — a popular Victorian motif. The name probably was meant to appeal to patriotic feelings. It is also printed with the name "Ellis Thayer & Son" of Pawtucket — probably the retailer who sold it, although unfortunately there is no listing in the 1877 New England Business Directory for Thayer or for Union Carpet Sweeper Co.

**II-7.** — "New Idea", Bissell Carpet Sweeper Co., Grand Rapids, MI, 1882. 4"H x 13"W x 12"D. The "New Idea" has a pulley mechanism similar to "Hatlinger's Champion" of c.1874. Friction from 2 sets of rubber-covered wheels rotate a single brush via a leather pulley strap; 2 tin dustpans swing down independently for emptying. Case decorated with ice blue & rose red hand-painted flowers, with gold stenciling. Handle socket somewhat unusual in placement.

**II-8.** — "Paragon", Grand Rapids Brush Co., Grand Rapids, MI, 1884. 3-3/4"H x 14"W x 8-1/2"D. The "Paragon" is handsomely decorated with hand-painted yellow & red flowers, and gold & black stenciling. It differs greatly from other sweepers in that the whole front half of the sweeper opens to empty the single dustpan. Note heavy wire clamp.

**II-9.** — *"Prindle", The Prindle Mfg. Co., Aurora, IL, 1885. 4"H x 14-1/2"W x 10-1/2"D. The "Prindle" sweeper exhibits a bold & powerful new look. The large cog wheels, that drive a single brush, rise above the top of the wooden sweeper case. The rounded top is covered with a black, red and gold paper label, with a version of a Barnum (as in circus) typeface. Two tin dustpans swing downward independently for emptying. The sweeper is surrounded by a leather bumper which protects furniture. Prindle also made a model with smaller wheels.*

### The Standard Arrives

By the late 1880s, the standard form of carpet sweeper had evolved. Most companies constructed sweepers in accordance with this form, usually comprising the following elements:

- Wooden rectangular case.
- Two pairs of rubber-covered exterior wheels, which creates a friction rotation on wood or carpet, for the
- Single brush, running the long way.
- Wooden or metal side brackets protecting the two pairs of wheels.

- Two tin dustpans, located in front of and behind the brush.
- A lever on the top or side of the sweeper case which, when depressed, opens the dustpans downward.
- A leather, rubber or cotton cord bumper to prevent marring furniture or woodwork.
- A toggle link with a moveable bail attached to the case on either side, with a socket or screw to which a broomstick handle was secured.

When the standard was established, marketing and aesthetic design became more important. Sweepers were no longer simply brushes encased in boxes. Various price levels were developed for sweepers ranging from the mundane to the ornate and the exotic. Several different woods began to be utilized in construction, which made it possible to match the sweepers to furnishings in various rooms of the house, and make of them decorative accessories. Higher-priced sweepers were often hand-painted and gold-stenciled. Many had ornate cast iron toggle links, trim, and fancy openwork metal wheel hubs and brackets, which were often nickel-plated. Some wheels were painted scarlet, and the use of gold pin-striping (which was also used to add to the attractiveness of things as disparate as sewing machines, carriages and plows) was common on painted cast metal parts as well as cases. Besides simple brand names, companies sometimes used special model names to catch market attention by evoking desirable social status, popular sentiments, or well-known events or personages. Some of these model names have obvious appeal: "Ladies' Friend"; "The Reward"; "The Mystic"; "Parlor King"; "Mrs. Russell's Pet"; "Science" [referring to the newly dubbed "science" of housekeeping]; "Victoria" [at the time of Queen Victoria's 50th reign year Jubilee in 1888]; "It's a Daisy"; "Social"; "Housewife's Delight"; and many others.

With these fashionable machines, not only could women of the late 19th century clean their carpets effortlessly, they could do it in style.

**II-10.** — "Ladies' Friend No.2", Goshen Mfg. Co., Grand Rapids, MI, c.1890. 4"H x 13-1/4" x 8-3/4". The Goshen Mfg. Co. originated in Goshen, IN, in 1882, producing sweepers there until 1895. Goshen also operated a plant in Grand Rapids from about 1885 to 1897.

During the late 19th C, companies went beyond strictly functional sweepers. Marketing techniques which would appeal to women were incorporated. This "Ladies' Friend" and the "Housewife's Delight" shown next, are just two of many examples where the sales pitch is part of the design on the sweeper itself. Both these sweepers have rubber-covered wheels and a friction-rotated single brush. They are similar in that a light-color finish frames a slightly darker stained center panel with gold stenciling. The dustpans are different: the "Ladies' Friend" dustpans swing downward for emptying; "Housewife's Delight" has two stationary tin dustpans emptied by lifting a small tin panel on the left. It is not at all uncommon to find quite similar sweepers produced by different manufacturers.

**II-12.** — "Furniture Protector", Bissell Carpet Sweeper Co., Grand Rapids, MI, 1889. 4-1/4"H x 14-1/4"W x 8-1/2"D. The "Furniture Protector" was an upper-priced sweeper which serves as an excellent example of the increased efforts toward improving aesthetic design in the late 1880s. The Aesthetic Movement affected the design of many things — from books to furniture to clothing. "Furniture Protector" is a mundane name, but its case is constructed of solid black walnut, with hand-painted blue and rose-color flowers & gold stenciling. The metal wheels are partly enclosed within wooden side panels — bumpers to protect the furniture — that have rounded corners.

An interesting (bizarre? jarring?) touch on this beautifully hand-crafted sweeper is the toggle link, which is coated with red-orange paint! Today, we might think the colors clash, but this color is found on quite a few models of that time period.

**II-11.** — "Housewife's Delight", Plumb & Lewis Mfg. Co., Grand Rapids, MI, pat'd Sept. 19, 1876, Nov. 28, 1879, October 19, 1880, with others pending. This one from 1892. 4-1/4"H x 13"W x 8-1/2"D. Plumb & Lewis existed from 1880 to c.1892, when it merged with Bissell.

**II-13.** — "Furniture City", Sweeperette Co., Grand Rapids, MI, 1895. 4-1/4H" x 14-1/4W" x 9-1/4"D. Victorian in every American sense of the word, this sweeper has a solid mahogany case with high gloss finish & gold stenciling. The ornately-cast toggle link, wheel hubs, wheel brackets and trim are all nickel plated. Functionally, this sweeper utilizes the standard elements of most late 19th C sweepers.

The Sweeperette Co. operated in Grand Rapids [nicknamed "The Furniture City" because of the great number of furniture manufacturers located there] from 1895 to about 1905. Most of their sweepers incorporated some sort of ornate cast trim (almost always nickeled), and many were made of exotic hardwoods, or some domestic woods with a high figure (grain pattern). Some woods were found in the same tropical rain forests that are recognized as highly endangered today.

II-14. — "No. 4 Easel", Bissell Carpet Sweeper Co., Grand Rapids, MI, c. 1901. This 4-sweeper display stand, made of maple, ash, and cast iron, is an example of innovative marketing techniques that made Bissell so successful. The stand was included gratis with a retailer's first order of 12 or more sweepers. Top to bottom, the Bissell Carpet Sweeper Co. sweepers on the "easel" stand are as follows:

"Grand Rapids", c.1897, white oak. This was Bissell's most popular & long-lived model, produced from 1894 to about 1950! The form was similar for six decades, but materials varied. Cases were originally made from woods such as maple & oak; later models had tin bodies.

"Ideal", 1895. The "Ideal" was a medium to upper-priced sweeper similar in construction to the "Grand Rapids", but made with exotic woods chosen for the grain (or "figure") & color. It could be ordered in bird's-eye maple (pictured), curly birch, or California laurel wood.

"Superba", 1907. This was the top of the Bissell line in its time. The case was covered with a single piece of crotch mahogany veneer. The "Superba" was advertised as the "Highest Point in Sanitation"; supposedly there were no crevices where dust and germs could collect.

"Crystal Sweeper", 1909. Originally the glass-topped "Crystal Sweeper" was made as the "Display Sweeper" to be given to store-owners for purposes of demonstrating the efficacy of Bissell sweepers. It sparked such great interest in customers, who loved being able to see the dirt being brushed off the floor, that Bissell put the sweeper, with its thick beveled glass-top, into production for the retail customer.

**From Crumbs to Clippings**

The success of the carpet sweeper for private homes led to other applications. Just after the turn of the century, the concept was adapted to the tabletop, with the introduction of a mechanical crumb sweeper. These are much rarer than the mini dustpan and brush. Carpet sweepers were also made in large versions for sweeping big hallways in institutions, and in compact versions for narrow or constricted passageways such as those in railroad Pullman cars. In the 1890s, one company had the idea of making a lawn sweeper modeled after the home carpet sweeper. These are still being made today; some can be pushed, and some are pulled along behind a riding mower.

II-15. — "Crumb Sweeper", manufacturer unknown, [American], 1903. This small mechanical sweeper was intended for use on tablecloths, and was probably also used on other textile throws used on table- and piano tops. It is made of black-painted, heavy stamped sheet iron, and has a friction-rotated brush. Note the tapered but squared-end handle & the tiny front wheel. Case 3-1/2"H x 6"W x 3-3/4"D.

**II-16.** — *"Hercules", Onondaga Sweeper Co., Syracuse, NY, pat'd July 8, 1897, case 11"H x 36-3/4"W x 15"D. This industrial size carpet sweeper was for buildings with wide, long, mainly carpeted hallways, such as hotels or clubs. The heavy tin case houses a single brush driven by a cog system located on its 2 rubber-covered cast iron wheels. The 2 tin dustpans have to be lowered manually for emptying.*

**II-17.** — *"Apollo Lawn Sweeper", Greene Mfg. Co., Springfield, OH, c.1895-1905, 15"H x 25-1/2"W x 24"D. The name is cast into the wheel hubs, and a figure of its eponymous god is stenciled on the japanned tin lid of the grass-catcher. The "Apollo" was a novel variation of the carpet sweeper that for some reason does not seem to have been very popular at the time, for there is a lack of lawn sweepers from other companies.*

## Toys For Training Girls

Along with other variants, working toy sweepers were developed in the late 1890s. These sweepers were constructed almost identically to their 'parent' models and were fully functional. One company marketed their toy sweepers for "future sweeper users". Companies boasted that these toys were helpful in the household, and morally correct in teaching young girls proper housecleaning techniques they would use later in life.

Toy carpet sweepers, and toy vacuum cleaners, met with instant success and their popularity has continued throughout the years.

II-18. — *Clockwise from the bottom: "Little Helper", Bissell Carpet Sweeper Co., Grand Rapids, MI, 1933. "Midget", Bissell, c.1895. "Hoover" toy vacuum cleaner, All Metal Products Co., Wyandotte, MI, 1931. (Note: handles were cropped in photo—they are much longer in reality.)*

## Vacuum Cleaners

During the second half of the 19th century, both hand (and foot) operated and electric vacuum cleaners were developed. The hand-operated inventions did not create much excitement since their efficiency failed to exceed (or even meet) the energy exerted for operation. All types of motive power were utilized for the handvacs — from cranks and pulleys, to pumps and bellows.

Electric vacuums, though first developed at the turn of the century, did not gain popularity for household use until after 1907. In the beginning, the problem was to create sufficient suction. Once that was achieved, the units proved to be too large and heavy for practical use.

David E. Kenney of New Jersey developed improvements in scaled-down versions. He received most of the patents for early electric vacuum cleaners: the first was granted in 1907 and didn't expire until 1923. Therefore, most of the electric vacuums of the first quarter of the 20th century, regardless of manufacturer, were produced under Kenney's patents.

II-19. — *"The Whirlwind Carpet Sweeper", A.M. Carpet Cleaning Co., Boston, MA, pat'd 1869 [possibly by Ives W. McGaffey], 43"H x 13"W x 9"D. This handvac is a very early example of a hand-operated suction cleaner. A fan encased in the circular section, glimpsed here behind the triangular hood, is operated by a crank-pulley system. The suction created by the fan was supposed to pull dirt and dust through the wooden hood, front, to the large dustbag atop the fan case. It is exceedingly difficult to crank & steer simultaneously.*

II-20. — *"Hall's Air Draught", [Ives W. McGaffey, Chicago, IL], 1878, 49"H x 11-3/4"W x 10"D. This handvac, like the "Whirlwind", used a pulley system to operate the fan to created suction and pull dust through the hood. The tin body is painted green with gold stenciling. NOTE: The manufacturer's name was inferred from the model name — "Hall's; see the electric vacuum in the next picture.*

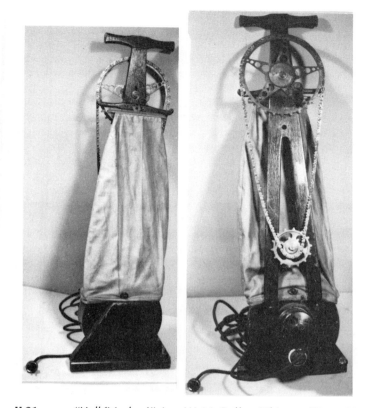

**II-21.** — — "Hall (Modern)", Ives W. McGaffey, [Chicago, IL], c. 1900, 44"H x 13"W x 9-1/4"D. Two views. This early electric vacuum is quite similar in appearance to the "Whirlwind" handvac. The fan located in the circular case behind the hood was started by a crank handle, and suction was sustained through electric current.

**II-23.** — Model name & manufacturer unknown. Built c.1895-c.1905, 49"H x 7-3/4"W x 4-1/2"D. This cylindrical handvac did not offer considerable relief from the drudgeries of housework. To operate it, the plunger handle was pushed down far enough through the cylinder to compress the large spring on the lower portion of the handle shaft. This created a vacuum of sorts inside the cylinder. Suction was created when pressure was released and the spring expanded upwards.

**II-22.** — Model name of this one is unknown. Mfd. by McGaffey, [Chicago, IL], c.1900-c.1905. Once again, this electric vacuum is extremely similar to the handvac in II-20. As with II-21, its fan is located in the circular case, and was started by a crank mounted near the top of the handle. Note the bicycle chain that links the large diameter crank wheel at top with the small wheel that in effect kick starts the fan. The fan's rotation, and the resulting suction were sustained with electric current. Dirt collected in the dustpan which could be emptied through a panel at rear left.

**II-24.** — "Ideal", American Vacuum Cleaner Co., NYC, NY, c.1895-c.1905, 47-1/2"H overall x 40"L. Canister is 10" in diameter. With this stationary handvac, suction was created by pumping the handle which operated bellows located in the middle portion. Originally a hose would have been attached to the nozzle on the front of the canister. This device looks as if it required the efforts of two people, but many such were advertised showing children operating them!

## Editor's Notes on Value Ranges

By Linda C. Franklin

Because so many of these sweepers and vacuums are exceedingly rare, market value for collectors is hard to estimate. As you know, for a general rule, early and other developmentally important examples are valuable; highly decorative examples in fine condition are on a par with their plainer but important predecessors. This excellent museum collection, which was assembled from the company's beginnings by the Bissell Carpet Sweeper Co. [now Bissell, Inc.], has very few examples with their original handles. Apparently thought to be unnecessary for historical purposes, and probably quite similar to any broom or mop handle with a threaded tip, the handles were all discarded as individual sweepers were added to the collection. This has to be considered a given in this collection. It is particularly unfortunate with some of the toys (though not those shown here), and detracts more considerably from their collector value, because they are traded in the very well-established, almost fanatically condition-oriented toy market.

Instead of lowering values because of the lack of handles, I have tried to neutralize their absence, and put the base value of each full-size sweeper within the quoted range. If you should find a particular sweeper with a provably original handle, the value is to be increased, but not substantially (i.e. more than $20.00-$25.00) unless the handle is unusual in shape or finish (add $30.00-$50.00), or has a maker's label (add $30.00-$60.00). Of course, the ideal is for all collectible tools to be complete and original. But we might logically take our lead from collectors of tools such as hammers and axes, who focus on business ends and not handles. An extra factor enters into the evaluation of the "easel" display rack shown in II-14, and that is the inflated prices of the highly competitive advertising collectibles market.

Price ranges for the depicted sweepers and vacuum cleaners are as follows, all based on very good to fine condition:

1) $125.00-$175.00
2) $100.00-$125.00
3) $70.00-$90.00
4) $175.00-$250.00
5) $175.00-$275.00
6) $125.00-$160.00
7) $150.00-$200.00
8) $125.00-$160.00
9) $175.00-$225.00
10) $70.00-$90.00
11) $70.00-$90.00
12) $150.00-$225.00
13) $150.00-$225

14) $125.00-$200.00 for stand; $45.00-$60.00; $60.00-$75.00; $65.00-$90.00; $125.00-$160.00
15) $85.00-$125.00
16) $175.00-$225.00
17) $175.00-$225.00
18) $35.00-$60.00; $40.00-$60.00 $85.00-$110.00
19) $250.00-$300.00
20) $150.00-$200.00
21) $200.00-$300.00
22) $160.00-$215.00
23) $90.00-$135.00
24) $125.00-$200.00

One writer on collectibles, Harry Rinker, says that we collect in order to recapture our childhoods. I suppose that is partly true. Some of my happiest (at least in retrospect) times in childhood were what seem now the eternally yellow and sunny hours spent in the breakfast room, ironing. This couldn't really be true; surely I had more fun running in the cornfields, or skipping rope with Tarley, or playing museum with my brother, Robbie, in the hayloft of the barn, in galleries laid out with chalk lines. But maybe not! After all, while I don't collect sadirons or laundry sprinklers, I do collect clothespins. And there's a tentative collection of ironing boards leaning against the basement wall, like actors at an audition.

It's a toss-up whether sadiron stands (or trivets), or the irons themselves, are the most collected item in this chapter. Collections of charcoal box irons and sadirons, with a few blue Colemans gathering dust too, may be the most visible as well as taken-for-granted collections in America. Think: Haven't you seen such a collection in the window of a local laundry or dry-cleaning establishment? Next to a droopy old philodendron with yellowed leaves? Laid out between the window and the person who does alterations? I know of at least three such collections in NYC, and that's only from my own neighborhood. Several books have been written (See Bibliography) on both the stands and the irons. Many trivets have been reproduced over the last 60 years; as far as I know, the irons have not been reproduced. However, a few basic old-fashioned types of simple cast iron flatirons and box irons, have been made up until modern times. So an old-fashioned look doesn't guarantee age; it also doesn't mean fake or reproduction with intent to deceive. Some people still use them. A "non-electric" catalog of household tools, put out by Lehman's Hardware for the Amish, is one of probably scores of sources today where new/old things such as sadirons can be bought. (Lehman's, 4779 Kidron Rd., Kidron, OH 44636)

Clothespins represent a very promising field because of relatively low cost, and great variety in design, material, age and size. They have been homemade, made by hand, and machine-made. Patented ones are difficult to find, probably because they were made in relatively small quantities. (See also page 163.)

Washboards have been collected for a long time, but by comparatively few people. Beginning in the mid 1980s, the more unusual of them — entirely of cast iron, or carved from all wood — began showing up at antique shows, displayed as sculpture would be. A famous art gallery owner in NYC assembled a large collection over a period of a very few years, and then had a big show of them, and sold his collection. (Now he's collecting coat hangers.) Some of the glamor-interest in washboards has died down again, so it's possible that you may find some interesting ones that haven't been uncovered.

**Blanket pin**, a large 'clothespin' to hold blankets or other heavy pieces of laundry to drying line. Turned wood, hole at head. Mark is cut into the wood — "J. P:", (J period, P colon), 8⅝"L, prob. 3rd or 4th quarter 19th C.
**$20.00-$25.00**

**Box iron**—See Iron, box, p. 70; also Iron, charcoal, pp. 67-68.

**Can for fuel**, for gasoline powered washing machine, cobalt blue enameled tin, with pouring spout, and white shield with name, "Maytag", Newton, IA, 20th C.• " 'Maytag Dive Bomber, eh? That's not the kind of a Maytag I want.' Ever notice how often the word 'Maytag' bobs up in the talk of the boys in the Army Air Forces? They call the little Piper Cubs that act as the eyes of the artillery 'Maytag Messerschmitts' or 'Maytag Dive Bombers.' The student training planes are nicknamed 'Maytag Hedgehoppers.' And when a cadet washes out he usually says he has 'gone through the Maytag.' Yes, MAYTAG has worked its way into the language of our fighting men — not because Maytag actually makes any of the army planes, but because, naturally enough, Maytag comes immediately to mind when any American thinks of washing or the sound of a washer. It's a touch of home for those boys out there — of millions of homes where Maytags have been doing the washing ever since they can remember. And when their war job — and ours — is done, they'll return to homes which can have new Maytags" *Better Homes & Gardens*, Sept. 1944. See also the wartime notes under Coffee mill (Coffee chapter), Fan, Toaster (both Electric chapter), in 300 Years of Kitchen Collectibles. **$35.00-$45.00**

**Can for oil**, tall cylinder with hooded pouring spout & cup-like strap handle, lithographed tin, blue, white, red & black, depiction of a muscle arm, an hourglass, & the name, Maytag Co., 6¼"H, early 20th C. **$12.00-$15.00**

**Charcoal iron**—See Iron, charcoal.

**Clothes dasher**, also called an agitator, clothes plunger or wash dolly, tin cone with wooden broomstick handle, a star is stamped on the tin, American, TOC or earlier.
**$25.00-$35.00**

**Clothes dasher**, copper funnel with wood shaft & lawnmower-like T-handle, "Oregon Wonder", 19"H, pat'd 1907, pat'd Apr. 20, 1909. **$60.00-$75.00**

**Clothes dasher**, copper pan with handle, no mark, American, 15¼"L x 8½" diameter, pat'd May 1890.
**$45.00-$65.00**

**Clothes dasher**, tin, cast iron & wood, you work a long wooden lever & 4 cups go up & down, supposedly quadrupling your personal horsepower, American, 22"H, 19th C. • German vocabulary — Waschestampfer: wash pounder. • I think in American usage, a "wash pounder" is something slightly different — a large heavy wooden pestle-like implement for actually pounding soap into heavy cloth inside the wash kettle or washtub.
**$60.00-$75.00**

**Clothes dasher**, tin funnel with wooden handle, "Rapid Washer", made by C.T. Childers, Galesburg, IL, 28"L, TOC. **$20.00-$35.00**

**Clothes dasher**, tin funnel & wood handle, with brass ID plate on the tin: "Little's Champion Washer", dated 1891.
**$45.00-$65.00**

**Clothes dasher**, tin, the struts & crosspieces below give it the effect of a spider web, American, 14½"L x 8¾" diameter, 19th C. • These dashers or dollies were used with wash tubs, both wooden ones and galvanized tin ones, and probably also with commandeered huge cast iron or old copper boilers. **$45.00-$65.00**

**Clothes dasher**, tin, water escape valves or sluices, brass ID plate: "The Perfect Clothes Washer", 15"H, pat'd Oct. 13, 1885. **$60.00-$75.00**

Clothes dasher, wooden with X frame & vertical handle, 18"L, dasher is 8" x 8", 19th C.                    $35.00-$45.00

Clothes dryer, wood umbrella tree, with cord strung around it. • "Back in the early stages of man's development, the limited clothing equipment of human kind was hung upon small trees to dry. ... The Hill dryer supplied an artificial tree, with lines arranged conveniently around it, and so constructed that both the air and sun could perform their functions. Constructed with 150 feet of line, the housewife is no longer forced to trudge up one line and down another, toting a heavy basket of clothes. ... The Hill dryer is so built as to permit its being folded up like an umbrella and removed." So wrote Orra L. Stone, in *History of Massachusetts Industries*, Boston, 1930. Hill Clothes Dryer Co., Worcester, MA, various sizes, est. early 20th C, still making them in early 1930s. $22.00-$40.00

Clothes dryer, wood & wire hanger, with 4 crosspieces that pivot out from central wire, with a clothespin at each end, for hanging 8 items to dry, no marks, prob. American, 16"L, TOC. See the chapter on "Closeting" for regular clothes hangers.                    $7.00-$15.00

Clothes dryer, wooden, works like umbrella, floor standing, American, 1904.                    $22.00-$30.00

Clothes dryers, of the 4 leg folding type called clothes horses, with simple frame & a number of dowel rods to hang the clothes on. Nowadays, these make good display easels for textile collections. American, various sizes, late 19th or early 20th C.                    $20.00-$100.00

> The clothes-horse is a noble steed,
> But very angular indeed.
> He is, as everybody knows,
> The only horse that can wear clothes.
> He never balks or runs away,
> But stands a lot on washing day.
> He is an inexpensive horse,
> Because he never eats, of course.

*House Furnishing Review*, July 1904. See picture III-8.

Clothes drying rack, actually for stockings, molded plastic in clear, or pearlized gulfstream blue, Martinique yellow, sea green & Caribbean rose, hinged scallop shell pulls down from wall mounted backplate (glued on to wall); 32 stockings could be hung by their toes through slots along ridges in the shell, "SafTdri", mfd by Donaco Plastics, Inc., Chicago, IL, 8"H, 1948. • Ad reads "Imagine! Hanging a whole bathroom full of washbasin laundry in just an 8 inch space! Stockings, sox, gloves, handkerchiefs and baby's diapers, too, can be hung compactly on a SafTdri. You don't need pins or clips and there are no snags or rust, SafTdri, offering lovely decoration, plus utility, also makes an ideal razor shelf, tie rack, or washcloth holder." To which I say, Hee Hee. Imagine 32 wet diapers hanging in only 8" of space! Gadz, they wouldn't be dry til the kid was 16.                    $6.00-$8.00

Clothes drying rack, folding with 10 arms, wood, made by the wringer company, stamped on front "Horse-Shoe Brand Clothes Wringers. Every One Warranted", mfd by The American Wringer Co., with trademark showing horseshoe arch with stacked "A W" inside, NYC, NY, TOC.                    $55.00-$70.00

Clothes drying rack, hangs on wall, 8 swingout rods, wood & cast iron, "Perfection", American, pat'd 1887 & made past TOC. • An early version, from the 17th & 18th Cs, was the blanket crane, mounted near the hearth. • Used to be, you could buy these racks for about $5.00-$15.00 because nobody wanted them.                    $55.00-$100.00

Clothes drying rack, or clothes tree, stamped steel, finished in 2 tone ("tu-tone") baked enamels, grays or ivory & green, and nickel, looks like 4 legged stool with 16 folding arms, also enameled, radiating from seat, "Dixiedri-Rack", Sommers Brothers Appliance Co., Saginaw, MI, about 28"H with 2' L arms, c.1930s.                    $12.00-$30.00

Clothes drying rack, wall rack, wire with 6 arms, "The All-Metal Clothes Dryer", 21½"L arms, pat'd 1915.                    $35.00-$45.00

Clothes hamper, wicker woven over vertical steel rods (new in late 1940s, after WWII), a pearlized plastic covers the lid & panels in front, various colors, Pearl-Wick-Ware "Duroweve", Astoria, Queens, NY, various sizes, 1940s to 1950s. • In NYC, if you walk south along the East River on the wonderful "boardwalk" starting about 20th Street, you can look across and see the Pearl-Wick factory.                    $8.00-$12.00

Clothesline reel, green painted wood, homemade, American, 19th C. • **Futurewatch.** — These are just beginning to pop up at flea markets. Might make a nice collection, along with clothespins. • **The Clothes-line belonging to Col. M'Allister,** Fort Hunter, on the Susquehanna above Harrisburg, in 1828. "A household convenience worthy of imitation," reported visitor Judge Buel. "The Clothes-line we saw had been six years in use, without sensible injury, though it had remained all this time in the open air. It had always been wound up, upon a small windlass, as soon as the clothes had been taken from it, where it was protected from the rain by a roof. Several posts, with notches near their tops, were placed in a range upon the grass plat, upon which the line could be drawn and fastened in two minutes, and from which it could be loosened and wound up in as short a time. It is but a small affair, but such small affairs make a large aggregate in ordinary life. 'Take care of the cents, and the dollars will take care of themselves.' " *The Farmers' Cabinet*, Vol. I, No. 1, Philadelphia, July 1, 1836.                    $15.00-$25.00

Clothespin, also called a clothes peg, carved bone, no decoration, American or English, 5"L, early 19th C.                    $55.00-$65.00

Clothespin, carved bone, very simple, beading or rings carved at neck & bottom, ball top, American or English, 3¼"L, early 19th C.                    $35.00-$45.00

Clothespin, carved & lathe-turned walrus or whale bone, round with interesting drilled holes through body in 2 places, lower hole, almost like a tooth, acts as grip, top hole was drilled to facilitate inserting saw blade in order to saw the lengthwise split; the hole also probably helps keep it from cracking apart when used by adding a small tolerance, head is truncated pyramid, extremely handsome, American (?), 4"L, early to mid 19th C.                    $100.00-$125.00

Clothespin, carved walrus bone or whale bone, no turning, big & fat in shape, American, 5"L, early 19th C.                    $135.00-$150.00

Clothespin, homemade, 2 part, pale bleached smooth wood, copper rivets, English (?), 7 5/18''L, late 19th C. **$9.00-$12.00**

Clothespin, large, oak, very smooth, spring clip, no mark, American, 6 11/16''L, late 19th C. **$20.00-$30.00**

Clothespin, molded pale green plastic, sort of a snowbaby doll's face knob, ''Rogers Clean-Grip'', American, 3 7/8''L, ''patent pending'', c.1940s or 1950s. **$3.00-$5.00**

Clothespin, pale wood, tacked-on tin band about¼''W holds 2 separate halves together, English, about 4'' to 5''L, late 19th C. • **Caveat.** — First of these clothespins I saw I got all excited, but after seeing hundreds of them, I'm not excited at all, and feel the price is way too high at $8.00, which is what everyone seems to ask. The only thing about them is they are made by hand, and each is slightly different. Still and all, they could be manufactured items. Sometimes you see a bit of printing on the tin, so you know that they were recycling old lithographed tins in a pleasantly thrifty way. See p. 163. **$6.00-$8.00**

Clothespin, small patented spring clip type. Seen from side it looks like a large wooden V with a relatively large circle of wire, which is the spring. American, only 2 5/8''L, late 19th C. **$15.00-$22.00**

Clothespin, smooth red plastic, 1940's ad says ''easy to find when dropped in the grass'', looks sort of like a strange big paperclip or 2 clothes pegs somehow joined together sharing center, can be used either direction — both ends are business ends. Mfd by Ratchford Corp., Dayton, OH, c.1948. **$2.00-$3.00**

Clothespin, smooth turned wood, rounded ends, very fat, brass holding band, rubber pads inside jaws for gripping, probably for hanging carpets or rugs from line, no mark, American, 6½''L, late 19th C. SEE the Blanket pin at beginning of this chapter. **$15.00-$22.00**

Clothespin, wooden with brass band, ''Lockwood'', American, Feb. 1877. • It's hard to find patented & marked examples of clothespins. **$10.00-$12.00**

Clothespins, 144 pins in original one gross printed cardboard carton, hardwood spring clip type, both the gripper & handle ends come to chisel point, wire spring goes through hole in one half of pin & forms a hook, United States Spring Clothes Pin Co., Montpelier, VT, pat'd June 28, 1887, still being sold in 1906. Single: $1.00-$2.00; gross: **$25.00-$30.00**

Clothespins, or clothes pegs, as the ones with no moving parts are sometimes called, mostly machine carved wood, most with knobby ''heads'' — which makes them ideal for clothespin dolls. American, mid 19th C to present. • **German vocabulary** — Wasche-klammer: clothes peg. • I don't know how they'd prove it, but hand-carved wooden pegs made by Shakers would be worth upwards of $25.00 each. • For common everyday pegs: **$1.00-$3.00**

• **An article about the manufacture of non spring clip pins** (or clothespegs) from 1906 is still instructive: ''It is estimated that no less than 1,250,000 five gross boxes of clothes-pins are manufactured in the United States alone, the great centre of the industry being Vermont.'' (This is 900,000,000 pins — amazingly enough, exactly the figure quoted in the *Wall Street Journal* in 1984, as the ''number of clothespins of both types'' sold in the U.S. every year in the mid 1980s.) ''The growth of the business has been enormous during the past few years, and if it were not for machines that are almost human in action, the demand could not be met.

''Interesting are the various processes whereby big birch logs from the rugged mountain sides are rapidly worked up into the clothes-pins of everyday use. During the winter great piles of logs are [stacked] about the mills, to feed the immense saws which snip them into 2½-foot lengths as easily as though they were so many matches. These lengths are rapidly split by another saw into thin slabs, ... in turn converted into long square strips by gang saws. Deft hands toss these strips onto a revolving drum, which bears them against still other saws and turns them out in the form of oblong blocks. Falling upon a moving belt, the blocks are whirled away to a number of lathes, which turn them into the desired shape at a high rate of speed.

''From the lathes a belt conveys the clothes-pins to a 'slotter,' which rapidly cuts the slot; the pins emerge with two symmetrical legs, and are swiftly borne by still a third belt to the upper floor, where they are dried in vast heaps at a high temperature .., bleached with sulphur, and finally polished with sax [probably some kind of powdered rock] in a huge revolving drum. Thence they descend again to the packers. Here they receive a final inspection, and all the pins that are not rejected are packed in boxes labelled 'A' or 'B', according to quality.

''The rate of production is amazing; yet very few are injured in the making, nearly every pin and handle emerging, after its tortuous journey, in perfect, polished form.'' *House Furnishing Review*, June 1906. See also p.160.

Clothespins, original package of wood & metal pins, mfd by Lewis M. Mann & Son, marked only with place, ''West Paris, ME'', this package prob. TOC. Company still making them in the 1940s. • This company also made toy clothespins, some sold packed in ''miniature barrels'' made also of wood. **$10.00-$12.00**

Clothespins, pine knot wood, 13 pins in slightly different eccentric forms that capitalize on shape of the wood, carved supposedly by Civil War soldier from Texas, or at least that story was passed down in family, along with an accompanying carved wooden cup, American, about 5½''L, 19th C. **$50.00-$80.00**

Clothespins, wooden, marked ''Maytag Washers'', 20th C. • **Ahoy, You Laundry Hobbyists.** — The first washing machine that the Maytag Co. built was called the ''Pastime'' model. That was 1907. Eighty years later, according to current company literature, Newton, IA, the hometown of Maytag, is known as the ''Washing Machine Center of the World.'' **$10.00-$15.00**

Clothespin bag, embroidered & appliqued linen with word ''Clothespins'', green & yellow, homemade, TOC. **$10.00-$12.00**

Clothespin bag, embroidered cotton, flowers, saddlebag or double pocket type, American, each half about 5'' x7'', 20th C. **$7.00-$10.00**

Clothespin bag, made from a Purina chicken feed sack, American, 20th C. **$10.00-$12.00**

Clothespin bag, made from old chicken feed sack, in very good bright condition, sort of a saddlebag with 2 pockets, hangs on line, ''Purina'', c.1920s-40s. **$12.00-$20.00**

Clothespin bag, pieced & printed cottons, rickrack trim, sewed in shape of bust of floppy eared rabbit — the head stuffed with batting, little collared shirt made of rabbit-printed fabric is open at the neck & is actually the receptacle. Small snap tab on back of head is for hanging on clothesline. Homemade but probably from a magazine project. American, 8''H, c.1940s. **$10.00-$15.00**

Clothespin bag, saddlebag type made from old flour sack, ''Big Jo'', 20th C. **$7.00-$10.00**

Fluting block, 2 part, wooden, English or American, 6'' x 4'', early 19th C. **$95.00-$120.00**

Fluting iron, also called a crimping iron, 2 parts, cast iron simple base with only 13 flutes, very slightly convex, simple iron with knurled handle, ''The Best'', American, late 19th C. **$75.00-$115.00**

Fluting iron, cast iron, wire clip, 6⅛''L, c.1870s. **$65.00-$75.00**

Fluting iron, rocker type, 2 part cast iron, no brass, corrugated bed or base plate with 15 rather fat corrugations, and corrugated rocking iron with handle. This was operated by heating bed, putting fabric over it, mating the grooves of top and bed and rocking the iron. A later version had a higher base, like a sculpture pedestal, with very slightly convex top, which — like the rocker — had a layer of brass. It was used like a box iron, in that a heated slab of iron was put inside the bed before using. This type was very popular and was being sold more than 30 years later by Sears Roebuck. ''Geneva Hand Fluter #1'', pat'd by Charles A. Sterling, mfd by Wm. H. Howell Co., Geneva, IL, pat'd Aug. 2l, 1866, but made (with changes) to c.1920. **$90.00-$120.00**

Fluting iron, rocker type, cast iron, corrugated or fluted curved rocking iron with handle, separate flat corrugated base plate, ''The Lady Friend'', American, pat'd 1875. • I believe the **first fluting irons** or fluting machines were patented in the United States in 1866, two years after an Englishman patented his. There is a puzzler from 1829, called a ''Machine for straight and spiral fluting,'' but this wasn't necessarily for cloth. A. H. Glissman states that ''many patents were issued between 1860 to 1900'', but as he doesn't specify examples prior to 1866, and I can't find any in the *Subject Index to Patents,* I suppose some qualifier was left out of his caption. He does say, and maybe someone is working on it, that ''a book could be written on fluters alone.'' **$85.00-$100.00**

Fluting iron, rocker type, rectangular and slightly arched cast iron base to which is bolted a wavy fluted copper plate, the hand held rocker has an arched sole with copper fluted plate, ''Howell Wave Fluter #2'', made by maker of the Geneva Hand Fluter, W. H. Howell, who made Wapak hollowwares for cooking. Geneva, IL, pat'd Aug. 21, 1866. • See also Pleater. **$125.00-$150.00**

Fluting machine, cast iron, heavy steel spring affords adjustability, 2 brass fluting rollers work like a wringer, sits on big saucer pedestal base and has crank action. Possible that the base was either in the public domain, or adapted from something else, so that only the ''fluting-machine rollers'' were patented. Unmarked with name, but rollers pat'd by H. G. Pearson, NYC, NY, pat'd Dec. 21, 1869. • A fluting machine was pat'd by H. B. Adams, also of NYC, just the week previous. It'd be nice to compare the two, and to know if Pearson & Adams were friends or rivals! So many stories hidden in the pages of the *Official Gazette.* (A third was patented Dec. 14 by F. Hewitt of Bloomfield, NJ.) **$145.00-$165.00**

Fluting machine, on rectangular stand, 2 adjustable corrugated cast brass rollers, black painted & pinstriped cast iron, round crank wheel at stanchion end, 4 long cast iron 'cigar' slugs to be heated (2 in, 2 out at any time), and the original long knitting needle-like tongs, foldaway screw clamp to base, ''Crown'', North Brothers Mfg. Co., Philadelphia, PA, pat'd Nov. 2, 1875, by Hermann Albrecht. • Another was found with same brand name & date, but marked by earlier (?) company — ''American Machine Co.'', also Philadelphia. • First I've ever seen with the slugs *and* tongs. **$145.00-$175.00**

Fluting machine, tabletop pedestal base with simple fluted rollers and crank, cast iron and brass, ''Excelsior No. 1'', mfd by Geo. Hovey & Son, NYC, NY, rollers are 5''L (the No. 2 has 7''L rollers), c.1870. • ''**Crimping machines** are for performing a kind of plaiting or fluting on frills with much greater regularity and expedition than could be practised by hand. This is done by grooved rollers, heated like the Italian iron.'' (ED.note: this looks like what we are accustomed to calling a goffering iron, but see below.) ''The process is performed merely by putting the articles between the rollers, and turning the handle.'' Webster & Parkes, *An Encyclopedia of Domestic Economy.* 1848 NY edition of 1845 English book. • ''The Italian iron affords a very neat and expeditious way of ironing certain articles, as frills, that require to be puffed. It is a hollow tube, and is heated by a cylindrical piece of iron made red hot and inserted in it. The articles to be ironed are drawn over the iron, instead of passing the iron over them.'' ibid. • Furthermore, the article continues, ''**Gauffering machines** differ from those used for crimping only by having the grooves much larger and less regular.'' ibid. **$125.00-$150.00**

Fluting machine, very small, cast iron platform with single stanchion at crank end, 2 brass fluted rollers, ''Eagle'', American Machine Co., Philadelphia, PA, rollers only 3¼''L, (they also made one with 5''L rollers), 4th quarter 19th C. • American Machine Co. also made several sizes of an 1870 (re-issued 1877) fluter called ''The Original Knox'', named after patentee Mrs. Susan R. Knox, who was granted her first patent with someone else, in 1866. It has 2 stanchions, a screw clamp swiveling attachment, and on the nearly flat rectangular base, centered in the middle, is an oval cartouche with a portrait of Mrs. Knox herself. The sizes varied by length of roller and number of corrugations. The ''Original Knox'' would be worth more than the ''Eagle''. **$130.00-$150.00**

Goffering iron, also spelled gauffering, iron & brass, has original cast iron slug insert. 15''H x 7½''L, late 18th C. **$180.00-$220.00**

Goffering iron, cast iron with brass barrel, simple round base, snaky shaft, iron has wooden handle, only mark is number ''13'', English, TOC. • Goffering irons of this type were made into late 1920s in England. This helps to account for the large quantity of them showing up now. **$75.00-$90.00**

Iron, box, cast iron ''box'' in rounded wedge shape, to contain heated slug — put in & removed through a sliding opening in the back, wooden handle, signed ''Hodges'', English (?), very late 18th C or early 19th. **$85.00-$110.00**

• ''**The box iron**
is an old fashioned implement, less used than formerly, but ingeniously constructed. As considerable pressure is frequently useful, this iron is made large and heavy; and to retain its heat longer, it is made hollow, the cavity con-

taining an iron heater which is made nearly red hot occasionally as the iron cools. To keep this heater in its place, an iron slider is made to shut down in front. Accidents of burning have sometimes happened by lifting these irons negligently, without seeing that the slider was down, so as to allow the heater to fall out.'' Webster & Parkes, *An Encyclopedia of Domestic Economy*. 1848 NY edition of English book of 1845. • **Box Iron Slug.** — At a flea market in Pennsylvania, in 1989. I bought an attractive piece of forged iron which I did not recognize. It is shaped like a sadiron — a rounded wedge — and has curious marks on top and bottom flat sides, made with a hammer and some kind of punch when the iron was still hot and being wrought. The design is a very abstract Tree of Life. Finally I realized that I had bought a slug or ''heater'' for a box iron, probably a very old one. It is 6''L and is about an inch thick, and I paid $22.00 for it, which seems a bargain for its beautiful design.

Iron, charcoal, cast iron, heated with hot charcoal from inside, ''Peerless'', John W. Lufkin, Boston, MA, 10''H x 11''L, 19th C. **$65.00-$90.00**

Iron, charcoal, cast iron, high body, with side vents for interior charcoal chamber, arched handle, cast iron lion on prow of iron, prob. German, perhaps mid 19th C. **$60.00-$75.00**

Iron, charcoal, chrome plated iron, red enameled wooden handle with gilded figures, German (?), late 19th or early 20th C. **$60.00-$70.00**

Iron, charcoal, high body with wooden handle, rather large cast rooster latch to hold top to bottom, large half-round ventilation holes on both sides of compartment inside body, unmarked, German (?), early 20th C. • **Rooster Latches.** — The most popular box iron found in general dealers' ads in the late 1980s (and it'll probably continue), has a cast rooster latch — standing, so to speak, on the prow of the high boxy iron. The weight of this useful ornament, like that of the heads of heroic people, swans, doves, etc., caused the latch to close securely and automatically, so that the hinged bottom wouldn't open and release the heated slug to bomb the ironer's foot. On page 27 of A. H. Glissman's so-far unparalleled book, *The Evolution of the Sad-Iron* (Carlsbad, CA: author, 1970) is a page of these ''rooster irons'', about which Mr. Glissman says that most of them were made in Germany, at least one from Austria (because of the handle style), and ''we know that one came from Polynesia and one is a Japanese reproduction made for the decorator trade.'' Well, I tend to get a bit paranoid about repros, but I bet most of the ones being sold today are Japanese (or other) reproductions, or quite recent German irons. Apparently few of these irons are marked, but according to Glissman a ''G'' (for the Grossag company in Germany) or a ''K'' (for Kaltschmidt) is occasionally found on them. • Glissman also shows a reproduction page from a 1955 German catalog showing a rooster latch as one of the multiple choices, along with handle types, you had when ordering. **$40.00-$75.00**

Iron, charcoal, sheet & cast iron, with a figural head of the iron & fire god — Vulcan — on damper, mfd by Bless & Drake, Newark, NJ, pat'd March 30, 1852, by Nicholas Taliaferro & William D. Cummings.• Bless & Drake is one of commonest manufacturers found today, despite age of the irons. The name is often found misspelled in ads — especially as ''Bliss & Drake'', but also ''Bliss & Blake'', etc. **$65.00-$80.00**

Iron, electric, ''Hotpoint Model R'', Edison Electric Appliance Co., 6½''L, pat'd Oct. 25, 1910, June 11, 1918, May 26, 1925. **$15.00-$25.00**

Iron, electric, very streamlined body, clear colorless Pyrex® glass (including handle) with colored plastic insert inside the clear glass of the body, meant to hide internal works & give decorative appearance. Inserts came in red, cobalt blue, also green, clear, and — according to some reports — in other colors, as well as silver & gold. Only the clear would not have hidden the innards. Chrome-plated metal sole. ''Silver Streak'', mfd first by OEM Co. with Corning Glass Pyrex® , according to Corning. Yonkers, NY, c.1946, 1947. • Other writers say mfd possibly by Continental Electric Co. of Geneva, IL c.1946, and then by Saunders Corp., and marked ''Model 1038''. **$800.00-$1400.00**

Iron, electric, with stand, nickel plated, 106-114 volts, Universal Landers, Frary & Clark, '' #E-909'', 7''L, 20th C. **$30.00-$40.00**

Iron, electric steam, cast aluminum, settings for Rayon, Wool, Linen, Silk, Cotton. Hole & stopper for water for the steam, very sculptural, ''Steam-O-Matic'', a Titeflex Product, mfd by Waverly Tool Co., Sandusky, OH, 10½''L, 1939 patent #1,178,512. • Hard to tell how much of the value is for Art & how much for Iron. **$70.00-$80.00**

Iron, fluting—See Fluting iron, also Fluting machine.

Iron, gas, black enameled sheet metal, with gas tank & pump, ''Coleman #609-A'', Wichita, KS, 1940. **$20.00-$30.00**

Iron, gas, cast iron with brass fuel tank, wooden handle, ''Monitor'', mfd by Bertus A. Lake, Big Prairie, OH, early 20th C. **$20.00-$28.00**

Iron, gas, with stand, blue enameled sheet metal, body pointed at both ends, with blue painted gas tank, brass pump, in original box, tin stand, ''Coleman Instant-Lite, Model 4A'', Coleman Co., Inc., Wichita, KS, 10½''L, 1929 patent #1718473. • Various models from 1925 to 1940. See also Stand for gas iron. **$60.00-$85.00**

Iron, gasoline, plated cast iron, double pointed shape, high handle with turned wooden grip attached to removable cover plate, horizontal cylindrical gasoline tank at one end, (this was also available with an alcohol burning system), embossed casting on top: Sun Mfg. Co., ''The Iron That Sizzles'', South Bend, IN, 7''L, tank 2¼'' diameter, early 20th C. **$50.00-$70.00**

Iron, gasoline, turned wooden handle, gas tank elevated behind end of handle, plated cast iron, ''Diamond'', mfd by Akron Lamp & Mfg Co., Akron, OH, c.1920s-30s. **$20.00-$30.00**

Ironing board, almost homemade looking, pencil marks for sawing it out show underneath, hardware also looks a bit make-do, tiger maple board very pointed but with truncated end, 2 adjustable heights — take center folding axle out and reinsert to change height, no mark, late 19th C. **$30.00-$50.00**

Ironing board, wood, has rectangular asbestos-lined metal insert with ridges & holes at the wide end of the board to create an iron rest, no mark, American, insert is 7½'' x 4½'', late 19th C. **$55.00-$75.00**

Ironing board, wooden, adjustable heights & folds quite flat, 30''L, pat'd Sept. 20, 1921. • Though many interesting patented ironing boards exist, (99% made of wood, with some metal hinges or fixtures), so far the ''market value'' for most of them is static. **$25.00-$50.00**

Ironing boards, usually pine, some pine & maple, wood left plain & unfinished on board, sometimes legs are shellacked or varnished, folding legs with varying degrees of mechanical sophistication — it may simply be an all wood sawtoothed ratchet & pawl, or wire & wood, or all metal, some are marked, some not, American, late 19th C to c.1930s. • The oldest ones are the most desirable, and tend to have wider top boards that are not pieced from two boards. They are often striking in design. • **Futurewatch.**— Although old all-wood ironing boards occasionally showed up at shows and flea markets in the late 1970s and early 80s, I believe that 1984 marked the beginning of a trend toward collecting them. Dealers in old kitchen things use them for display, and so do collectors. The biggest error in judgment is to varnish or stain or Minwax® or Briwax® them. They are not pieces of furniture. For that matter, old furniture oughtn't be permanently stained either, except as a last resort. **$20.00-$50.00**

Ironing machine, also called a <u>mangle</u>, cast iron 4 footed base & frame, with table plate & 2 wide adjustable rollers of turned hardwood, horizontal wheel & spring to adjust is under table, crank to turn rollers is at side, "The American Mangle", 3 hand power sizes: 21"L (4" diameter ); 23"L (5"D), 26½"L (5"D); & 1 motorized one also 26½"L (5"D). Folder claims pat'd Mar. 30, 1863, but this was Monday not Patent Tuesday. **$225.00-$300.00**

Ironing machine, heated by gas or gasoline, cast iron tabletop frame, 4 slightly arched legs, adjustable double mangle rollers with very large spoked cranked wheel, "Gem", Domestic Mangle Co., Racine, WI, TOC. **$125.00-$150.00**

Ironing sleeve board, small wooden thing shaped like a bicycle seat, padded in muslin, iron screw clamp, instructions read "A long needed arrangement for the ironing board or table. To use in ironing or pressing sleeves, children's garments, caps, etc. It saves one half the labor in ironing shirtwaists. Does away with the crease in the sleeve, which is caused by being obliged to iron double as heretofore. Can be used in any sleeve. It is constructed so as to enable you to iron in any direction without turning the garment." "Acme Sleeve-Board", mfd by C. H. Smith & Co., Boston, MA, pat'd June 3, 1899. **$30.00-$40.00**

Irons—See also Sadiron; Sleeve iron, Fluting iron.

Keeler or washtub, a shallow, coopered tub with pine staves, iron bands, nice & tight, iron ear handles, 15"H x 23" diameter, mid 19th C. **$225.00-$350.00**

Lacework dolly, a very small tabletop washing machine for lace, turned wood container & turned wood dasher, with lid-apron like a churn lid, prob. European, 11"H x 4½"D, early 19th C. **$165.00-$125.00**

Laundry bag, handmade embroidered cotton, fancy script letters reading, "Laundry", American (?), late 19th C. **$15.00-$18.00**

Laundry bag, small, made rather like clothespin bag, colorful printed ginghams joined & appliqued to form a little girl in a wide skirt & cape, with little feet on bottom seam, loop handle, for hanging over hanger or hook. This is related to the pajama or nightgown bag. American, 22"L, 1920s or 1930s. **$3.00-$8.00**

Laundry bucket, large galvanized sheet iron bucket, horseshoe shape from above, with angled built-in corrugated zinc washboard soldered from top edge of flat side, down to bottom, wire bail with wooden grip, Home Laundry Bucket Co., Cortland, NY, late 19th C or early 20th. **$15.00-$22.00**

Laundry sprinkler, blue & white ceramic, cat shape, American, TOC or early 20th C. **$12.00-$18.00**

Laundry sprinkler, ceramic woman, crudely handpainted decoration, polkadotted blouse, apron, marked underneath "Myrtle — The Pfaltzgraft Pottery Co.", York, PA, 20th C. **$15.00-$20.00**

Laundry sprinkler, figural clothespin bottle with happy face, yellow glazed pottery, American, 20th C. **$30.00-$40.00**

Laundry sprinkler, figural clothespin, molded plastic, foil label, "Sprinkle Pin — From the Studio of Jay & Sunny Originals", Hollywood, CA, c.1950s or 1960s. **$12.00-$18.00**

Laundry sprinkler, figural elephant, trunk up, glazed ceramic, Cardinal China Co., American, mid 20th C. **$25.00-$40.00**

Laundry sprinkler, figural sadiron with ivy, ceramic, Funny, this image. Nice if you could leave the ironing so long that ivy could grow over the iron! American, 20th C. **$28.00-$35.00**

Laundry sprinkler, figural Trylon & Perisphere from World's Fair, ceramic, American, 1939. • Some crossover competition here from World's Fairs & Expos people. **$40.00-$50.00**

Laundry sprinkler, galvanized tin, L-shaped cylindrical vessel, the perforated sprinkling head being screwed to the short piece, the long piece, held horizontal in use, lengthened more by tapered tubular handle at end. This long piece has a small metal screw-on cap for filling, and a push button exactly where the thumb would lie. It's obviously a sprinkler, but not until I found a How-to in a metal workers' trade journal did I understand the innards. First devised by "H. J. W.", Chicago, IL, 9"L, 1890s. • "For the benefit of my brother 'chips,' (tinsmiths) I send drawings of a clothes sprinkler which I have just gotten out. ... The material used in the manufacture of this sprinkler may be either zinc or brass, according to the taste of the manufacturer. If brass be employed I would suggest that it be tinned on the inside." He goes on to explain that a coiled spring inside holds a disc against a valve made at the elbow of the L, and it holds this disc in place until that is pushed away by pressing on the thumb button near the end. "The arrangement of this device is such that the water cannot escape from the sprinkler except by pressing with the thumb upon" the lever. "This device for dampening clothes results in a great saving of time and labor compared with the old fashioned method of sprinkling with the hand, and it is, I am sure, an improvement on the plan employed by the maligned 'Heathen Chinee,' who fills his mouth full of water and squirts it through his teeth on the clothes. The rose of the sprinkler is made from a water pot head (rose), and can be unscrewed for cleaning if necessary. This device is intended [to be] an article of use rather than ... beauty." *The Metal Worker*, Oct. 11, 1890. See III-116. **$15.00-$22.00**

Laundry sprinkler, girl with blonde hair, white blouse & green pants, ceramic, 20th C. **$12.00-$15.00**

Laundry sprinkler, hand painted ceramic Chinese laundryman, brass sprinkler head, "Cleminson Brothers" (I've seen this misspelled by sellers as Clemenson and Clemson.), CA, mid 20th C. **$18.00-$25.00**

Laundry sprinkler, in shape of sadiron, ceramic, depicts woman ironing in sort of sgraffito design on sole plate of iron, American, 1950s. **$10.00-$12.00**

Laundry sprinkler, moldblown glass with bulbous shape, American, 19th C. **$15.00-$20.00**

Laundry sprinkler, molded bright yellow plastic, in form of woman with arms akimbo, hands on hips, long skirt & apron, screw cap is her cap, paper label says "Merry Maid Clothes Sprinkler", mfd by Reliance, 6½"H, c.1940s. • Another, without label, is of molded red plastic, the face painted in pink tones, white apron, same yellow cap as other. **$6.00-$12.00**

Laundry sprinkler, of Chinese man, blue & white ceramic, long skirt, head comes off to fill, water sprinkled out of man's cap's top not a metal screw-on cap, American (?), c.1950s. **$12.00-$15.00**

Laundry sprinkler, pieced tin can with slightly flared sides, perforated top, filled through the tubular side handle with cork in end, not marked, but called the "Chi-Nee" sprinkler, mfd by Syracuse Stamping Co., Syracuse, NY, holds pint of water, c.1908. **$15.00-$20.00**

Laundry sprinkler, pieced tin, canister with cork and pierced holes, painted tan, slightly tapered tubular side handle, capped at end, American, 4"H x 7½"L including handle, c.1870s to 1880s. • Some of this type are actually tools used by paper hangers, to keep their work wet. See III-118. **$30.00-$45.00**

Laundry sprinkler, pieced tin, sort of a can with truncated end capped off with latched lid with perforations, slightly tapered tubular handle with capped end, American, 19th C. **$20.00-$30.00**

Laundry sprinkler, sitting-up Siamese-like cat, ceramic, glazed in shades of tan & brown, brass sprinkler top looks like cap on head, Cardinal China Co., 8½"H, mid 20th C. **$18.00-$25.00**

Patent model wash boiler, tin, with official tag made out in wonderful old hand, one of three pat'd by C. E. Miller, Indianapolis, IN, Model (and patent) #80651, dated Aug. 4, 1868. • Hundreds of thousands of patent models were submitted with specifications and applications, as required during most of the 19th C. There were so many, and they presented such a storage problem, that officials of the U. S. Patent Office decided that drawings would suffice in most instances. This was after two fires. First, in 1836, about 7000 models, dating back to at least 1823, were consumed by fire, along with all the original drawings and other papers. Models of what are now some of the most famous inventions of America were destroyed. Then a second horrible fire at the Patent Office, on the 24th of Sept., 1877, destroyed "87,000 models. Among them were several thousand known as 'pending' and 'issue' cases. The former are those cases in which the applications are still pending in the examiners' rooms, and the latter belong to that class of cases allowed by the examiners, and still awaiting the payment of the final fees. The loss of these falls on the inventors. The loss of rejected models is not serious." *Official Gazette*, Oct. 9, 1877. • There have been several sales of patent models in the 20th C; they are still being sold in dribs and drabs, at what are sometimes very high prices, particularly for the fun things. • This household type uncommon; when available the range is very wide for patent models: **$175.00-$900.00**

Pleater, brass, iron, in original box, with instructions for use, "The Simplicity", TOC. • See also the Fluters. **$10.00-$15.00**

Polishing iron—See also Sadiron, polishing, next page.

Polishing sadiron, cast iron, with slightly convex sole & beveled edges, rope design edge to top plate. This iron could put a high polish or glazed appearance on fabric, "N. E. Butt", mfd by New England Butt Co.,Providence, RI, 5"L, 1880s. The company made butt hinges for doors. **$25.00-$40.00**

Sadiron, alcohol burner, also called a spirit sadiron, cast iron, tall handle, fancy design with A & O in laurel wreath, raised edge of pointed toe, triangular top to hold alcohol or other spirits that could be lit to heat iron, marked "Adre. Odelin", for Andre Odelin, French, early 1800s. **$75.00-$90.00**

Sadiron, alcohol burner, nickeled cast & sheet iron, revolving soleplate, presumably to have a hot fresh iron every few minutes (heat rises), nice turned handle, pat'd by J. Conrad, Apr. 2, 1878. **$75.00-$90.00**

Sadiron, cast iron, clip-on handle, R. W. Weida, (I saw this recorded once as Weidas, but Patent Index has without the "s"), Philadelphia, PA, 6"L x 3"W, marked "pat'd 1870" but actually pat'd Sept. Aug. 22, 1871. • **Boo Hoo. Why "Sad"?** — There are three explanations of the word sad in this context: **(1)** That it is a sad iron because the ironer was not happy about her work; **(2)** That the very old meaning of the word sad was heavy; and **(3)** That the term sad applied to cast objects that were flat and cast in a one-part mold (or a relatively flat mold), as opposed to hollowware. • **Mangled nerves.** — A mangle is "a valuable domestic machine, employed for the purpose of smoothing such linen as cannot be conveniently ironed. Mangles are highly useful in preventing the necessity of ironing all plain articles of linen or cotton, which is a serious and laborious task on a warm day in the United States, and the source of much indisposition among females. Mangles are made in Philadelphia by Wright, Cherry Street." Anthony Florian Madinzer Willich, *The Domestic Encyclopedia; or A Dictionary of Facts & Useful Knowledge...* 1st American edition, Philadelphia: W. Y. Birch & A. Small, 1803-04. **$35.00-$40.00**

Sadiron, cast iron sole & handle, soapstone body, "Hood's Patent", pat'd by P. B. Hood, of Milford, NH, pat'd Jan. 15, 1867. **$85.00-$100.00**

Sadiron, cast iron, with detachable handle, "WAPAK #5", mfd by Wm. H. Howell Co., Geneva, IL, late 19th C. **$25.00-$35.00**

Sadiron, cast iron with detachable wooden handle, "Mrs Potts #3", no maker given, 1870-71. • **Mrs. Mary F. Potts' iron,** first patented on May 24, 1870, was made by several companies: Chalfant Foundry, Enterprise Mfg. Co., American Machine Co., Kenrick & Sons (England), Grossag (Germany), and Colebrookdale Iron Foundry, Pottstown, PA — this last one until 1953. • **Great Minds Think Alike.** — A woman's lamentation in the May 1871 *American Agriculturist* was a long instructive piece about making a homemade hotpad to be used with sadirons. "Mrs. W." suggests that to quilt one with layers of newspapers inside is better than cotton stuffing; and to quilt one filled with sawdust would be much better, "wood being a non-conductor to a great degree, the hand is not so injuriously affected by heat as from the old-fashioned metal handle and a common holder. I wish some woman would invent a movable wooden handle for flat-irons, which would be easily adjusted on taking an iron from the fire. Some woman, whose husband is a blacksmith, and would make her models, perhaps might succeed." Of course, there may have been some connection between Mrs. Potts and the Mrs. W. who wrote this, and perhaps the latter knew that Mrs. P. had already got her patent a year before, and was boosting its renown. • **Restored Handles.** — Ads from the late 1980s claim that the old Potts'-type arched wooden handles are "restored like new" by David Caraway, Antique Farm, 1315 Dollarway, Ellensburg, WA 98926. You can write him, using an SASE, if you are interested in finding out more.

**$25.00-$35.00**

Sadiron, cast iron with high detachable wooden handle, rather like Mrs. Pott's iron, "The Sensible", mfd by Nelson R. Streeter, Groton, NY, pat'd 1887. **$50.00-$60.00**

Sadiron, cast iron with stepped base, wonderful coiled wire heat dissipating handle has loops on both verticals, mfd. by W. M. Ferris, St. Louis, MO, pat'd Oct. 6, 1891.

**$25.00-$40.00**

Sadiron, cast iron, wooden handle & hood, cast iron slug or core, "Dover #912", The Dover Mfg. Co., Canal Dover, OH, pat'd May 22, 1900. **$20.00-$30.00**

Sadiron, cast iron, heavy, detachable iron handle with the same kind of raised tubular hand grip found on many tea kettles, rather wide & thick sole, marked only with date: "Imp Nov. 1865", but none to be found in Subject Index to Patents. **$30.00-$40.00**

Sadiron, cast iron, possibly sleeve iron, narrow body pointed in front, rounded end, diamond "quilted" cast handle attached by S-curved rods, "Sweeney #4", pat'd by Mary Sweeney, 7"L, pat'd July 18, 1899.

**$24.00-$28.00**

Sadiron, cast iron, with detachable handle, mfd by Shreiber & Cormar, late 19th C or early 20th. • **German vocabulary** — Biegeleisen: flat iron. • Most commonly found German maker's name is Grossag, in existence since 1863 in Schwabisch-Hall, Germany. They were still in business in 1970, probably still are. **$22.00-$30.00**

Sadiron heater, cast iron, fits over range eyes, "R. M. Merrill's #9", pat'd Jan. 11, 1876. **$40.00-$55.00**

Sadiron heater, long oval pan with very wide flat lip, rather shallow, nice carrying handles at each end, cast iron with smooth finish, also advertised as being useful for "some cooking purposes", Favorite Stove & Range Co., Piqua, OH, 3 sizes: No. 7, 18⅝"L x 8¼"W; No. 8, 21¼"L x 9½"W; No. 9, 23½"L x 10¾"W, late 19th or early 20th C.
**$35.00-$65.00**

Sadiron heater, stove top, openwork iron in pyramidal shape, holds 3 irons, all openings had to be covered by an iron, so you had to have 4 irons, with 1 in use and 3 heating up, at all times, "Dome", mfd by Shepard Hardware Co., Buffalo, NY, pat'd Feb. 23, 1886. **$25.00-$35.00**

Sadiron heating stove, kerosene fueled, cast iron, very small, 9¾"H x 4" x 7½", TOC. **$90.00-$150.00**

Sadiron, polishing, cast iron all in one piece, odd jaunty shape, with back-angled thick handle, & calla lily leaf-shaped sole, complete with little rib up center of top, it almost looks one-of-a-kind instead of a production piece, marked "McCoy", American (?), 4¼"L, 3rd or 4th quarter 19th C. **$45.00-$55.00**

Sadiron, polishing, cast iron, elliptical oval, toe or "prow" convex, heel like badly rundown shoe, very rounded, "M. A. B. Cook #1", pat'd by Mary Ann B. Cook, Boston, MA, 5¼"L x 2½"W, pat'd Dec. 5, 1848. • Glissman, *The Evolution of the Sad-Iron* (1970), says that "this is the earliest patent we have been able to obtain on any type of ironing device." But that could refer to the extreme difficulty of getting the early, sometimes unnumbered, patent records from the Patent Office. **$50.00-$65.00**

Sadiron, polishing, cast iron, entirely convex rocker sole plate, high handle with big handgrip, "J. & J. Siddons", (Joseph & Jesse), West Bromwich, Staffordshire, England, company est.1846 & made this iron up to 1939 (Glissman, p.134). **$30.00-$50.00**

Sadiron, polishing, cast iron, smooth polished fine diamond waffle pattern on sole, a scored diamond pattern on handle grip. About the waffling on the bottom, A. H. Glissman, in **The Evolution of the Sad-Iron,** says Mahony "does not claim patent rights for the shape of the irons, which are usually called French polishers. He claims only … an improved smoothing sad-iron, and an improved polishing sad-iron [one is pointed on front, other is completely round at front]. He experimented with many configurations [for the sole pattern] — elliptical, circular, wavy, star-shaped, etc. — but found the polygons with their diameters parallel to the center line of the sole, to be the most successful." (p.139.) Marked "Mahony", pat'd by Michael Mahony, "Troy", NY, only 4½" x 2", pat'd Nov. 28, 1876. **$35.00-$45.00**

Sadiron, polishing, cast iron with detachable wooden handle, deliberately uneven sole, "Enterprise Star Polisher #72", mfd by Enterprise Mfg. Co., Philadelphia, PA, pat'd Jan. 17, 1877. • I can't find this in the c.1893 to 1900 Enterprise catalog. But the Star Polisher No. 77 is in it; it has a stationary japanned perforated cast iron "cold handle" that can't be removed, and a rounded edge & bottom so that it can be rocked & rolled while ironing.

**$30.00-$40.00**

Sadiron, polishing, thick cast iron, detachable iron & wooden handle, short toboggan shape with upturned front, straight heel, "Mrs. Streeter's No. 2 Gem Polisher", N. R. Streeter Co., Groton, NY, 1870s.

**$40.00-$50.00**

Sadiron set, 3 double pointed irons, with single detachable fits-all handle, cast iron & wood, a Mrs. Potts-style iron, "Enterprise irons Outfit No. E32", with No. E30 irons in sizes 1, 2 & 3, Enterprise Mfg. Co., TOC. • Added value with the original wooden box with the handle and the bent wire holder stand. Even more valuable would be the Outfit No. 330, with nicer wooden box that has handles at each end, holding five graduated irons, 4 double ended, one more like modern iron — No. 82, 90, and the 3 sizes of No. 50 irons, also the wire stand, 3 handles, and a star & heart triangular stand with handle. **$45.00-$50.00**

Sadiron set, nickel-plated cast iron detachable hood or cover & black shaped-wood handle, 3 cast iron cores. Set includes the rarely-found-together square asbestos insulated stand (or trivet), all in original finger-jointed wooden box as if it had never been used, "Asbestos, #70", Dover Mfg. Co., Canal Dover, OH, hood is 4¾"L, c.1900 to 1913 (when word Canal was dropped from name). • The best information on Dover sadirons is in "Dover Hall of Fame", by Carol "The Iron Lady" Walker & Timmy Walker, that appeared Sept. 7, 1988 in the *Antique Trader Weekly*. I can't reprint it here, but you can always buy the ATW yearbook of articles if you missed it. • The Iron Lady's address is 100 N.E. 5th St., Waelder, TX 78959. If you write to ask a question, please enclose an SASE, as you do whenever asking for information. **$55.00-$65.00**

Sadiron set, with 3 irons, cast iron, single wooden handle, "#1, #2, #3", A. C. Williams Co., Ravenna, OH. **$35.00-$50.00**

Sleeve iron, cast iron, long skinny sole, Ober Mfg. Co., Chagrin Falls, OH, 8"L x 2¾"W, TOC. **$55.00-$65.00**

Sleeve iron, cast iron, possibly it was given as a premium of some kind, by "Grand Union Tea Co." **$30.00-$40.00**

Sleeve iron, pointed cast iron, narrow body, marked only "HUB" (probably nothing to do with Arthur Hubbell, who invented an iron mfd by Enterprise), PA, 7"L, 19th C. **$40.00-$55.00**

Sleeve or flounce iron, sleek narrow cast iron, blued steel finish, blunt front point, rounded at edges like polishing iron, high rising handle with big cast grip with curved uprights made of heavy flat bands of strap iron, name & place cast on top "Walker, Orlynch", (which Glissman says may be O. R. Lynch), "Boston", 4"H x 6"L, c.1870s (?). • The same type of iron, with markings not known to me, was being made through the 1920s & probably even later. **$50.00-$70.00**

Smoothing board, carved wood, stylized horse handle fitted into end, carved with 6 petal flower and interesting marks that look like religious symbols with initials, old green paint, red molding around outside (not applied but carved), handle never painted, rest of paint mostly worn off, smooth underside but repaired with old wood putty, probably by early owner and user, marked only "ANNO 1797", European, Canadian, or, less likely, American, 21¾"L, 1797. **$800.00-$1200.00**

Soap dishes—See Bathrooms, though used elsewhere.

Soap grater, tin, "Super", 20th C. **$3.00-$5.00**

Soap saver, metal, "Fels Naptha", Fels & Co., Philadelphia, PA, early 20th C. **$8.00-$12.00**

Soap shaver, tin, with wire handles, like a carrot grater but with even bigger round slits. For making shavings of hard laundry soap to be mixed with hot wash water, or to be put into a soap "saver" for swishing through hot water to make suds. embossed "Sunny Monday — Saves Soap & Labor", American, 10 ¾"L x 4"W, 1st quarter 20th C. • This qualifies as a "confusable": it might be mistaken for a food grater if you didn't know that Monday was washday. • Federal Washboard Co. of Tiffin, Ohio made a washboard with same name ... but that doesn't mean Federal made the shaver: the expression might have been used for many laundry-related products. **$14.00-$18.00**

Sock dryer, or what is often called a <u>stocking dryer or stretcher</u>, maple, small child's size, 19th C. or early 20th. **$15.00-$25.00**

Sock dryer, tiger maple, for man's socks, 19th C. • **Reproduction alert.** — Look for good patina on wood, and no fakey "early American" varnishing, overdone distressing, or use of exaggerated knotty pine. • <u>Added value</u>: A pair would bring a lot more. **$25.00-$35.00**

Sock dryers or stocking stretchers, a pair, flat cutouts of birch wood, shape of foot & leg, "H & W", American, 21"L, TOC. **$35.00-$45.00**

Sock dryers or stocking stretchers, bent wood outline of foot and leg, with a slat of wood across top (where the sock band would be) keeps ends together, natural finish, not the common type you see, marked "W. C. 9" and "Size 10½", American (?), early 20th C (?). **$45.00-$65.00**

Stand for gas iron, cast iron, "Pitner #90", early 20th C. 12.00-$15.00

Stand for gas iron, cast iron, footed, double pointed, with rail open slightly at each end. Great figural design of the iron itself, on a scrolly nouveau background, marked in border: "Double Point IWANTU Comfort Iron", Strause Gas Iron Co., Philadelphia, PA, 20th C. • <u>Classic.</u>— Not rare, but because of great design, it's still a thrill to see. There is also a single point stand for the Strause Gas Iron. **$25.00-$45.00**

Stand for gas iron, cast iron, triangular shape with openwork design with scrolls, 3 feet, initial forms central design, with low relief depiction of gas iron, "R", & around edge "Rosenbaum Mfg. Co., NY, UNEEDIT GAS IRON", 1"H x 7"L x 4"W, late 19th C. **$25.00-$35.00**

Stand for gas iron, cast iron with star-like flower and ring-pattern handle, American, late 19th C. **$30.00-$40.00**

Stand for gas iron, nickel (?)-plated cast iron, 3 short legs, image of gas iron in openwork pattern on face plate of trivet, "The Modern Home Gas Iron", mfd by Koenig Gas Iron Co., Philadelphia, PA, TOC. **$22.00-$30.00**

Stand for sadiron, brown glazed pottery, 3 stubby peg feet, fat pointed end shape, marked "J. M. G." then either a "10" (or "TO" or "IO"?) inside 2 concentric rings, then "M. G." underneath, American (?), 7½"L, and ⅝" thick exclusive of feet, c.1870s (?). **$25.00-$50.00**

Stand for sadiron, carved soapstone, rectangle with gothic arch shape depression carved out for the iron, magnificent looking, American, 7" x 6¼" x 1" thick, 3rd quarter 19th C. • When I saw it it was only $15.00 and I AM A DOPE FOR NOT HAVING BOUGHT IT. **$55.00-$70.00**

Stand for sadiron, cast brass, in scroll, heart & double tassel pattern that looks like 2 brooms, but are actually funereal tassels. Pattern is called "Lincoln Drape". Inaccurately called "Grain and Tassel" by the foundry that was making reproductions in the 1950s (and perhaps even later). A "drape" design of swagged heavy draperies of the type used in the 19th C to stage viewings of coffins, was also used in some commemorative objects for the assassinated Garfield. • "Grain & Tassel" is another pattern — the space between the tassels are an abstract of the head of a stalk of wheat. American, 8¾"L. (A cumbersomely cast Wilton 'reproduction' is only 5¾"L), late 19th or early 20th C (?). Problematic to date. **Reproduction alert I.** — Many cast brass sadiron stands are repros of old patterns, the molds being copies (hence slightly fatter & sloppier). Brass became *de rigeur* in the "Colonial" revival in the 1920s, and this "Lincoln Drape" pattern (which I at first mistook for two brooms) was copied early on. In the 1920s, no less now, antiques were for decoration, and brass is usually considered more "for nice" than cast iron. Signs of polishing and wear are not proof of 19th C. origin, only of frequent good care, possibly for as few as 35 years. <u>Old cast iron stands</u> will not have little holes in the bottoms of the three tiny feet; these are a sign of newness, because modern makers of reproductions bow to modern housekeepers who buy these as living room decoration, by putting tiny rubber guards, shaped sort of like thumbtacks, on the tips of the feet. <u>Sheet brass stands</u> should reveal these signs of age: tiny scratches going in myriad directions from polishing; slight unevenness in thickness; and evidence that the feet were separate and were riveted on. • **Alert II.** — Griswold made at least 6 reproduction stands of cast iron, which they called "trivets", in old styles, all with short handles. They include Tassel & Grain (4 legs, rectangular), Eagle & Laurel (wreath), Tree of Life (4 legs), an extra fancy Cathedral (the only decidedly sad iron 3 legged trivet), an openwork star in round rim with "I X L", and a round gearwheel one with 8 circles in rim and snowflake star. These all date to the 1950s, and had rubber tips on feet when new. **$45.00-$65.00**

Stand for sadiron, cast iron, "R C O", Rosenbaum Mfg. Co., NYC, NY, 3"H x 10½"L x 6"W, 19th C. **$45.00-$65.00**

Stand for sadiron, cast iron, "American Foundry", St. Louis, MO, TOC. **$15.00-$18.00**

Stand for sadiron, cast iron, "H. R. Ives", Montreal, CAN, late 19th C. **$15.00-$20.00**

Stand for sadiron, cast iron, 3 legs, extremely plain, has low railing, American, 6¹/₁₆"L, late 19th C. **$18.00-$22.00**

Stand for sadiron, cast iron, "Cathedral" pattern, very lacy openwork that makes the pointed triangular shape with interior scrolls, look like a church window. Because the scrolls form what looks like a heart, pointing toward the handle, this stand or trivet is often classified with heart designs, among several makers is Griswold, Erie, PA, late 19th C (?). **$25.00-$45.00**

Stand for sadiron, cast iron, gothic arch shape, interior cutout with urn, 3 short feet, embossed around edge "Ferrosteel Cleveland", Cleveland Foundry (?), OH, ¾"H x 6"L x 4¼"W, TOC. **$18.00-$25.00**

Stand for sadiron, cast iron, gothic openwork design of 12 hearts encircling 5 petal flower, short straight handle ending in circle with pinwheel (called a <u>fylfot</u>), beautiful casting, marked on back "W. R. Rimby", Baltimore, MD, dated 1843. • Rimby also made a round stand with short feet & nearly straight short handle, with intertwined tulips & stems, marked only with his initials and date 1843. Either one: **$125.00-$150.00**

Stand for sadiron, cast iron horseshoe rim, with 6 point star within, has 3 legs — the 2 at tips of horseshoe are L-shaped, short loopy scrolled handle, motto "Good Luck to All Who Use This Stand", is part of the ornate openwork, no railing, filed flat and smooth, American, 7⅝"L x ⅜"H, late 19th C. • <u>The 6-point star</u>, can mean something besides a patriotic star, but not necessarily. Coins, state seals & old US seals often have 6 point stars. This stand is considered fairly scarce. **$35.00-$50.00**

Stand for sadiron, cast iron, horseshoe shape with motto "God Bless Our Home" around edge. I'm afraid I don't know if this one is the same as the other God Bless stand. American, dated 1892. **$45.00-$65.00**

Stand for sadiron, cast iron, horseshoe with date in center, 3 short legs, short handle, American, 7½"L x 4"W, "1884". **$60.00-$75.00**

Stand for sadiron, cast iron horseshoe, with maritime icons — anchor & cross, plus an openwork border with a star & a motto, "GOD BLESS OUR HOME", American, 6¼"W x 6"L, late 19th C. • Dick Hankenson, in his book *Trivets, Old & Reproductions, Book 2*, calls this design "Sailor's House Blessing". **$50.00-$70.00**

Stand for sadiron, cast iron, in star & rayed rising sun design (some people refer to it as star & fan design), "The Cleveland Foundry", Cleveland, OH, late 19th C. **$15.00-$18.00**

Stand for sadiron, cast iron, initial forms decorative pattern in center, the outer rim cast with full name, no handle, "F", Fanner Mfg. Co., Cleveland, OH, late 19th C. **$25.00-$30.00**

Stand for sadiron, cast iron, triangular arch shape, fancy script "E" in center, 3 short feet, embossed around edge with name "ECONOMY", & place "Syracuse, N. Y.", 6"L x 4½"W, late 19th or early 20th C. **$18.00-$22.00**

Stand for sadiron, cast iron, urn shaped (also looks like a lyre), called "Lacy Urn" pattern, has truncated end, 3 legs, simple scalloped railing to hold iron in place, was also made with plain, unscalloped railing, American, 5 ¹³/₁₆"L x ¾"H, late 19th C. **$35.00-$50.00**

Stand for sadiron, cast iron with copper finish, screw clamps to board, openwork pattern is a large "G", for W. H. Glenny & Co., Rochester, NY, c.1904. **$15.00-$25.00**

Stand for sadiron, cast iron, with crown & Maltese cross pattern cutout in center, 3 feet, full name around border, "Colebrookdale Iron Co.", looks English, but made at Pottstown, PA. Company also used keystone mark, 5¾"L x 4¼"W, late 19th C. • Another, with the exact same crown & cross design, has words "N. R. Streeter, Groton, N.Y." around edge. The English foundry <u>Coalbrookdale</u>, operated by Abraham Darby in Shropshire, England, is sometimes confused with the American <u>Colebrookdale</u>. **$25.00-$35.00**

Stand for sadiron, cast iron with image of George Washington's bust, nice shield shape with longish bifed handle, low railing, 3 feet, American, poss. c.1876 for Centennial, maybe later. • **Shall I Stand by my Trivet?** I had almost been convinced by the redoubtable Didsbury, a.k.a. Ray Townsend, that to use the term *trivet* was to be a recreant. Hmmm. Because so many original source materials, in this case manufacturers' catalogs, called the little three-legged stands for sadirons *stands*, and not *trivets*, Ray was persuaded that to call them trivets was to err. Even though trivet means three-footed, which most stands are. • I recently read an interesting article by Dorothy H. Jenkins, entitled "Trivets", published by *Woman's Day*, back in March 1965. In it she presents her case for calling the generic stands by two names — trivets and quads, depending on the number of feet! This is a useful terminology, but that the terms have to be qualified to tell what this particular quad or this particular trivet was meant to hold. If a stand is neither strictly a trivet nor a quad then call it a stand. For example, those "trivets" of twisted wire used under hot platters or tea kettles on the table. (I use mine for hot casseroles out of the oven, to save the Formica.) I guess they ought to be called stands, as many of them have as many little feet as there are scallops, twists, loops or spokes of wire. • There are a number of large four-legged stands called footmen, which stood by the fire to keep utensils, like teapots, warm. I'm not sure I'd be comfortable calling them quad footmen …

but maybe it'll catch on. • Carl W. Drepperd, whose *A Dictionary of American Antiques* I quote a few times in this book, writes that a trivet is "properly a three-legged flat-topped stand. Innumerable varieties, and not all three-legged. Some stand a foot or more high, have box tops, and are of brass and wrought iron. Some are tiny, low, and of cast iron, made for a miniature flatiron. Some are of tile, pottery, or glass, but generally of silver, silver-plated base metal, brass, copper, or iron." • If you feel this subject warrants more argument, please write, and I'll share with Ray what you say. (And don't forget those S.A.S.E.s if you want an answer. Yes, even though I've asked for your letters.) **$45.00-$75.00**

Stand for sadiron, cast iron, with pattern formed of the monogram "Y M CO" over a sort of half-gear shape, low railing, "Ypsilanti Mfg. Co.", Ypsilanti, MI, TOC. **$22.00-$30.00**

Stand for sadiron, cast iron, with slot at one end for stove lid lifter, made in oblong shape, scalloped railing, 6 holes & word "SENSIBLE" spelled out in openwork, mfd by Nelson R. Streeter, early 20th C. • There is a child size version of this, but the word is embossed rather than cut out. The child's version is priced about the same as the bigger one. **$22.00-$35.00**

Stand for sadiron, commercial size, nickeled cast iron, huge and massive rounded triangle with 3 legs, all one piece casting, longitudinal ridges cast on face plate along with name, "D. E. F. KOENIG GAS IRON 131 N 7", Philadelphia, PA, 3½"H x 9"L, early 20th C. **$20.00-$30.00**

Stand for sadiron, cutout heavy tin, abstract floral design, American, TOC. **$45.00-$55.00**

Stand for sadiron, double-sided, 3 heavy coiled iron springs sandwiched between 2 triangular plates of tinned sheet iron. Why you'd want your iron to bounce, I don't know. If the iron were really heavy, I guess it might save a calorie of effort every time you picked it up. Reminds me of a hair comb I bought new the other day, with a flexible rubber handle. The package stated that it would "prevent fatigue". Oh, gosh. I do get sooooo tired when I comb my hair. "Universal", Landers, Frary & Clark, 1½" thick x 7¼"L x 5"W, (another reported 12⅞"L), pat'd June 16, and June 30, 1914. **$7.50-$12.00**

Stand for sadiron, fine, almost fragile looking forged iron triangular body with 2 hearts, pointing away from each other, 3 short feet, turned wooden handle, Pennsylvania (?), looks sort of English, 2⅛"H x 12½"L overall x 4½"W, 19th C. • Robacker May 1989 price: **$1050.00**

Stand for sadiron, finely cast iron with chubby turned wooden handle, 3 nice little feet, slightly bowed triangle with 3 zigzag lengthwise bars, of a type commonly seen since the invention of containerloadism, English, 9 1/16"L, (saw one that was 8½"L), c.1870s to 1880s. • I saw one recently with broken-off foot (and it wasn't even there to be repaired) for $45.00, which is way too much. I've bought damaged pieces with missing parts all my collecting life, if they were cheap, because I use them as a tangible record, but collectors should strive for either good to fine condition, or early repairs. **$55.00-$65.00**

Stand for sadiron, flat topped cast iron, in interesting open-work pattern formed by connected images of various blacksmith tools, including a rasp, hammer, anvil, calipers, compass, square (some are Masonic symbols, or

at least like them), and a 3 link chain (definitely an Odd Fellows symbol), so this is some kind of workman's circle or fraternal order piece. This piece cannot be identified by its mixed symbols. Has wonderful tongs as the handle, low railing, American, 8½"L, 19th C. **$125.00-$175.00**

**• Fraternal Orders' Symbols.** — Basically <u>Freemasons</u> use masonry tools, viz. the trowel, crossed squares, a level, a plumb rule or bob, a mallet, a pickaxe, an iron rod, along with the all-seeing eye, a radiant sun, stars & comets, moon, 3 steps, a triangle, 3 triangles forming 9 point star, 3 columns of various architectural orders, representing Wisdom, Strength and Beauty, a bee hive, an incense pot, anchor & ark, hourglass with wings, a scythe, crossed hammer & spade, Aaron's budding rod, a coffin, a cord, a shoe, crossed keys, crossed quill pens, crossed swords, & other subjects. • <u>Knights Templar</u> symbols are possibly fewer in number (?), and use a paschal (Passover or Easter) lamb with a banner, a Maltese cross, a cross with long vertical, triangles, coffins, tents, etc. • The <u>Odd Fellows (I.O.O.F.)</u> seem to have the most emblems & symbols; they use an all-seeing eye, skull & crossbones, three-link chain, often with initials F. L. T. inside links, scythe, bow, arrows & quiver, bundle of rods, heart in palm of hand, an axe, a globe, the Ark of the Covenant, golden pot of manna, Aaron's budding rod, a serpent, scales & a sword, the Bible, an hourglass (sometimes with wings), a coffin, 3 pillars representing Faith, Hope & Charity (sometimes Faith, Love & Truth — F. L. T.), as well as Wisdom, Strength & Beauty of Religion, an open tent, an altar of sacrifice, tables of stone (10 Commandments), a Pilgrim's scrip, sandals & staff, a crown, a Shepherd's crook, sword, a sun, an owl, a huge sheep-looking lamb with a cross, half-moon, crossed gavels, baton, 5 point star, crossed quill pens, crossed wands, burning torch, & possibly more. The woman's <u>Rebekah degree of Odd Fellows</u> uses a bee hive, a dove, the moon & 7 stars, & a lily. They also use the image of Rebecca at the well. • Confused? How about Shriners; Woodmen of America; <u>Improved Order of Red Men</u>; various <u>Knights</u> ..., such as <u>Knights of Pythias</u>, ... <u>of Maccabees</u>, ... <u>of the Orient</u>, ... <u>of Malta</u>, and ...<u>of the Red Cross</u>!

Stand for sadiron, forged iron, shaped like abstract Christmas tree, 3 feet, marked "O. P. Frost", American, 19th C. **$225.00-$300.00**

Stand for sadiron, homemade of heavy sheet iron, 3 bent iron legs, handle riveted on, triangular platform, sawtooth railing, truncated tip, American, 11½"L, to hold iron 6¾"L, late 19th C. **$30.00-$40.00**

Stand for sadiron, homemade of wood & sheet copper beaten over a wood form to get rail, painted gold underneath, part of iron's support slides out from underneath, American, 7¾"L, late 19th C. **$55.00-$75.00**

Stand for sadiron, made of 2 gauges of iron wire, the plate, handle & arched body & frame of heavier gauge, the plate composed of front-to-front (confrontal) S spirals forming heart with scrolled lobes, the fine wire twisted in zig zag to form rail, American, prob.1870s. **$80.00-$95.00**

Stand for sadiron, nickeled steel, pointed shape with a scroll pattern inside assembled from bent & curled lengths of flat steel, long rod from point curls back under so stand can be slipped securely over edge of ironing board, W. H. Glenny & Co., c.1904. **$15.00-$25.00**

Stand for sadiron, or for a kettle?, forged iron, fat teardrop shape with 3 peg feet, 5 cutout hearts & 2 diamonds, no handle but very small round hanger where ordinarily a handle would be. The roughly triangular shape into which most heart trivets fit, makes it easy to assume that they are sadiron stands, but possibly they were used for pots or tea kettles. American, prob. PA, 1⅝''H x 8⅜''L x 4⅞''W, early 19th C. • Robacker May 1989 price: **$325.00**

Stand for sadiron or tea kettle?, brass plate in rounded triangle shape, 3 shaped feet (front one replaced), punched design of 2 concentric rings with 6 point star within, very short handle with hanging hole, marked ''C. Stedman'' on underside, PA (?), poss. related to Simeon Stedman of Hartford, CT, 1⅝''H x 8⅜''L x 4¼''W, 19th C. • Robacker May 1989 price: **$100.00**

Stand for sadiron, sheet iron, cut out with crossed keys & initials ''U C M'', sawtooth railing, ''U. C. M.'', 9¾''L, early 20th C. **$18.00-$22.00**

Stand for sadiron, twisted wire, rather elaborate approximation of the triangular 3 footed & short handled trivet common in cast iron or brass, each looped piece of wire secured to the frame & center axis, with twists of very thin wire, flimsy looking but surprisingly sturdy, American, about 10¼''L, 1890s. **$30.00-$50.00**

Stocking stretchers—See Sock or stocking dryers.

Tailor's iron, cast box iron with twisted handle, the box held a slug (now missing) of iron which was heated red hot before inserting into the iron, marked ''Cannon'', Cannon Co. Ltd., Bilston, Staffordshire, England, weighs 12 lbs, mid-19th C (?). • This is one type hard to date because it was being made at least from the 1830s through the 1920s, and probably the 1930s. In Glissman's *The Evolution of the Sad-Iron*, pages from an 1840 Cannon catalog are shown. **$40.00-$55.00**

**Trivet**—See Stand. Also see Trivet chapter for non-laundry types in <u>300 Years of Kitchen Collectibles</u>.

Wash bat or stick, a narrow form of washboard, corrugated maple board with handle, American or European, 35''L, early 19th C. **$245.00-$290.00**

Wash bat or stick, carved wood with scalloped ends, 21¾''L, early 19th C. **$175.00-$200.00**

Wash dolly—See Clothes dasher.

Wash fork, wood, primitive, used to stir the heavy heavy laundry in a huge wash kettle, American, 19th C. **$60.00-$70.00**

Wash stick, hand carved wood, pivoting handle grip, nice patina from years of work with lye soap, 38''L, early to middle 19th C. **$80.00-$95.00**

Wash stick, iron 2-pronged fork with wooden handle, for moving clothes in the washtub, American, 19¼''L, pat'd Dec. 5, 1916. **$30.00-$45.00**

Wash stick, wood, 2 pronged, 32''L, prob.19th C, but rural homes have used them well into 20th C. **$35.00-$45.00**

Washboard, all metal, zinc, Quapaw Zinc Products, Quapaw, OK, 20th C. **$50.00-$60.00**

Washboard, all wood, big fat rounded corrugations, cutaway so it'll fit against your stomach while you rub-a-dub-dub, English or Portugeuse, 22¼''H, 19th C. **$80.00-$90.00**

Washboard, all wood, corduroy effect with varying sizes of dowels, relatively deep soap shelf, 21''L x 13¼'', 19th C. **$95.00-$120.00**

Washboard, all wood, rather crude or primitive, poss. South American or Mexican, 24½''H, although very worn, prob. 20th C. **$50.00-$65.00**

Washboard, all wooden (for the WWII metal conservation effort), 18'' x 12''W, 1940s. **$12.00-$18.00**

Washboard, also called a scrub board, all wood, wood dowels, drilled out soap holder, very long cross pieces in H shape to fit over top rim of tub, poss. Shaker manufacture, prob. MA, 29½''L, scrub surface 13⅜''L, 19th C. **$95.00-$125.00**

Washboard, blue glass in wooden frame, ''Soap Saver, No. 197'', 24½''H, early 20th C. **$80.00-$90.00**

Washboard, blue-sponged yellowware, pine frame, no marks, American, 1870s-80s. **$350.00-$450.00**

Washboard, brass board, stamped in sort of dense criss-cross pattern instead of rows of grooves, set in wooden frame, with soap shelf with slot for front draining, ''Paragon Brass, Manufactured for Paxton & Gallagher Co.'', Omaha NE, TOC. **$28.00-$35.00**

Washboard, brass crimp-ribbed board, wooden frame, slotted soap shelf for front draining, ''Maid-Rite, Standard Family Size Brass No. 2062'', mfd by Columbus Washboard Co., Columbus, OH, 20th C. They made tin & brass ''Maid-Rite'' boards at least to 1981. • Interesting how many variations there are with basic materials being brass, glass, enameled iron, zinc & tin. More interesting is how similar some models by same company are, and their evocative names — undoubtedly a marketing ploy to appeal to various customers. **$30.00-$38.00**

Washboard, brass in wooden frame, ''National No. 80l'', mfd by National Washboard Co., Memphis, TN, 20th C. • Others of similar age, value & size (about 24'' H x 12''W), are ''Sunset'', ''Standard Family'' & ''Best Made''.some have mixed metals, with tin soap savers at top. **$26.00-$32.00**

Washboard, brown Albany slip glazed ceramic, ''The Common Sense Washboard'', Western Reserve Pottery Co., Warren, OH, late 19th C. **$245.00-$275.00**

Washboard, brown glazed ''Bennington'' or ''Rockingham'' type pottery, wooden frame, no mark, American, 23''H x 12''W, third quarter 19th C. • Some chips & glaze wear. Hard to find in perfect condition; the wonder is that any have survived. I saw one in 1986 with the panel OK, set into replaced frame made from a fruit crate, one part stenciled ''—W Fruit Growers Inc., Los Angeles, CA'' and the price was an astounding $850.00. Forced to comment, I'd say the price is a combination of things — the rather high value of the pottery scrub boards, and the charm of the repair, mixed, unfortunately, with hubris on dealer's part. **$180.00-$250.00**

Washboard, cast iron in wooden frame, has bumps on scrub surface, not ridges, ''W. Hill'', East Smithfield, PA, overall length is 22''L, iron part is 12'' x 9½'', including lips or prongs, pat'd Aug. 6, 1861. **$120.00-$140.00**

Washboard, cast iron, reversible, sharpish corrugations, soap depression, American, prob. from a Pennsylvania foundry, 21¹⁵⁄₁₆''H x 10¼''W, mid to 3rd quarter 19th C. **$125.00-$150.00**

Washboard, cast iron, wonderful cabriole or crookt (bent 'knee') legs, daisy pattern flowers at top, rounded corrugations, American, 21⅜''H x 11¾''W, mid 19th C to 3rd quarter. **$140.00-$175.00**

Washboard, cobalt blue agateware, wooden frame, ''The Enamel King'', Memphis (?), TOC. **$55.00-$65.00**

Washboard, cobalt blue enamel with zinc soap saver at top, wooden frame, printed on back in red & black is this testimony: ''Porcelain Enamel Washboard. The washing surface is made from a sheet of steel into which has been fused a coating of porcelain enamel (a composition of fine glass). It is durable, sanitary and flexible and will not rust or corrode and is not affected by alkali or strong washing compound.'' Marked with an eagle war-time mark: ''N. R. A. Member — We Do Our Part'' (NRA here is National Recovery Act). ''The Soap Saver, #197'', American, 1941 patents #52766 and 1283148. • Zinc oxide has been used for about a century in the porcelainizing or enameling of iron. **$55.00-$65.00**

Washboard, cobalt blue enameled board in wavy basketweave ribs, set in wooden frame, soap shelf drains in back, reads ''Porcelain Enamel Made from a sheet of steel into which as been fused a coating of porcelain enamel, a composition of fine glass''. ''National Washboard Co. #420'', Memphis, TN, (Chicago also seen as address.) TOC. **$45.00-$60.00**

Washboard, double-sided brass board in wooden frame, large size, one side for lingerie. Front draining, ''Brass King — Top Notch Soap Saver— Sanitary Front Drain'', mfd. by National Washboard Co., 20th C. **$55.00**

Washboard, dovetailed wooden frame, wooden scrubber & soap holder, 20½''L x 12''W. **$45.00-$55.00**

Washboard, for laundry & making music, corrugated herringbone tin in wooden frame, with color printed paper labels (front and back) pasted into soap shelves area with picture of Mickey Rooney, aged about 18 to 22, marked ''Mickey Rooney's One-Man Band'', American, 18''H x 8¾''W, 1930s-40s. • I don't know if this was just a marketing ploy, or if it were sold to amateurs wanting to set up a jug band. **$75.00-$90.00**

Washboard, for lingerie, ''Scanti Handi'', prob. 1930s-40s. **$12.00-$18.00**

Washboard, for lingerie, aluminum, rubber bumpers on stubby legs, ''Morton's Speedi Wash'', American, about 11''H, 20th C. **$20.00-$25.00**

Washboard, galvanized tin, ''Sanitary'', 24¼''H, early 20th C **$35.00-$45.00**

Washboard, glass & wood, ''The Glass King'', mfd by National Washboard Co., 20th C. • Another glass one of same value is the ''Good Housekeeper'', manufacturer not known to me. **$20.00-$30.00**

Washboard, gray graniteware in slightly arched bentwood frame, American, TOC. **$70.00-$100.00**

Washboard, hand carved wood, all made from one plank of wood, scrubbing surface on one side only, American or European — recent imports confuse provenance, 18''L x 8¼''W x 1⅝'' thick, 19th C. **$145.00-$175.00**

Washboard, hand carved wood, recess at top for soap, beautiful patina, American (?), early 19th C to mid-l9th C. **$250.00-$350.00**

Washboard, handmade, carved oak with maple frame, wood has heavy zinc plated or galvanized wire poked through holes and bent over on the back side, the thick loops on front providing a scrub surface. Large carved soap holder, American, 21½''H x 14''W, mid 19th C to about 1870s. **$120.00-$150.00**

Washboard, ''Little Monarch'', 16''L x 7''W. **$15.00-$20.00**

Washboard, mold blown glass with original label, actually toy candy container, ''Midget Washer'', 8½''L x 6''W, TOC. • Add $10.00-$20.00 for the little candies, if present. **$35.00-$50.00**

Washboard, ribbed glass with herringbone pattern, wooden frame, with zinc soap trough at top, name stamped in large letters, ''Soap Saver, No. 190, National Washboard Co.'', and ''National'' cast into intermittent grooves in the glass, Memphis, Saginaw, Chicago , c.1918? • The last patent number is 1283148, which is 1918 if it's a regular patent, or 1941 if a design patent. Although glass products proliferated (to save metal) during WWII, it seems more likely that this is 1918, as many glass boards were being made by early 1900s. National was in business since late 19th C., and started with all-wood boards. **$15.00-$22.00**

Washboard, thick heavy wood frame with corrugated tin wash surface, looks homemade, 24''L x 11''W, TOC. • About the only washboards collected by people outside the field are the home- or handmade ones, especially those carved of wood. They are often charged with a lot of feeling, angular, leaning to one side or the other, worn and smooth and given a lovely patina by use. Most of the homemade ones are about the size of manufactured ones; occasionally one is found that is either much larger (say 30-34''H), or very small, probably a toy. Values range from about $100.00 to $300.00 or so. **$40.00-$50.00**

Washboard, tin board in wooden frame, soap drains in front, ''The Silver King No. 824'', National, Memphis, TN, pat'd 1918. • There were many shiny tin boards named ''Silver'', viz. ''Flyer Silver'', ''Silver Cup'', ''Silver Prince'', ''Royal Silver'', ''Dixie Silver'', ''Excelsior Silver No. 60'', ''Rid-Jid Silver'', & ''Mission Silver''. **$15.00-$22.00**

Washboard, tin scrub board in wooden frame, with inset brushes,''Brush Board'', American, 20th C. **$65.00-$80.00**

Washboard, very little, with zinc corrugation, cotton tape strap on back to slip hand through, printed with directions: ''WARNING! WASH SILK HOSIERY ON THIS SPECIAL WASH-BOARD ONLY! Rub only toes, heels, and soles. Use Ivory Soap Flakes exclusively following special instructions ...'', Real Silk Hosiery Mills, Indianapolis, IN, early 20th C. **$25.00-$35.00**

Washboard, ''White Hen'', mfd by National Washboard,Memphis, TN, pat'd 1918. **$25.00-$35.00**

Washboard, wood, curves to fit inside wash tub, ''corrugations'' are actually rollers, rather like abacus boards, no mark, American, 24''H x 13''W, TOC. **$110.00-$135.00**

Washboard, wood frame, ''Shapleigh's'', poss. not made by the hardware firm, but perhaps the printed name commissioned, late 19th or early 20th C. **$10.00-$18.00**

Washboard, wood frame, slightly trapezoidal in shape, shiny corrugated tin scrub board, no mark, 20¼''H, TOC. **$50.00-$65.00**

Washboard, wood with brass scrub board, "King Cotton", prob. National Washboard, because Memphis is where Cotton was/is King, 20th C. **$25.00-$32.00**

Washboard, wooden frame, brass scrub board, "Brass Lion", mfd by White Wood Products Co., Bogalusa, LA, 24"H x 12½"W overall, 11" x 12" face, early 20th C. **$15.00-$20.00**

Washboard, wooden frame & brass scrubber, frame with stenciled scene of the Pilgrims, "National", 24"H x 12½"W. **$18.00-$25.00**

Washboard, wooden frame, cobalt blue graniteware scrubber, one maker of this type was Ingram-Richardson Mfg. Co., Beaver Falls, PA, late 19th C. **$45.00-$65.00**

Washboard, wooden frame, glass scrubber, "Atlantic No. 15", American. **$15.00-$25.00**

Washboard, wooden frame, stenciled with picture of the Capitol building, zinc scrubber, "Capitol", American, TOC. **$18.00-$25.00**

Washboard, wooden frame, tin scrubber & soap saver, "Junior", early 20th C. **$12.00-$18.00**

Washboard, wooden frame, turned wooden spools on rods laid in close rows form spinning scrub surface, instructions are interesting because they reflect the concern with standardized, interchangeable parts found more typically in cast iron tools and gadgets. "The only washboard made that can be repaired." There's also concern for health: "Place tub high enough for operator to stand erect. Backaches are unnecessary." "Mother Hubbard's Patent Roller Washboard", American, late 19th C. **$110.00-$135.00**

Washboard, wooden frame with brass scrubber, "Standard Family", 20th C. **$20.00-$25.00**

Washboard, wooden frame with stencil of tree stump, glass scrubber, 18" x 8¼"W. **$18.00-$25.00**

Washboard, wooden frame with tin scrubber & tin soap saver, with a funny name when you think it might have been used to wash those dainty step-ins! "National Knickerbocker", poss. made in NY, 20th C. **$25.00-$35.00**

Washboard, wooden frame & wood scrubber surface, large size, Columbus Washboard Co., OH, 19th or early 20th C. **$18.00-$30.00**

Washboard, wooden frame, zinc scrub board, boogaloo while you wash, with the "Silver Beam", mfd by White Wood Products Co., Bogalusa, LA, "laundry size" is 25"H x 13½"W overall, 13" x 12" face, early 20th C. • Size range: "Large Family" is 24"H x 12½"W overall; "Small Family" is 24"H x 11½"W, with scrub face 1" smaller both ways. White Wood also made "Dixie Dandy, Goldenbeam, Dixie Maid, Southern Belle", and offered to make private brands — actually the same boards, printed with private brand names (see the Shapleigh's above). **$15.00-$20.00**

Washboard, zinc face in wooden frame, "Zinc King — Lingerie, Do Not Rub Hard, The Board Will Do the Work", National Washboard Co., Memphis, TN, 18"H x 8¾"W, 20th C. **$12.00-$15.00**

**ZINC.**— When "zinc" is used to describe a washboard face, or the lining of a dry sink, or ice box, it almost always means galvanized iron or steel, which is iron or steel with a zinc coating. You will see "zinc" used as if it meant pure zinc sheet metal, but so far as I know the only zinc sheet metals are zinc alloys. Some washboards may be zinc alloys; others are galvanized sheet iron. "The pro-

cess of galvanizing," states the author of *The First Hundred Years of The New Jersey Zinc Company* (NY: 1948), "or the coating of iron or steel with zinc to prevent it from rusting, is older than the zinc industry in the United States. As far back as 1778, in France, zinc was applied as a coating to iron utensils. In 1805, in England, a patent was taken out which recommended the use of 'nails coated with zinc' and, in 1837, also in England, the first patent on hot dip galvanizing was issued. The galvanizing industry in the United States started in 1864. ... Zinc is the most effective coating for preventing ... [rust] because zinc protects iron electrolytically. As a result, corroding agents in air, water and the soil attack zinc in preference to iron. ... This action is ... important when ... a small area of the base metal is exposed....The base [is] protected from corrosion as long as sufficient zinc remains." • **"Hot dip galvanizing and electrogalvanizing** are very different methods of applying zinc coatings, each...suitable for certain applications." He adds that hot dip galvanizing is used "when the product is to be bent and formed after coating, ... wire is a familiar example of such an application." • I suspect that most "zinc" or "galvanized" products known to housewares collectors — washboards, pails, corrugated waste cans, and so-called "linings" of dry sinks or refrigerators — are formed before galvanizing, and therefore were electrogalvanized. Zinc alloy castings are found inside washing machines, refrigerators and some electrical appliances. • **Zinc-coated?...galvanized?**— Visual and tactile comparisons must be made with tinned, nickeled or chromed objects. Worn galvanized metal tends to look dark and somewhat mottled, and feel almost like soapstone — very smooth, yet with just a hint of drag or grab to the touch. Really corroded zinc gets a rather unpleasant white powdery film on the surface. Sort of like mealybugs on the aspidistra.

Washboard, zinc (galvanized steel) in tiny brick-wall like pattern, thick wooden dowel legs fit into tubular sides of board, "Sani-Steel Washboard", (Jamestown Metal Products?), (Jamestown, NY?), 20th C. **$45.00-$55.00**

Washing machine, copper & cast iron, wood, "Laundry Queen", American, TOC. **$100.00-$175.00**

Washing machine, copper with wooden & copper cone-shaped dasher or dolly , American, TOC. **$75.00-$85.00**

Washing machine, electric, enameled metal, with clamped-on wooden wringer, "Mighty-Magic", 20th C. • By now, it's possible that the **club for collectors of old major appliances** envisioned by collector Charles Diehl, Jr., may be a reality. Write him, with an SASE, at 13 S. Potomac St., Baltimore, MD 21224. **$125.00-$145.00**

Washing machine, electric, painted iron skeletal frame, 4 legs on double casters, big copper drum body, ovoid cylinder, top loading with 2 iron handles, wringer mounted above, with slanted water trough leading back into washer, motor mounted underneath body, shaft up left side leads to drive for the wringer, Coffield Motor Washer Co., Dayton, OH, c.1920. • A funny ad for a 1928 washing machine, the "ABC Spinner", touts it as "beautiful as a Baby Grand, compact as a Spinet Desk, safe as a Baby's Toy and fast as the Twentieth Century." **$85.00-$125.00**

Washing machine, electrified, copper tub, cast iron gears, mfd by Judd, (Wallingford, CT?), pat'd 1909. **$100.00-$120.00**

Washing machine, floor standing, non electric, large globular aluminum body in heavy wire frame, top loading, fill with up to 4 lbs clothes, water & soap, close tight-fitting lid, and crank. ''The secret of this ingenious washer lies in its ability to build up a high pressure within a compressed area which surges the soap or detergent through your clothes.'' ''Pressure-O-Matic'', mfr unknown, American, 18'' diameter, c.1964.     **$5.00-$8.00**

Washing machine, heavy metal tub type with wooden handle, ''Burlingame'', 34''H x 23''D, TOC.     **$75.00-$100.00**

Washing machine, large wooden body slightly upcurved at ends, in A frame attached to large rockers, flat sides to body, interestingly curved wood forming top and bottom, top loading, appears to have small wheels at one end, ''The Perfect Washing Machine'', mfd by L. O. Lein, Albion, WI, pat'd March 29, 1889. • **How many & how much?** — The fact that a collector can have too much of a good thing (ie. too many huge cumbersome washing machines) means that how much a dealer can get is limited. This is a great looking machine, but at about four feet long, how many could even the barn-owning collector keep?     **$300.00-$500.00**

Washing machine, pieced tin ''pig'' body, actually looks like slightly deflated football, set in high red painted wooden frame with bracket feet, neat fitted square corner tubular handles, brass hexagonal nut closes off end, the piece is a tinner's tour de force, American, prob. PA, 35''H, body 46''L, late 19th C. • I went to a show in Hamburg, PA, in a small rented car. Dealer Ursula Friedrich had this fabulous piece, for only $75.00. I hung around admiring it, patting it; we talked about using it as a clothes hamper in my one-room apartment, or as a cat hidey-hole. I went out to look at the car twice; it wouldn't fit, I thought. I drove away, got 10 miles and came back. Went in, looked, decided again there was no way. It was later bought, ran through 3 or 4 dealers or collectors, ended up at $700.00. But the right person, who was obviously me (!), never happened upon it again, and it was sold at auction in 1988 for about $150.00. QUICK! What is the moral of this tale? (Answer: there is none.) **$200.00-$250.00**

Washing machine, portable electric, aluminum body with iron handles, clip-on wringer, tub: 14½''D x 10½''H; wringer: 9½'' x 3⅞'', 20th C.     **$65.00-$80.00**

Washing machine, tin tub, wooden dasher & iron crank, American, 1883.     **$125.00-$145.00**

**Do You Feel Tired?** Read This for Cure: **''Hints to Housekeepers.**— Rise early in the morning, or you will not get a fair start with your business. Rise earlier on Sunday morning than any other day, that the children may be at Sunday-school in time; and domestics have time to so arrange their necessary business as to be able to attend Divine service. Do all the cooking for Sunday on Saturday, or, if it is absolutely necessary that some cooking be done, have it all completed at breakfast, and the fires extinguished for the day. Have the house cleaned and every thing put in order on Saturday. On Sunday only make the beds, and do such things as are absolutely necessary On Monday it will be necessary to spend more than the usual time in cleaning and setting things to rights. On Monday evening look over the soiled clothes. Mend, and put on buttons and strings. Select out the white articles, and put them to soak. Have a separate basket or bag for keeping towels, napkins, and table-cloths. Put them to soak in a vessel to themselves. The soaking will soften the grease, and make it easier to wash out. Have the water drawn in barrels, if possible. Exposure to the air will soften the water, and will give time for the sediments to settle at the bottom. This will be found an excellent plan, particularly where there is limestone in the water. Have the wood cut and every thing in readiness, so that on Tuesday the washing may be carried through without interruption. Wash colored clothes first, and take them in as soon as they dry. The practice of some washerwomen is to wet colored clothes too late to dry them, and then pack them away damp until morning. This is a severe and unnecessary trial to colors. Some colors fade from being long exposed to the sun. The ironing of course follows the washing, and should be done with as little delay as possible, and the cloths assorted and put away. Stockings and socks should be darned when brought in from the wash. System and order must be strictly observed in all household arrangements.'' *Mrs. A. P. Hill, Mrs. Hill's New Family Receipt Book*, NY: 1870. (P.S. Don't try to write a book, read a book, learn to play the piano, take evening classes, walk the dog, or anything else. P.P.S. Just how much ''grease'', for example, accumulates in just one week in all those towels and napkins?)

Washing machine, wooden box with iron crank, box on 2 legs, slide-out tub rack has 2 legs to rest on the ground, ''Columbia Hand Washer'', (possibly made by H. F. Brammer Mfg. Co., (Davenport, IA), 14''H x 12'' x 10'', pat'd Dec. 3, 1895.     **$200.00-$220.00**

Washing machine, wooden, rocking churn type action, on legs, ''Rock-A-Bye'', American, TOC.     **$125.00-$300.00**

Washing machine-powered churn, aluminum, Maytag, 15''H x 13½''D, early 20th C.     **$75.00-$90.00**

Washing or dry-cleaning machine, white enameled metal oblong box, with clamped on lid, set at crazy kitty-corner angle on cranked axis, in a simple metal 4 legged frame, to be loaded with ''things'' requiring dry cleaning, after which you ''pour on the non-explosive Duette fluid, turn the machine for two minutes, and out come [your] things beautifully fresh and clean. They require no pressing, either. The Duette also washes ... especially good for the baby's things.'' ''Duette'', Duette Mfg. Co., Chicago, IL, about 22''H x 25''L, c.1929. • Added value.— A gallon or half gallon can with original label if not with ''non-explosive'' contents, would add to the price. **$35.00-$50.00**

Washtub, 12 staves of wood, wood bound, American, 11 ½''D x 5''D, early 20th C.     **$45.00-$65.00**

Washtub, a really superior piece. A big galvanized tin tub, ribbed all the way around with pattern of ribbing meant to direct the water so it would flow back down to bottom, back splash scrub board for doing hand wash, soap dish on side, ''Rub-A-Tub Senior'', 17½'' diameter, provisional patent #25762, prob. TOC.     **$75.00-$125.00**

Washtub, old blue painted wood, staved, white painted inside, 3 metal bands, heavy wire side handles, American, late 19th C.     **$65.00-$85.00**

Wringer, all wood but for iron crank & 2 springs, ''Hall's Little Washer'', 28''L, marked ''pat'd Sept. 7, 1859'' (?). • No such Tuesday. And while there was a Sept. 7 Tuesday in 1852, 1858 and 1869, there's no ''Hall''.     **$45.00-$55.00**

Wringer, all wood, with crank handle, 6 rollers, including 3 corrugated. This would really do the job, American, dated 1871.     **$65.00-$85.00**

**III-1.**
**Etching of washerwomen,**
*by Kate Finley, mid-1930s. Plate size 6" x 9". Finley was, at the time, a student at the Art Students League in NYC, while working at the New York Public Library, Mott Haven branch. The woman on the right was modeled by Mary Mac Wilson Franklin, another librarian. The picture represents an early washday style; outdoors with a large cast iron cauldron over a fire, and a pair of tubs and a washboard. Clothesline hung with wash have long had great visual appeal for me, whereas one of my painting teachers once told me it was not a fit subject for art. Harrumph.*

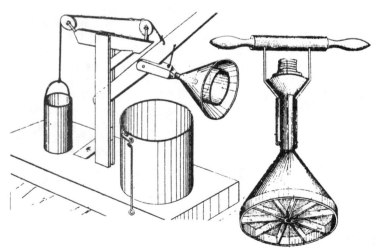

**III-2.**
**Clothes pounder & washing machine patents.**
*(L) Washing-machine pat'd 12/6/1881, by August E. Appelt, Round Mountain, TX. At left is a "weight bucket"; disappearing into upper corner is the long lever used to work the "pivoted pounder" inside the tub. (R) The clothes pounder was pat'd 11/22/1881, by Frank A. Huock, Holden, MO, assignor of one-half to William M. Coventry, same place. According to the claim, a valve & valve chamber are in the upper part, and the flared base has "a series of radial vanes," making it look like an apple segmenter in the drawing. Official Gazette.*

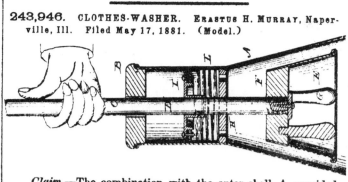

**243,946. CLOTHES-WASHER.** ERASTUS H. MURRAY, Naperville, Ill. Filed May 17, 1881. (Model.)

*Claim.*—The combination, with the outer shell, A, provided with a perforated diaphragm or partition, H, and centrally-perforated cap B, of the reciprocating rod D, inner shell, E, beaters F, piston I, and spiral spring L, all arranged to operate substantially in the manner specified.

**III-3.**

**Clothes-washer patent,**
along the lines of a washing dolly & dasher. Pat'd 7/5/1881 by Erastus H. Murray, Naperville, IL. The upper chamber had a valve, and was separated from the lower portion by a "perforated diaphragn or partition." Note the springs, and the individual pestles fitted to the bottom of the pounder. This would have been used in a washtub. <u>Official Gazette.</u>

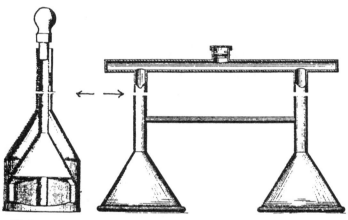

**III-4.**

**Clothes-pounder patents.**
(L) A truncated cone with a plunger within, pat'd 5/1/1877, by William T. Robertson, Asheville, NC. #190,372. On the same day, Robertson was given a patent for another pounder, that one with radial wires at the bottom, and another Robertson, Harvey O., also of Asheville, patented a washing machine with a segmented rocker. (R) A double stemmed pounder connected by a strut and by a horizontal handle, in the center of which is a valve. Pat'd 10/25/1881, by Margaret P. Colvin, Battle Creek, MI. NOTE: Both patent drawings, to save space, were published in the <u>Official Gazette</u> with the tubes shortened. The customary way to indicate this was to leave a space between the two parts — where I've drawn the arrows.

**III-5.**
**Clothes washer.**
The "Perfect," mfd. by Masters & Masters, Athens, OH. Pat'd 10/13/1885. Illustration from undated flyer.

**III-6.**
**Clothes washer or wash dolly.**
Tin with brass name plate, "The Perfect Clothes Washer," pat'd 10/13/1885. 15"H. Water escape valve is in the hooded little thing above the body, and kept water from splushing into user's face. Photographed in Bob "Primitive Man" Cahn's booth at the Stella Show, NYC, December 1985. Value range mine, not Cahn's.
**$60.00-$100.00**

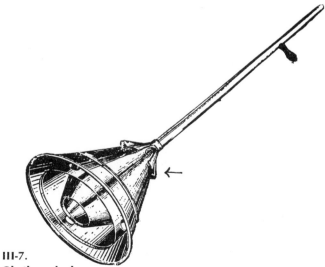

**III-7.**
**Clothes dasher.**
"Rapid Vacuum Washer," heavy tin, beechwood handle with cross handle bolted on. Handle 40"L. Note hooded covers near top of cone, which cover air holes meant to "introduce air into the water, forcing steam, water and air through the clothes thoroughly cleaning them." From catalog of Excelsior Stove & Mfg. Co,. Quincy, IL, c.1916.
**$35.00-$60.00**

**III-8.**

**"The Clothes-Horse,"**

*of the poem transcribed in one of the "clothes dryer" listings. More like a bogey-man. From House Furnishing Review (HFR) 7/1904.*

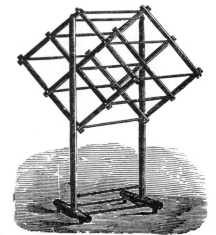

**III-10.**

**Clothes dryer.**

*(Creak, creeeeaaak, crRASH.) "To the many devices for holding clothes while drying, we add this one that gives a large amount of hanging room for the floor space it occupies." Hardwood foot pieces and upright standards, light pine kite-box frame. Folding. Published as a do-it-yourself project in American Agriculturist, 4/1881. See also III-21.* **$55.00-$70.00**

**III-9.**

**Clothes dryer patent,**

*called a "clothes-frame of the lazy-tongs type," by the inventor, A.B. Jaquith, Boston, MA. Pat'd 10/13/1874, #155,952. The feet are "set in rockers," and — like most clothes horses or dryers of the wooden dowel type — it folds up.*

**III-11.**

**Clothes-dryer patents.**

*(L) Pat'd 8/25/1874, by C.A. Meekins, Norton, MA. #154,409. Tripod with radial arms that can be folded against the centerpole. (R) Pat'd 7/5/1887, by Nathaniel J.M. Heck, Hazleton, PA, assignor of one-half to Charles Krapf, same place. #366,096. The application for this handsome folding horse, with stop blocks on the half-round center part of one of the crossed legs, was submitted with a model — meaning that it may still exist somewhere.*

**III-12.**

**Clothes-dryer or rack (right, two views).**

*Pat'd by William A. Bode, Orange, NJ, depicted in Scientific American, 12/14/1895. Combination of umbrella-tree form of dryer and horse-type.* **$125.00-$250.00**

# THINK

## About It

She can easily raise the clothes to the ceiling where the heat is greatest, and where they will be out of the way. She can easily move the "horse" hung with clothes about the room.

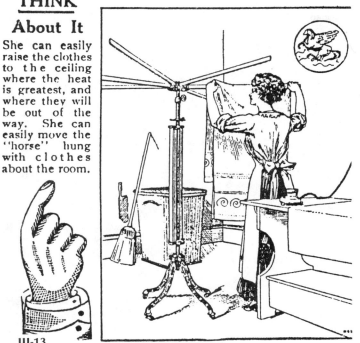

**III-13.**

**"Elevating Portable Clothes Horse,"**

obviously of the umbrella-tree type. But the trade name — "Pegasus", the flying horse — eloquently spoke of what it did. Hardwood racks, each 32"L with malleable cast iron base on casters, steel tubular adjustable-height upright; 5' to 9'H. Mesha Mfg. Co., Wyandotte, MI. *HFR* ad, 5/1911.

**$125.00-$200.00**

**III-14.**

**Clothes dryer,**

homemade from a "light buggy wheel that has served its time in its first field of usefulness, mounted on a low post." "An ingenious improvement on the ordinary styles of drying horses in use at the back door of every thrifty farm-house...At the door where we saw this one, were two of these wheel-driers — one for cloths (sic) and the other for dairy utensils. As the maid stands with her pile of pans or handful of cloths, she places them on the wheel one by one, revolving it to suit her motions." *American Agriculturist,* 1/1879.

**III-17.**

**Clothes dryer.**

"Superior," mfd. by C.A. Chapman, Geneva, NY, and meant for "drying clothes from a Window, Balcony or Veranda." The building shown at left is typical of late 19th C tenements, which originally didn't have quite the perjorative meaning the word has today. *HFR* ad, 2/1908.

**III-15.**

**Clothes dryer.**

"Hawse's Patent," strung with either 120 or 150 feet of clothes line, and sold without the post, which cost extra. "Portable, elevating, folding and revolving." *American Agriculturist* ad, 8/1861.

**Hill's Clothes Dryers**
For the yard or balcony
*They please everybody*
*A million people use them*
Ask your Hardware Dealer or send for Catalogue F. We pay the freight.
**Hill Dryer Co., Worcester, Mass.**

**III-16.**

**Clothes dryer.**

"Hill's," mfd. by Hill Dryer Co., Worcester, MA. This ad claims they're for the "yard or balcony"; a year later an ad said "lawn or balcony," adding that it did away with "unsightly Posts and dangerous pulley lines." *Ladies' Home Journal (LHJ)* ad, 12/1901. According to Orra L. Stone's History of Massachusetts Industries (Boston: S.J. Clarke, 1930), Vol. II, "Back in the early stages of man's development, the limited clothing of human kind was hung upon small trees to dry, and taking advantage of this precedent, the Hill dryer supplied an artificial tree...Constructed with 150 feet of line, the housewife is no longer forced to trudge up one line and down another, toting a heavy basket of clothes." Made well into 20th C. **$20.00-$35.00**

**III-18**

**"Clothes dryer for a Mantle Shelf."**

*Shown in American Agriculturist article by L.D. Snook, of the Yates Co., NYC. 11/1876. Self-explanatory, and meant to allow, by use of two brackets mounted underneath, the "mantle shelf original-ly built" over a fireplace, even when that fireplace has been permanently or temporarily closed up because of the owners now having a stove. (Actually, most people seem to have put their stoves partly into the old fireplace, venting the pipe up the chimney.)*

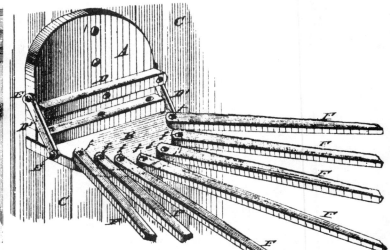

**III-20.**

**Clothes dryer patent.**

*Pat'd 5/5/1885, by George A. Spross and Rolla Meeker, Toledo, OH. #317,236. Stationary part was secured to the wall or other sturdy support, and the bracket held the arms in upright position when not in use. Official Gazette.*

**III-19.**

**Clothes dryer patent.**

*Pat'd 1/23/1877, by A.A. Peterson, Chicago, IL, assignor of one-half to N.J. Nelson, same place. #186,612. Could be raised and lowered by the cord through the pulley. The arms were removable but not folding. Official Gazette.*

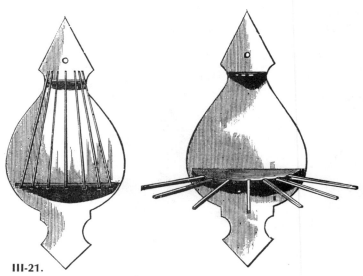

**III-21.**

**Clothes dryer or rack.**

*After an Oak Hill, NY reader of American Agriculturist saw his 5 April 1881 issue, he wrote the magazine about the drying rack he had devised which he thought was superior to the rack depicted in April (see III-10)—both because it could be folded against the wall when not in use, and because "when properly constructed, (it is) quite a pretty kitchen ornament." The reader said that the back plate "can be formed to suit the fancy, and made of whatever wood is preferred; if of pine or bass-wood, it may be stained."*

**III-22.**

**Clothes dryer patent,**

*for use around a stovepipe. Pat'd 8/23/1881, by Thomas Liddon, Yorkville, Ontario, Canada. #246,160.*

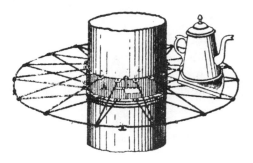

Conceals 32 feet of Drying Line

**III-23.**
**Clothes dryer.**
*"Dixiedri-Rack," mfd. by Sommers Brothers Appliance Co., Saginaw, MI. Steel with baked-on enamel in two tones. Served also as a stool, with nickel-plated seat. Rubber feet.* Good Housekeeping, *4/1931.* **$12.00-$30.00**

**III-25.**
**Clothes dryer & laundry stove,**
*"for residences, flats and institutions." At right is the stove, with large wash boiler on top. It heats the huge closet-like dryer, into which the racks slid. Only one fire required to do it all, including heating the flat irons! Mfd. by Chicago Clothes Dryer Works, Chicago. Made in any size, apparently of wood. Note the neat iron sinks at left on cast iron pedistal legs. Ad in* Century, *5/1893.*

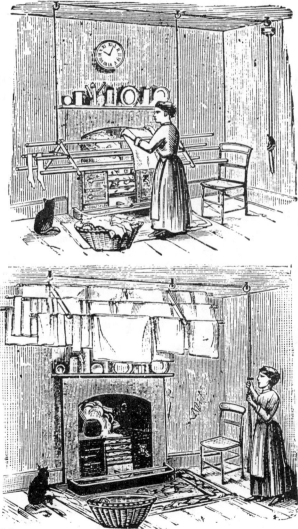

**III-26.**
**Clothes dryer,**
*similar to previous one, although the stove isn't mentioned in the ad. "No need of the sun...dries clothing in from 10 to 24 minutes, according to kind of heating system used." "The Canton," mfd. by Canton Clothes Dryer & Mfg. Co., Canton, OH. Ad in* Harper's, *10/1904.*

**III-24.**
**Clothes dryer & airer.**
*"The Barnes' Patent." Upper picture shows the dryer in down position, to receive clothes. Note pulley at ceiling at far right. "By merely turning one of the poles the Dryer will expand, and, if necessary, go flat, to meet the difficulty where kitchens are low." Came in five sizes — from 6'L to 10'L. The six foot one was "equal to 30' of clothes line." Pictures from 1895 catalog of Harrod's Stores, Ltd., Brompton, London.*

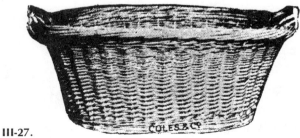

**III-27.**
**Clothes basket.**
*"French whole wicker," made in five sizes: 11"H x 24" x 19"; 11"H x 27" x 20"; 12"H x 19" x 22"; 13"H x 31" x 23"; 13"H x 34" x 25". In D.J. Barry hotel supply catalog, 1924, but of old type. Picture marked "Coles & Co." — mfr.? or photographer?* **$30.00-$75.00**

**III-28.**
**Clothesline reel.**
*Wire & turned wood, elegantly simple. Others may have a crank, or be entirely of wood. The ad for this one says "simply turn the crank and your line will wind up easily and neatly. No awkward overhand motion or blistering of fingers." But I don't know where the crank action is. From F. W. Seastrand mail order retail catalog, c.1910s.* **$15.00-$30.00**

**III-29.**
**Clothesline holder.**
*Galvanized malleable cast iron, to be mounted to wall or post. Probably should have been cast brass, like the ships' hardware it resembles.* Hearth & Home, *10/21/1871.* **$5.00-$15.00**

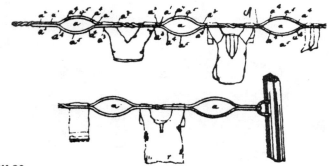

**III-30.**
**Clothesline patent.**
*Pat'd 9/20/1887, by Herbert E. Percival, Spokane, WA, assignor of one-third to Myron C. Percival, Lynn, MA. #370,348. Some people preferred rope, others liked galvanized iron for clotheslines; this one may have taken its inspiration from the gentler kinds of barbed wire, consisting of links of twisted wire, with "nipping-jaws" to hold the clothes. The apparent swarm of bees on the clothes at left are actually a plethora of small letters, used to identify parts in the original patent drawing.* Official Gazette.

**III-31.**
**Tradecard** showing fanciful line of clothes.
*One of a large series of highly imaginative and humorous chromolithographed cards issued by Kendall Mfg. Co., Providence, RI, for their washing powder — "Soapine." 1880s.* **$5.00-$10.00**

**III-32.**
**"Whipping it out"—**
*a newly-made candlewick spread or "quilt" after hanging on the clothesline. "They will wash. It is only necessary to fasten them strongly with clothes pins to a high line, and frequently whip them out while drying." From article in "The Household," in* American Agriculturist, *6/1867. How would you like to whip it out in heavy clothes like these dresses?*

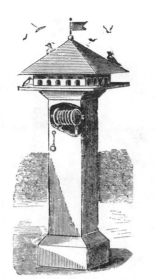

**III-33.**

**Combination clothesline reel & bird-house.**

*I happen to have a few lengths of line strung from angled posts on the back deck. The bird feeder is but a foot away, but a tree is even closer. So far, so good, but how'd you like to have a clothesline the only resting place for a hotel of martins? American Agriculturist, 7/1876.*

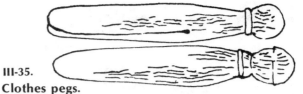

**III-35.**

**Clothes pegs.**

*Lathe- & hand-carved of whalebone, very simple style, early 19th C, about 5"L. Market value per peg:* **$90.00-$125.00**

**III-36.**

**Clothespin.**

*Handmade of wood, with iron nails to keep it from splitting. Early 19th C. Worth the most with some kind of carved decoration, even initials. Such clothespins or clothes pegs, are often said to be a type of love token.* **$30.00-$45.00**

**III-34.**

**Logo.**

*for Lewandos — a "cleansers, dyers and launderers" chain begun in Boston in 1829, and thereafter established all over Massachusetts, and in Connecticut, Maine, Rhode Island, Philadelphia, and NYC and Albany, NY. Ad in the back of Fannie Merritt Farmer's 1915 edition of A New Book of Cookery.*

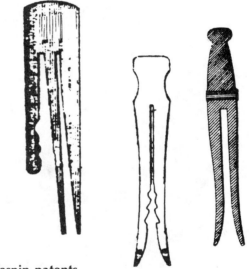

**III-37.**

**Clothespin patents.**

*All one piece of wood. (L) Pat'd 10/31/1876, by William H. Mayo, St. Joseph, MI. Has a "rigid corrugated thumb on one side, a rigid finger on the other side, and an intermediate flexible finger" in the middle. (M) Pat'd 11/28/1876, by Albert G. Cummings, Chicago, IL, assignor of one-half to Jonathon R. Talcott, North Williston, VT. Has "a series of beveled notches on the inside of the prongs, for different sizes clothes-lines." (R) Pat'd 12/23/1884, by Thomas W. Wheatley, Wilkes-Barre, PA. Has a "strengthening tube open at both ends, inserted through the body just above the prongs and transversely to the plane of the slot forming the prongs, (with) its ends flared" (like a rivet). Official Gazette.* **$5.00-$15.00**

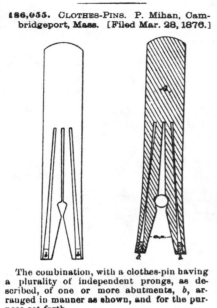

186,055. CLOTHES-PINS. P. Mihan, Cambridgeport, Mass. [Filed Mar. 28, 1876.]

The combination, with a clothes-pin having a plurality of independent prongs, as described, of one or more abutments, *b*, arranged in manner as shown, and for the purpose set forth.

**III-38.**
**Clothespin patent.**
*Pat'd 1/9/1877, by P. Mihan, Cambridgeport, MA. Has a "plurality of independent prongs." Official Gazette.* **$5.00-$15.00**

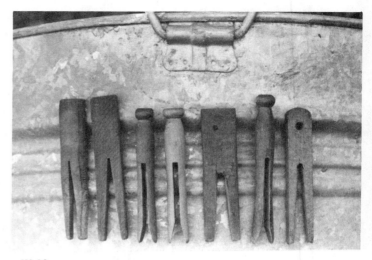

**III-39.**
**Clothespins,**
*homemade and commercial, from one piece of wood. Tallest is 4 3/4"H; shortest is 4"H. Late 19th C into early 20th. Photographed against galvanized washtub.* **$2.00-$6.00**

**III-40.**
**Clothsepin.**
*"Double-fast pin," pat'd by E. Seaver, 5/5/1868, and possibly marked with stamped patent date along one side. "It is doubly secure, — is made from selected throroughly seasoned kiln-dried rock maple, in two equal parts, which are securely fastened together, is entirely free from metallic springs, or machinery of any kind; and in every stage of its manufacture the utmost care is exercised to secure a finish superior to that of any other." Mfd. by American Clothes-Pin Co., Boston. Flyer from early 1870s.* **$5.00-$15.00**

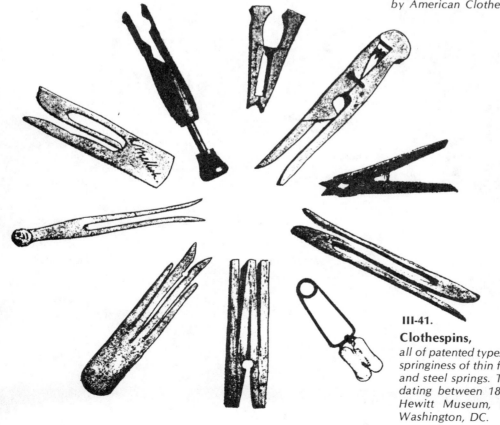

**III-41.**
**Clothespins,**
*all of patented types. Mostly of wood, several utilizing the natural springiness of thin fingers or prongs of hardwood; others use wire and steel springs. These are full-size patent application models dating between 1856 and 1875. Photograph courtesy Cooper Hewitt Museum, NYC, division of Smithsonian Institution, Washington, DC.* **$10.00-$30.00**

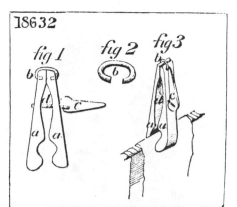

**III-42.**

**"Clothes clamp" patent.**

*Pat'd 11/17/1857, by L.H. Cushman, Monmouth, MO. #18632. Wood & wire.* Official Gazette.

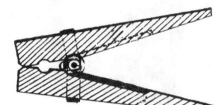

**III-43.**

**Clothespin patent.**

*Pat'd 2/13/1877, by William N. Lookwood, Campbille, CT. Wood, steel spring, and "flat metallic strips secured on the sides of the jaws."* Official Gazette.

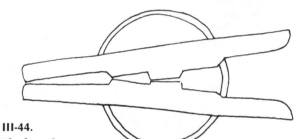

**III-44.**

**Clothespin.**

Two separate wooden jaws with a spring wire ring connecting them. 2 3/4"L, late 19th C or early 20th C. Courtesy Dorothy M. Zinniger, Dallas, TX. **$6.00-$10.00**

**III-45.**

**Clothespin.**

*"U.S. Spring," mfd. by United States Clothes Pin Co., Montpelier, VT. "Clasps the clothes on the line and holds them until unlocked." Pat'd 6/28/1887, and made until at least 1909. Ad in HFR, 5/1906. A similar ad in Iron Age, 1/7/1909. Date may be stamped along edge.* **$2.00-$5.00**

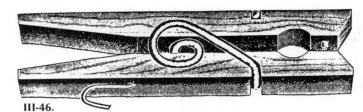

**III-46.**

**Veneer manufacturers' clip, like a clothespin.**

*"Holdfast," mfd. by Demeritt & Palmer Packing, Co., Waterburg, VT. "This is especially adapted for holding thin pieces of board in place while being glued together. The spring is exceptionally strong, and as shown in the illustration, has a steel brad between the ends of the jaw, which gives it great holding power." Note also the hanging hook. This company also made clothespins, letter clips, photographer's clips and others, specially designed and made to order. Ad from* Iron Age, *1/7/1909.*

**III-47.**

**Clothespin.**

*"U.S. Spring Clothes Pin," mfd. by U.S. Clothes Pin Co., Montpelier, VT. Two pieces kiln-dried hardwood, galvanized spring steel wire. Pat'd 6/2/1887. Ad in* HFR, *4/1906.* **$2.00-$4.00**

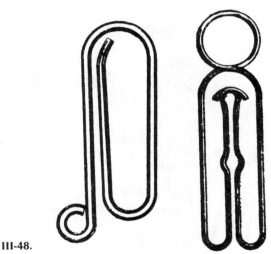

**III-48.**

**Clothespin patents.**

*(L) Pat'd 1/16/1877, by William S. Davis, Pittsfield, MA, assignor of one-half to Warren L. Parks, same place. (R) Pat'd 3/13/1877, by D.B. Sanderson & D.H. Linscott, Lewiston, ME.* **$4.00-$7.00**

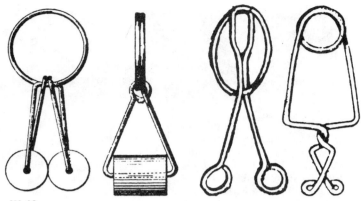

**III-49.**

**Clothespin patents.**

*(L-1 & 2) Pat'd 2/6/1877, by S.B. Hunt, NYC, assignor to A.W. Bill-ings, Brooklyn, NY. Bent wire with wooden rollers that form the clamp. Great idea! (M) Pat'd 10/28/1890, by George W. McCord, Baker City, OR. (R) Pat'd 8/1/1876, by George A. Lambert, Worcester, MA. Another item patented the same day by Lambert was a sort of jailor's keyring with a ring to fit around arm at the crook of the elbow, suspended from which was a partially-closed ring over which one slipped the small loop of his wire clothespins.*
**$5.00-$15.00**

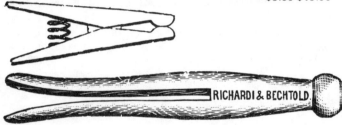

**III-50.**

**Clothespins.**

*Two types offered by D.J. Barry in their hotel supply catalog, 1924. A choice of the "American" or "U.S." spring pin, above, this one must be the American; or the non-mechanical peg type, the "Daisy," mfd. by Richardi & Bechtold. The pegs were offered in three styles, all "first quality." The "Boss" or the "Eclipse" were 5"L, and the "Daisy" which was 4 1/2"L.*
**$2.00-$4.00**

**III-51.**

**Clothespins.**

*"Busy-day" may be trade name, or it may be "2-4-1". Red plastic, two-ended. Ratchford Corp., Dayton, OH. 1948 ad in Better Homes & Gardens.*
**$2.00-$3.00**

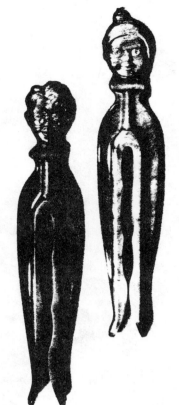

**III-52.**

**Clothespins.**

*Molded acrylic plastic in various colors — some opaque (medium sky blue, cherry red, avocado green, purplish gray or mauve), and at least one semi-transparent (pink). "Rogers' Clean-Grip," 3 3/4" to 3 7/8"L, c.1940s-50s. "Patent Pending."* **$3.00-$5.00**

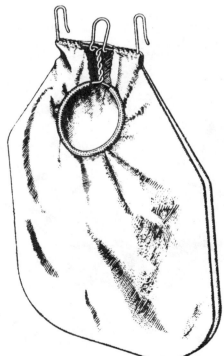

**III-53.**

**Clothespin bag patent.**

*Pat'd 8/9/1887, by William Jamieson, Saratoga Springs, NY. #368-091. Clipped over clothesline, apparently had rigid outer frame. Hand-hole looks small, but maybe the bag was huge. Official Gazette.*

**III-54.**

**Clothespin bags.**

*Composite picture made up from two ads. (L) "Ever-Handy Clothes-Pin Pocket," mfd. by Hook Mfg. Co., Baltimore, MD. HFR ad, 6/1906. (R) Socks, towel and "Glenny's" bag — from Glenny's "Monday and Tuesday line, which is a very popular line with the house furnishing trade. Made in serveral sizes and grades to sell from 10– to 25–. W.H. Glenny & Co., Rochester, NY. HFR 10/1904.* **$4.00-$7.00**

**III-56.**

**Fluting machine.**

*Elegant classic "Geneva Hand Fluter," mfd. by W.H. Howell, Geneva, IL. Cast iron, about 6"L. Marked on underside "Heat this." Pat'd 8/21/1866, but made for about six decades. This is a fairly early version, with no brass. Mfd. by same company that made a variety of sadirons, as well as WAPAD cast iron cookwares. Photograph courtesy Waltraud Boltz Auction House, Brandenburger Strasse 36, Bayreuth 8580, Germany, which conducts outstanding auctions in this field, as well as many others, and publishes really grand catalogs, in German. From the Loecherbach Collection, auctioned May 1987.* **$90.00-$150.00**

**III-55.**

**Clothespin bags.**

*"Vandy-Handy," made of "water-proof Khaki cloth" or "very serviceable white fabric." Two types, used with two kinds of clotheslines — a pulley line from a window, and a post-strung line. Vandy-Handy Co., no place given. HFR, 8/1910.* **$4.00-$7.00**

# DIAGRAM OF ROLLS
## For Fluting Machines.

The following diagram shows the size, as to coarseness and fineness, of the rolls used in the different machines

### FLUTING ROLLS.

No. 10

No. 12

No. 15

No. 18

No. 22

No. 26

No. 30

No. 40

No. 50

### CRIMPING ROLLS.

No. 126

No. 130

No. 140

No. 150

No. 160

# Fluting Machines.

**"CROWN."**
4½, 6, 8-inch Rolls.
10 to 160 Flutes.

**"KNOX."**
4½, 6, 8-inch Rolls.
10 to 160 Flutes.

**"AMERICAN."**
5, 6, 7-inch Rolls.
12 to 160 Flutes.

**"EAGLE."**
3½, 5½-inch Rolls.
15 to 22 Flutes.

The Rolls are of Brass, accurately cut and highly polished in various sizes and styles shown on opposite page. The machines are handsomely finished and are furnished with four heating irons and tongs.

Descriptive circulars of Fluting Machines, also Hand Fluters and Plaiting Machines, mailed free on application to

**NORTH BROS. MFG. CO., Philadelphia, Pa.**

III-57.
**Fluting machines & corrugations chart.**
The machines at right are all from North Brothers Mfg. Co., Philadelphia, PA. At left is diagram of 14 different patterns of cast brass rolls to be selected for use in the cranked machines, to provide flutes or crimps. All from North Brothers' cookbook-catalog, "Dainty Dishes For All the Year Round," by Mrs. S.T. Rorer, 1912. The machines: **$115.00-$175.00**

# EXCELSIOR FLUTING MACHINE.
## CHEAPEST AND BEST IN THE MARKET.
### WARRANTED
TO GIVE
### PERFECT SATISFACTION
*PRICES.*
No. 1, 5 in. roller, **$6.00**
No. 2, 7 in. roller, **8.00**
Sent by Express, *C.O.D.*
Illustrated Circular sent free on application.
Agents wanted in every part of the United States.
**GEO. HOVEY & SON,**
*309 East 22d Street, New York.*

III-58.
**Fluting machine.**
"Excelsior," mfd. by George Hovey & Son, NYC. Their address at the time of the 1870 Peterson's Magazine ad was 309 E. 22nd Street; it gives me a special frisson to read that because I lived only one block from there for many years in the 1970s, and must have passed to old Hovey building many times. **$115.00-$150.00,**

**III-59.**

**Fluting machine.**

"Champion Fluter," advertised as "largest in the market." Cast iron, fully nickel plated, walnut handle, malleable cast iron shank on roller, complete with two long cylindrical heaters inserted within roller. 8"L x 4"W plate; roller is 1 7/8" diameter x 4"W. Available through 1882 catalog of, and possibly manufactured by, Heinz & Munschauer, Buffalo, NY. Probably patented before that, and made for decades. **$90.00-$125.00**

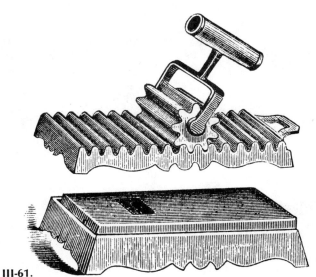

**III-61.**

**Fluting machine.**

"Standard," mfd or sold by Heinz & Munschaeur, Buffalo, NY. Nickeled cast iron plate & roller, base or stand is japanned. Base 6 1/2"L x 3 1/4"W; roller 1 1/2" diameter x 3 1/4"W, came with two flat oblong heaters. Original price only $7.00 a dozen! **$70.00-$115.00**

**III-60.**

**Fluting machine.**

"Empire Fluter," mfd. & sold by Heinz & Munschauer, Buffalo, NY. Nickeled cast iron plate & roller, wooden T. handle. Hinged base plate, two heating plates. Base 6 3/4"L x 3 1/4"W; roll 2 1/2" diameter x 3 1/4"W. **$90.00-$125.00**

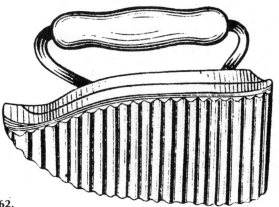

**III-62.**

**"Combined Corrugated Glossing & Molding Iron,"**

that at first glance might appear to be part of some kind of fluting machine. Pat'd 12/3/1878, by Wallace W. Nixon, #210,551. Used to polish and stiffen a starched item of linen, calico or muslin, and give it a gloss. "It is requisite that only a small surface of the glossing iron should come in contact with the fabric, and hence, in most laundries the favorite is the 'heel-iron,' which is shaped somewhat like an oridinary sad-iron with its heel rounded. To produce the gloss, after the articles are ironed and slightly moistened, the point of the 'heel-iron' is elevated, and the article rubbed with the oval part of the iron." This iron has what its inventor described as "alternate oval heels or ridges, and oval grooves" so that "each heel produces its own gloss, independently of the other." To use: "After the shirt is stretched over the board it is an improvement to rub the bosom, previous to using the iron, with a clean white towel dampened with soft water." Wallace W. Nixon, The Chemical Laundry Guide, Lynchburg, VA: J.P. Bell & Co., 1879. **$35.00-$60.00**

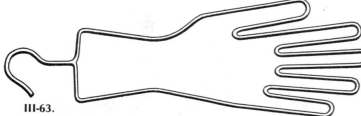

**III-63.**
**Glove drying frame.**
*Wire finished in blue pyroxolin enamel. "Used to dry rubber kitchen gloves, also drying fabric gloves." The Washburn Co., Worcester, MA & Rockford, IL. 1927 "Sno-Cap" Androck catalog.*
**$4.00-$8.00**

**III-64.**
**Goffering iron,**
*or gauffering iron, on stand. Cast & wrought iron. Supposedly NY provenance, c.1820. Best details are the twist-for-rigidity in the heater's handle, and the faceted finial to the "S" curve. Nice large penny feet. 9"H. Photograph courtesy Litchfield Auction Gallery, Litchfield, CT. Ex-Harol Corbin Collection, auctioned 1/1/1989.*
**$650.00**

**III-65.**
**Heating slug,**
*called a* **Gluhbolzen** *for a* **Plattglocken** *in German (that is, a heat-bolt for a pressing iron of a particular type. (See description in price listing for Iron, box.) One at (L) is quite similar to one described that I bought, and has the Tree of Life, or* **Lebensbaum,** *motif. About 6 1/4"L. (R) Also cast iron, monogrammed J R, decorative motif is a vine or tendril,* **Rankenmotif.** *About 5 3/4"L. Both are 19th German. Similarly marked irons are found with two holes, where a 2-standard handle was fitted in, or with the handle in place. These are highly polished on the bottom. Photograph courtesy Waltraud Boltz Auction House, Bayreuth, Germany. From the Loercherbach Collection, auctioned May 1987.*
**$50.00-$80.00**

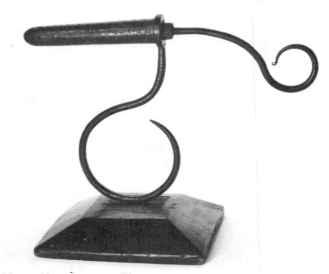

**III-66.**
**Goffering iron,**
*on stand. Forged iron. Very superior to one sold the year before in every regard, but maybe it's too simple to draw the attention. About 10"H. Photograph courtesy Litchfield Auction Gallery, Litchfield, CT. Ex-Harold Corbin Collection, auctioned 1/1/1990. Price realized:*
**$475.00**

**III-67.**
**Goffering irons,**
*or* **tolleisen** *in German (literally, crimper), without heaters. Cast iron, highly polished, one with round base. English, mfd. about 1822 by William Bullock & Co., West Bromwich. A little over 7½"H. (R) Also English, about 7¼"H. Photography courtesy Waltraud Boltz Auction House, Bayreuth, Germany. From the Loecherback Collection, auctioned May 1987.* **$120.00-$175.00**

**III-68.     Chinese charcoal iron.**
*Cast iron pan-like utensil with no lid, and with carved rosewood handle in form of Chinese Goddess of Mercy, Kuan Yin. The wood has been painted to resemble ivory. Glowing charcoal was put in the pan, which — thus heated — was smoothed over the fabric. 1974 photograph courtesy of Ayer Public Relations, NYC; the iron itself was (perhaps still is) from the A.H. Glissman Collection — a renowned collection by the author of the best book extant on irons. (See Bibliography) I am not going to attempt to evaluate irons pictured from this collection which are not found in other books.*

**III-69. Box iron & heating slug.**
*This cast iron box with wooden handle is shown with the lid raised and turned to reveal interior. In foreground is cast iron slug, shown with an   Enterprise stove lid (or heating slug) lifter. The iron was made by Nelson Streeter Co., Groton, NY., about 1876. It probably came originally with its own lifter. 1974 photograph courtesy of Ayer Public Relations, NYC; the iron itself was (perhaps still is) from the A.H. Glissman Collection.*     **$50.00-$70.00**

**III-70.**
**Box iron.**
*French, cast brass, late 19th C. Note the "garage door" is down in the back, holding the heated slug in. 1974 photograph courtesy of Ayer Public Relations, NYC; the iron itself was (perhaps still is) from the A.H. Glissman Collection.*     **$60.00-$90.00**

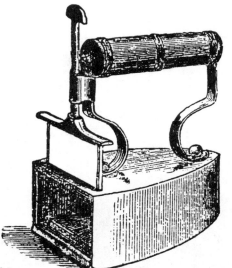

**III-71.**
**Box iron.**

*English, cast iron, late 19th C, but in form common through last half 19th C into the 20th. Shown with door up, revealing iron slug, which was heated before inserting. Irons came with two of them usually, so one could always be on the stove. This one came in three sizes: 4 1/2"L; 5"L; and 5 1/2"L. From ironmongery department, Harrod's Stores Ltd., Brompton, England, 1895 catalog.* **$35.00-$55.00**

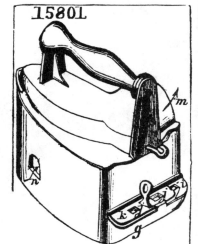

**III-73.**
**Self-heating smoothing iron patent.**

*Irons that were heated by something within, even if that had to be tended or heated, were called self heaters. Box irons with slugs, charcoal irons, all the way to a Coleman gas iron are all considered self-heating irons. This charcoal iron pat'd 9/30/1856, by William D. Cummings, Washington, KY. "The nature of this invention consists in providing the rear end with a trough (g) which serves to receive the ashes.* Official Gazette.

THE SELF-HEATING **FLAT IRON** solves the ironing problem. No stove necessary. No heating of room in hot days. **Absolutely safe.** No tubing or connections with gas or electric fixtures. Always hot. Handle cool. **5 hours' ironing costs but 1c.** The only satisfactory self-heating iron. Booklet, testimonials and prices free on request. **The Self-Heating Flat Iron Co., 24 E. Randolph St., Chicago**

**III-74.**
**Self-heating flat iron,**

*of the alcohol-burning type. The Self-Heating Flat Iron Co., Chicago, IL.* Ladies' Home Journal *ad, 6/1902.* **$30.00-$45.00**

**III-72.**
**Charcoal iron.**

*Mexican, cast iron with "black granite coating." Cast dove on the latch, looking out over the expanse of wrinkled cloth ahead. Top is hinged at back. Half-moon openings are vents.* **$40.00-$80.00**

**III-75.**
**Self-heating charcoal irons.**

*Both shown with curved heat shield for hand. Big one with angled front is a tailor's iron of same type. From Russell & Erwin Mfg. Co., New Britain, CT, 1865 catalog.* **$50.00-$90.00**

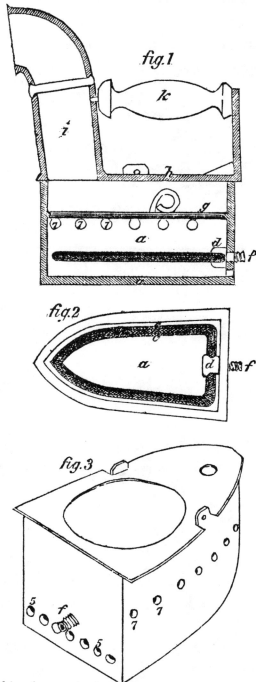

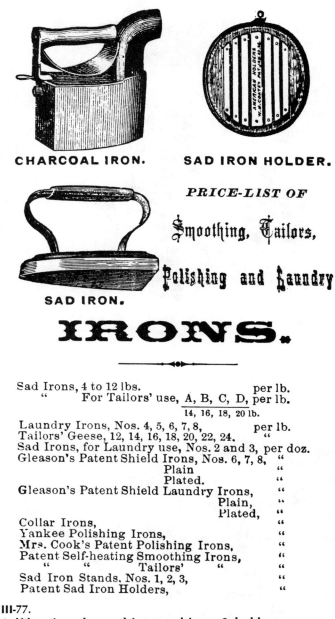

**CHARCOAL IRON.**  **SAD IRON HOLDER.**

*PRICE-LIST OF*

𝔖𝔪𝔬𝔬𝔱𝔥𝔦𝔫𝔤, 𝔗𝔞𝔦𝔩𝔬𝔯𝔰,

𝔓𝔬𝔩𝔦𝔰𝔥𝔦𝔫𝔤 𝔞𝔫𝔡 𝔏𝔞𝔲𝔫𝔡𝔯𝔶

**SAD IRON.**

# IRONS.

Sad Irons, 4 to 12 lbs.      per lb.
    "    For Tailors' use, <u>A, B, C, D,</u> per lb.
                            14, 16, 18, 20 lb.
Laundry Irons, Nos. 4, 5, 6, 7, 8,      per lb.
Tailors' Geese, 12, 14, 16, 18, 20, 22, 24.    "
Sad Irons, for Laundry use, Nos. 2 and 3, per doz.
Gleason's Patent Shield Irons, Nos. 6, 7, 8,    "
                        Plain            "
                        Plated.         "
Gleason's Patent Shield Laundry Irons,    "
                        Plain,         "
                        Plated,        "
Collar Irons,                           "
Yankee Polishing Irons,              "
Mrs. Cook's Patent Polishing Irons,     "
Patent Self-heating Smoothing Irons,    "
    "               "     Tailors'       "
Sad Iron Stands. Nos. 1, 2, 3,          "
Patent Sad Iron Holders,            "

**III-77.**

**Self-heating charcoal iron, sad iron, & holder.**

*Page from catalog of Stuart, Peterson & Co., 1875. Philadelphia, PA. They made stoves, various kinds of holloware for cooking, as well as irons.*

**III-76.**

**Smoothing iron patent.**

*Pat'd 10/3/1857, by J. Goodlin, Jr., Cincinnati, OH, #18543. Charcoal iron with venting chimney sticking up like periscope.* <u>Official Gazette</u>.

**III-78.**

**Charcoal iron.**

*"Ne Plus Ultra", Twin chimneys with cast handle & heat shield. 7 1/4"L. Pat'd 1902 by George Finn, Newark, NJ. Photograph courtesy Waltraud Boltz Auction House, Bayreuth, Germany. From the Loecherbach Collection, auctioned May 1987.*

### III-79.
**Self-heating spirit iron.**
*"Brilliant," alcohol-burning, nickeled iron with wooden handle. Pat'd by Joseph Feldmeyer, Wurzburg, Germany, and manufactured all over Europe and in the U.S. Iron dates probably to late 19th C. 1974 photograph courtesy of Ayer Public Relations, NYC; the iron itself was (perhaps still is) from the A.H. Glissman Collection.* **$50.00-$80.00**

## Purchasing a "UNEEDIT" Family Gas Iron Means

A SATISFIED operator
A PLEASED customer
Distinctive work
A short day
SMALL GAS BILL

Exclusive features proved by it being adopted by the largest gas companies in the United States and abroad and passed by laboratories of Gas Companies, and approved by Good Housekeeping Institute.

Write for prices and sample.

**Rosenbaum Mfg. Company,** 33-37 Bleecker Street New York City

### III-81.
**Gas iron,**
*modeled very like a charcoal iron with the vents and heat shield. Note the long tube at the rear, to which the rubber gas tube was fitted. "Uneedit," mfd. by Rosenbaum Mfg. Co., NYC. HFR, 8/1915.* **$50.00-$70.00**

### III-80.
**Self-heating spirit iron,**
*mfd. by The Coleman Co., Philadelphia. "Beveled edge for easier ironing of pleats, around buttons. Iron in comfort anywhere — indoors or outdoors." This indoor-outdoor concept appears also in connection with some washing machines, this chapter, and is a captivating one. I think it would be a pleasant chore, if it could be done outside, under a tree, in the cool of a summer morning. Ad from* Farm Journal*, 4/1947.* **$50.00-$70.00**

### III-82.
**"Enjoyable Minutes with an Electric Iron."**
*Illustration of behatted smiling woman in January 1912, ironing in a tiled & painted room on a table covered with cushioning cloth. Note small stand; also the small cord, which disappears below the table instead of up into ceiling fixture, as was more common at the time. Illustration from Maud Lancaster's* Electric Cooking, Heating & Cleaning*, 1914.*

MRS. POTTS IRON

COMMON IRON

POLISHER

FLOUNCE IRON

GAS IRON

ELECTRIC IRON

**III-83.**
**Various kinds of irons.**
*This illustration is from* Approved Methods for Home Laundering, *by Mary Beals Vail. Cincinnati: Procter & Gamble, 1906. Relative prices were given to help the consumer decide on an iron: 2" sad irons, 8 lbs., 40¢ each; 2 sad irons, 6 lbs., 30¢ each, 1 sad iron, 4 lbs., 20¢; 1 flounce iron, narrow and long, 25¢; 1 or 2 polishers, 45¢ each; set of 3 irons, with detachable handle, 98¢; gas or alcohol iron, 95¢; electric iron, $4.50 to $6.00*

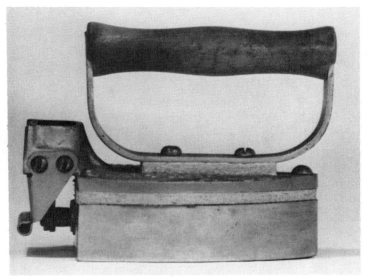

**III-84.**
**First General Electric iron,**
*dates to 1904. Nickeled cast iron, wood. Photograph courtesy General Electric.* **$35.00-$60.00**

**III-85.**
**Electric iron.**
*"Pelouze", with high & low heat control. Note early streamlining to handle. Pelouze Mfg. Co., Chicago. Ad in Hardware News, published by Buhl Sons Co., Detroit, 4/1912. Value range dependent on approach — aesthetics or historical.* **$40.00-$70.00**

**III-86.**
**Electric traveling iron.**
*"Prom", mfd. by British Prometheus Co. It can "be used, by altering the position of the connecting block at the back, with any electric supply at voltages between 100 and 250." Sold with flexible cord and "adapter for connecting to any lamp-socket." Lancaster,* Electric Heating, *1914.* **$35.00-$60.00**

**III-87.**
**Electric iron.**
*Westinghouse. Note stand with what might be thought of as upsidedown position of the rounded 'feet'. Lancaster,* Electric Home, *1914.* **$35.00-$50.00**

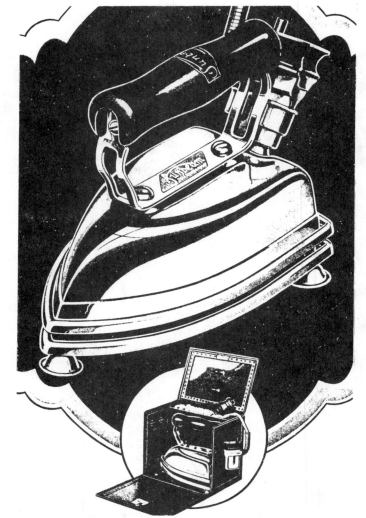

**III-89. Electric iron,**
*on stand. "Sunbeam," 1928. Shown in this catalog picture in its original fitted box, which should add to value. Mfd. by Chicago Flexible Shaft Co., Chicago.* **$20.00-$35.00**

**III-88.**
**Electric steam iron.**
*General Electric, 1924. Photograph courtesy of GE.* **$20.00-$30.00**

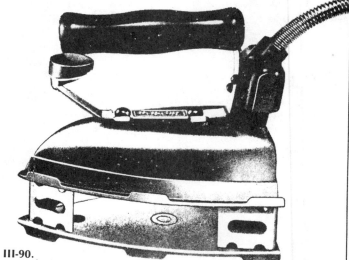

**III-90.**
**"Special Model" electric iron,**
*"made available to care for the needs encountered in traveling and to afford the advantages of Hotpoint ironing to homes where 320 volt home lighting plants provide the current. Large heat storage capacity assures quick, satisfactory ironing." Nickeled iron, black wood "through-bolt" handle with thumb rest. Permanently attached cord; pressed steel stand. 575 watts. Mfd. General Electric. 1935-36 catalog.* **$15.00-$30.00**

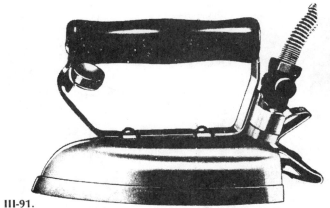

**III-91.**
**"Special Model" electric iron,**
with adjustable voltage. Plug connection adjustable for voltage ranges of 100 to 125, or 200 to 250. Mica core unit. Angled thumb rest. Note heel stand. Detachable "long-life cord set with miniature appliance plug and G-E moulded rubber attachment plug." 330 watts. "Hotpoint," mfd. by General Electric. 1935-36 catalog.
**$15.00-$30.00**

**III-93.**
**Electric iron.**
"Moderne", catalog No. 119F83 or 119F84, weighing 3 1/2 lbs. and 6 lbs. respectively. Alternating current, 115-125 volts, 1000 watts. General Electric catalog, 1935-36. Very "aero-dynamic" streamlined styling adds a little value. **$15.00-$28.00**

**III-92.**
**Electric irons.**
Both mfd. by Knapp-Monarch. Top: A non-automatic iron — that is, without thermostat, so it continues to get hotter and hotter until unplugged. Below: an automatic iron, with thermostat. The regulator is set for the "degree of heat you wish. It may be marked with the words, artificial silk, silk, wool, cotton, or linen, which is the order of ironing different materials from a heat standpoint." Or, it may be "marked high, medium and low, or simply by lines, letters or numbers." Pictures from E.S. Lincoln's The Electric Home, NY: Electric Home Pub'g Co., 1936. **$15.00-$22.00**

**III-94.**
**Electric irons.**
"Tru-Heat," mfd. by General Mills Home Appliances, Minneapolis, MN. (T) "This truly modern beauty does a better job faster with lots less pushing, twisting, lifting." Touted are "larger soleplate," tapered heel; and the projections on the side which enable the iron to be rested "safely on its side." 3-3/4 lbs. (B) Same iron with the "new Steam Ironing Attachment which instantly changes (it) into a steam iron...This attachment produces steam in 2 to 4 minutes for professional steam ironing." Betty Crocker was used in advertising this iron, albeit with a portrait less than a half inch high. Ad in Better Homes & Gardens, 12/1948. With the attachment: **$25.00-$45.00**

**III-95.**
**Ironing board.**

Reader of <u>American Agriculturist</u>, Maggie Martin, Sussex County, DE, wrote editor in July 1871 issue about her method: "Take a board five or six feet long, one foot wide, and an inch and a half thick. The board is covered with two or three folds of woolen material, and over this is put a piece of linen or flannel, which is lightly tacked on, in order that it may be taken off and washed when necessary. The ends of the board rest upon two chairs, or they may be supported at the proper height in any other convenient manner." Martin liked this board because on it a skirt could be ironed without rumpling — a problem we still have when the skirt gets caught up on the legs.

**III-96.**
**Ironing table patent.**

Pat'd 3/6/1877, by R.S. McEntire, Burlington, IA. Combined table with lift-up lid, and a sliding board. The term "ironing table" was used much more frequently than "ironing board" in the 19th C. <u>Official Gazette</u>.

**III-98.**
**Ironing table patents.**

(T) "Ironing board and table," pat'd 4/28/1885, by Ann A. Wysong, Baltimore, MD. A combination of a chest, an ironing board, and a supporting door (the little one seen front left near top. It looks like a child's delight. (B) Pat'd 10/21/1890, by Andrew A. Wagon, Whitewright, TX. The treadle appears to assist in raising or lowering the angle of the board. <u>Official Gazette</u>.

**III-97**
**Ironing table patent.**

Pat'd 10/20/1885, by Moses J. Jerome, Newburg, NY. A model of this was submitted with the patent application. The vertical piece at far left represents a permanent or fixed support — probably a wall, or the side of a cupboard. The table is the folding 3-board assemblage, including a "locking piece", and a "staple" that holds it to the wall. <u>Official Gazette</u>.

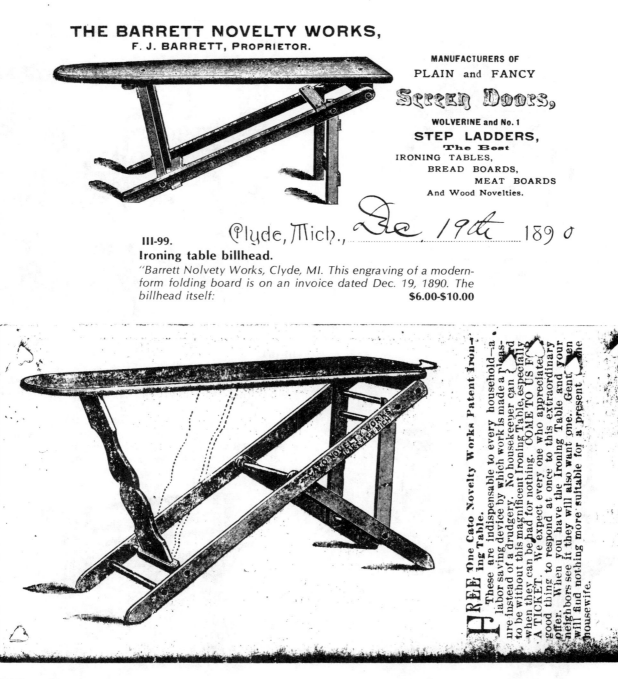

## THE BARRETT NOVELTY WORKS,
### F. J. BARRETT, PROPRIETOR.

MANUFACTURERS OF
PLAIN and FANCY

Screen Doors,

WOLVERINE and No. 1
**STEP LADDERS,**
The Best
IRONING TABLES,
BREAD BOARDS,
MEAT BOARDS
And Wood Novelties.

Clyde, Mich., Dec 19th 189 0

**III-99.**

**Ironing table billhead.**

*"Barrett Nolvety Works, Clyde, MI. This engraving of a modern-form folding board is on an invoice dated Dec. 19, 1890. The billhead itself:* **$6.00-$10.00**

**III-100.**

**Ironing table tradecard.**

*A "Cato Novelty Works Patent Ironing Table" is depicted with a description on one side of a 3-1/8" x 5-5/8" tan card. The heart-shaped holes are punched holes, which show (on the reverse) that the holder of the card had bought of Wheeler Brothers General Merchandise...and Dry Goods Store, MI, one 10¢ purchase and five 50¢ purchases—working toward a total of $25.00 in order to qualify for a free Cato ironing board. Date not given, c.1890-1910. Card:* **$9.00-$15.00**

**III-101.**

**"Ironing stand,"**

*The "Diana," mfd. by Aten Lumber & Mfg. Co., Monroeville, OH. "Top can be raised without the legs collapsing." Ad in HFR, 1/1909.* **$25.00-$40.00**

**III-102.**
**Ironing table.**
"Rid-Jid" open end folding ironing table. Cannot wiggle, wabble, jiggle, slip or slide. Look at the picture. It is reproduced from an actual photograph. Did you ever see a folding ironing table that would support a 153-lb. woman on its open end without tilting it? Never!" 57"L x 15"W; "only 2 1/2" thick when folded." In c.1916 Excelsior Stove & Mfg. Co., Quincy, IL, catalog. This kind of advertising reached a sublime absurdity when an ironing board ad showed a very fat man standing up there on the board. **$18.00-$30.00**

**III-104.**
**"The mangled Tybalt!"**
"Act 5, Sc. 3" is printed directly below the picture of a humorous play on words, showing Tybalt flat as a sheet. Mangle or mangling machine gears and crank visible. "Mangle" is very old word, dating back to about 1200. The picture is from an unidentifiable c.1830 English book, a single page of which I bought for a dollar at a print shop. Poor Tybalt was a nobleman, cousin to the fated Juliet, and killed by Romeo himself in Shakespeare's _Romeo & Juliet_.

**III-105.**
**Ironing machine or mangle.**
"The American," pat'd 3/30/1863. From Haley, Morse & Co., NYC, c.1863 flyer. Text goes on, "In England and other parts of Europe, Mangling is considered an absolute necessity in every household." It was "for ironing clothes without heat in one-quarter of the time required by the Flat Iron," and "is adapted to Hand or Steam Power." **$225.00-$350.00**

**III-103.**
**Ironing board,**
called the "Standpat Skirtboard." This one is one of four models offered by Simplex in their c.1916 brochure. It is No.3, having some of the features of No. 1, and "with electric iron." It cost a whopping $31.00. The other three are: No. 1. "has removable main board, new patented swivel sleeve board, iron, rest, sponge and water cups." No. 2 is "same with gas burner for keeping two irons hot." No. 4 is a combination gas & electric board. One of the new plus ultras of ironing! **$40.00-$60.00**

## WARD'S AMERICAN MANGLES.

### FOR IRONING CLOTHES WITHOUT HEAT.

Suitable for Families, Institutions and Hotels. More work can be done in an hour with a Mangle, than in half a day with the sad-iron, and the clothes will look fresher and more glossy. Also the celebrated **UNION WASHING MACHINE AND WRINGER,** acknowledged to be the best and most durable ever made. Warranted to *wash perfectly* without soaking, rubbing or boiling—it gives unbounded satisfaction everywhere.

Fluting Machines of every style. Wringers of all kinds repaired. Send for Circular.

**J. WARD & CO.,**
No. 31 (formerly 23) Courtlandt St., N.Y.

**III-106.**
**Ironing machine.**

*"Ward's American Mangles," by J. Ward & Co., NYC. It is very like the previous one by (?) Haley, but there are fewer spokes to the crank wheel as well as to the wheel underneath, which apparently adjusts the tension. Peterson's magazine, throughout 1870.*
**$225.00-$350.00**

**III-108A.**
**Ironing machines.**

*Both mfd. by Standard Laundry Machinery Co., Boston & NYC. (L) A floor-standing model with wooden-top table, with two polished metal rollers. (R) A tabletop model to be fastened with clamp or bolt. As with other traditional mangles, "the smoothing (is) done entirely by pressure." American Agriculturist, 10/1876.*
**$150.00-$300.00**

## Ironing Easy
### GEM Ironing Machine

Heated by gas or gasoline — 1½ cents per hour. 10 hours' work in 1 hour. Especially designed for families and hotels. Write for FREE illustrated booklet, "Modern Methods in Ironing."

**Domestic Mangle Co., Box E, Racine, Wis.**

### A Labor and Time Saver for Women

For convenience nothing can compare with using

**The GEM Ironing Machine**

It absolutely saves nine-tenths time, great amount of labor and all worry. Economical, practical, durable. Only 1 cent per hour to heat by gas or gasoline. Sent FREE—Illustrated booklet, "Modern Methods in Ironing." Write to-day. **Domestic Mangle Co., Box E Racine Junction, Wis.**

**III-107.**
**Ironing machines.**

*"Gem" tabletop model and one with its own stand, mfd. by Domestic Mangle Co., Racine, WI (and then Racine Junction, WI). Originally tiny ads from Century, in 1901 and 1902.* **$125.00-$175.00**

## 'SAFETY'
### Wringer and Mangle.

**Framing Unbreakable, being made of Wrought Iron.**

### PRESSURE INSTANTLY APPLIED OR RELEASED.

**Breakdowns Impossible.**

A PERFECT MANGLE.

*Send for Illustrated Catalogue, containing 61 different sizes and varieties of Machines. Post free.*

Patentees and Sole Makers:
**ENTWISLE & KENYON, Accrington.**

**III-108B.**
**Mangle & wringer combined.**

*"Safety," mfd. by Entwisle & Kenyon, Accrington, England. Chambers' Journal, 11/1/1884.* **$150.00-$300.00**

**III-109.**
**Ironing machine.**

*"Stratton's Gas Heating Mangle (that) irons all plain goods with or without heat...the only three-roller mangle so constructed." "Dampen the pieces uniformly, then fold to a suitable width, to the length of the rollers. Place one end between the rollers; turn the wheel slightly,...straighten to prevent any fold or wrinkle. A cloth should be spread under the Mangle, on the floor, to avoid long pieces from getting soiled, in passing backward and forward in mangling. Care should be taken not to allow the pieces to run out of the Mangle until sufficiently smoothed. Turn on gas-light on end of roller. Turn off gas when not mangling." American, but maker not mentioned. Hand-or power-operated models were available. 1881 flyer.*
**$200.00-$350.00**

**III-110.**
**Ironing machine.**
*Skeletal cast iron model with casters. From Vail's Approved
Methods for Home Laundering, 1906.* **$150.00-$200.00**

**III-111.**
**Lacework dolly.**
*Turned wood. A small hand-washing machine used for dainties
such as handkerchiefs and lace collars. They were put inside with
soapy water and gently agitated with perforated dasher. 11"H x
4 1/2" diameter. Early 19th C. Formerly in the Keillor Collection.*
**$165.00-$250.00**

**III-112.**
**Ironing machine.**
*"Simplex Ironer." Massive cast iron frame, electric motor. Note
the clock: she's done by 9:00—undoubtedly a.m. Simplex
booklet, c.1916.* **$100.00-$200.00**

**III-113.**
**Laundry marker.**
"Triumph," pat'd 11/14/1871. Silverplated, in box, with "bottle of indelible ink, pad, nippers, and three complete sets of type, with periods, spaces, etc. It can also be used for printing cards." This was available as a premium to subscribers of *American Agriculturist* magazine who brought in two $1.50 subscribers, or who sent a dollar to the magazine! It is but one of many types of premiums offered — an interesting practice lost in history. *1883-84 Premuim List.*                    **$15.00-$30.00**

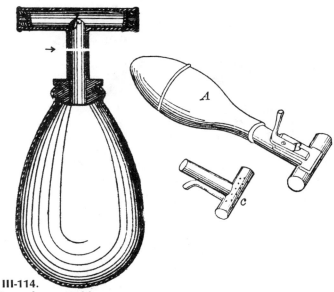

**III-114.**
**Laundry sprinklers,**
both of bulb type. (L) Pat'd 6/19/1877, by Edward K. Walker, Exeter, NH, and Thomas Roddick, Stranraer, Scotland. It sprinkled out of the perforated "T pipe." Break in pipe indicates it was really longer. (R) "Sprinkler for Clothes and Flowers," pat'd 1/15/1867, by Dana Bickford, Boston, MA. "An elastic bulbous reservoir in connection with a pipe and a rose, acting on the principle of a syringe." *Official Gazette.*

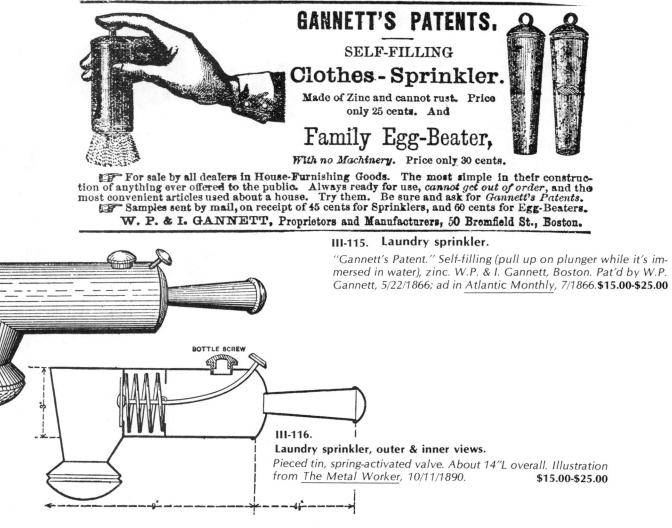

**GANNETT'S PATENTS.**

**SELF-FILLING**

**Clothes-Sprinkler.**

Made of Zinc and cannot rust.   Price only 25 cents.   And

**Family Egg-Beater,**

*With no Machinery.*   Price only 30 cents.

☞ For sale by all dealers in House-Furnishing Goods. The most simple in their construction of anything ever offered to the public. Always ready for use, *cannot get out of order*, and the most convenient articles used about a house. Try them. Be sure and ask for *Gannett's Patents.*
☞ Samples sent by mail, on receipt of 45 cents for Sprinklers, and 60 cents for Egg-Beaters.
**W. P. & I. GANNETT,** Proprietors and Manufacturers, 50 Bromfield St., Boston.

**III-115.   Laundry sprinkler.**
"Gannett's Patent." Self-filling (pull up on plunger while it's immersed in water), zinc. W.P. & I. Gannett, Boston. Pat'd by W.P. Gannett, 5/22/1866; ad in *Atlantic Monthly*, 7/1866.**$15.00-$25.00**

**III-116.**
**Laundry sprinkler, outer & inner views.**
*Pieced tin, spring-activated valve. About 14"L overall. Illustration from* The Metal Worker, *10/11/1890.*                    **$15.00-$25.00**

**III-117.**
**"Liquid spraying bellows."**
*"The Woodason." "Invaluable to poultrymen and cattle owners for spraying kerosene and other liquid insecticides...Invaluable for laundry work. Throws a spray as fine as smoke." Available from garden supply catalog of Joseph Breck, Boston, 1905.*
**$15.00-$25.00**

**III-118.**
**Sprinkler.**
*The illustration comes from a 1902 billhead of Reilley Brothers, NYC, who manufactured "painters" wood and metal sundries, and paper hangers' tools." This is a sprinkler intended for a paper hanger, but probably the same thing was used for laundry.*
**$15.00-$30.00**

**III-119.**
**Laundry sprinkler.**
*"Chi-Nee Clothes Sprinkler," mfd. by Syracuse Stamping Co., Syracuse, NY. Pint capacity, corked tubular tapered handle for filling. HFR ad, 3/1906.*
**$15.00-$20.00**

**III-120.**
**Laundry sprinkler.**
*Embossed stamped aluminum, 6"H, 9 1/2 ounce capacity. "Mirro," mfd. by Aluminum goods Mfg. Co., Manitowoc, WI, 1927 catalog.*
**$7.00-$12.00**

**III-121.**
**Polishing iron.**
*"Mrs. Erickson says that shirt bosoms and collars, when new, have a smoothness and gloss which she cannot impart to them afterwards. She has tried spermaceti (whale 'grease' of waxy consistency), gum (gum tracanth), and other things, in the starch, and yet fails to get the gloss. Spermaceti and other forms of grease may help, but she has not yet tried the right kind which is elbow grease, and it is not put into the starch, but applied directly to the linen."* Clothing ironed the regular way first, then dried, dampened lightly, then rubbed "and rubbed hard" with a polishing iron. The iron itself must have highly polished sole and well rounded edge. *American Agriculturist*, 5/1875.
**$20.00-$30.00**

TUESDAY.

**III-122.**
**Tuesday's chores tradecard,**
*part of a set of housekeeping depictions. (See Monday washing, III-158, and the Friday housecleaning one at end of Chapter I.) Chromolithograph, 1880s.*
**$6.00-$10.00**

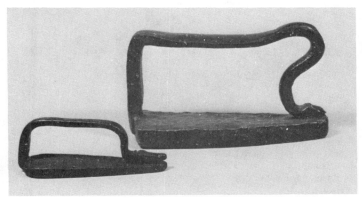

**III-123. Sadiron.**

*Forged iron, both snake-handled. Large one is somewhat unusual, even in this rare subcategory of collecting so-called primitive irons, in that the snake's head is attached to the plate. 5-1/2"L and 3-5/8"L. Collection of Carol Walker. Look for an authorative, definitive and well-illustrated book on all kinds of irons by Carol Walker in the next few years.*

**III-124. Sadiron.**

*Forged iron, unusual high-arched tail-like grip, causing the iron to be handled differently in use than most irons. Would have been very good for a seated person to use. 4 1/4"L. Collection of Carol Walker.*

**III-125. "Tattle-tale" sadirons.**

*These are also known as "slave" or "bell" irons. There is an iron ball loose inside the hollow handle which was supposed to signal when the iron was in use. Forged iron, early 19th C, perhaps earlier? According to collector, "This type is exceptionally rare in the 3 1/4" child's size. The larger 6 1/4"L adult size is more common, but still prized by collectors." Collection of Carol Walker. NOTE the striations visible in the side of the larger iron; these are like geological strata, and visual proof of the hand-hammering that went into making this forged piece. This kind of mark is found on all sorts of blacksmith-made tools.*

**III-126. Sadiron.**

*Forged iron with handle twisted while still red hot. The twist serves three purposes: one intent is to give the handle rigidity and extra strength (and was therefore often used on long handles of fireplace and hearth tools); it also provides a better grip; and is somewhat heat-dissipating. 7"L, probably 18th C. Collection of Carol Walker.*

**III-127. Sadirons.**

*Forged iron with twisted 'braided' handle, 17th or 18th C German. Photograph courtesy Waltraud Boltz Auction House, Bayreuth, Germany. From the Loercherbach Collection, auctioned May 1987.* **$200.00-$300.00**

**III-128. Tailor's iron,**

*sometimes called a* **tailor's goose.** *Cast iron, with knopped handle providing a good grip, much as twisted handles on early forged irons did. Despite look of age, this one is probably mid 19th C, and was mfd. by Savery, of Philadelphia. About 12"L. By the way, the German word for casting or founding is* **guss** *('guß' is somewhat like how it appears typographically), and I suspect that "goose" is a phonetic corruption of* **guss.** **$60.00-$90.00**

### III-129.
### Sadiron,

with pointed front. Cast iron handle and cast bronze plate. Incised or engraved words and calligraphic decoration as well as filed decoration. Maker's name and date: "Gabriel Spalt in Breisach Anno 1660" — Gabriel Spalt, of Breisach (South Germany), in the year 1660. Almost 6"L. Photograph courtesy Waltraud Boltz Auction House, Bayreuth, Germany. From the Loercherbach Collection, auctioned May 1987. Estimated to sell for thousands of dollars; realized price not known by me.

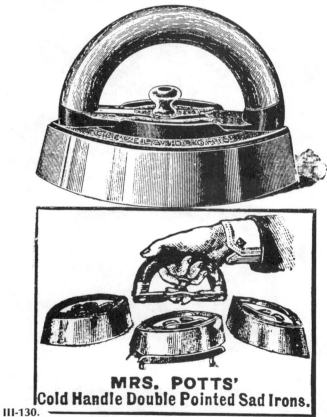

### III-130.
### Sadiron set.

"Mrs. Potts" double-pointed sadirons with detachable curved bentwood handle that fit all three irons. Top is picture of the iron as made by the Cleveland Foundry, Cleveland, OH, with "tinned trimmings." Cleveland was one of many companies over the years that made, presumably under license, Mrs. Potts' patented iron. Ad from The Metal Worker, 2/6/1892. Lower picture is from an Enterprise Mfg. Co. catalog, as advertised in 1882. Value depends on completeness, and I suppose on foundry origins and age. The first was pat'd 5/24/1870.                     **$25.00-$40.00**

### III-131.
### Sadiron set.

"Pott's Pattern Flat Irons" as advertised by Butler Brothers, a huge mail order house in Chicago, in their 1899 catalog. Note that stand is scalloped. "Three double pointed irons, detachable, always cool handle, (cast) iron sad stand." They also could be had nickel plated, and you could order extra handles of walnut-finished hardwood.                     **$25.00-$40.00**

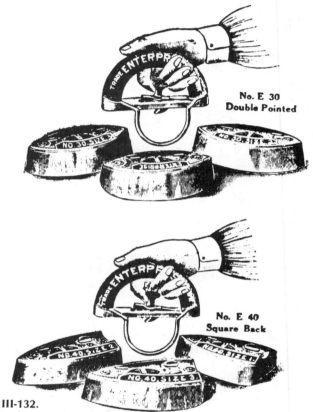

### III-132.
### Sadiron set.

Enterprise Mfg. Co., Philadelphia, weighs in with their own double-pointed set with detachable handle, and a set with square backs. From Enterprise catalog, early 20th C.                     **$25.00-$40.00**

### III-133.
### Sadiron set.

"Ideal" sadirons by Bless & Drake, Newark, NJ. Bentwood handle with cutaways, catch & spring release. Made double-pointed or square back. Picture from The Metal Worker, 5/17/1890.                     **$35.00-$50.00**

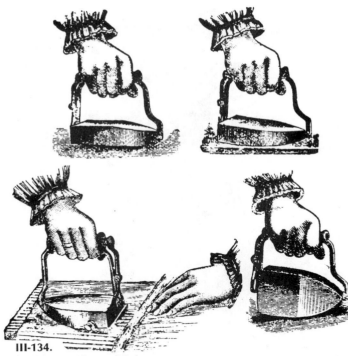

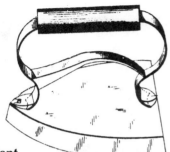

**III-136.**
**Sadiron patent.**
*Pat'd 7/26/1887, by Simgesmer Needles, Sedalia, MO. The patent is for a sadiron with detachable handle, the lower curved "horn" serving to pull the two uprights away from the raised projections on the iron itself. Official Gazette.*

**III-137.**
**Sadiron.**
*A cast iron flat iron with raised star mark — very commonly found today. It came in seven sizes, and was sold through 1895 of Harrod's Stores Ltd., Brompton, England.* **$10.00-$22.00**

**III-134.**
**Sadiron with multiple purposes.**
*"King", mfd. by Hewitt Mfg. Co., Pittsburgh, PA. Cast iron, pivoting on handle into three positions. The three smaller pictures, starting left top, show the King used for "plain" work; next flipped over for polishing or glossing; next used on its side as a "band iron." The bigger one below shows the iron being used with a corrugated soleplate, being used with the special corrugated board on the table. The description of this board is offhand, but I believe it was made up of narrow strips of half-rounds of wood, strung together much like the tambour front on an old rolltop desk. The iron is held backwards and the iron is drawn from left to right "instead of pushing from right to left as in ironing." Flyer c.1860s.* **$55.00-$80.00**

**III-138.**
**Sadiron.**
*Very heavy cast iron sadiron in intermediate weight "B" — 15 1/2 lbs. This is a tailor's iron, mfd. by S.H. German. Other sizes were AA (11 1/2 lbs.); A (12 1/2 lbs.); C (18 1/2 lbs.); and D (20 lbs.). From D.J. Barry hotel supplyer catalog, 1924.* **$10.00-$22.00**

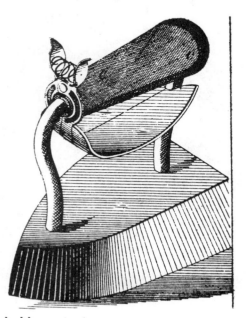

**III-135.**
**Sadiron holder patent.**
*Pat'd 11/13/1877, by William Reinhard, Eau Claire, WI. This invention appears to be a detachable heat shield which opens for removal when the two small pieces with the spring between are pinched. Official Gazette.*

**III-139.**
**Sadiron heater for gas stoves.**
*Cast iron, pyramidal shape. Shows a Mrs. Potts style iron, a plain sadiron, and an unidentified piece which I have marked with an arrow, which may be some kind of slug for a goffering iron or fluter. Cleveland Foundry ad in The Metal Worker, 2/6/1892.* **$35.00-$70.00**

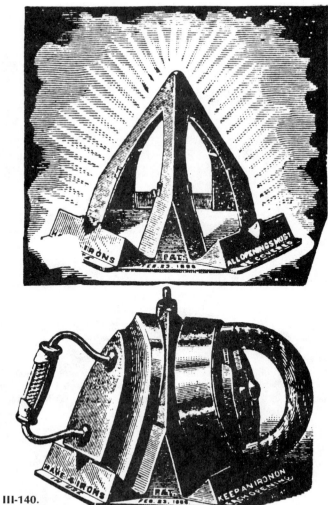

**III-142.**
**Sadiron heating stove,**
or **Laundry stove..** Cast iron; No. 1, with room for 8 (or 7?) irons. *The Union Stove Works, NYC. In dealer catalog, c.1880.*
**$200.00-$500.00**

**III-140.**
**Sadiron heater,**
for gas or gasoline stoves. "The Dome," mfd. by Shepard Hard-ware Co., Buffalo, NY. Pat'd 2/23/1886, and meant for 3 irons. "When covered with irons, it gathers up all the heat of a burner and distributes it over the entire surface of three flat-irons. It will heat three irons as fast and more evenly than two sat down on the flame, and is therefore a saving of one-third." You had to have 4 irons to use this, as the heater required being closed up by three irons. *The Metal Worker*, 12/27/90. **$35.00-$70.00**

**III-143.**
**Sadiron heating stove.**
Cast iron, with oblong top for oval washboiler perhaps. Maker not known. Picture from Vail's *Approved Methods for Home Laundering*, 1906. **$200.00-$500.00**

**III-141.**
**Sadiron heater,**
of type called a "flat heater," to be placed on top of a cookstove or any other kind that would hold it. The flatirons were placed inside. Three sizes: 7", 8" and 9". From Catalogue of Repairs and Attachments for Ranges, Stoves & Furnaces, Henry N. Clark, Boston, 1884. **$20.00-$35.00**

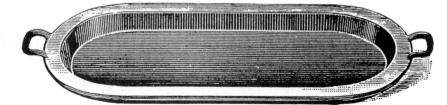

**III-144. Smoothing boards,**
*called* **Mangelbrett** in German. Both carved hardwood. Top: Horse handle, initials K E D," and lots of carved surface ornament in traditional motifs, 22-3/8"L. Norwegian, late 18th C. Bottom: Similar piece, but with more abstract horse, a large heart and the initials P M D, and the rosettes which are often called "hex signs" here in the U.S. 24"L. Danish, late 18th C. Photograph courtesy Waltraud Boltz Auction House, Bayreuth, Germany. From the Loecherbach Collection, auctioned May 1987. **$1000.00-$2500.00**

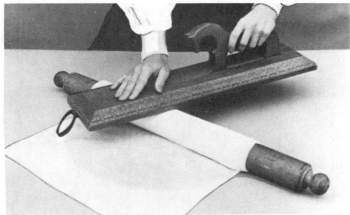

**III-145.**
**Smoothing board,**
*also called a* **mangling board.** *A simpler horse one from Scandinavia, used with a rolling pin-like roller onto which the material was rolled. Probably late 18th or early 19th C. 1974 photograph courtesy of Ayer Public Relations, NYC; the mangle board itself was (perhaps still is) from the A.H. Glissman Collection. This type of simple board:* **$700.00-$1500.00**

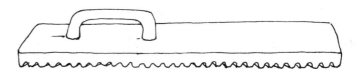

**III-146.**
**Smoothing board and scrubbing board,**
*two somewhat similar laundry items that have completely different uses. Smoothing board or manglebrett is Scandinavian, late 18th or very early 19th C. Lower picture is a corrugated wash or scrub board, usually made not quite so long as the mangle board.*

**III-147.**
**Stand for sadiron.**
*Homemade, sheet iron with zigzag rail. Handle & 3 legs riveted on. 11 1/4" overall. 19th C.* **$30.00-$60.00**

## III-150.
### Stands for sadiron.
*Japanned cast iron (I think they were also available plain). Russell & Erwin Mfg. Co., 1865.* **$30.00-$70.00**

## III-148.
### Stands for sadiron.
*Twisted wire, German, and although they look 1870s, the auction cataloguer says they date to c.1920-30. About 9-3/4"L. Photograph courtesy Waltraud Boltz Auction House, Bayreuth, Germany. From the Loecherbach Collection, auctioned May 1987.* **$40.00-$65.00**

## III-151.
### Stands for sadiron.
*Top: Cast brass, English, late 19th C. 10 5/8"L; bottom: whitesmithed iron, German, 19th C., 13 3/8"L. Photograph courtesy Waltraud Boltz Auction House, Bayreuth, Germany. From the Loercherbach Collection, auctioned May 1987.* **$45.00-$70.00**

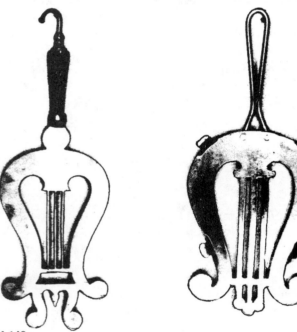

## III-152.
### Stand for sadiron.
*Japanned cast iron, very like bottom one in XX-150. German, late 19th or early 29th C., 11 1/8"L.* **$30.00-$45.00**

## III-149.
### Stands for sadiron.
*Lyre-shaped, German, early 20th C. (L) cast brass, wooden handle, 13 1/4"L. (R) Sheet metal with bent heavy wire handle, 12 1/2"L. Photograph courtesy Waltraud Boltz Auction House, Bayreuth, Germany. From the Loecherbach Collection, auctioned May 1987.* **$40.00-$70.00**

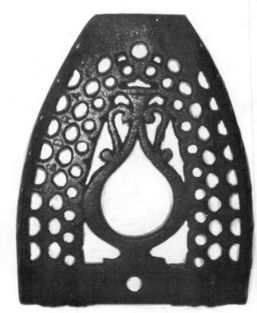

## III-153.
### Stand for sadiron.
*Cast iron with lyre-like urn design inside border of perforations. 5 -13/16"L. American (?), late 19th C. Courtesy Darwin Urffer.* **$35.00-$55.00**

**III-154.**
**Stand for sadiron.**
*Cutout sheet metal, 4 folded-down tab feet, about 7"L. American, late 19th or early 20th C.* $30.00-$50.00

**III-156.**
**Stand for sadiron.**
*Cast iron, 4 feet, 8 1/4"L overall. Design called "Grain & Tassell." There is some confusion about the name for this pattern, which is sometimes referred to as "Lincoln Drape," despite absence of any drapes. The tassels however belonged on funeral hearse. The first one I saw, I thought, Brooms! Late 19th C.* $45.00-$65.00

**III-155.**
**Stand for sadiron.**
*Cutout sheet iron, with crossed keys & phonetic "U C M" initials, sawtooth railing. 9 3/4"L, early 20th C.* $20.00-$30.00

**III-157.**
**Sinks.**
*Heavy molded white glazed pottery sinks. Top is one divided into soak, wash and rinse sections. Note that "wash boards & soap-cups (are) moulded in tubs." Bottom is long kitchen sink. Stewart Ceramic Co., NYC. Century magazine ad, 1/1891.*

MONDAY.

**III-158.    Monday washing chores tradecard.**

*Chromolithograph, part of set. (See III-22.) Note wooden laundry sink, hot water heater behind it, laundry basket on head of pigtailed woman at right, wooden washtubs on floor. 1880s.*
                                                    **$6.00-$10.00**

**III-159.
Suds dipper.**
*Galvanized stamped sheet metal, tapered tubular handle. 5"H x 7 7/8" diameter at top. From Central Stamping Co., NYC, catalog of 1920.*                                    **$15.00-$30.00**

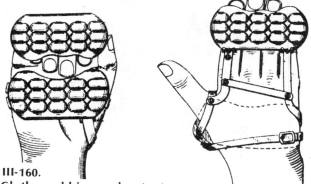

**III-160.
Clothes-rubbing pad patent.**
*Pat'd 6/23/1885, by William S.F. Dillon, Madeira, assignor of one-half to William E. Arnold, Madisonville, OH. A sort of glove to save the real knuckles. I don't know if it was to be made of wood or hard rubber, nor if it were ever made.*

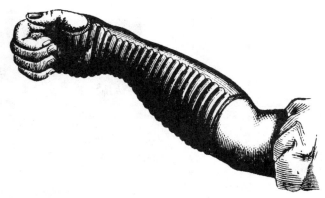

**III-161.
Washing shield,**
*"or armor." This one, depicted in Scientific American, 1/14/1871, actually did exist. It was pat'd 2/5/1867 by C.F. Lewis, Washington, DC. "In the rubbing of clothes by the hands, the skin is liable to be abraded from the mechanical action, which is greatly aided by the softening of the skin from the effect of the free alkali in the soap employed." I don't see how it would work, but mebbe so.*

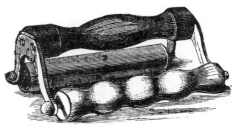

**III-162.**

**"Washing machine."**

*"U.S.,"* zinc-plated malleable cast iron frame, black walnut handle, bumpy roller in ash, the other is wood covered with rubber, 5 1/2" x 4 1/4". Mfd. in NJ. *"Use with any wash tub and board. Grasp the handle or rest the fingers on the cross piece, and rub the clothes backwards and forwards, pressing lightly. The friction of the corrugated rollers cleanses thoroughly. Dip the clothes or machine into the water as often as it is pressed out. Then ready to rinse, roll the machine over the clothes as they are drawn out of the water,"* in other words, use it as a wringer too! The column in which the story on this appeared is called *"Sundry Humbugs"* and was meant to enlighten readers on frauds. The general tone of the entire article implies that the editor did not believe in this roller, and thought that its best use would be on the woodpile under the wash boiler, helping to keep the fire hot. Looks like it would be great cellulite massager! *American Agriculturist,* 4/1880.                     **$20.00-$30.00**

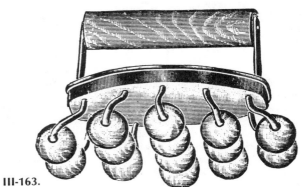

**III-163.**

**"Washing machine."**

*"Litta."* 14 wooden beads that roll. *"Roll over the wash on flat board or bottom of tub, instead of using knuckles or wash board."* Sold through catalog of Ritzinger & Grasgreen, importers of housewares, NYC, c.1906-07 catalog.          **$20.00-$30.00**

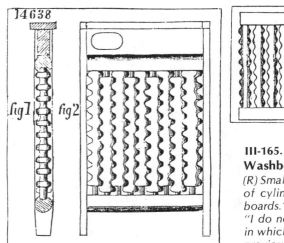

**III-164.**

**Washing tradecard.**

Chromolithograph card advertising Fisk & Co.'s *"Japanese soaps,"* and meant to be stamped by the individual store owners with their own name and address. *"Positively no filthy, putrid, tainted, disease-giving grease used, but the purest oils and tallow of our own refining."* Soap pat'd 10/11, 1875; 9/18/1877; card late 1870s or early 1880s.                     **$6.00-$10.00**

**III-165.**

**Washboard patents.**

*(R)* Small picture of one pat'd 1/15/1856, by Ira S. Parker. *"A series of cylindrical beaded bars, the ends of which are secured to boards."* *(L)* Two views of one pat'd 4/8/1856, by Royal Hatch. *"I do not claim the beaded rounds, irrespective of the manner in which they are arranged or fitted together, for they have been previously used; but I claim the beaded rounds"* are set in so that the ins-and-outs of the beads fit each other. Notice the soap holder in the top.

**III-166.**
**Washboard patents.**
*(L) Pat'd 1/30/1877, by Samuel A. Gould, Osgood, IN. Zinc with "serpentine ridges." (R) Pat'd 1/30/1877, by Thomas M. Webb, Norwalk, OH, assignor to L.T. Farrand, Norwalk. There are "acorn-shaped projections formed on the upper face of the board"; and "triangular figures embossed on the lower face." stamped sheet metal, the claim for which was based on the new patterns. Official Gazette.*

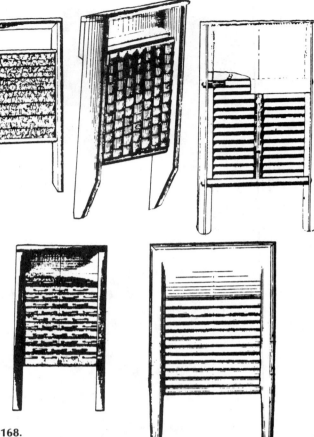

**III-168.**
**Washboard patents.**
*Top: (L) Pat'd 5/1/1877, by J.M. Gorham, Cleveland, OH. Crimpe metal, and "an irregularly-noduled or morocco-finished surface." (M) Pat'd 4/24/1877, by J. Poole, Cleveland, OH. "Formed with screw-like elevations or currugations in parallel rows or columns. (R) Pat'd 3/20/1877, by William Serviss, Sidney, OH, assignor to W.M. Serviss. Bottom: (L) Pat'd 10/6/1885 by Melvin Jincks, Conesus Centre, NY. He claimed as new "the combination of the rubbing surface provided with transverse equidistant channels, secured with staples, and so arranged that adjacent rows break joints, so as to direct the descending lather from one row to the lower row." Official Gazette.*

OFFICE OF

The Lapham-Dodge Co.

MANUFACTURERS OF THE

→NORTH STAR←

AND

RED CROSS

WASH-BOARDS,

COR. DETROIT AND STATE STREETS.

**III-167.**
**Washboard billhead.**
*"North Star," mfd. by Lahpam-Dodge Co., Cleveland, OH, pat'd in 1875 and 1877. Invoice dated 1890. The billhead itself.*
**$7.00-$10.00**

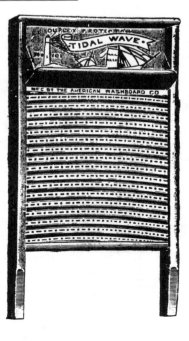

**III-169.**
**Washboard.**
*"Tidal Wave," mfd. by the American Washboard Co. Wooden frame with stamped metal face, perforated soap tray. Would be nice to find with name intact. Sold through Joseph Breck catalog, 1905.*
**$20.00-$40.00**

**III-170.**
**Washboard.**
*Cast iron, reversible, soap depression. Corrugations rather sharply defined. 21 15/16"H x 10 1/4"W. Photographed at booth of Bob "Primitive Man" Cahn, Stella Show in NYC, December 1985.*
**$125.00-$175.00**

**III-171.**
**Washboard.**
*Cast iron, Queen Annish legs, embossed pattern of daisies along top, rounded corrugations and round shoulders. 21 3/8"H x 11 3/4"W. Photographed at booth of Bob "Primitive Man" Cahn, Stella Show in NYC, December 1985.* **$140.00-$200.00**

**III-172.**
**Clothes stick.**
*"Eastlake." Tubular metal, pat'd 3/18/1879. Bauder & Co., Eastlake Works, Birmingham, Erie County, OH. Ad from Scientific American, 12/20/1879.* **$20.00-$40.00**

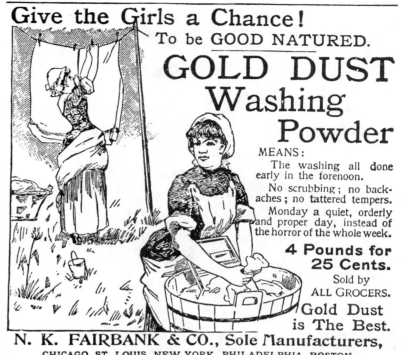

## Give the Girls a Chance!
### To be GOOD NATURED.

# GOLD DUST
# Washing
# Powder

MEANS:
The washing all done early in the forenoon.
No scrubbing; no backaches; no tattered tempers.
Monday a quiet, orderly and proper day, instead of the horror of the whole week.

**4 Pounds for 25 Cents.**
Sold by
ALL GROCERS.
**Gold Dust is The Best.**

**N. K. FAIRBANK & CO., Sole Manufacturers,**
CHICAGO, ST. LOUIS, NEW YORK, PHILADELPHIA, BOSTON, BALTIMORE, NEW ORLEANS, SAN FRANCISCO, PORTLAND, ME., PORTLAND, ORE., PITTSBURGH AND MILWAUKEE.

**III-173. Washing powder ad.**
*"Gold Dust," mfd. by N.K. Fairbank & Co., Chicago, etc. Fairbank was owner of various businesses related to the slaughterhouses, and presumably "Gold Dust" washing powder was of the "filthy, putrid, tainted...grease" that Fisk advertised as anathema to them. Ad in LHJ, 3/1892. Note wash basket, clothesline & pegs & pole to hold line up, small bucket for the pegs, and the washtub & washboard.*

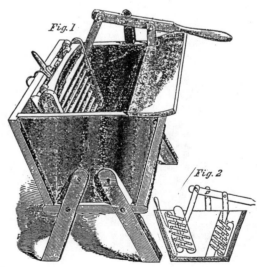

**III-174.**
**Washing machine.**
*"Price's" patent, pat'd 10/27/1857 by Thomas J. Price, Industry, IL. "Clothes are placed with water and soap in the tub, between the slats (of the two side), which are placed like blind slats in a frame and are moved back and forth by the lever." "The rods are loosely connected so as to give the slats the necessary motion, which is one peculiarly adapted to washing, combining the rubbing action of the knuckles with the continuous certainty of a machine." Scientific American, 10/9/1858. In those days, Scientific American had many notices of the wonders of household invention, not being devoted solely to quasars and quarks.*

118

**III-175. The "Metropolitan" Washing Machine,** *patented in 1858. The tub alone is 26"H. The dolly (this one of the mutant-cow-udder type) is provided with 16 replaceable pestles or pounders, which were fitted into the heavy round disk. Between the pestle and the disk was a spring. The two bowed wings are actually wooden 'springs', set into the base. The T-handle was worked with two hands, up and down, although they advertised that it could be done with only one hand.*

## Rubbing & Wringing done away.

METROPOLITAN WASHING MACHINE.
For sale by WM. FALKNER & SON, San Francisco, Cal.
Wholesale and retail by       LE ROY & CO.,
                              Hartford, Conn., and
       DAVID LYMAN, Middlefield, Conn.
Send for a circular.

**III-176.
Washing machine.**
*Also the "Metropolitan," as described two years later. It appears that the number of pestles has been increased, but this may have been artistic license. A special wringer is shown in place on the edge of the tub. American Agriculturist, 8/1860.*

# EAGLE WASHER

**III-177.
Washing machine.**
*"Eagle," mfd. by Oakley & Keating, NYC. Looks like a wringer at first glance, but it is a washing machine. Ribbed wooden cylinder, "oscillating roller frame with guiding guards," metal parts all galvanized or tinned or made of brass. Flyer c.1865-70.*

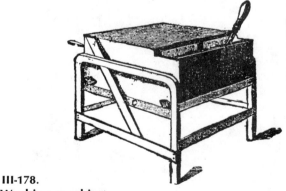

**III-178.
Washing machine.**
*"Railroad," mfd. by Ferry & Co., NYC. Like many other makers of washing machines & wringers, this company was located on Courtland Street in what is now the Wall Street area of the city. This one is somewhat unusual in that it has a lid. American Agriculturist, 6/1870.*

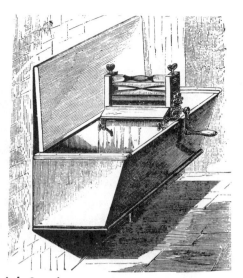

**III-179.**
**Washtub sink & wringer.**
*In effect, a washing machine. Sink is wooden, with two compartments. One lid, which doubled as an "ironing table." American Agriculturist, 12/1875.*

**III-180.**
**Washing machine.**
*"Walker," mfd. by the Erie Washer Co., Erie, PA. "The domestic labor-saving machine that, of all others, has been most generally accepted by the maid-servants, is the wringer; the utility of this was so manifest, and the contrast between turning a crank with ease, and wrenching the muscles of the arms and upper body, in twisting the water out of a large sheet, so great, that in most cases prejudice gave way and the wringer tolerated. Perhaps its resemblance to a wringer is one reason by the 'Walker Washer' has become so rapidly become popular." American Agriculturist, 4/1878.*

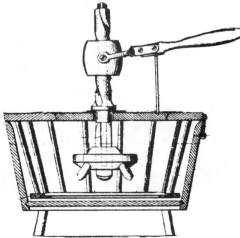

**III-181.**
**Washing machine patent.**
*Pat'd 11/3/1885, by Stephen C. Mortimer, Fort Wayne, IN. #329,760. Pivoting lever works the dolly up and down. Official Gazette.*

**III-182.**
**Washing machine.**
*"Western Washer," mfd. by Horton Mfg. Co., Fort Wayne, IN. Cranked dolly agitates clothes and sudsy water. LHJ ad, 10/1891.*
**$100.00-$200.00**

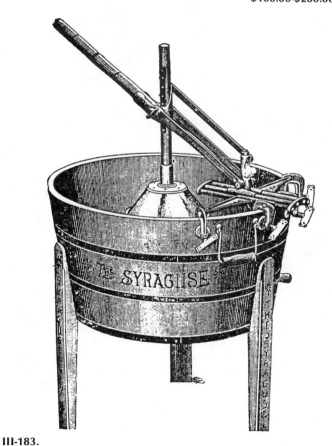

**III-183.**
**Washing machine.**
*"The Syracuse," mfd. by Dodge & Zuill, Syracuse, NY. Flyer from 1870s.*

OVER
NOW

70,000
IN USE.

**H. F. BRAMMER**
MANUFACTURING CO.,

MANUFACTURERS OF

**Washing Machines,**

CHURNS,

Ironing Boards and Clothes Racks.

Cor. Second and Ainsworth Sts.,

**DAVENPORT, Iowa.**

AGENTS WANTED IN EVERY CITY AND TOWN IN
THE UNITED STATES AND CANADA.

WRITE FOR TERMS, PRICES, &C.

**III-184.**
**Washing machine tradecard.**
*H.F. Brammer Mfg. Co., Davenport, IA, made washing machines
and churns. Card not dated, but c.1880.*

**III-185.**
**Washing machine.**
*"The New Becker," pat'd 9/1/1885 and 6/14/1887. Mfd. by N.C.
Baughman, York, PA.* The Metal Worker, *4/12/1890.*

**III-187.**
**Washing machine.**
*"Boss," mfd. in three sizes by E.H. Huenefeld, Cincinnati, OH.
Pat'd 7/7/1891; 6/9/1896; 10/20/1896. Two cylinders ran in opposite
directions. "It is so arranged that it is absolutely impossible to
tear the clothes, and works so simple and easy that a child can
work it without fatigue."* HFR, *10/1897. Picture here shows works
up, revealing one corrugated drum. Girl works wringer.*

**III-186.**
**Washing machines.**
*The "Boss" and the "Eli," both mfd. by Boss Washing Machine
Co. (R) Pat'd 7/7/1891.* Hardware, *2/25/1895.*

**III-188.**
**Washing machine.**
*"1904 Automatic," also mfd. by the Boss Washing Machine Co.,
first in 1904. This ad is from 1/1909* HFR.

**III-189.**

**Shaker washing machine,**

as depicted in <u>Scientific American</u>, 3/10/1860. The two tanks are alike, but shown cutaway at left, and with the board front in place at right. The clothes, water and soap are put into the tank at left, and the paddles agitate the contents by the movement of the swinging frame, which is put in motion by the crank seen at center. After sufficient washing, the water is drawn off and the clothes are pressed against the tank walls. It must have worked better than it would seem, because several big hotels used this machine — Boston's Revere House; Philadelphia's Girard House; and Washington's Willard's Hotel (which is still in business). Pat'd 1/26/1856, by David Parker, Shaker Village, NH.

Fig. 1.—WASHING MACHINE.

Fig. 2.—DRYING MACHINE.

Fig. 3.—STARCHING MACHINE.

Fig. 4.—BOSOM STARCHER.

**III-190.**

**Village laundramat of the 1870s.**

Front-loading washer, filled through the holes, closed up, then partly filled with hot water and soap. "The machinery is then started, and in a short time the clothes are washed. They are then rinsed, in the same machine, before being placed in the "rotary drier, in which they are freed from water." (Like a centrifugal water-expresser in a modern laundramat.) Next they are "carried to the drying-room, which is a large apartment heated by ranges of steam-pipes, and there; hung upon lines, they are quickly dried." Some are then put through the starching machine and then taken to the ironing room. A huge iron-heater, taller than a man, is not depicted here. <u>American Agriculturist</u>, 1/1874.

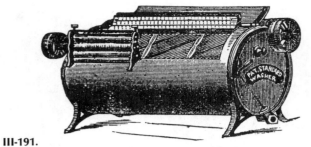

**III-191.**
**Washing machine.**

*"Superior," mfd. by Standard Laundry Machinery Co. Winner of various gold, silver and bronze medals at expositions. American Agriculturist ad, 1/1877.*

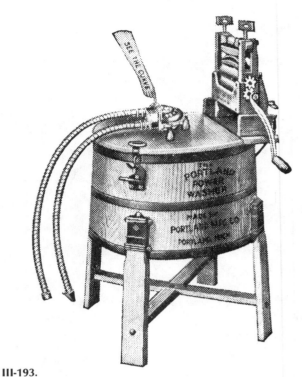

**III-192.**
**Washing machine.**

*"Motor High Speed," mfd. by Michigan Washing Machine Co., Muskegon, MI, for Paxton & Gallagher, Omaha, NE. Information on brass plate. Cast iron gears, wooden coopered tub, long lever action, wringer visible at back. Photograph courtesy Single Tree Antiques, Larry & Koralyn Kibbee, Manhattan, MT.***$100.00-$200.00**

**III-193.**
**Washing machine.**

*Water power washer showing water intake & outflow tubes. Worked with 15 lbs. of water pressure. "The Portland," mfd. by Portland Mfg. Co., Portland, MI. Hardware News 4/1912*
**$100.00-$200.00**

**III-194.**
**Commercial laundry tradecard.**

*Chromolith card, 3 3/4"H x 5 1/2"L, showing rotary machines at right. Notice Simon Legree in the doorway. Published by National Laundry Journal Press, Chicago, mid 1880s.* **$8.00-$15.00**

**III-195.**
**Washing machine.**
"Princess," mfd. Princess Mfg. Co., Cincinnati, OH. Water power, with "no internal springs, no motor troubles. Furnished with either Rub Board or Prong Dasher." *Iron Age* ad, 1/7/1909.
**$100.00-$200.00**

**III-197.**
**"Power washer for homes without electricity."**
Maytag 'Multi-Motor Washer," with built-in gasoline engine. Portable..."put anywhere — in the cellar or the kitchen — on the porch — out under a tree. It comes equipped with a long, flexible, metal exhaust pipe, so you can use it anywhere indoors." Ad in *Farm Journal*, 6/1920.
**$80.00-$150.00**

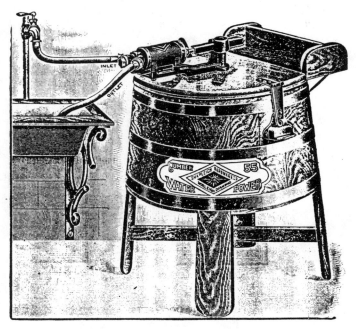

**III-196.**
**Washing machine.**
"Norleigh Diamond No. 55," mfd. by Shapleigh Hardware Co., St. Louis. From 1914 catalog.
**$100.00-$200.00**

**III-198.**
**Washing machine & wringer.**
"Apex," Hurley Machine Co., Chicago. Electric, washes by suction action. Maud Lancaster, *Electric Heating*, 1914.**$80.00-$150.00**

**III-199.**
**Washing machine.**
"The Locomotive Special," designed by William Remmert, mfd. by Remmert Mfg. Co., Belleville, IL. Gas or oil burner to keep water hot, otherwise electric power. The obling boiler (shown with cutaway side here) moves "back and forth 120 times a minute. This action continually forces the hot suds through the meshes of the fabric."
**$100.00-$150.00**

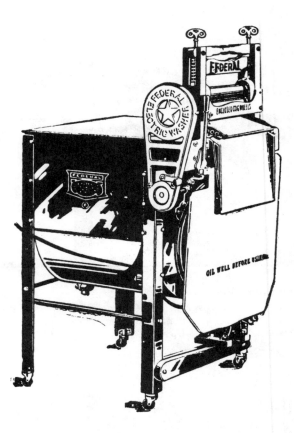

**III-200.**
**Washing machines with wringers.**
*(T) "Maytag," electric powered by motor underneath, double wringer. On casters. (R) "Federal," mfd, by Federal Sign System, Chicago. Also mounted on casters, with small motor underneath that drives the cylindrical oscillating tub and the reversible wringer on top. "All gears and moving parts are protected by a metal shield so that there is no risk of accident." Both from Lancaster's* Electric Heating, *1914.* **$80.00-$150.00**

**III-201.**
**Laundry room,** *with electric washing machine. "A-B-C Super Electric." Square cabinet of metal, but within is a "white maple cylinder (that) reverses at the end of every revolution, forcing hot suds through the clothes 44 times per minute." Mfd. by Altorfer Bros. Co., Peoria, IL. The ad, from 2/1920* LHJ, *is one of a charming black & white series showing mother and daughter.* **$80.00-$150.00**

**III-204.**
**Washing machine with wringer.**
*Maytag electric, Cast aluminum tub, steel frame with casters.*
*Better Homes and Gardens.*

**III-202.**
**Washing machine with wringer.**
*"2-in-1," mfd. by Minier Mfg. CO., Minier, IL, using GE motors. About 32"H. Sturdy hi-tech rolling platform with what is pretty much old-fashioned washer. About 1924. Photograph courtesy. GE.* **$80.00-$150.00**

**III-203.**
**Personal dry cleaner.**
*"Duette," Chicago, IL. For countertop use. "You just put in your things, pour on the non-explosive Duette fluid, turn the handle a minute or two, and out come your things — clean! Require no pressing either." Came with 2 gallons of fluid — "enough for 8 to 10 dresses." House Beautiful, 12/1930.* **$30.00-$45.00**

**III-205.**
**Personal washing machine.**
*"Pressure-O-Matic," non-electric, floor-standing (legs seen cut off here at halfway point). "Exclusive internal pressure action." Maker not known. Picture from House Beautiful ad of 1964. A tiny picture in the ad shows woman in her living room, reading a book while the machine is going. But what makes it work!* **$30.00-$45.00**

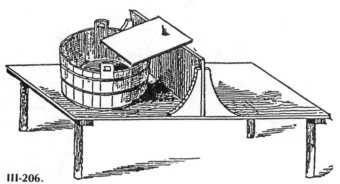

**III-206.**

**Washing bench with tub.**

*"The attention of house-keepers is called to a wash bench with a very simple attachment that will hold the wringer firm and steady, and save changing it from one tub to the other. It is a board as long as the bench is wide, and three inches higher than a common tub, attached to the center of the bench by curved cleats. At the top near the center is driven a piece of wire projecting upward. A light board is hung upon this wire. The wringer is attached to the upper side of the cross-board as well as upon either side of the horizontal board."* I still don't get it, but the drawing is beautiful. *American Agriculturist*, 4/1883.

**III-207.**

**Wringer and wash bench with ghostly tubs.**

*"Keystone Folding Bench Wringer"* rises in the center on shoe feet. The bench part folds up when not in use. Mfd. by American Wringer Co. — Note the horseshoe tag they hung on their products. Rubber rollers, reversible drain board just below wringer frame can be directed to either side so that the water runs into one tub or the other. Catalog of Excelsior Stove & Mfg. Co., c.1916. **$65.00-$90.00**

**III-208.**

**Wash tub, keeler & boiler.**

(L) Cedar tub with hoops, cast iron handles, c.1900. (R) "Model" copper bottom wash boiler, lid, wooden handles. Three sizes, all 12 3/4"H; 20 1/2"L x 11 3/8"W; 21 1/2"L x 12 1/4"W; and 23 3/4"L x 12 3/4". (B) "Puritan" galvanized sheet metal, red-painted band, brackets for wringer attachment. Three sizes: 10 5/8"H x 19 3/4" diameter; 10 5/8"H x 22 1/4"; and 11 1/8"H x 25". Model & Puritan from Central Stamping Co. catalog, 1920. **$20.00-$100.00**

**III-209.**
**Washtub.**
*Galvanized iron, riveted iron handles, top rim has reinforcing wire. Four sizes — all either 10"H or 10 5/8"H, and 20", 21", 22 3/4" and 24 5/8" in diameter. Matthai-Ingram catalog fragment, c.1890. This has gotta be in near perfect condition, and completely non-rusted, to be worth anything* **$20.00-$40.00**

**III-210.**
**Wash boiler.**
*"Iron Horse," mfd. by Rochester Can Co., Rochester, NY, c.1930. Heavy tin, copper bottom, top edge reinforced with wire, wood handles. Slightly tapered sides, so it's "nestable" — a good feature for retailers. Also available all copper except lid, and also in heavy galvanized steel. Two sizes: 13"H x 22 1/2"L and 13"H x 24"L. The original printed paper label would add to value. Value range for copper one with original label:* **$90.00-$150.00**

**III-211.**
**Washtubs on lazy susan bench.**
*This great picture is actually one lesson, on photo-retouching, from the Federal School of Commercial Designing, Inc., Minneapolis. I bought it with a folder showing what the rusted, banged up tub at left should look like when finished — brilliantly galvanized. Mounted on heavy cardboard, the photograph showed both tubs dented and rusty. The one on the right was retouched.*

128

**III-212.**
**Wash boiler washing machine.**
*"Harment" Patent Self-Acting," mfd. by A. Harmens, London, England. Water spewed out of perforations in a central tube, acting rather like a giant percolator for clothes. Ad in* The Queen, *1888.*

**III-214.**
**Washboard & washtub combined.**
*"Rub-a-Tub Senior," heavy galvanized tin, ribbed all the way around with pattern of ribbing directing water flow. (T) This view shows the built-in washboard for doing hand wash. A long-handled wash dolly was used for bigger stuff. This one also has built-in soap dish along edge. (B) Another example, without the soap dish. 17 1/2" diameter. "Provisional patent #25762." Turn of century or early 20th.* **$75.00-$100.00**

**III-213.**
**Wringer.**
*David Lyman's wooden wringer set on edge of tub (See III-175, 176). The upright frame has two very fat wooden rollers inside that are connected by simple cogwheels, cranked by a crank extending from the axle of the lower one. Editor of* American Agriculturist, *in August 1860, wrote "A month ago Mr. Lyman sent us from Yankeedom (Middlefield, CT) a small apparatus, 14 inches high, 12 inches wide, and 5 inches thick, and wished us to set it upon the edge of our Metropolitan wash-tub, or any other, and try it for wringing out clothes. It did not strike us very favorably at first. However, as it cost us nothing, not even the express charges, (which is more than we can say of many a useless gim-crack sent to us), we could do no less than take it home for a trial. Well, we like it; our better half likes it; and — to say a big thing in its praise — our 'help' liked it on the first trial, though she is constitutionally opposed to any new-fangled machines about the kitchen. Next to the sewing machine, we consider it the greatest woman's labor-strength-and-health-saving-implement."*

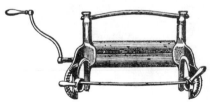

**III-215.**
**Wringer.**
*"Putnam Self-Adjusting," mfd. by Putnam mfg. Co., NYC & Cleveland, OH. Galvanized iron, no wood. Made with and without cogwheels. "It took First Premium at Fifty-seven State and County Fairs in 1863." H.W. Putnam, of Cleveland, got two "clothes-wringer" patents: 12/17/1861 and 9/16/1862. Ad in* American Agriculturist, *1/1865.* **$65.00-$80.00**

**III-216.    Evolution of the Wringer.**

*Four interior scenes as depicted in The March of Invention, Dubois & Dubois, 1891. Top (L) is very earliest type of Blue Monday, with water heated in kettle in fireplace. Top (R) represents the "first United States patent for a wringer, issued in 1847." It was pat'd 5/8/1847, by I. Avery, of Tunkhannock, PA. Bottom (L) is "the famous roller wringer, invented in 1862." and the fourth, with the cast eagle atop the frame, was pat'd in 1878. According to the book, in 1891 "there are about 75 wringer factories in operation in the United States."*

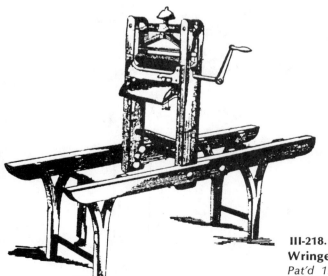

**III-217.
Wringer.**
*Galvanized iron, with cog wheels. "Sherman's Improved," available through, and possibly mfd. by Haley, Morse & Co., NYC. Came in four sizes — two "Family" ones, with rollers either 10"L x 1 7/8" or 11"L x 1 7/8"; and two "Hotel" ones, with rollers 12"L x 2 1/4", and 14"L x 2 1/4". Flyer c.1863.*   **$40.00-$90.00**

**III-218.
Wringer & bench patent.**
*Pat'd 12/16/1884, by Henry Baumgartel (poss. missprint for Baumgarten), Sturgis, MI. The side rails on the bench seem to be what Henry was patenting.*

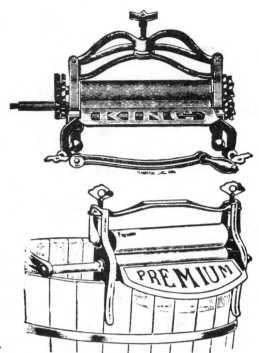

**III-219.**
**Wringers.**
*(T) "King," mfd. by National Wringer Co., Canton, OH. Galvanized iron frame, cog wheels. Note bowed top of frame, and the single central screw for changing tension between the rollers. (B) "Premium," by Colby Wringer Co., Montpelier, VT. Iron & wood, with tension-tighteners on both ends. Both ads from* Hardware, *2/25/1895.* **$30.00-$60.00**

Good Work in the Laundry

CANNOT BE DONE WITHOUT A

# Horse-Shoe Brand
# Clothes Wringer

TRADE **AWC** MARK

THEY ARE THE ONLY LONG-WEARING, EVEN-SQUEEZING, CLOTHES-SAVING, BUTTON-KEEPING, DRY-WRINGING, TIME-REDUCING WRINGERS MADE.

Our little book, " *The Wring of Sense,*" and attractive novelty, " *It's All in the Rubber,*" sent free on postal request.

## THE AMERICAN WRINGER CO.
99 Chambers Street, New York

**III-220.**
**Wringer.**
*"Horse-Shoe Brand," mfd. by American Wringer Co., NYC. Ad from* LHJ, *2/1901.* **$20.00-$40.00**

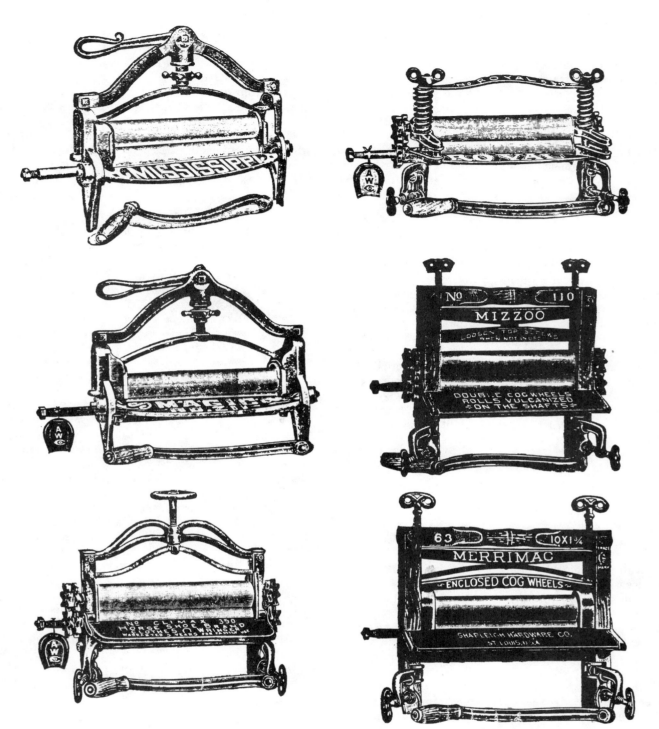

**III-221.**

**Wringers.**

*(L) to (R) top to bottom. (1) "Mississippi," mfd. for or by Sears & Roebuck. Note the monkey-tail lever at top. Galvanized malleable cast iron and steel. "Instantly attached to the tub throwing over the top lever, which, at the same time, by the same movement, adjusts the pressure on the rolls. Rollers 11"L x 1-3/4" diameter. Sears catalog, 1908. The remaining five are all from Shapleigh Hardware Co., Chicago, catalog of 1914. (2) "Royal No. 530," mfd. by American Wringer Co. Galvanized malleable cast iron frame and gears, steel springs. Some versions have ball bearings. Rollers range from 10"L to 14"L, and weighed from 19-1/2" to 28 lbs. (3) "Magic," mfd. by AWCo. "Comes with eccentric top lever, which adjusts the pressure and also clamps the wringer to the tub." One size only, with 11" rollers. (4) "Mizzoo No. 110," possibly by Shapleigh. Rock maple frame, hard rubber pressure spring, galvanized iron clamps & gears, white rubber rollers. Cheapo — no warranty, whereas on better ones, the rollers were warranted for 3 years or 1 year. (5) "Climax No. 350," mfd. by AWCo. Handsome iron frame. Came in three sizes, with rollers 10"L, 11"L and 12"L. (6) "Merrimac No. 63," mfd. by Shapleigh Hardware. Rock maple frame, steel springs, galvanized cast iron clamps, "elastic & durable white rubber rollers," 10"L.* **$20.00-$80.00**

132

# IV. MENDING & CLOTH COLLECTIBLES

This is a new category for me. Often I find things related to housekeeping that don't fit in elsewhere, so I've put them here. There are **Futurewatches** placed on appliance covers, aprons and pot holders.

Sewing tools are listed in the most simplistic way because it is a recognized separate field of collecting with a large number of old-time collectors and a number of very good books. Of the things included in my little chapter, thimbles are perhaps the most widely collected. I fancy sewing birds, but can't really afford them. I do have a small collection of 1920s and '30s diecut printed cardboard needle cases; the colors and the somewhat naive designs depicting happy people sewing, or tumbling kittens playing with spools of thread, are as charming as the much earlier trade cards of the 1880s, such as those that sold thread.

Figural things remain very important in the collecting world, and here it is tape measures shaped like real objects in miniature that best fulfill the desire for real shapes. (For buttons, the term is ''realies''.)

**TOC** = turn of century (about 1900).

Appliance cover, for a mixer, quilted white plastic vinyl with turquoise poodles in 3-D vinyl applique, ''E-Z Fit Mixmaster Cover'', no maker's name, 1950s. • Appliance covers are only distant cousins, thrice removed, to tea cosies whose purpose was not to disguise or costume the pot but to insulate it. • **Futurewatch.** — This unnamed company also caused to be made (probably abroad) a matching toaster cover & a ''Broilquick'' cover. The value I've assigned them may seem high, but these are now about 40 years old, they are highly emblematic of a period, they would not survive use & washing well; and in perfect condition they're rare. It's up to you to decide if you think they are also desirable! • Another type, from the same period and earlier, are such peculiarities as ''toaster dolls'', or cloth ''rag'' dolls — the skirts of which cover the toaster. **$5.00-$10.00**

Appliance cover, for a toaster, Black Americana appliqued & embroidered cotton cloth, ''Mammy'' with red polkadot dress, American, prob. 2nd quarter 20th C. • May have been commercially manufactured, or perhaps featured in a 1930s or 40s needlework magazine as a home craft project. **$35.00-$50.00**

Apron, blue & white check cloth, probably handwoven, long with short tie straps to be pinned to dress, 19th C. • **''A necessity in the kitchen,** because it is a great protection against clothes taking fire, is a large kitchen apron made full length with bib, and sleeves if wished, the skirt to button close around the dress-skirt. ... Have two large pockets in your kitchen apron, and in one of them always keep a [pot] holder.'' *Practical Housekeeping*, Minneapolis: 1884. • A better protection against the skirts catching fire was a skirt protector, like a fire screen for the fireplace, screening in a nearly waist-high metal frame with two lower side screens. The woman could stand in front of the fire inside the screen. This household convenience was offered in an F.A. Walker catalog of the 1870s. Apron: **$85.00-$100.00**

Apron, embroidered & appliqued cotton cloth, sunbonneted women, mid 20th C. • **Futurewatch.** — Aprons make a wonderful collection, and can even be matted and framed to hang on the wall. There are eight major categories: (1) Ethnic or costume aprons, not necessarily for the kitchen, (2) Souvenir aprons bearing the name and/or picture of a place or event, (3) Advertising aprons (which include those made from livestock feed sacks), (4) Joke, Motto or Legend-bearing aprons, (5) Made-to-pattern and/or magazine project aprons, (6) Homemade, one-of-a-kind aprons, (7) Men's aprons (many of which bear jokes or mottos), and (8) Professional chef or bartender aprons, which are the least collectible. Look for special details in applique motif or technique, decorative stitching & trim, amusing or evocative prints (especially those which are exemplary of fabric design for the period), oddly-shaped pockets, personalized designs, and one-of-a-kind designs, which at their best can be folk art. Condition of cloth, printing & trim is important to value. A neatly darned hole, however, may actually add to value as living proof of a thrifty soul. **$15.00-$20.00**

Apron, or coverall, cotton printed with adv'g message, ''Mother Hubbard Flour, Worth the Difference'' American, TOC. **$12.00-$20.00**

Apron, tucked & pleated white cotton, long length, crochet insert & scalloped hem, 1890s. **$25.00-$35.00**

Apron, white cotton, full skirt, wide tie, pinafore top with angel wing ruffles over the shoulders, white cotton, 2nd quarter 20th C. • How I wish I still had some of these flutterby pinafore aprons — some in printed calicos, some in old sheet material — that my mother wore in the 1940s. We always loved the Mary Petty cartoons, from the New Yorker, with upstairs and downstairs maids flying hither and thither, indoors & out, in these winged aprons. After I learned to iron napkins, I graduated to handkerchiefs, tablecloths and simple skirt aprons, and at last pinafore aprons, before finally reaching the summit (?) — at which time I was allowed to iron shirts and blouses. I recall ironing in the breakfast room, with the back door open and the sun coming in, listening to Arthur Godfrey and the Andrews Sisters. If ironing were as pleasant now as then, I would still love to iron. **$15.00-$22.00**

Buttonhole scissors, iron, marked ''Henry Sears & Son'', no place, & I couldn't find name in *Subject Index to Patents*. Pat'd 1865. **$30.00-$40.00**

Clothespin bags—See in Laundering chapter.

Darner, also called a darning egg. Black wooden egg, either ebony or bog oak, mounted to ornate hollow silver handle, like serving piece flatware handle, pattern may be recognizable to silverware experts, no mark except ''Sterling'', American, 6½''L, c.1880s to 1900. No matter how many scratches the needle makes on an ebony or bog oak egg, it remains black. Many imitation ebony darners, made of black-painted wood, were made in the same period; unless they've been fixed-up with black shoe polish, you can see the lighter wood where the egg is scratched. The ebony and bog oak ones also tend to be a bit heavier. Bog oak, by the way, is ancient oak in Ireland that has been immersed in dark peat bog water. It was a very popular material throughout the 19th C for decorative accessories. **$45.00-$65.00**

Darner, blown glass, very fancy with flower inside, loopy swirled colored handle, blue, pink, white & clear, no mark, English (?), 6''L. prob. early to mid 20th C. • See information on this type of glass under Rolling pins, in Mold chapter of my kitchen book. **$175.00-$225.00**

Darner, hollow cast brass egg head, openwork cast brass handle, head rather large relative to handle length, 6½''L, early 20th C (?). **$30.00-$45.00**

Darner, red & white plastic, casting seam long way around egg, shapely handle, American (?), prob. 1920s. **$15.00-$22.00**

Darner, turned wood handle, hollow egg-shaped wooden head, American, 7''L, 19th or 20th C. • There are many variations on this. Look for differences in color, and in turning of handle, & size of egg. **$12.00-$30.00**

Darner, turned wood, some bands on handle painted a la Mexican wares, Mexican (?), 1930s-40s. • Confusable with a small percussion instrument — a maraca, which should have a nearly round head, not an egg-shaped one. **$8.00-$12.00**

Darner, unusual gourd, somewhat egg shaped, dried, hollow with rattling seeds inside, turned wood handle with varnish overall, American, 8''L, late 19th or early 20th C. **$10.00-$18.00**

Dish towels—See Kitchen towel; also Tea towel.

Doily, crocheted cotton, reads "B R E A D", American (?), 10''L x 5''W, TOC. • A lot of old-fashioned crocheted food-related items are newly made. Nice, decent needlework, and if cotton, & washed a few times, I don't know how you'd know from old ones, which might go back to 1890s or so. Contemporary doilies, perhaps old in style, are sometimes made of synthetic fibers, or cotton blends. However, Chinese crocheted doilies in all cotton are common in craft & sewing shops. **$20.00-$30.00**

Doilies, paper lace, in various shapes & sizes, including round, oval, square, rectangular, & heart shaped, also paper lace tablecloths, all diecut paper, white, metallic gold or silver, or colored, usually also embossed, to give a feel of real lace, American, French, prob. German & English too, a few inches to at least 14'', as well as sizeable tablecloths, began 2nd quarter 18th C — for bon bons or Valentines. Still made. • Added value. — Prices would be highest for original stacks of doilies, still in original packages. There is great variety, and paper doilies look beautiful when framed against dark paper. This would be a great thing to collect when traveling, here and abroad. I recall from a 1965 trip that the dimestores in Munich were stocked with a huge variety of smalls, sundries and stationery supplies for everyday German life, and I bought many things. That would have been a great place for doilies. I usually try to stop at small five 'n dimes of the general store type still found in hundreds of small towns across America, if they look as if they have been there forever, and may have old stock. One such place in Maine yielded everything from 1940s oxfords and men's hats to cheap old toys. **50¢ to $10.00**

Doilies, washable plastic vinyl, very lacy and intricately diecut (or molded?), one ad claims theirs have 'the look and feel of fine lace'' (oh?), oval for a bread tray. Spelled doily or doilie or doiley; plural doilies. These particular ones made in Italy, but apparently marked only on a now-missing stick-on label. The bread tray size is 10''L x 5½''W, 1973 ad. • This ad lists 9 shapes & sizes: bread tray doily; serving tray doily 13'' x 9'' oval; cake plate doily 11'' diameter; place mat 18''L x 11½'' oval; place mat 16'' diameter round; place mat 17'' x 11'' oblong; table cloths 36'' and 48'' square and 50'' diameter round. The original price range was 59¢ to $5.99. This is definitely a **Futurewatch** situation! No matter what you think about plastic doilies on your table, there's no question that they are amazing tours de force from a manufacturing point of view, and are actually a very amusing use of plastic. I can't tell you how long they've been in production, nor where most of them have been made, but I suggest vinyl and paper doilies as a collectible. **25¢-$5.00**

Fabric & hem measurer, black painted metal, gold pinstriping, decal decorations, Measuregraph Co., St. Louis, MO, 1925. **$30.00-$40.00**

Feed sacks or bags, for chicken or livestock feed, colorfully printed sacks or bags of somewhat coarse cotton, supposed to have inspired farmers' wives to create colorful aprons, tablecloths, dresses, and pillow slips. Usually sort of calico prints, but also larger floral designs, the original paper labels just stuck on, American, various sizes, from 5 lbs up at least to 50 lbs, early 20th C., poss. late 19th. • Old bags or sacks may look fresh and rather new if unused, but more likely will be faded (from sun, washing or age), and will have stretch marks, or sag marks where weight of seed has stretched fibers of cloth. • See also clothespin bags & laundry bags in Laundering chapter. • **Reproduction alert.** — I thought that surely these wouldn't have enough money in them to reproduce, but it seems, from an ad in *Antique Trader*, May 3, 1989, that you can now buy ''Frontier Feed & Flour Bags. A fast selling item for crafters & seamstress. Reproductions of old bags in bright colors. 6 diff. designs $6 ea. Wholesale inquiries welcome. Oneida Chicken Scratch, Will-Hite Seed-Watermelon, Bewley's Best Flour, Frontier Beans, Race Horse Oats, and Hudson Cream Cow.'' The company who placed the ad is in Missouri. I'm quite surprised, as the startup costs for printing textiles (or paper, for that matter), is extraordinarily expensive, because each color gets a printing roller or plate, and all of it involves a lot of handling. • **Haute Purina.** — The March 1949 issue of *National Geographic Magazine,* has a picture of three young women in Memphis, TN, wearing capelet frocks made of feed sacks. Cotton printed with bunches of violets, bright red & yellow flowers, and a sort of blue dimity make up the dresses, while huge sacks of ''chow'' and ''laying mash'' are lined up behind the women, showing a green calico, a stripe, a purple calico, and a vivid floral print. See book published by Books Americana on the subject of feed bag clothing, etc. **$3.00-$18.00**

Hatchel, or hetchel or heckel for combing flax to remove seeds, chaff, etc., cutout wood repaired with old forged iron hardware including tulip hinge, mustard paint, hatchel spikes bound by 2 iron bands, this one without the box cover (that were made to slip securely over the spikes, and sometimes decorated like their hatchels), Pennsylvania (?), 32''L x 8''W board, early 19th C. • **German vocabulary** — Flachskamm: flax comb; also Hecheln: flax comb. **$275.00-$300.00**

Kitchen towel, also called a dish towel, Black Americana, appliqued cotton cloth, ''Mammy'' at stove, pancakes, etc., American, 20th C. **$20.00-$25.00**

Kitchen towel, linen, natural unbleached/undyed, wide woven border design in blue (also came in red, green & gold with natural), depicts a coal scuttle, a broom & dust pan, & a kerosene lamp. Irish, 30"L x 22"W, early 1930s. • At the same time you could buy a more moderne design, of a pair of stemmed glasses, a sort of Fiesta ware teapot, and a bull's-eye decorated china plate and cup woven into the panel. The original cost for these was $4.75 a dozen, which amazes me. Price range is for each. See also Tea towel.                    **$8.00-$12.00**

Maids' uniforms, long or short sleeved dresses, of various materials — to quote from a Macy's 1931 ad: "broadcloth, chambray, rayon, crepe de chine or Celanese acetate", mostly fitted, with a trim set (collar & cuffs) and apron to contrast or match. One fancy long-sleeved depicted uniform is black crepe de chine, with a gored skirt, pointed white lace cuffs & deep pointed collar (pinned or basted on, as they were washed every day), with black taffeta apron. The apron hem & the dress's bodice have 6 or 7 rows of closely-spaced stitching, all in all a very handsome outfit originally costing $16.00. An acetate one has an embroidered organdy apron, cuffs & collar, even a cap. Colors available were black, green, blue, grey & lavendar; sizes up to 46. American, 1931 *House & Garden* ad. • **Decoratively Maid.** — Wealthy people in maid-surfeited households liked their staff to look sharp, even match the decor. These "Costumes of the hour for well-dressed Maids" are sometimes found in thrift shops, especially in large cities. I once found a bundle of about 10 trim sets — embroidered organdy cuffs and collars — together with a few aprons, still starched to the hilt. Occasionally you will find the older, more interesting uniforms for sale through vintage clothing dealers. • A company who manufactured uniforms, Oliver A. Olson, advertised "Delightfully Different Maids' Uniforms & Accessories", and you could request a "Portfolio of 'Modish Maids Wear' for free. (NOTE: That printed portfolio of designs would probably be worth $35.00 or more by itself!) Olson's Feb.1929 *House Beautiful* ad makes funny reading. They claimed their outfits "gracefully solve the problem of correct attire of your maids. For true harmony in the color scheme of your house beautiful — Olson offers charming uniforms and accessories in all the modern colors. Or to add a note of cheerfulness and quiet distinctiveness to a tea or bridge party, a costume of soft washable silk in a new shade of brown, orchid or perhaps green for the serving maid finds great favor among smart women everywhere." • The 2 value ranges are (1) collar, cuffs & apron, (2) dresses alone.        **$3.00-$20.00, $5.00-$50.00**

Napkin, white linen damask, Illinois Central RR's logo woven in center, 19" x 19", 20th C.        **$5.00-$8.00**

Needlecase, cardboard printed in black on orange, cut in shape of salt box, adv'g "Worcester Iodized Salt", 3"Lx1 3/4" W, 20th C.        **$10.00-$12.50**

Needlecase, diecut cardboard in shape of kitchen range,adv'g "Buy a Household Range", 3" x 4", 20th C.        **$12.00-$18.00**

Paper napkins, 48 in original cardboard box, cocktail size, soft-feeling cream-colored creped paper, scalloped diecut edges, printed with borders & rather widely spaced polkadots, an assortment of red, green, yellow & blue dots, European, early 1930s. For all:        **$2.00-$5.00**

Placemats, 2 hammered aluminum oblongs, very shiny & reflective, with narrow bands of copper at each end, American, 18"L, 1930s.        **$12.00-$15.00**

Pot holder, appliqued cat's head, very fanciful, c.1930s.        **$7.00-$10.00**

Pot holder, appliqued cloth, blue & white gingham around edge, white cotton center, red stitching, a clock face with every other numeral, tab hanger at top, 5" diameter. Pattern appeared for this in Summer 1941 McCall's Needlework magazine. • In the same how-to article appeared a wonderful cozy little armchair-shaped pot holder of calico. Also a great man's shirt with red tie, the sleeves and shirt tails forming irregular outline on basic round shape. I've never seen either one, but would like to!        **$7.00-$10.00**

Pot holder, appliqued cotton, hearts and diamonds, red & green on white, brass hanging ring at corner, c.1930s.        **$5.00-$7.00**

Pot holder, appliqued cotton, pig motif, 20th C.        **$10.00-$12.00**

Pot holder, appliqued & cutout felt, very odd, or rather Amish, color combinations, which are modern in appearance, cotton flannel backing, all bound in red cotton tape, c.1880s to 1890s.        **$25.00-$30.00**

Pot holder, appliqued in layers & embroidered, Black man's face, with frayed fringe hair, red wool jersey lips, white jersey eyes, flappy ears, not a nice caricature, but interesting handicraft in Black Americana mode, 8" diameter, c.1890s to 1910s.        **$90.00-$110.00**

Pot holder, bargello needlepoint, backed with printed cotton, geometric pattern, c.1880s.        **$13.00-$15.00**

Pot holder, Black Americana needlepoint with simple depiction of a dancing black man & woman who nearly fill the space, also "Any holder but a Slave holder", • Made for Frederick Douglass by Lena Irish, 5½"H x 6½"W, mid 19th C. • Dealer Bernie McManus, Woodbury House, Woodbury, CT, offered this punning piece in 1985, along with a manuscript letter by Douglass. •In Feb. 1989,Windham Antiques in Shepherdstown, WV, advertised a "potholder by freed slave (NC, circa 1865), red, black, white cross-stitch on gray wool (Confederate uniform), red" binding and hanging loop. It has a dancing Black man and woman very small in center, and the same motto, but with all 6 words with initial capital letters, and measures 5½" x 6". • Price range mine, after trying to separate out the pot holder from the letter, which on the autograph market might bring many thousands of dollars. The "Douglass" pot holder:        **$350.00-$450.00**

Pot holder, chicken with upstanding head, to use for grasping handle of teapot (wings to fold around the handle), mustard & ochre cotton sateen, green floss knots around neck, blue eyes, Mennonite, 5⅜" diameter, c.1900.        **$95.00-$140.00**

Pot holder, cotton, Black Americana theme of cook or chef, American, 1940s or so.        **$18.00-$22.00**

Pot holder, crazy quilt silk & satin, probably for parlor use while pouring tea or coffee, c.1870s to late 19th C.        **$18.00-$22.00**

Pot holder, crocheted cotton, caricature face of an Oriental, yellow with red lips & black hair, pigtail braided & attached, 6" diameter, c.1930s to 1940.        **$7.00-$10.00**

Pot holder, crocheted cotton in white with red outlines, shaped like little house with colored windows & door, crocheted hanging ring is chimney, about 5″H, patterns for these advertised 1940-41.                    $7.00-$10.00

Pot holder, crocheted cotton, round, with appliqued flowers & leaves crocheted separately from red, green & yellow cotton. Hanging ring of metal. American, 6″ diameter, c.1930s-40s.                          $6.00-$12.00

Pot holder, embroidered cotton, depicts a house, c.1920s-30s.                              $20.00-$25.00

Pot holder, fine needlepoint on canvas, one side is a rebus with ombre shaded lettering in red on green background, with black kettle picture, reads ''Genie put the (kettle) on & we will all take tea'', obverse has flowers, vases, dog, cat, scissors & a wreath on black background, English (?), 5″ x 4 ³⁄₁₆″, c.1860s to 1880s. • Being a rebus collector, this attracted my attention immediately. It is a fine piece of needlework, as well as being a puzzle, and appeals to various kinds of collectors.          $100.00-$150.00

Pot holder, for handle of parlor teapots, velvet parrot without wings, only body, tail & simple head with beak, body folds over the handle, green velvet with pale tan silk lining, embroidered with mother of pearl button eyes, poss. English, certainly High Victorian, 7″L, c.1880s-90s. • Another one, an inch longer, was teal blue velvet with beige silk lining.                    $30.00-$45.00

Pot holder, for teapot in parlor, needlepoint in dark green & red, brown polished cotton backing, design is a rebus poem, pictures given here in parens: ''Except the (Tea Kettle) Boiling (B), Filling the (Tea Pot) Spoils the (T)'', prob. American, close to 6″ square, c.1830s to 1850s. • **Reproduction alert — a Craft Lookalike.** — In the Feb. 1925 *House Beautiful* there is a short piece on using a commercial pattern to make a cross stitch (or maybe needlepoint?) pot holder with this rebus puzzle motif. The illustration with the column is so clear that a clever needleworker could make her own pattern, which would account for some slight variations. The editor writes, [We bring you a] ''canvas pattern for a teapot holder which I am sure many of you will enjoy doing in cross-stitch. It is a pattern which our Grandmothers used, and I have one at home in crimson wool, with the figures in black, which is very old. The work is of the simplest, and I should think little girls would like to make these useful bits of needlework. The pattern itself is 6 inches square, and it is priced .35 cents.'' Old ones:          $85.00-$125.00

Pot holder, knitted or crocheted (?) thick cotton yarn, red & green, with interesting wiggly woven look to top side, brass hanging ring sewed on corner, 4″ x 4″, c.1920s.                              $5.00-$8.00

Pot holder, needlepoint, pink, red & blue, design of tree of life, printed brown calico backing, Mennonite, 5⅜″ x 5 ⅝″, c.1870s.                          $45.00-$55.00

Pot holder, printed cotton & muslin butterfly, the wings to be folded around the handle, 6″W wingspread, c.1920s.                              $5.00-$7.00

Pot holder, tan wool flannel, red cotton tape binding, tiny red braid machine stitched in floral pattern on front, back plain, (another example done on gray wool flannel), supposed to be Amish, c.1880s to 1890s. • **Reproduction alert.** — I heard in 1989 that some immigrants from India who settled in Pennsylvania are sewing things that are being sold as Amish. I don't know if they are using old cast off materials, or things bought in thrift stores, or new fabrics. **More Repros — March**

**1992 update:** The Washington Post. 3/19/92, had important long article on quilt reproductions. It has info on applique work being done in PA, and elsewhere, by hundreds of Laotian Hmong immigrants, for Amish & Mennonite shops. Also, using American fabrics, some 500,000 pillow shams & rugs are made each year in People's Republic of China, many as repros, for sale in the USA.          $15.00-$18.00

Pot holder rack, plywood cutout, Black Americana theme, a painted ''Mammy'' with blue & white gingham checked apron & kerchief of cloth, white thumbtack eyes, paper glued-on lips, thumbtacks in legs to hold 2 pot holders, American, 7″H, ¼″ thick ply, c.1940s.          $18.00-$22.00

Quilt clamp, forged iron variant of a C clamp, very decorative whitesmith work, hammered, polished & cut, with heart-like thumb piece for screw clamp part, American, about 4½″H, 3″ throat, early 19th C. • The simplest bring close to bottom of value range. Fancy ones, especially with animalistic forms or specially shaped thumb screws would bring up to 10 times the top value.          $35.00-$70.00

Sewing bird, also called a hemming bird or a gripper, cast iron, fine smooth finish, screw clamps to table, bird's wings out & swept back, very pointed figure, parrot-like beak, no mark, American, 4⅝″H, mid 19th C. • Robacker May 1989 price at auction:          $175.00

Sewing bird, cast bell metal or bronze (?), screw clamp with Roman-type acanthus leaf along back, bird has wings out & swept back, parrot-like beak, red plush cushion on back, American (?), 6½″H, bird is 3¾″L, mid 19th C. • One of the differences you start to notice, besides the metal used, is in the **birds' beaks** — some longish & pointed, like a sparrow, swallow or canary, some short and slightly hooked like a parrot. Canaries were very popular birds in the 19th C, and perhaps the yellow brass so often used was meant to resemble a yellow canary's plumage.          $185.00-$235.00

Sewing bird, cast iron, a bit chunky, painted with daubs of metallic gold & yellow on wings and head, plain clamp, American, mid 19th C to 3rd quarter.          $175.00-$225.00

Sewing bird, cast iron, duck's or swan's head with looped neck, screw clamps to table, American (?), approx. 4″H, c.1870s.                          $200.00-$350.00

Sewing bird, cast iron, sleek wings slightly out and swept back, knurled knob for screw clamp, no pincushion, prob. PA, 4¼″H, bird 3⅝″L, c.1840s-60s.          $200.00-$350.00

Sewing bird, cast & machined brass, very small, upturned curve to body, wings out & swept back, screw clamps to table, American, mid 19th C. • **Reproduction alert.** — According to *Schroeder's Price Guide for 1990*, a brass sewing bird has been reproduced in the late 1980s. I have no other information.          $160.00-$200.00

Sewing bird, cast & stamped brass, screw clamps to table, a couchant (head up, but reclining) curly-haired dog (retriever?), original red velvet pincushion along back, mouth is clamp to hold material, heart cutout thumb screw, American, c.1870s. • This dog & pincushion, with the clamp missing, was for sale at a 1989 show for over $600.00. But it was that kind of show.          $300.00-$400.00

Sewing bird, forged iron screw clamp, stamped 3-D bird with forked tail, hollow body, no wings, American, mid 19th C.                          $160.00-$200.00

Sewing bird, ornate cast brass clamp, with ''fire gilt'' brass very detailed bird, many feathers in detail, wings out and swept back, red plush pincushion with pedestal, American, mid 19th C. • **Fire gilding** is a term that usually refers to plating silver with gold. This is also called wash gilding or mercury gilding, & is accomplished by painting a mercury and gold amalgam [mixture] on the surface, then heating so as to cause the mercury to leave, with a thin gold "wash" bonded to the surface. The term is used, although perhaps not accurately, for lightly gilded brass called gilt latten.                    **$160.00-$200.00**

Sewing bird, polished or planished iron, slender bird like a swallow, wings close to body, thumb screw is heart shaped, no pincushion, just a leaf spring between clamp & body so when you press down on the tail, the beak opens to hold cloth, American, about 2 3/8"L beak to tail, early 19th C, prob. c.1820s.          **$200.00-$275.00**

Sewing bird, stamped brass with fine detail of feathers on top, sides & underneath, swept back delicate wings, silvery plated finish, probably nickel, 2 red velvet or plush pincushions in different sizes: larger one below the very slender bird's breast, tiny one in middle of back, (another was found with old black cotton pincushions on back & under breast, possible replacements of early date), not marked with his name, but design patented by C. Waterman, Meriden, CT, 5⅛"H overall, bird 3¾"L, pat'd Feb. 15, 1853. • I have also seen this stamped out of another sheet metal (probably tin), with a gilded finish, a very brummagem *golden yellow, easily distinguished from polished brass, and only slightly less easily-distinguished from lacquered brass, if the lacquer has any yellow color in it. See bottom of page.          **$250.00-$300.00**

Sewing bird, stamped & cast metal, fancy screw clamp, 2 pincushions — on back & below breast — in blue cloth, approx. 5"H, dated 1867, but I can't find one listed in *Patent Index* with that date. • In fact, the only four "sewing-bird" patents in the 1790 to 1873 *Subject Index to Patent*, are definitely "mid century". Viz. (1) C. Waterman, Meriden, CT, Feb. 15, 1853, design patent 546; (2) J. North, Middletown, CT, May 29, 1853, des. pat. 710; (3) J. E. Merriman, Meriden, CT, July 26, 1853, design pat. 582 (despite later date); and (4) A. Gerould & J. H. Ward, Middletown, CT, Aug. 2, 1853, design pat. 589. Connecticut was the center of the stamped, machined & cast brass smalls industry, so it is to be assumed that these patents were all for brass birds. Mr. Merriman also got a regular (as opposed to a design) patent for a sewing bird on Feb. 7, 1854, #10,509.          **$145.00-$175.00**

Sewing bird, wrought iron, dog instead of usual bird, screw clamps to work table, English or American, about 3½"H, 19th C. • The Smithsonian's Museum of American History on the Mall in Washington has a case full of sewing birds.          **$200.00-$275.00**

Sewing box, wood, mustard grain painting, 2 hinged lids on either side of carved centerboard, which has heart cutouts, little turned knobs on lids, Amish, prob. PA, 4"H exclusive of centerboard x 13½"L x 9½"W, c.1870s to 1880s. • The dealer called this a sewing box, but it looks just like a cutlery box; perhaps the dealer knew for sure.          **$500.00-$600.00**

Sewing clamp, turned wood, screw clamps to work table edge to hold fabric, American (?), 2½"L, 19th C.          **$40.00-$55.00**

*Brummagem** is a corruption of word Birmingham. Brummagem goods, of cheap gilded brass, were made for centuries in Great Britain's brass capital, Birmingham.

Show towel, cross-stitched linen, embroidered in red and blue with Tree of Life motif and other designs, made not for use but as a show piece just for sche, and typically hung on a door to display its full length, name "Ramsey Happel", PA German, dated 1832.          **$465.00-$600.00**

Tablecloth, blue damask, flowers & ribbon band border, 48" x 48", late 19th or early 20th C.          **$40.00-$50.00**

Tablecloth, colorfully-printed cotton, Black Americana images of small children playing banjos, "Mammy" with a chicken, cotton boll border design, c. 1930s. Old stereotypes & cliches extending well into the 20th C.          **$40.00-$50.00**

Tablecloth, cotton, red & white woven check, some small neatly-darned patches, 12 feet long — good for church picnics or large family reunions, early 20th C.          **$40.00-$50.00**

Tablecloth, cotton printed with poinsettias and other Christmas motifs, 72" x 56", 1940s or 1950s.          **$18.00-$22.00**

Tablecloth, cream-colored Quaker lace, 70" x 55", TOC.          **$65.00-$80.00**

Tablecloth, cutwork damask, white linen with green floral border, 12 matching napkins, 85" x 55", 19th C. • **1892 Damask Pattern Names.** — J. N. Richardson, Sons, & Owden, Ltd., of NYC, advertised in the Dry Goods section of *Century Magazine*, August 1892, "a few of the Patterns to which the attention of Purchasers is specially directed" in their "Richardson's Damask Table Cloth" line. They are all British made, with a trademark of a rampant lion, and were said to be "Designs by the Best Artists … Woven in their own Looms and Bleached on their own Greens." The 28 patterns and their design numbers are listed below, all spellings as in the ad. • No. 941. *Black Thorn;* 944. *Jessamine;* 764. *Wild Rose, Asparagus, Bignonia;* 769 *Chrysanthemum and Acacia;* 509. *Rose and Fern;* 531. *Gothic 534; Early English;* 550½. *Hibiscus and Tiger Flower;* 852. *Primrose;* 860. *Persian;* 861. *Flax;* 862. *Palm and Stephanotis;* 863. *Wheat;* 869. *Autumn Fruit;* 964. *Passion Flower, Rose and Palm;* 574. *Birds and Fishes;* 578. *Japanese;* 583. *Pompeian;* 883. *Mistletoe and Oak;* 975. *Egyptian;* 976½. *Assyrian;* 979. *Moire Antique;* 598 7/8. *Classic Greek;* 598. *Egyptian Water Lily;* 607. *Japanese Fans;* 608. *Australian Plants and Birds;* 620. *Arum Lily;* 24E. *Rose, Shamrock and Thistle.* • Although numbers go up into the 900s, and a few are followed by fractional numbers, we can't assume there were 900 + choices of patterns. For cloth & napkins:          **$120.00-$250.00**

ching napkins, Irish, 74" x 55", 20th C.          **$75.00-$125.00**

Tablecloth, damask dinner cloth, white, with name woven right into center, "Burlington Route" Railroad, American, 50" x 40", 20th C.          **$18.00-$25.00**

Tablecloth, damask, heavy dark rusty orange ground with salmon colored border, monogram mark in border, "U P R R" (Upper Peninsula Rail Road), 40" square, 20th C.          **$15.00-$20.00**

Tablecloth, damask, peach colored cotton, with center monogram design, with 2 napkins in white, "Illinois Central Railroad", 42" x 36", 20th C.          **$18.00-$25.00**

Tablecloth, damask, pink & white with border of dominoes & checkers, then larger border of children playing, girl holding doll, with 4 matching napkins, American (?), smaller than card table size, for child's tea party table, late 19th C to c.1910s.          **$100.00-$200.00**

Tablecloth, damask, turkey red cotton with fringe, fruit & flower design in white, reversible, very silky, 19th C.          **$125.00-$140.00**

Tablecloth, damask, white with name forming decorative design, "Rio Grande Railroad", 42" x 36", 20th C. **$18.00-$25.00**

Tablecloth, embroidered white cotton with blue & white chain-stitched teapot & teacups, 4 matching napkins, American (?), a little bit bigger than card table size, early 20th C. **$30.00-$45.00**

Tablecloth, feed sack printed cotton, made from wonderful colorful old sack, depicts happy chickens, eggs, wicker basket, "Nutrena Egg Mash", c.1920s to 1940s. **$20.00-$40.00**

Tablecloth, filet lace, 72" x 55", TOC. **$35.00-$50.00**

Tablecloth, handwoven linen, cream color, two 120"L x 30"W bands sewn together side by side, mid 19th C. • Still as lively feeling as when it was made, if not more so. Nothing like oft-washed heavy old linen. **$45.00-$60.00**

Tablecloth, Jacquard weave cotton, navy & white Greek Key border design, nice overall floral pattern, not a formal cloth, but extremely handsome, 90" x 90", 19th or early 20th C. **$60.00-$70.00**

Tablecloth, lace on netting, floral design, ecru color, 64" x 48", TOC. **$45.00-$60.00**

Tablecloth, printed cotton, map of California with all the tourists' sights, c.1940s. **$15.00-$22.00**

Tablecloth, printed cotton, map of Florida with all the sights, multi-color on white ground, souvenir of Florida, 48" x 48", c.1940s. • A collection could be made of **map tablecloths,** depicting states, cities, parks & natural wonders. **$15.00-$18.00**

Tablecloth, printed linen, with 6 matching napkins, colorful depictions of a square dance & farm, 54" x 54", c.1930s-50s. **$40.00-$50.00**

Tape measure, champagne bottle in cooler figural, wind-up, c.1880. **$160.00-$180.00**

Tape measure, coffee mill figural, homemade of cardboard, covered with brown satin, wire & wood crank in top coming out of hopper, which is cardboard, cloth tape comes out of slot in one side, American, 1 1/4" square, 1880s. **$18.00-$25.00**

Tape measure, Hoover vacuum cleaner figural, plastic, spring wound, 20th C. • There are hundreds of figural & fancy tape measures; the only ones represented here are figurals relating to the rest of our kitchen & closet & household chores field. **$45.00-$60.00**

Tape measure, lithographed metal, adv'g "General Electric" refrigerators, 20th C. **$12.00-$15.00**

Tape measure, lithographed metal, adv'g "Frigidaire", 20th C. **$20.00-$28.00**

Tape measure, plastic, adv'g "G E Vacuum Cleaners", 20th C. **$25.00-$30.00**

Tape measure, sadiron figural, TOC. **$135.00-$150.00**

Tape measure, sewing machine shape, wind-up, 1880s. **$80.00-$100.00**

Tape measure, tea kettle figural, TOC. **$20.00-$25.00**

Tea cosies — Old ones from the 19th C as well as those made before the 1940s are collectible. They are made from all kinds of cloth, mainly cotton or wool, and are usually padded (like quilts) with some kind of felting or batting. Best are those with unusual designs or nifty stitches. **"Tea-Pot Cosey.** — The English cosey for covering the tea-pot to keep it hot, is a great comfort, and can be made of any thick material. The handsomest are of silk sateen, with a border of plush, but for ordinary uses, those of cloth or smooth flannel are best. The shape resembles a cap, and the size is governed by that of the tea-pot it is to cover. The cosey can be decorated with embroidery or with Japanese figures in bright colors cut from cretonne, and transferred upon dark flannel. Others have merely lettering, as 'Take a cup and drink it up, and call the neighbors in,' or 'The cup that cheers, but not inebriates.' For the lining cut out two caps of chamois, the same size as the cloth, baste a layer of cotton on these, and afterward join all together at the bottom of the cosey." American Agriculturist, Jan. 1885. • For most cosies: **$15.00-$35.00**

Tea towel, embroidered blue & white check cloth, outline of several dishes with word "DISHES", American, early 20th C. **$10.00-$20.00**

Tea towel, embroidered white damask, depicts a knife, fork & spoon outlined in red chain stitch, American, early 20th C. See also Kitchen towels. **$10.00-$20.00**

Thimble, aluminum, "Frigidaire", 20th C. **$4.00-$5.00**

Thimble, blue plastic with black lettering, adv'g "Sunbeam Bread with a Bonus", 20th C. **$2.00-$2.50**

Thimble, silver, very small — child size, embossed "For a Good Girl", mid 19th C. **$8.00-$15.00**

Thimble case, small wooden rolling pin, "Mrs. Love", early 19th C. Possibly a sailor's love token. **$75.00-$100.00**

Yardage estimator, metal, wood, in original box, "Putnam", (probably Putnam Die Co., St. Charles, MO), early 20th C. **$15.00-$20.00**

Yarn winder, fabulous, spectacular cast iron precision tool, painted black with gold stenciling, mounted to flat base, a sort of ferris wheel, with high upside down L-bracket, curved brace, and the wheel with 6 rods with wide ends screwed on, short crank out from axle of revolving "wheel", mfd by Brown & Sharpe, the tool-makers, Providence, RI, about 16"H, 19th C. • I've seen only a picture, in May 1989 Maine Antique Digest, of Clair Dounoucos' of Schenectady, NY, show booth. Her price was $285.00. Seems below the money. **$285.00-$500.00**

**IV-1.**
**Aprons.**
Clockwise from top (L): (1) Heavy linen tea room apron, with long streamer ties, edges trimmed with white rickrack. Small pocket on both sides of skirt, making the apron reversible. (2) Heavy linen reversible apron with pin-back waistband. 27"L from waist. (3) Linen full-length apron, pockets inside & out making it reversible. 38"L x 44"W. (4) and (5) White cotton soda & tea room aprons, with streamer ties. Pointed bottom one 17"L; pleated one, 18"L. Not reversible. All from Albert Pick-Barth Co. hoteliers supply catalog, 1929.    **$4.00-$6.00**

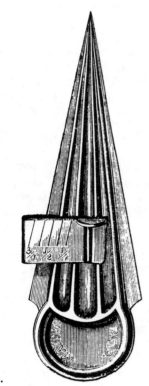

**IV-3.**
**Bottonhole cutter.**
"Graduated" cutter, corrugated steel blade shaped like an arrowhead, one cutting edge. "When used, the gauge is placed on the cutter, at a point where the blade is as wide as the hoe to be cut. The point of the cutter is then placed on the cloth, at the spot where the hole is to begin, and pressed through the cloth. The one sharp edge will cut away from the point of beginning until the gauge touches the cloth. Any-sized holes—from the smallest one needed for a doll's pinafore (if they are to wear pinafores this season) to the biggest hole required for a pea-jacket of a stevedore—can be cut by this." Hearth & Home, 10/21/1871.
**$5.00-$10.00**

**IV-2.**
**Apron.**
Blue chain-stitch picture on white cotton, of sunbonneted girl hanging clothes on line. Small drawing below shows style of apron and placement of embroidery. 1920s-30s.    **$8.00-$12.00.**

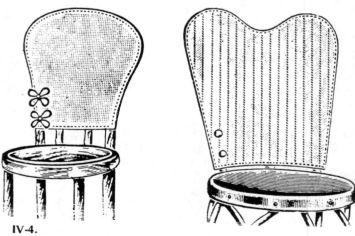

**IV-4.**
**Chair back covers,**
actually meant for restaurants, ice cream parlors and tea shops, but found in homes too. (L) Heavy white duckcloth for wire-back or bentwood chairs, with decorative ties. (This was also available in heavy muslin and in blue, rose, tan, gray or green muslin.) (R) Striped damask, two-tone ecru color, with buttons. For bow-back wire chairs or bentwood chairs. Pick-Barth Co. catalog, 1929.
**$5.00-$10.00**

# Queen Stocking Darner

Nickel-plated steel spring ring holds stocking or other fabric firmly in place, and does not require readjusting until work is completed. The darning surface is 2¼ inches in diameter and slightly convexed---just the proper shape for doing good work. Made of light colored wood and finely finished. Price....... **15 Cents**

**Postage 5 cents extra**

**IV-5.**
**Stocking darner.**
"Queen." Turned wood with nickeled spring steel ring to slip over once the stocking is pulled on. These rings are usually missing. A.E.Rayment Co., Rockford, IL, c.1910-20 catalog. **$7.00-$12.00**

**IV-6.**
**Glove darner.**
Silverplated metal with two different-sized tips. 4 1/2"L. Could be engraved with owner's name. Theodore A. Kohn & Son, Jewelers, NYC, c.1890. **$7.00-$15.00**

**IV-7.**
**Paper lace doily.**
"Cluny" lace pattern, square in five sizes (5", 6", 8", 10", 12"). Original cost was from 26¢ to $1.00 per gross. In D.J. Barry, NYC, 1924 jobber's catalog of hotel supplies. **5¢-$5.00**

## VINYL LACE DOILIES AND PLACE MATS
### THE LOOK AND FEEL OF FINE LACE • WASHABLE • MADE IN ITALY

| | | | |
|---|---|---|---|
| Bread tray size | 5½"x10" | .59 | (2-S1.00) ppd. |
| Serving " " | 9"x13" oval | .79 | (2-S1.50) ppd. |
| Cake plate " | 11" rd | .79 | (2-S1.50) ppd. |
| Place mat oval | 11½"x18" | 4-S3.99 | (8-S7.50)* |
| Place mat rd | 16" | 4-S3.99 | (8-S7.50)* |
| Place mat oblong | 11"x17" | 4-S3.99 | (8-S7.50)* |
| Table cloth | 36" sq. | $3.99* | |
| Table cloth | 50" round | $5.99* | |
| Table cloth | 48" square | $5.99* | |

*Send 50c post. for Place Mat and Table Cloth Orders
No C.O.D.'s  Fla res. add 4% tax.

P.O. BOX 667    SUSAN-LYNN DESIGNS    HALLANDALE, FLA. 33009

**IV-8.**
**Vinyl lace doily or placemat.**
White vinyl, embossed, washable. In various sizes—from bread tray size (5 1/2" x 10") to various other ovals (placement is 11 1/2" x 18") and oblongs. Also tablecloths, 36" and 48" square and 50" round. Made in Italy. Advertised in House Beautiful, 4/1973. **50¢-$5.00**

**IV-9.**
**Doily.**
Very fine linen, silk embroidery in shades of purple & lavender, and hand-made aria-type lace. 12 1/2"W edging. Late 19th or early 20th C. **$10.00-$28.00**

**IV-10.**
**Doily.**
Natural fine linen with scalloped edge finished by sewing machine, but with hand embroidery in shades of green & scarlet. 10 1/2" square. Early 20th C. **$5.00-$12.00**

GLASS TOWEL

UNION HUCK TOWEL

ALL COTTON TOWEL

DAMASK TOWEL

**IV-11.**
**Kitchen towels.**
Irish linen, Jacquard designs woven in color on natural ground. Blue, gold, green or red designs. "If yours is a modern cookery choose the towel with border of glass and chinaware." The bottom one, with coal scuttle, dustpan & whisk broom, and tin lantern, "is for a provincial setting." Maison de Linge ad in House & Gardens, 6/1933. **$7.00-$15.00**

**IV-13.**
**Kitchen towels.**
Counterclockwise from top (L). (1) Woven linen red or blue border design, meant for drying glasswares. 21" x 29". (2) Called in the catalog a "Union Huck" towel. "Huck" refers to the biscuit weave of the cloth. Half linen & half cotton, with red woven border. For drying dishes. Three sizes: 17" x 32"; 20" x 38"; and 22" x 44". (3) Jacquard- woven damask towel with long fringe, red & white threads. Came in all linen, or half linen, half cotton threads. Four sizes, from 19" x 39" to 23" x 48". (4) Cotton towel with fancy neo-classical woven border in red. "It may also be used as a dresser or table cover." 20" x 38". All from Albert Pick & Co. catalog of 1909. **$2.00-$25.00**

**IV-12.**
**Kitchen curtains.**
So far I've found six panels—in matched sets of 4 and 2, done by different hands. Evidently following a pattern from a magazine, which I wish I could find. White cotton, dark blue cotton bird facing yellow bird. Embroidered beaks, eyes & topknots, with chain-stitched legs & feet. Made from long narrow strips, some cut in curves, some straight. Actual size 9"L. 1930s-40s. **$5.00-$15.00**

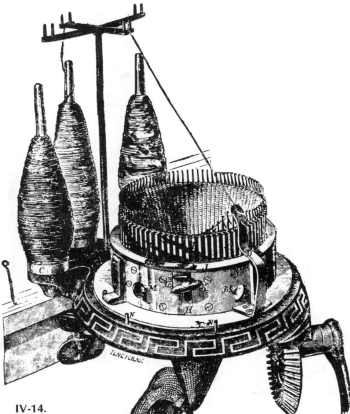

**IV-14.**
**Knitting machine.**
*"The Bickford Family Knitting Machine," mfd. by D. Bickford, Boston & NYC. Japanned cast iron, steel, clamps top table edge, cranked. Used for knitting stockings and mainly simple knit goods, "from a watch cord to a bed blanket." Bickford held at least four knitting-machine patents—dated 9/10/1867; 7/21/1868; 7/6/1869 and 9/17/1872—as well as some related patents. This as from* American Agriculturist, *7/1871.* **$25.00-$50.00**

**Bickford Family Knitter.**
Knits everything required by the household, of any quality, texture and weight desired. Sold on installments. Pair of small stockings sent on receipt of 10 cents.
**A. M. LAWSON.**
**783 BROADWAY, N.Y.**
[Mention HOUSEWIFE.]

**IV-15.**
**Knitting machine.**
*Also the "Bickford Family Knitter," but as it appeared in an ad 20 years later from* The Housewife, *7/1891. Other knitting machines were made; and there are over 300 machine patents prior to 1873.* **$25.00-$50.00**

**IV-16.**
**Maids' uniforms or apron dresses.**
*Flapper styles for maids or waitresses. (L) Wraparound colored cotton with contrasting trim. (M) Buttonless V-neck pullover apron dress, also in choice of navy, French gray, old rose or natural tan color, with detachable belt that is pinned on. Heavy natural color linen or white twill. All came in three sizes: small, medium & large. Pick-Barth catalog, 1929.* **$4.00-$10.00**

**IV-17.**
**Maids' uniforms.**
*A lot more stylish. (L) Celanese acetate dress with set-in belt & embroidered organdy apron & cap set (originally $8.94 and $7.94). (M) Crepe de chine, yoke front, gored skirt, and taffeta apron with stitching. (Original cost, $11.94 and $3.69.) (R) Rayon dress with gored skirt and point d'esprit apron & cap (originally cost $5.54 & $2.74). All available in black or green; middle one also in gray; left one also in blue. Macy's, NYC, ad in* House & Gardens, *3/1931.* **$3.00-$20.00**

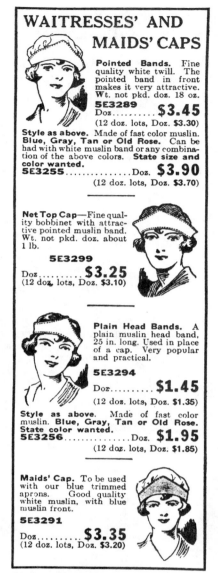

# WAITRESSES' AND
# MAIDS' CAPS

**Pointed Bands.** Fine quality white twill. The pointed band in front makes it very attractive. Wt. not pkd. doz. 18 oz.

**5E3289**
Doz......... **$3.45**
(12 doz. lots, Doz. $3.30)

**Style as above.** Made of fast color muslin. Blue, Gray, Tan or Old Rose. Can be had with white muslin band or any combination of the above colors. **State size and color wanted.**
**5E3255**.............Doz. **$3.90**
(12 doz. lots, Doz. $3.70)

**Net Top Cap**—Fine quality bobbinet with attractive pointed muslin band. Wt. not pkd. doz. about 1 lb.

**5E3299**
Doz......... **$3.25**
(12 doz. lots, Doz. $3.10)

**Plain Head Bands.** A plain muslin head band, 25 in. long. Used in place of a cap. Very popular and practical.

**5E3294**
Doz......... **$1.45**
(12 doz. lots, Doz. $1.35)

**Style as above.** Made of fast color muslin. Blue, Gray, Tan or Old Rose. **State color wanted.**
**5E3256**.............Doz. **$1.95**
(12 doz. lots, Doz. $1.85)

**Maids' Cap.** To be used with our blue trimmed aprons. Good quality white muslin, with blue muslin front.

**5E3291**
Doz......... **$3.35**
(12 doz. lots, Doz. $3.20)

**IV-18.**
**Maids' or waitresses' caps.**
*From Pick-Barth catalog, 1929.*                $1.00-$2.00

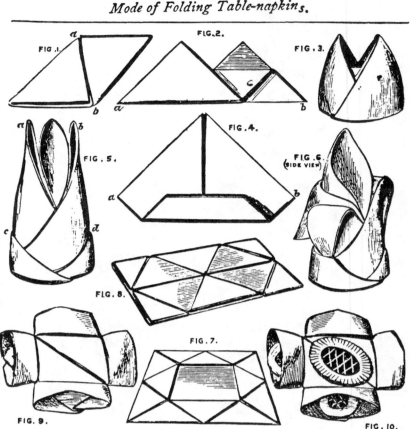

*Mode of Folding Table-napkins.*

*To Fold the Mitre.*—The napkin must be folded in three, thus :—Fold one third over, turn it *backwards*, and thus make the three folds. Fold both ends to meet in the middle. Take the left-hand corner, *a*, and fold it across in a right angle. Take the opposite corner, *b*, on the left hand at the top, and fold it in the same manner ; you will thus form figure 1. Turn over and fold in halves lengthwise ; open the points, and you will have figure 2. Bend the point, *a*, towards the right, and tuck it in the groove, *c* ; turn the point, *b*, backwards towards the right hand, and tuck it in as at *a* ; you will then have figure 3—The Mitre.

*The Water Lily.*—Have a square napkin and fold it like a half handkerchief. Then take the two opposite points and make them meet on the centre one, which forms a square. Take the bottom corner, opposite the points, and roll it up as at figure 4. Turn the napkin over, and roll point *a* to about the centre. Take point *b*, and tuck it in the groove ; raise it, and you have figure 5—the Water Lily. Turn the corners over, and tuck them in at *c* and *d*. Turn back the second fold at the top—fig. 6.

*Napkin Folded for small arts at the side and a Cake in the middle.*—Have a perfectly square napkin ; turn the corners over so that they meet at the centre. Turn the four corners back to the edge, and you will have figure 7 ; carefully turn the napkin without unfolding it ; turn it over from two opposite sides into the centre at figure 8 ; turn it over again and make the other two ends meet in the middle  you have then figure 9.

**IV-19.**
**"Mode of Folding Table-napkins."**
*Page of instructions from Warne's Model Cookery and Housekeeping Book. Complied & edited by Mary Jewry. London: F. Warne & Co., 1868.*

**IV-20.**
**Dinner napkin.**
*Jacquard-patterned damask, red & white cotton, 18" square.*
**$4.00-$10.00**

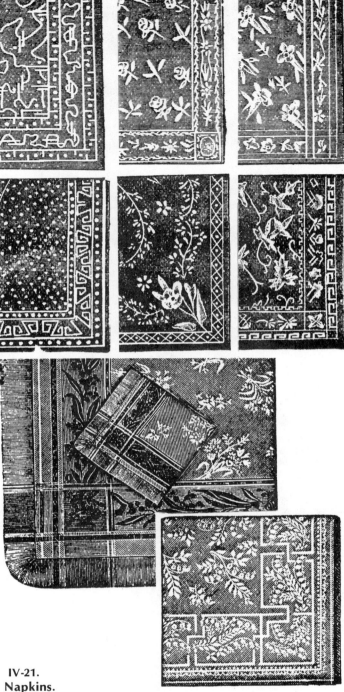

**IV-21.**
**Napkins.**
*Various damask napkins from Bogg & Buhl's catalog of fashions & linens, Allegeny, PA, 1894. The only two colors mentioned in the catalog are "turkey" and "scarlet" (both reds) and white. (L) to (R) from top: (1) & (2) John S. Brown's Irish bleached damask, 2 sizes. (3) German bleached damask, luncheon size only. (4) & (5) German bleached damask, 2 sizes. (6) "Heavy German" bleached damask. Luncheon size. (7) Fringed damask table set with "2 rows open work," tablecloths either 6' x 7 1/2' or 6' x 9'. (Original costs ranged from about $1.25 to $7.00 a dozen for napkins, to $5.00 for the huge tablecloth & napkins.) Value ranges here for 4 napkins in very good condition.* **$10.00-$30.00**

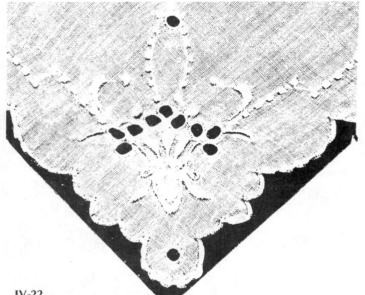

**IV-22.**
**Tea or luncheon napkin.**
*Cotton lawn, machine embroidered, 8″ square. 1910s-1930s. Set of four:* **$5.00-$10.00**

**IV-23.**
**Luncheon napkin.**
*Cotton, cut & embroidered by hand, 9″ square. These, I know from personal history, to be from the 20s-30s. Set of four:* **$4.00-$8.00**

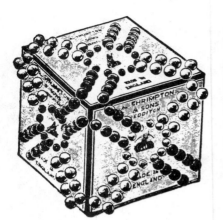

**IV-24.**
**Pin cube.**
*"Toilet Pin Cube," blued steel pins, white & black glass heads, stuck in patterns into cardboard cube covered with white paper. From Alfred Shrimpton & Sons notions catalog, c.1900, but cubes may go back 30 years before that.* **$5.00-$10.00**

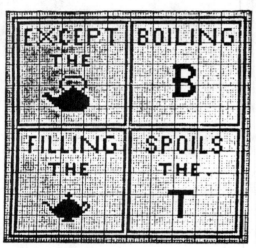

**IV-25.**
**Pattern for teapot holder.**
*Cross-stitch pattern (also seen done in needlepoint) "which our Grandmothers used, and I have one at home in crimson wool, with the figures in black, which is very old." 6″square.* House Beautiful, *2/1925. For one from the 1920s or 30s:* **$5.00-$15.00**

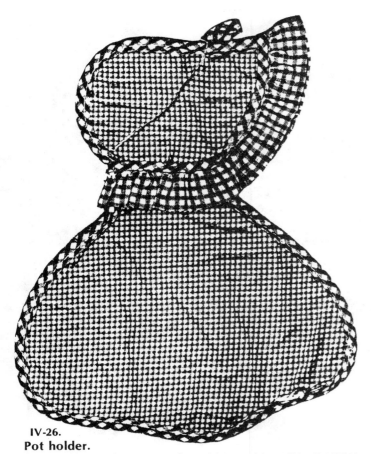

**IV-26.**
**Pot holder.**
*Machine stitched cotton gingham, blue & white. 9"H x 7 1/4"W, c.1940s.*
**$3.00-$5.00**

**IV-28.**
**Pot holder.**
*Pieced cotton, handsewn. Blue feedsack calico, white cotton muslin or flour sack material, pink & black thread embroidery. Cotton batting inside. White plastic ring. 5 5/8" x 6 1/4", c.1930s-40s.*
**$3.00-$5.00**

**IV-27.**
**Pot holder.**
*Pieced cotton butterfly, handsewn with brown & white check, dark brown border, tan inside, black & gold floss embroidery. 5 3/4" x 7 1/8", c.1930s.*
**$3.00-$5.00**

**IV-29.**
**Pot holders.**
*"Can be made up quickly in quantities for a kitchen bazaar table. The holders themselves are from the five & dime store. Each, however, is decorated with an applique vegetable (of cloth or felt) from McCall transfer No. 708. Squash, bets, carrots, pepper, tomato. McCall Needlework, Summer 1941.* **$3.00-$5.00**

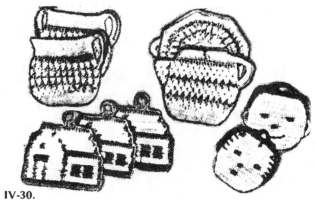

**IV-30.**
**Pot holders.**
*This is the kind of ad I like to find in old magazines because it depicts something I've bought and am trying to date. These crochet patterns, for "sugar & cream" sets of 4 holders, plus the houses and faces, are from* <u>McCall Needlework</u>, *1941.* **$3.00-$5.00**

**IV-32.**
**Pot holder.**
*Cotton crochet fancy pants, front shown, back is plain. White with red trim. Has self button & loop, and would be terrific for a certain size doll. 5 3/4"H x 8 3/4"W. 1940s.* **$3.00-$7.00**

**IV-31.**
**Pot holder.**
*Here's one of the houses from above. Red & yellow crochet, 2 layers, same on both sides. 7 1/4"H x 7 1/8"W, c.1941.* **$3.00-$5.00**

**IV-33.**
**Pot holders.**
*Cotton crochet. (T) Daisy in green & white, 6-1/8" diameter. (B) Red & white, 7" x 5-5/8". Both with covered curtain rings as hangers. 1940s.* **$3.00-$5.00**

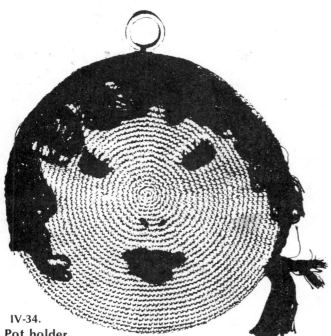

**IV-34.**
**Pot holder.**
*Cotton crochet, yellow with embroidered details; red lips, black eyes & hair. Celluloid ring. 6" diameter, late 1930s (?).***$3.00-$5.00**

**IV-35.**
**Pot holders.**
*Cotton with appliqued crochet flowers & chain-stitched stems. (L) Yellow & red square, possibly woven on one of those old pot holder frames with pins. Crochet edging. 6 3/8" square. (R) Crochet in white with green stems & leaves, varicolored flowers & crocheted edging. 7 1/8" diameter. 1940s.* **$4.00-$6.00**

**IV-36.**
**Pot holder.**
*Pieced cotton cutout of white cat, loose buttonhole or blanket stitch around edge. Bow is pink, embroidery in black, blue, red. Blue & white shirting on back. 6 1/4" x 6 3/8", 1940s.***$4.00-$6.00**

**IV-37.**
**Pot holders.**
*"Scrap bag pot holders we call these. You make them from leftovers." Embroidered cutout shapes. McCalls Needlework, Summer 1941.*
**$3.00-$5.00**

**IV-38.**
**Pot holder.**
*Souvenir woven-pattern terrycloth holder with cotton edge. 1939 World's Fair in NYC, depicts 2 most typical sights, both having coined names: the 700 foot high trylon, and the 200 foot wide perisphere. Tan, blue & rust cotton. 6 3/4" x 6 1/2". 1939 or 1940.*
**$3.00-$5.00**

**IV-39.**
**Sewing clamp.**
*Cast iron, not marked, screw clamps to table edge. Measures approx. 9" diagonally, as shown. Late 19th C. From collection of Carol Bohn, Mifflinburg, PA.* **$60.00-$90.00**

MISS PRETTYMAN

**IV-40.**
**Sewing bird, depicted on playing card.**
*This badly damaged card is one of nine remaining (?) in a card game resumably called "TAILOR," which I found at a flea market. I had to use a magnifying glass to see it, but I feel sure that the object in "Miss Prettyman's" hand is a sewing bird, of the type from the late 1840s. The engraved & hand colored pasteboard cards, blank on one side, depict "Caudle's Sunday Coat," "Scratchem His Clerk," "Errand Boy," and "Mrs. Fuzby," seem to fall into three suits—the suitcoat of Caudle, a pair of tailor's shears, and an ink bottle. 3 5/8" x 2 1/2". I'd like to know more about them; anyone know? I paid for each:* **$2.25**

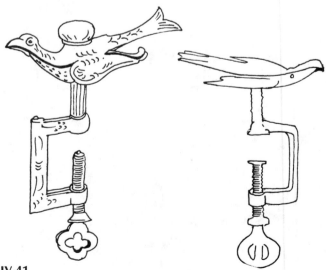

**IV-41.**
**Sewing birds.**
*(L) Gilded cast metal, possibly firegilt brass, with green plush pincushion. Bird may represent a gold finch. About 5 1/2"H. 1840s. (R) Steel, no cushion, very sleek bird, 6"H, 1830-50s.* **$160.00-$225.00**

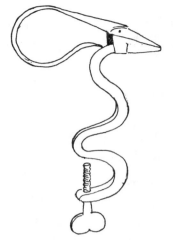

**IV-42.**
**Sewing bird.**
*Forged iron & steel, 7"H. Drawing done from photograph of piece advertised in 1990 by Garrison House Antiques, Summit, NJ, who specialize in unusual sewing & other tools. This type of handmade 'bird' is much rarer than the stamped & cast brass ones. Value range mine, not Garrison House's.* **$250.00-$400.00**

**IV-44.**
**Detail of stenciled luncheon tablecloth.**
*Cotton & rayon (?) crepe, stencil-printed in bright abstract patterns. This is the center design, in black, deep blue, red & gold on creme. One of many patterns found in this material, napkins & tablecloths. Best are the wildly abstract patterns that resemble pre-WWII Czechoslovakian china decoration, very vivid & very Art Deco. 40" square, c.1920s (?).* **$15.00-$65.00**

**IV-43.**
**Spool holder.**
*"Dressmakers are in the habit of continually losing their spool of cotton. Generally the spool is placed on a nearby table, where it can be readily knocked off and lost." This simple bent wire pin & hook can be "secured to the garment, where it can be most conveniently reached." These came in 2 sizes — for one or two spools. Jewelry & Jewelry Novelties catalog of Royal Novelty Co., Attleboro, MA,n.d., c.1910-15.* **$3.00-$5.00**

**IV-45.**
**Tea cosy.**
*Called a "Tea-Pot Cosey," in the American Agriculturist, 1/1885.*
*"The English Cosey for covering the tea-pot to keep it hot, is a great comfort, and can be made of any thick material. The handsomest are of silk sateen, with a border of plush, but for ordinary uses, those of cloth or smooth flannel are best. The shape resembles a cap, and the size is governed by that of the tea-pot it is to cover. The cosey can be decorated with embroidery or with Japanese figures in bright colors cut from cretonne, and transferred upon dark flannel. Others have merely lettering, as 'Take a cup and drink it up, and call the neighbors in.' For lining, cut out two caps of chamois. Baste a layer of cotton on these, and afterward join all together at the bottom." Condition, charm of the design, and skill of work all contribute to value. These are often found in wool flannel, complete with moth holes.* **$15.00-$35.00**

**IV-46.**

**Damask yardgoods.**

*All are from 1894 catalog of Boggs & Buhl, Allegheny, PA. As with the napkins, the catalog doesn't state what colors various patterns came in, if any, although one listing states choices of "turkey red" or "scarlet" patterns. It is possible that some of these only came in shades of natural or "cream". All are imported. (L) to (R) from top. First 3 are all "Cream Table Damask." (1) 58 in. wide; (2) 60 in. wide; (3) 54 in. wide; (4) "Finest Scotch Satin Table Damask, 72 in. wide;" (5) "Best Irish Damask, 72 in. wide." The next three are all "Irish Bleached Damask": (6) 60 in. wide; (7) 66 in. wide; (8) 72 in. wide; (9) "Grass Bleached German Damask, 72 in. wide;" (10) "Scotch Double Bleached Damask, 72 in. wide." For dinner cloth:* **$30.00-$150.00**

**IV-47.**

**"Finger Guard,"**

*or thimble of different type. The ad doesn't explain, but if you find one, at least you know what it is, and who made it — National Finger Guard Co., NYC. American Agriculturist, 1871.***$1.00-$5.00**

**IV-48.**

**Tea or dish towel.**

*Red-embroidered white damask showing crossed flatware. Monogrammed "A K." Sewn-on hanging loop of cotton tape. 25 1/2"L x 24 1/2"W, probably turn of century.* **$12.00-$20.00**

# V. Some Old-fashioned HOUSEHOLD HINTS

**A surprising** thing is that household hints, especially those of a homey type ringing with the pride and surprise of discovery, haven't lost any of their importance to housewives so many generations after the first ones were published in receipt books. No matter how much housekeeping psychology, not to mention technology, is claimed to have been advanced, there is still room for the quirky, useful, often cheap (or even free!) and almost always technologically retro ways to do something.

With the escalating interest in treating Mother Nature with some loving kindness (i.e. without harsh chemicals and wasteful resource depletion), household hints have really gone mainstream. Whole books are written on how to organize your life, your closets, your thoughts. Magazine articles abound on ways to help yourself become happier, healthier, richer, thinner, more self-reliant. We are told how to make something out of something else, just as our forebears were told in their magazines and weekly papers. We're all aware that many safe and supposedly effective substitutes for all the whizzing globs and fizzes that come in spray cans and vacuum-formed plastic packages, are proposed by many organizations who hope to save the Earth for future generations. I'm sure the manufacturers of those fancifully-named, magic products that make holes in the ozone and pollute ground water while doing other jobs like cleaning ovens and removing catsup stains and unclogging toilets, are wishing they'd spent a few millions developing friendlier ingredients. When you read some of the following receipts, you'll see that harsh chemicals aren't all new: oxalic acid, for example, was recommended for cleaning brass; look at the labels of popular metal cleaners today. Turpentine was a popular ingredient for cleaning — not exactly Nature neutral.

The following are a short selection showing the range of useful tips found in old cookbooks, housekeeping books, and periodicals, as credited. I don't offer any guarantes of effectiveness, and certainly you can't call all of them labor-saving!

## Soda for Washing

"To five gallons of water add a pint and a half of soft soap and two ounces sub-carbonate of soda. Put the clothes (after soaking over night) into the mixture when at boiling heat, rubbing the parts most soiled with soap. Boil them one hour — drain — rub, and rinse them in warm water, after being put into indigo water, they are fit for drying. Half the soap and more than half the labor is saved by washing in this manner." *The Farmers' Cabinet*, October 1, 1836.

## Keep a Notebook

"Every farmer should have a book for inserting all these useful hints which are so frequently occurring in conversation, in books, and gathered in the course of his reading, or in a practical management of his farm." *The Farmers' Cabinet*, January 1, 1837 (And so should a farmer's wife!)

## How to Save Time

"Have a place for every thing, and when you have done using it, return it to its place. This will save much time in hunting after articles which are thrown carelessly aside and lie you know not where." *The Farmers' Cabinet*, February 1, 1837.

## A New and Cheap Paint

"More impervious to the Weather than Common Paint. Take of unslacked lime a quantity sufficient to make two gallons of white wash when slacked — mix it with a due quantity of water — add to it two and a half pounds of brown sugar, and about three ounces of salt. The exact proportion of each will be best ascertained by experiment. This, when applied as a paint, becomes perfectly hard and glossy. By mixing either ivory black, or lamp-black, with the ingredients, a beautiful lead color may be had, or a yellow, by mixing suitable ingredients. This paint is now almost altogether used at the south for houses, fences, &c. *The Farmers' Cabinet*, February 15, 1838.

## To Blacken the Eye-lashes

"The simple preparations for this purpose are the juice of elder berries, burnt cork, and cloves burnt at the candle. Another means is, to take the black of frankincense, resin, and mastic. This black will not come off with perspiration. It is also equally as good for the hair of the head." *The American Family Keepsake: or People's Practical Cyclopedia, 1848.*

## To Make the Hair Curl

"At any time you may make your hair curl the more easily by rubbing it with beaten yolk of an egg, washed off afterward with clear water, and then putting on a little pomatum before you put up your curls; it is well always to go through this process when you change to curls after having worn your hair plain." *The American Family Keepsake*

## Cure for the Itch

"Take half a pound hog's lard, four ounces spirits turpentine, two ounces flour sulphur, and mix them together cold. Apply it to the ankles, knees, wrists, and elbows, and rub it in the palms of the hands, if there be any raw spots. Apply a little three nights when going to bed." *The American Family Keepsake.*

## Sore Throat Cure

"Inhale through a funnel the steam of hot vinegar, in which sage leaves have been steeped." *The American Family Keepsake*

## New Life for Disgraced Furniture

"If you have in the house any broken-down arm-chair, reposing in the oblivion of the garret, draw it out — drive a nail here and there to hold it firm — stuff and pad, and stitch the padding through with a long upholsterer's needle, and cover it with the chintz like your other furniture. Presto — you create an easy-chair." *The American Woman's Home* by Catharine E. Beecher & Harriet Beecher Stowe, 1869

## Making Your Own Soap in the Backyard

"The ashes should be strong (hickory is best), and kept dry. When put in the hopper, mix a bushel of unslacked lime with ten bushels of ashes; put in a layer ashes; then one slight sprinkling of lime; wet each layer with water (rain water is best). A layer of straw should be put upon the bottom of the hopper before the ashes are put in. An opening in the side or bottom for the ley [lye] to drip through, and a trough or vessel under to receive the ley. When the ley is strong enough to bear up an egg, so as to show the size of a dime above the surface, it is ready for making soap; until it is, pour it back into the hopper, and let it drip through again. Add water to the ashes in such quantities as may be needed. Have the vessel very clean in which the soap is to be made. Rub the pot over with corn meal after washing it, and it is all discolored, rub it over with more until the vessel is perfectly clean. Melt three pounds of clean grease; add to it a gallon of weak ley, a piece of alum the size of a walnut. Let this stew until well mixed. If strong ley is put to the grease, at first it will not mix well with the grease. In an hour add three gallons of strong hot ley; boil briskly, and stir frequently; stir one way. After it has boiled several hours, cool a spoonful upon a plate; if it does not jelly, add a little water; if this causes it to jelly, then add water to the kettle. Stir quickly while the water is poured in until it ropes on the stick. As to the quantity of water required to make it jelly, judgment must be used; the quantity will depend upon circumstances. It will be well to take some in a bowl, and notice what proportion of water is used to produce this effect.

"To harden it: Add a quart of salt to this quantity of soap; let it boil quick ten minutes; let it cool. Next day cut it out. This is now ready for washing purposes.

"To prepare it for hand-soap. Scrape off all sediment; shave it very thin; put it in a tin-pan, and hardly cover it with water. Set it on the fire; mash it to a jelly, and perfume with lavender, sassafras, or anything preferred. It will be nicer if it is melted in water and cooled two or three times before shaving it.

"Soap will improve by age if kept well boxed in a cool, dry place." *Mrs. Hill's New Family Receipt Book*, by Mrs. A.P. Hill, 1870

## Removing Grease Spots

"To remove grease spots from Calicoes, Muslins, etc., cover the spots with the yolk of an egg; then wash off the egg after it has remained half an hour; use no soap on the spot, but wash in suds." *Mrs. Hill's New Family Receipt Book*

## Where the Colors are Doubtful

"Bran-water is excellent to use in washing colored cottons or delaines, when the colors are not fast. Boil a peck of wheat bran and a pint of salt in five gallons of water, an hour; let it settle; strain the water; wash the articles through it, and rinse with water into which forty drops of elixir vitriol to the gallons is mixed. Wash all such articles on a clear, windy day, so that the air will dry them rapidly; take them in immediately." *Mrs. Hill's New Family Receipt Book.*

## Removing Tar Stains

"Tar and pitch can be removed by greasing the place with lard or sweet oil. Let it remain a day and night; then wash in suds. If silk or worsted, rub the stain with alcohol." *Mrs. Hill's New Family Receipt Book*

## Removing Scorch Stains

"Boil scorched articles in milk and turpentine, half a pound of soap, half a gallon of milk. Lay in the sun." *Mrs. Hill's New Family Receipt Book*

## Making a Cheap Carpet

"To make a cheap passage or kitchen carpet, whip together the edges of coarse, strong homespun; press the seam until it lies flat and smooth. Stretch it well, and keep it tacked; paste some pretty pattern of wall paper upon it as if preparing a wall. When perfectly dry, varnish with two coats of varnish." *Mrs. Hill's New Family Receipt Book*

## Cleaning Brass

"If stained, rub over with oxalic acid or strong vinegar; polish with rotten-stone pulverized and whiskey or sweet oil, or turpentine; then rub with soft leather or buckskin. In the beginning of warm weather, when there is no farther use for andirons, wrap them carefully in tissue paper or old silk. I have seen them wrapped so tastily with the former as to make a handsome parlor ornament." *Mrs. Hill's New Family Receipt Book*

## Preventing Fly-blown Frames

"To prevent flies from settling upon picture frames, brush them over with water in which onions have been boiled." *Mrs. Hill's New Family Receipt Book.*

## To Expel Fleas

"Use penny-royal or walnut leaves; scatter them profusely in all infested places." *Mrs. Hill's New Family Receipt Book*

## To Get Rid of Ants

"Wash the shelves with salt and water; sprinkle salt in their paths. To keep them out of safes: set the legs of the safe on tin cups; keep the cups filled with water." *Mrs. Hill's Family Receipt Book*

## To Prevent Moths in Woolens

"To prevent moths from troubling woolen goods, leaves of the China tree [*Melia azedarach,* also called a Chinaberry tree or a Pride of India tree] strewed among woolen garments prevent moths troubling them." *Mrs. Hill's New Family Receipt Book*

## Tooth Powder Receipt

"Powdered orris root, half an ounce; powdered charcoal, two ounces; powdered Peruvian bark, one ounce; prepared chalk, half an ounce; oil of bergamot or lavender, twenty drops. These ingredients must be well worked up in a mortar, until thoroughly incorporated. This celebrated tooth-powder possesses three essential virtues, giving an odorous breath, cleansing and purifying the gums, and preserving the enamel; the last rarely found in popular tooth-powders." *The Practical Housekeeper,* edited by Mrs. E.F. Ellet, 1873.

## Polish for Tables

"One pint of linseed oil, half a pint of turpentine, two ounces of beeswax, sixpence worth of white rosin. Boil the mixture in a saucepan, and put it in a bottle for use." *The Practical Housekeeper*

## Removing Ink Spots

"Remove ink spots by soaking the part in milk immediately; then wash out in cold water without soap." *The Practical Housekeeper*

## To Repel Moths

"In May and June, the little millers that lay moth eggs, begin to appear. Brush your woolens, and pack them away in a dark place covered with linen; pepper, red cedar chips, tobacco, and best of all camphor, or any strong spicy smell, will keep moths out of your chests and drawers." *The Practical Housekeeper*

## To Preserve Pencil Marks

"If you see anything drawn or written with a lead pencil that you wish to preserve from rubbing out, dip the paper into a dish of skimmed milk. Then dry it, and iron it quickly on the wrong side." *The Practical Housekeeper*

## Cleaning Japanned Trays, Urns, &c.

"Rub on with a sponge a little white soap and some lukewarm water, and wash the waiter [tray] or urn quite clean. Never use hot water, as it will cause the japan to scale off. Having wiped it dry, sprinkle a little flour over it; let it rest awhile, and then rub it with a soft dry cloth, and finish with a silk handkerchief. It there are white heat marks on the waiters, they will be difficult to remove. But you may try rubbing them with a flannel dipped in sweet oil, and afterwards in spirits of wine." *The Practical Housekeeper*

# VI. RUB-A-DUB-DUB:

## COLLECTIBLE WASHING MACHINES

With a heritage of religio-philosophical beliefs in the sanctity of order and cleanliness, Americans have sought improvements in washing machines that would, as their primary business, wash vast volumes of clothing and linens with great efficiency, and —secondarily— ease the truly back-breaking work of women.

Not counting washboards, wash boilers, and a few related items, ''washing-machines'' and ''clothes washers'' were patented by the hundreds, between what I think is the earliest date — March 28, 1797 (awarded to N. Briggs for ''Clothes, washing.'') and the end of 1873 (when my index quits). Approximately 1750 washing machines were patented in that time period, a small percentage of them being combo-contrivances such as ''washing machine & corn sheller'' or ''washing machine & churn'' or ''washing machine & wringer.''

Many of them are not what we would call a machine today, dependent as they are entirely on human bicepial motive power, greased with the elbow. Included in this non-mechanical type are what collectors today are likely to call ''clothes pounders.''

But even if we estimate that as many as a third of the 1750 were such non-machines, that leaves over a thousand, which we can roughly divide into five types, of which most were hand-powered.

**CYLINDER** — This kind worked by having a revolving cylinder or drum within the washtub itself. This perforated cylinder might be made of wood, galvanized iron, or —much later— aluminum. Some were porcelainized iron. The cylinder was made to revolve with a crank usually, although a few could be fitted up with pulleys to animal power, usually with a sheep or mule or a large dog on a treadmill. The revolving cylinder type is one of the two commonest types of washing machines made today. (See VI-7)

**TURBINE** — This type has a tub with a revolving or reciprocating propeller-type agitator that not only stirs the clothing inside the tub but also stirs the water from the bottom up, constantly creating a sudsy mix. Many modern washers use this principle. (See III-188 in Chapter 3)

**OSCILLATOR** — This type has a metal or wooden tub usually with corrugations or projecting parts on the inside like a washboard. In the simplest type, there are no movable parts, and the tub itself is made to rock or tip back and forth; some have springs, some have pulleys and weights. In a more complex type, a levered mechanical substitute for the user's hands or arms pushes the clothes back and forth across the corrugations, saving the hands from hot caustic water, but demanding much of the woman's arms. (See VI-9, VI-11)

**VACUUM-CUP** — A circular tub is within the body of the machine, and funnel-like or conical cups work up and down, pushing water and suds through the clothes, then sucking the mixture back up through the clothes again. This kind could be made with a crank or a lever. Vacuum cup washers could be had separately, and were used in any kind of washtub. (See III-183)

**DOLLY or PESTLE** — This type has one or more agitators fitted in the lid so that they project down into the tub, or they come up from the bottom. Each agitator may be shaped like a pestle or beetle, or might be more like a cow's udder (in wood) or a milking stool, or otherwise meant to replace a sturdy hand with many rigid fingers. The dolly could be given, by ingenious mechanics, a combination of up and down and semi-revolving motions. (VI-5; III-175)

As you may have noticed, two types of washing machines are closely related to churns, specifically the oscillating and the dolly (or dasher) types. Probably about half as many churns were patented in the same 80-year period as were washing machines; some inventors thought of both, and some companies manufactured both.

''Motor'' driven washing machines were introduced in the last quarter of the 19th century with water motors — the psi (the measurement of pressure in pounds per square inch) of the water drove the gears that either turned the inner tub, or tumbled the clothing, or moved the dollies up and down. A pressure of from 25 to 50 pounds was needed, and water pressure not only differed from community to community, but was often erratic during the day, depending on the whole community's usage.

Gasoline engines, steam engines, and later electric motors were attached to what were pretty much unchanged washing machines. About 1908, a man named C.W. Swanson, president of the Apex Appliance Co. of Chicago, became convinced that electric washing machines were destined for general use, along with other electric appliances. In a February 1917 article in *House Furnishing Review*, Swanson was quoted as saying ''I realized there was a new era coming. The home had been neglected, where the shop and office had adopted new and labor-saving devices, and I believed the day was at hand when electrical appliances, like vacuum cleaners, washing machines, and ironing machines would go far to eliminate the drudgery of the home. I was particularly interested in the washing machine, because washing by hand is the hardest work in the home, and I felt that a machine that would do away with this cumbersome labor would win. I became interested in the oscillatory type..., as I believed this to be the most effective principle.'' Merchandizing of motorized washing machines capitalized on women's memories of the old-fashioned ways they, or their mothers, had had to use.

In a 1911 article on the ''selling points of washing machines'' in *House Furnishing Review* the writer said ''The washing machine [whether hand-power, water-motor, electric, or belt-driven with animal or windmill power] does the rubbing, squeezing and stirring of the clothes in a closed tub, from which no steam or hot water escapes to scald the hands and parboil the face.''

The same article said that there were ''184 manufacturers on file, and we have reason to believe that there are probably as many more of whom we have no record.'' An ample field for today's collectors!

The collector market for these washing machines is still quite small, probably because most people don't have the room to display them. This does not deter some collectors, and I know a few who even collect old electric washing machines (and driers) from the 1930s to 1960s, and restore them to operation.

155

Because collector interest is recent and limited, and because the oldest machines have probably long since been burned for fuel or melted down, prices are still pretty much under $100.00. Exceptions are for especially attractive machines with good patina, early paint (if wooden) or made in a desirable metal (such as copper), or in a form or shape which somehow transports the lowly washing machine into another orbit. I'm thinking specifically of the torpedo-shaped one on wooden frame depicted in this article, VI-11.

NOTE: This article is adapted from one that appeared in *Fine Tool Journal*, Winter 1990/1991. If you are interested in subscribing, send SASE for information to the publisher, Vernon Ward, Iron Horse Antiques, Inc., RD 2, Box 245B, Pittsford, VT 05763.

**VI-1. — Four Stages of Blue Monday** — *from washtub on bench, through a variety of mechanical washers up to c.1880s. Pictures from* The March of Invention, *a short how-to-invent & patent booklet published by Dubois & Dubois in Washington, 1891.*

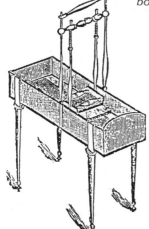

**VI-2. — Elegant Patented Machine**, *pat'd by Aaron F. Wright of NYC, in 1836. This is one, out of the 1750 I have the names for, which I can't find in the Official Gazette index, nor in the index to unnumbered patents. It was awarded a Premium at the 9th Annual Fair of the American Institute, held October 1836 in NYC. The inventor claimed that "By this machine, one person can perform a washing which would require three or four persons, by the ordinary method, in the same time, and with greater ease — and also with less wear to the article than the rub-board or the hand." Picture from the* Journal of the American Institute

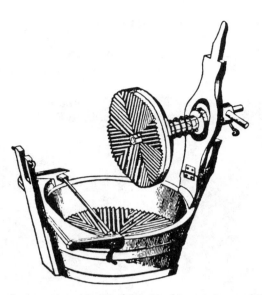

VI-3. — **Improvement in Washing Machines**, *patented October 21, 1856 by Charles N. Tylor. The corrugated "washing disk" rubs the clothing against the corrugated bottom of the tub, when the crank is turned. The distance between the two surfaces was adjustable.* Official Gazette.

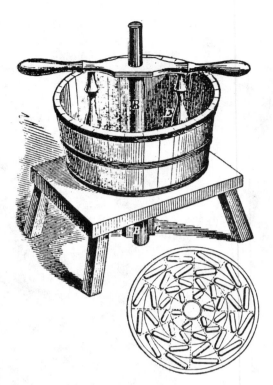

VI-5. — **Allen's Washing Machine**, *as depicted and described in* American Agriculturist. *It was patented September 14, 1858 by the Reverend John Allen, Galena, MD, who had it for sale shortly thereafter. It is hardly a machine at all, requiring lots of work by its user, although at least she was saved from assuming "any unnatural or unhealthy position" by the fact of the bench. The disk shown below the machine is the dolly or pestle, "provided with artificial knuckles upon which the clothes are rubbed."*

VI-4. — **Swan's Churn, Washing Machine, & c.** *"Will wonders cease?" wrote the* Scientific American *editor in the December 11, 1858 issue. He went on, "We have had combinations of all kinds, and nearly every machine or process has been added to some other by the genius of inventors; so that operations that were once long and tedious, have become easy and quick." It has been forcibly argued that with the march of progress in household appliances, the housewife, whose work was formerly pretty much "done" on Sundays, had even more demanded of her. As a woman in a piece goods shop said to me recently, "When I was growing up, my father said we were either the cleanest or the dirtiest people in town, from the amount of washing my mother did."*

VI-6. — **Doty's Clothes Washer** — *"The most popular, best, and cheapest...ever invented." It was awarded the first premium at the American Institute Fair of 1865. It cost $12.00 in 1866, according to the ad in* American Agriculturist.

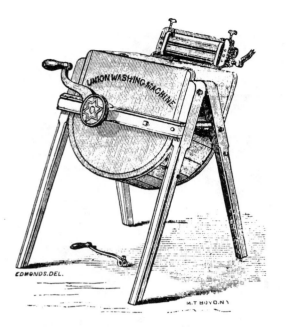

**VI-7.** — **Union Washing Machine & combined wringer,** *made by Haley, Morse & Co. of NYC. This won a "large prize medal" at the International Exhibition in July 1863, a prize medal at the American Institute in 1863, and a prize at the Paris Exposition of 1867. Picture is from a small flyer, c.1870.*

**VI-9.** — **"Infantile Power Washing Machine,"** *patented by John Highbarger of Sharpsburg, MD, September 10, 1867. The tank is shown cutaway here to show the ribbed sides. "The clothes are washed by the oscillation of a rocking chair, with ribbed rocker bottom, the rocking being effected by the hands of the operator, which grasp a hand bar. This plan of utilizing baby power is certainly novel, and is, no doubt, amusing to the operator, and we are sure it will be to our readers," wrote the editor of Scientific American, March 4, 1871. Two counterweights are shown, fore & aft.*

**VI-8.** — **"The Excelsior"** *on bench, with "patent flange cogwheels on both ends of the rolls, also the Patent Oscillating Board, for conducting the water into either tub as desired, which saves much hard labor, as no shifting of the tubs is necessary." This was manufactured by the Bailey Washing & Wringing Machine Co. Early 1870s flyer.*

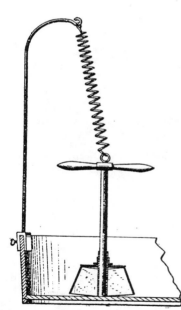

**VI-10.** — **"Clothes-pounder,"** *patented by Leonard Study of Plum Hollow, NY, October 11, 1881. This has real elegance, and to me there's as much "machine" to it as to many others, with that spring and clamp. Official Gazette.*

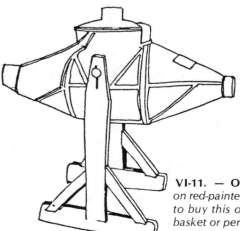

**VI-11.** — **Oscillating or rocking washer,** *pieced tin 'pig' body on red-painted wooden frame. 35"H x 46"L overall. I really wanted to buy this one, to use in my one-room apartment as a laundry basket or perhaps a cat hideaway, but it wouldn't fit in the rental car.*

# THE BOSS WASHING MACHINE CO.

### MANUFACTURERS OF

## ALL THE LEADING AND BEST WASHERS

*Cincinnati, O., January 1st, 1909.*

## TO THE TRADE

AT THIS season we desire to express our appreciation for the many and substantial evidences of Good Will shown us in placing your orders for our productions and to thank you for your valuable patronage, which we trust we shall be favored with in the future as in the past, and which we assure you it will be our aim to merit a continuance of the same.

WISHING YOU A HAPPY AND PROSPEROUS NEW YEAR,

We remain, respectfully yours,

THE BOSS WASHING MACHINE CO.

## BOSS WASHING MACHINES

### Made in Eleven Different Styles

including all machines that are in demand and possess merit. Jobbers can save capital invested, also stock room, by ordering assorted carloads from one factory, and dealers are also benefited by being able to get assorted styles from their jobber. Machines are not genuine without our label.

THE BOSS WASHING MACHINES have stood the test for over 15 years, and are still conceded to be the only Washers constructed on the true principle of washing clothes.

It sells readily and at good profits. It has less competitors than any other style of washer. Our label on each machine stands for quality — *Look for it.* Order the "BOSS" from your jobber.

We advertise to the consumer for the benefit of the dealer, therefore each dealer should carry the "BOSS" in stock to supply the wants of his customers.

Write for nearest distributing point to your city, copy of late catalogue, giving prices, etc.

The "BOSS" is not in the catalogues of catalogue houses, therefore the dealer's profits are assured.

**VI-12. — "Boss" Washing Machines,** *lookin' old, but dating to 1908-09. Advertisement in Iron Age, 1/07/1909. There's the "Boss," "Banner," "New Standard Champion," "Boss Quick," "Uneeda" and "Cincinnati".*

159

*The following is Part One (of a two part article) that appeared May 17, 1884 in Charles Dickens' wonderfully eclectic magazine All the Year Round. There is much of interest to collectors of clothespins, also called clothes-pegs, and clothes wringers, skewers, kegs and other household items that Dickens thought uncommonly interesting despite their commonness. All the items were imported into England from the United States.*

# VII. ''Curiosities of Trade''

## by Charles Dickens

I have had occasion just lately to look through a large number of the London and Liverpool Bills of Entry, and in trying to find what I wanted, I could not help noticing the many queer articles that are brought into the country. Now a large number of readers will know perfectly well what a bill of entry is. But there must be a great many who are not so well informed, and therefore, for their instruction, let me at once describe it.

This is a daily publication appearing at our chief ports. It contains the names, tonnage, number of hands, port of departure, etc., etc., of all the vessels arriving here the day before, and to each vessel is appended a description of its cargo in detail—a table of contents, in fact. Besides this there is also a list of all goods exported yesterday, with the place of destination, and a variety of shipping information generally. My concern, however, is not with our exports; it is imports alone with which I have to do. It will be understood at once that amongst these there will be seen by the merest inspection a vast quantity of goods whose presence there is a matter of course. Nobody is surprised to find that we receive from the United States, wheat, Indian corn, cattle, dead meat, cotton, petroleum; tea and silk from China; palm-oil from the West Coast of Africa; wine from France, Portugal, and Spain; currants from Greece, and so on. But there are many articles which, though considerable in the aggregate, are of less importance than these. At first sight they seem odd, but are not so in reality when we come to think over the matter. Perhaps some of these items will strike my readers with the same sense of queerness as they did me.

Who would expect, for instance, to find in the cargo of one of the magnificent New York liners three thousand boxes of clothes-pegs? Yet such an entry is common enough. ''Bless my soul!'' somebody will say, just as I did when I noticed it, ''are we dependent on the States for such things?'' Pursuing my investigations further, I found that this was only one out of many of the same kind. It is evident, therefore, that it pays to cut down timber, convert it into the manufactured article, pay carriage to a port, shipping charges, freight, landing charges, carriage to inland towns anywhere in England, commissions to several—a score, for anything I know—intermediaries, in order that the British materfamilias may buy a dozen clothes-pegs for three-halfpence, which is what my wife tells me she paid last. I never saw the boxes as imported, but I should imagine they would be large, and hold several hundreds each—thousands, may be.

Does not this give us an idea of the enormous quantity that must be turned out every year in the States? I presume even there the washerwoman is not yet emancipated from the tyranny of the clothes-peg, and this being so, just fancy what a lot must be consumed by fifty millions of people. Yet they are able to supply, not only their internal demand, but to send them to us by the million. Likely enough they will send them as well to some other European countries, though the demand there will not be so great as here, if only from the fact that the weekly wash is not such a national institution.

One cannot help thinking what has been is, and will be, the effect of this large importation on the home-made article. It is possible from such an insignificant stand-point as the clothes-peg to soar into the highest politico-economic regions. Are our native clothes-peg makers free-traders, or fair-traders, or protectionists, and if so, why so? and if not, why not? I pause for a reply! But none is forthcoming, for I don't know a soul in the trade. If I did I have no doubt he would glow with the fervour of his convictions. But the trade is, I fancy, modest and retiring in its nature; nobody ever hears of its grievances in the House, or through long letters in the Times. And yet the native clothes-peg maker has to live; it must be a serious question with him whether the trade is being driven out of the country by foreign imports, or whether it still defies competition. Perhaps the demand has out-stripped his powers of supply, or perhaps he holds his head up proudly, and asserts boldly that if you want a really first-rate article you must still come to him. Perhaps the trade has quietly died out and made no sign. I should not be surprised to hear this. If my recollection is to be trusted, the present clothes-peg did not make its appearance here till some twenty or twenty-five years ago. Everybody who can look back so far will remember that the clothes-peg to which he was accustomed was evidently a piece of a branch peeled, shaped, cut in two, and then bound together with two or three inches of tin, which were fastened by a bit of wire driven in. Such was what I may term the pre-American, or the antique clothes-peg.

I cannot assert with confidence that this ancient style has disappeared, for I confess that I do not keep my eyes open purposely to study clothes-pegs. But this much may be allowed: the antique is not prominent; possibly it yet lingers in out-of-the-way and old-fashioned places. In the centres of civilisation, however, it is conspicuous by its absence, its place seems to be taken by the modern article. This, as is well-known, is all in a piece, and might be pronounced artistic, were it not evidently made in a machine, and therefore, according to Mr. Ruskin, an utter abomination. How one thought leads to another. To mention a machine makes one wonder whether prices have fallen or advanced, since the American machine-made article came in. Flour is pretty much the same price it was then, beef and mutton, butter and cheese, are dearer, as everybody knows; what has been the effect on clothes-pegs? I don't find them in prices current, yet there must be a market for them somewhere—at Liverpool, I should fancy. If you want the statistics of the trade, where would you go to? The name does not appear in the Board of Trade returns. Can it be that the article is ignominiously classed under wool or sundries? The old Roman in the play could say that nothing that was human was foreign to him. Let me imitate him, and say that nothing commercial is insignificant to me. And yet I must acknowledge that clothes-pegs are not a leading or an important article. The great commoner could awe the House with "Sugar—sugar—sugar, Mr. Speaker," but I am afraid it would have laughed even at him if he had begun "Clothes-pegs—clothes-pegs—clothes-pegs."

It is unnecessary to tell my readers that America sends us enormous quantities of wood, both in the rough and manufactured. The shapes in which the latter appears are numerous and peculiar at first sight. And here I may as well state that each of my illustrations is but a single instance out of hundreds and thousands of similar entries during a year. The same steamer which brings the clothes-pegs carries also two hundred and eighty oars. Just imagine all these piled up against a boat-house; what a lot they would look! And where on earth do they all go to? Whence, too, should we have got them if we had not had the States to go to?

Still keeping to the States and to wood, what do I light upon next? Why, nine hundred and ninety-five maple rollers. What in the world can these be for? Think again, sweet sir; can't you guess? No, I can't. Well, I begin to think that Mr. Puff was right in saying that the number of people who give themselves the trouble of thinking is inconsiderable. Did you ever see a washing and wringing machine? Haven't wringing-machines rollers? Don't you remember, in your youthful days, seeing the process of wringing gone through by the washerwoman, usually assisted by one of the servants, and on blanket-washing occasions, possibly by the whole strength of the establishment? That, as you know very well now, is all done away with; the poorest cottager has a machine, and what used to be a severe strain on the muscles of the arm is now as easy as grinding an organ. Thanks to mechanical inventors, washing-day has been deprived of half its terrors by losing all its trouble.

Thus it will be seen that every one of us over thirty or thereabouts, has witnessed the origin and development of a new branch of industry, and one, moreover, which brings comfort to the poorest of us, a consideration not to be lightly esteemed. To whom occurred the happy thought of using in common life the appliances well known in large industrial establishments we know not, but, whoever he was, he proved himself a benefactor to this species. To go back somewhat, let us suppose the wringing-machine invented, we could not have supplied ourselves with the wood necessary for the rollers. With us sycamore is comparatively scarce, and of considerable value. The price of the rollers alone would have prevented the use of the machine by the working man, or even by the better class. For it must not be supposed that any wood will do. Certain qualities are required, which sycamore alone combines in itself. It must be fairly close-grained, it must turn well, it must not warp in the transition from hot to cold, or from wet to dry, and it must not wear out quickly. Last, and most important, it must be cheap. Now steps in America. "I can give you all this; the maple, a sister to your sycamore, is perhaps the commonest tree in my northern and middle states, and fulfills all these conditions. Give me your orders, and you shall be well served, and therefore well satisfied." Hence the trade. After this disquisition, nobody will be surprised to hear that the next entry is fifty-six casks of handles. Wood again. Washing-machines, of course, need wooden handles, and innumerable other things want them as well. Here is an outlet for the smaller pieces— we shall see that every part of the tree is used to advantage. Short lengths, which are unfit for large work, such as rollers, can be converted into good-sized handles at any rate.

All of us know that "wooden head" is a term of reproach applied to human beings. It may be thought that we have already quite enough of them in the country, and the arrival of four thousand four hundred and eighty-two from America will be hailed with anything but satisfaction. But there is no occasion to grumble, on the contrary, for this consignment is merely intended to supply casks with heads. But this is not all. If we get heads from America, why not get staves as well? We do. One steamer from New Orleans brings us, amongst other goods, an assorted lot, comprising seventeen thousand seven hundred and ten pieces pipe, two thousand nine hundred and fifty-five pieces hogshead, three thousand five hundred and eighty pieces claret, four thousand one hundred and seventy-eight peices barrel, and ten thousand seven hundred and thirteen pieces keg staves. Each of these five descriptions is of a different size from the others, cut to a regulation length, and thickness. The trouble of the English cooper is reduced to a minimum; if he has orders for pipes, hogsheads, or kegs, he chooses from his stock, bought in Liverpool, the requisite number of staves, which are already of the right size in every respect, and the proper number of head-pieces, which are also cut to certain well known lengths. He has simply to put the whole together, and fasten on his iron hoops. For these last we need not say he has not to go abroad. But if it is necessary that his casks be bound with wooden hoops, for these he is to a great measure dependent on the foreigner. Enormous quantities arrive every week from Rotterdam; such an entry as nine hundred and forty bundles is of almost daily occurence at London or Liverpool. Staves and heads from a very large article of export from almost all the North American ports from New York to New Orleans.

Charleston is best known to Englishmen as the great cotton-port; but it also holds high rank as an exporter of timber, in the shape of staves and trenails. Perhaps it may be as well to say that the latter are what may be described as large wooden nails, used in many operations of carpentry. Anyone who has ever seen a ship building must have noticed the big wooden nails projecting all round the hull. For such purposes a wood is wanted which must above everything be tough, and this quality is found to perfection in the locust-tree which flourishes abundantly in the Carolinas. We find in one steamer fifteen thousand locust trenails.

Does not everyone remember a few years ago how the British joiner was going to be ruined by the importation of doors, window-frames, and what not from Sweden and Norway. The native artisan, however, has gone on since then in pretty much the same way as before, and his trade is by no means extinct. One gets used in time to these lamentations, especially when one recollects that a great many men still living have known the whole country going to be ruined more than once. The import of manufactured wood from the Scandinavian ports is not yet at an end, and is further supplemented from a source still farther off. We find a New York steamer bringing two thousand five hundred and forty-seven doors. Another New York steamer carries ninety-four cases of spokes, and two cases of hubs — material here for a good many waggons or carriages, as the case may be. But my feeling is, that after the clothes-pegs, there is no room for surprise at anything, and, therefore, an entry of four cases of umbrella-sticks from Philadelphia passes almost unnoticed; simple enough from all their wealth of wood to choose the best-looking branches, and send them over to us. Bobbins, too, thirty cases of these create no surprise; but stay, what is the next item that catches the eye? Why, four cases of mousetraps. These must be some Yankee notion, the latest patent, warranted to contain one or more victims every morning. We are dimly conscious of having seen in a shop-window somewhere a mouse-trap all wood, into which no mouse could avoid falling, and out of which it could not possibly get; perhaps this was one of the lot, per British Prince, from Philadelphia. There must surely be in these some superiority of design or execution, or, however could it pay to send them so many thousand miles? One would think it would be impossible to compete with the home-maker in an article which is made from all sorts of odds and ends. Of course the States have also their odds and ends, and the mousetraps are a pretty good proof that they make the most of them. But there remains still an entry to show to what an extent they try to turn everything to advantage. What do you think of fifty-six barrels of skewers? Barrels, of course, mean flour-barrels; only imagine fifty-six of these full of skewers. Let me see, what are skewers used for? Oh, fowls are trussed with them, and only yesterday I had to utter an anathema on the cook for leaving one in. Butchers, though, must be the great consumers; don't we see in the shops sheep stuck all over with them? And that reminds me that many years ago some ingenious gentleman wrote to Notes and Queries to point out that Shakespeare was probably a butcher, or at any rate was well up in the technicalities of the trade, as he appears to have been with every other trade, on the strength of his having written:

There's a divinity that shapes our ends,
Rough hew them as we will.

And to shape the ends is still the correct expression for the butcher - boy when making his skewers. I wonder if butchers still make their own skewers? Hardly, I should think, in large houses where they can buy them ready made, or be waited on by salesmen eager for orders. Depend upon it, the butcher of to-day adapts himself to the improved conditions of the times, and looks upon the days when he made his own skewers as we all look upon the times when there were no railways. Such is the march of progress. The butcher-boy no longer has his soul vexed at the thought that when he has carried out all the meat, and cleaned the blocks, and swept up, the remaining hours will be employed in whittling out skewers for the morrow. Happy boy! he has nothing to do with skewers except use them, and if he knew where they came from he would bless America.

It will be difficult to imagine anything brought into the country much more insignificant than skewers, unless it were shavings, and I must say that I have not yet found that we import these. But I have found that we import large quantities of firewood, and from the form of the entry, I should not be surprised to learn that it comes in ready cut for use—chips, in fact. Entries such as forty fathoms firewood are common enough in the London Bill of Entry. This, however, does not travel so far as the skewers, it comes to us from Norway, and gives us an idea of the value we must be to our Scandinavian cousins, who thus find a ready market for what is rubbish to them. There they are wondering what on earth to do with their odd bits, here we are crying out for something to light our fires with. Somehow or other the two are brought together, and a further link welded in the chain of commerce, which brings all nations closer together. As everybody has heard of the enormous pine-forests in Norway and Sweden, we expect to find large quantities coming in, in all sorts of shapes. We are all acquainted with the Swedish matches, which are to be found everywhere. These, however, are not made from fir, but from the aspen, also a very common tree. One vessel from Gothenburg brings forty-one thousand nine hundred and thirteen props, nine thousand three hundred and forty poles, and one hundred and ninety-seven thousand eight hundred and sixty-six fir-staves. The first of these may cause surprise to many, but to those who are acquainted with the coal districts, it is a matter of course; they are used in enormous quantities for props in coal-pits. As to the next, one has only to think of building operations and scaffolding-poles, and there is no mystery in the matter. Gothenburg also a vessel brings twenty-three thousand four hundred and thirty-six bundles of laths, and Frederickstadt sends us thirty-nine thousand seven hundred and sixty-seven pieces of flooring-boards. If any of my readers, therefore, wants to build, he will have a good idea where his timber comes from, but if he wants to fence his garden or his park, he must go farther, for I find part of a cargo from St. John's, New Brunswick, to consist of six thousand nine hundred and forty pieces of palings.

So far I am content to mention the commonest wood and wooden articles we import. It is unnecessary to do more than state the fact that of furniture, ornamental and dye woods, large quantities arrive from abroad. There is, however, no novelty or oddity in these. But there is an often - recurring entry which at first sight struck me as peculiar; the first one I met with was three hundred and forty-six empty casks from Alexandria, these, of course, might have held anything. But my suspicions were confirmed by the next entry, which was one hundred and eighty-nine hogsheads, one hundred and twelve barrels, and five hundred and fifteen kilderkins from Malta, consigned to Bass, Allsopp, and Worthington. There could be no possible mistake, they were empty beer-barrels, and these we know are to be found wherever Englishmen do congregate. An odd-looking entry, too, was fourteen casks of empty bottles, from Alexandria, consigned to J. Schweppe and Co. Nobody need be told what these were. It used to be said in the old overland route days that the path across Egypt could be traced by the soda-water corks lying about. Whatever may be done with the corks, the bottles at any rate get returned. One can fancy the Egyptian boy, in his leisure hours, amusing himself by prowling along the Canal looking out for empties.

---

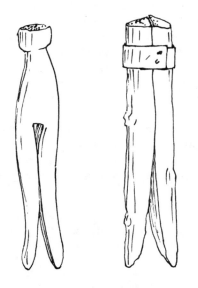

**VII-1.**
**Manufactured clothes-peg & "pre-American" clothes-peg.**
*(L) A turned peg made "all in a piece" from American timber and exported to Europe. Dickens thought this type of clothes-peg made its first "appearance" in England about 1860 to 1865. Before that, (R) the type he termed "antique" or "pre-American" was common. It is a piece of peeled branch cut in two lengthwise, then bound back "together with two or three inches of tin" held in place with a small wire nail or two. This latter type, about which Dickens wondered if it were still being made and used in "out-of-the-way and old-fashioned places", is prevalent at antique shows in America today, especially at dealers who buy shares in or whole container loads from the British Isles. (It has been recently said that these pegs are made by gypsies in England and peddled door-to-door. Whether that means used-to-be or still-is, it isn't ever said. But from the modern appearance of some of the lithographed tin, I'd say it's not a dead art). It is amusing that the imbalance of trade described in ironic fashion by Dickens more than a century ago is perhaps being balanced again! Whereas the machine-made pegs from America were apparently profitable for Americans to retail by the millions in England for 1 ½¢ per dozen in 1888, thousands of the antique pegs, handmade in England, are apparently profitable to retail in America for about $42.00 to $96.00 a dozen in 1992. And that's not adjusting for inflation! (By the way, the "Great Commoner" Dickens refers to on page 161 was William Pitt, sometimes considered the greatest orator ever of the House of Commons, who was a distinguished member of the House by age 21 [1780]).*

## VIII. "THE LAUNDRY, in 1886"

From *Practical Housekeeping. A Careful Compilation of Tried and Approved Recipes*
Minneapolis, MN: Buckeye Pub'g Co., 1884

————

When inviting friends to visits of a week or more, try to fix the time for the visit to *begin* the day *after* the ironing is done. The girl feels a weight off her mind, has time to cook the meals better and is a much more willing attendant upon guests.

Do not have beefsteak for dinner on washing or ironing days—arrange to have something roasted in the oven, or else have cold meat also.

Do not have fried or broiled fish. The smell sticks, and the clothes will not be sweet; besides the broiler and frying-pan take longer to clean.

As for vegetables, do not have spinach, pease, string-beans, or apple-sauce. All these good things take time to prepare, and can be avoided as well as not. Have baked white and sweet potatoes, macaroni, boiled rice, parsnips, sweet corn, stewed tomatoes, any canned vegetables in winter. For dessert, baked apples and cream, bread-pudding, or something easily prepared.

When removed from the person, clothing, if damp, should be dried to prevent mildew, and articles which are to be starched should be mended before placing in the clothes-basket. Monday is the washing day with all good housekeepers. The old-fashioned programme for a washing is as follows: Use good soft water if it can be had. If not, soften a barrel-full of well-water by pouring into it water in which half a peck or more of hard wood ashes have been boiled, together with the ashes themselves. When enough has been added to produce the desired effect, the water takes on a curdled appearance, and soon settles perfectly clear. If milky, more ashes and lye must be added as before, care being taken not to add more than is necessary to clear the water, or it will affect the hands unpleasantly. On the other hand, if too little is put in, the clothes will turn yellow. Gather up all clothes which are ready on Saturday night, and the rest as they are taken off; separate the fine from the coarse, and the less soiled from the dirtier. Scald all table linen and articles which have coffee, fruit, or other stains which would be "set" by hot suds, by pouring over them hot water from the tea-kettle and allowing them to stand until cool. Have the water in the tub as warm as the hand will bear, but not too hot. (Dirty clothes should never be put into very hot clear water, as it "sets" the dirt. Hot soap-suds, however, has the opposite effect, the water expanding the fiber of the fabric, while the alkali of the soap softens and removes the dirt.) Wash first one boiler full, taking the cleanest and finest through two suds, then place in a boiler of cold water, with soap enough to make a good suds. A handful of borax to about ten gallons of water helps to whiten the clothes and is used by many, especially by the Germans, who are famous for their snowy linen.

This saves in soap nearly half. For laces, cambrics, etc., an extra quantity of the powder is used, and for crinolines (requiring to be made stiff), a strong solution is necessary. Borax, being a neutral salt, does not in the slightest degree injure the texture of the linen. Its effect is to soften the hardest water. Another way to whiten clothes is to throw a handful of tansy into the boiler in which clothes are boiling. It will make the water green, but will whiten the clothes. Let them boil, with cover off boiler, *not more than five or ten minutes*, as too long boiling "yellows" the clothes. (Some advocate strongly no boiling.) Remove to a tub, pour over them cold water slightly blued, and turn all garments, pillow-slips, stockings, etc., wrong-side out. (If there are more to boil, take out part of the boiling suds, add cold water, and fill *not too full* with clothes. Repeat until all are boiled. The removal of part of the suds, and filling up with cold water, prevents the suds from "yellowing" the clothes.) Wash vigorously in this water (this is called "sudsing"), wringing very dry by hand, or better with the wringer, as the clear appearance of the clothes depends largely on thorough wringing. Rinse in another tub of soft water, washing with the hands, *not* simply lifting them out of the water and then wringing, as is practiced by some, because all suds must be rinsed out to make them clear and white. Wring and shake out well and put into water pretty well blued, putting in one article after another until the first boilerful is all in. Stir up occasionally, as the blue sometimes settles to the bottom, and thus spots the clothes. (This time well-water may be used if soft water is difficult to obtain.) Wring out again and for the last time, placing the clothes which are to be starched in one basket, and the rest, which may be hung out immediately, in another. While the first lot of clothes is boiling, prepare the second, take out first, put second in boiler, and "suds" and rinse first. In this way the first is finished and hung out while the later lots are still under way. Have the starch (see recipes) ready as hot as the hand can bear, dip the articles and parts of articles which need to be very stiff, first "clapping" the starch well in with the hands, especially in shirt-bosoms, wristbands, and collars, and then thin the starch for other articles which require less stiffening. When starched, hang out on the line to dry, first wiping the line with a cloth to remove all dirt and stains. Shake out each article until it is free from wrinkles, and fasten securely on the line (with the old-fashioned split clothes-pins), being careful to hang sheets and table-linen so that the selvage edges will be even. The line should be stretched in the airiest place in the yard, or in winter a large attic is a better place for the purpose. (Freezing injures starch, and for that reason it is better in winter to hang clothes out unstarched until dry, then taking in, starching and drying indoors.) When dry, remove from line to clothes-basket, place clothes-pins as removed in a basket kept for the purpose, take down and roll up the line, remove basket, line, and pins to the house, and put the two latter into their proper places. The clothes-line should always be carefully put up out of the weather when not in use. Wipe it carefully with a clean cloth before hanging out clothes, and always count clothes-pins when gathering them up. Every housekeeper ought to provide a pair of mittens for hanging out clothes, to be used for this purpose and no other. Cut them from clean flannel (white seems the most suitable), and line them with another thickness of flannel, or make them double, if the flannel is thin. These should be kept in a clean place ready for this particular business, and nothing else. A good and handy place to keep them is in the clothes-pin bag. Turn all garments right side out, shake out thoroughly, sprinkle (re-starching shirt-bosoms, wristbands, and collars if necessary). Shake out night-dresses and under-garments so as to free them from creases, and if they are ruffled or embroidered, dip them in thin starch, pull out smoothly, fold first, and then, beginning at the top of each garment, roll up, each by itself, in a very tight roll, and place in the basket; fold sheets without sprinkling, having first snapped and stretched them, and lay on the rest; over all spread the ironing blanket, and let them stand until next morning. Next day iron, beginning with the sheets (which, as well as table linen, must be folded neatly and carefully, so that the selvage edges will exactly come together. Or, another way to fold and iron a sheet is to bring bottom over top, then bring back bottom edge to edge of middle fold, leaving top edge; iron the upper surface, then turn the whole sheet over, fold the top edge back to the middle edge, and again iron upper surface; this leaves the sheet folded in four thicknesses; now bring the selvage edges together and iron the upper surface, and the sheet is done), and taking shirts next, cooling the iron when too hot on the coarse towels. In ironing shirts a "a bosom-board" is almost indispensable, and an "ironing-board" is a great convenience for all articles. The former is a hard wood board an inch thick, eighteen inches long, and eight wide, covered with two thicknesses of woolen blanket stuff, overlaid with two more of cottton cloth. The cloth is wrapped over the sides and ends of the board and tacked on the back side, leaving the face plain and smooth. The ironing-board is covered in the same way, but is five feet long, two feet wide at one end, and narrowed down with a rounded taper from full width at the middle to seven inches at the other end, and the corners rounded. This board may be of any well-seasoned wood which will not warp, and should be about one inch thick; on this all the clothes are conveniently ironed. Always use cotton holders for the irons. Woolen ones are hot to the hand, and if scorched, as they often are, the smell is disagreeable. In ironing a shirt or a dress, turn the sleeves on the wrong side, and leave them until the rest is done, and then turn and iron them. In this way the bosoms are less likely to become rumpled. Pull muslin and lace out carefully, iron it over once, and then pull into shape, pick out the embroidery and proceed with greater care than before. Embroideries should be ironed on the wrong side over flannel. Always have near a dish of clean cold water, so that any spot which has been imperfectly ironed may be easily wet with a soft sponge or piece of linen, and ironed over again, or any surplus bit of starch removed. As fast as articles are finished, they should be hung on the clothes-dryer until *thoroughly dry*, especial care being taken with those which are starched stiff, as they retain the starch much better if dried very quickly. **Thorough** airing is necessary, twenty-four hours being none too much.

If a machine is used in washing, it is better to soak the clothes over night in warm soft water, soaping collars and wristbands, and pieces most soiled. Have separate tubs for coarse and fine clothes. In soaking clothes for washing Monday, the water should be prepared Saturday night, and all clothes which are ready thrown in, and the rest added when changed. If washing fluids are used, the recipes which follow are the best.

Another method is to half fill tubs Saturday night with clear, soft water, warmed a little if convenient, but not too hot, made into a weak suds; in one put the finer articles, such as muslins, cuffs, collars, and shirts; in another put table-linen; in another bed-linen; in another the dish-cloths and wiping towels, and in still another the coarsest and most soiled articles: always put the most soiled articles of each division at bottom of tub; cover all well with water and press down. Rub no soap on spots or stains, as it will "set" them. Of course, articles which can not be had on Saturday night are put in the next day as they are changed. Monday morning, heat not very hot a boiler full of clean soft water, add to it water in which soap was dissolved Saturday night by pouring hot water over it, and stir it thoroughly; drain off the water in which the clothes were soaked after shaking them up and down vigorously in it, pressing them against the sides of the tub to get out all the water possible. Then pour over them the warm suds, and wash out as before described, washing each class separately. If found impracticable to make so many divisions, separate the coarse and fine, and the least soiled and the dirtiest.

In the summer, clothes may be washed without any fire by soaking overnight in soapy soft water, rubbing out in the morning, soaping the dirty places, and laying them in the hot sunshine. By the time the last are spread out to bleach, the first may be taken up, washed out and rinsed. This, of course, requires a clean lawn.

Before washing flannels shake out dust and lint; use soft, *clean, cold* water in winter merely taking the chill off. Let the hard soap lie in the water, but do not apply it to the clothes. Wash the white pieces first, throw articles as fast as washed into blued cold water, let them stand twenty or thirty minutes, wash them through this water after dissolving a little soap in it, wring hard, shake, and hang up. Wash colored flannels in the same way (but not in water used for white, or they will gather the lint), and rinse in several waters if inclined to "run." When very dirty, all flannels should soak longer, and a little borax well dissolved should be added to the water. This process is equally good for washing silk goods and silk embroideries. Calicoes and fancy cotton stockings may be washed in the same way, except that no soap should be used in the rinsing. Wash gray and brown linens in cold water, with a little black pepper in it, and they will not fade. For bluing, use the best indigo tied in a strong bag made of drilling.

TO CLEANSE ARTICLES MADE OF WHITE ZEPHYR.—Rub in flour or magnesia, changing often. Shake off flour and hang in the open air a short time.

TO REMOVE INK-STAIN.—Immediately saturate with milk, soak it up with a rag, apply more, rub well, and in a few minutes the ink will disappear.

# IX. CLOSETING:

## TAKE IT OFF & HANG IT UP

I warned you in the introduction to the Housecleaning chapter: I'm not neat. I know the philosophy of "Don't put it down. Put it away." But it's awfully hard! To make up for my lack of neatness, my lack of closeting compulsiveness, I collect coat hangers. Some are for closets, some are to be used as small, very portable drying racks, some are for traveling, some are for dolls and children. Hangers are more visible at antique shows and flea markets now; the word is getting out. In 1989, I predicted that there would be a major show of them in NYC art gallery. Two years later there was.

Bootjacks have been collected for many years, and hence have been documented in articles. A few — most notably the Bug or Beetle bootjack — have been reproduced in the last 40 years or so; I suspect that many more have been reproduced in the last five years, when cast iron began to take off. For collectors, a bootjack sort of falls between a sadiron stand and a doorstop.

A **Futurewatch** should be placed on shoe shine boxes. If you can't justify having more than one, remember they can be used as footstools!

Bootjack, all wood, folds, American, 11"L, TOC. • A couple of patented bootjacks from the *Subject Index of Patents*, that may never have been made but I'd love to see them, are: a combination Boot-jack & burglar-alarm, patented by F. C. Goffin of Newark, NJ, April 6, 1858, & a Boot-jack, nut-cracker, tack-hammer, & tack puller combination, the brainchild of G.R. Osborn and J. Crandell, Ilion, NY, patented April 17, 1866. All through the 1850s to 1870s, and to some extent later, there were thousands of combo patents, many with functions so unrelated as to amaze readers of the *Official Gazette*. **$30.00-$40.00**

Bootjack, carved wood, shaped oblong, with huge cutout of heart in the foot plate; angular "U" jaws, most unusual for wood, & especially because it is signed, "S. Ashmead", Philadelphia, PA, 24"L, 19th C. • Robacker May 1989 price is way under the money. **$65.00**

Bootjack, cast iron, adv'g "Musselman's Plug Tobacco", TOC. **$135.00-$150.00**

Bootjack, cast iron device with horseshoe-like opening, openwork handle, a stiff brush on one tip of the "Shoe", & 2 short feet. Multipurpose, viz. to take boots off, then the brushless forked jaws of the horseshoe used to pick out dried mud, the brush for applying boot blacking, pat'd by H. J. Miller, Nashua, NH, patent date on jack as "March 3D 68" (1868). **$65.00-$80.00**

Bootjack, cast iron, fancy openwork casting, "Boss", American, 15"L, 19th C. • **German vocabulary** — Stiefelknecht: bootjack. **$125.00-$140.00**

Bootjack, cast iron, flat, cutout foot plate with words "TRY ME", American, 12"L, late 19th C. **$65.00-$90.00**

Bootjack, cast iron, heart & other geometric cutouts, foot plate shaped like sole of shoe, "U" jaws with outward curved, rounded ends, American, 13¼"L, prob. 19th C. **$90.00-$115.00**

Bootjack, cast iron, impish devil figural, his high curving high horns forming the jaws, cutout round eyes and triangular nose, belly cutout, legs bent slightly & out at knees, little boots, American, 10½"L, (another one found measuring 10⅝"L), 19th C. • Pictured in Jean Lipman's *American Folk Art In Wood, Metal and Stone,* 1948, there is a picture of one of these jacks made of cast brass. According to information in the book, it was found in Massachusetts, is 10¼"L, and was formerly in the possession of the Downtown Gallery, NYC. Lipman also says "early 19th C", but I disagree. • In ads I have seen one very like this described as a boot scraper, but I fail to see how it would

work as such. I have also seen the same figure from the waist up. (One of these partial figures, 8¼"L x 3¼"W, from the Robacker Collection sold at the May 1989 auction for an under the money $100.00.) • For the full figure: **$180.00-$235.00**

Bootjack, cast iron, openwork design of simple tree in an arch for the foot plate, small cutout heart, with "U" jaws for boot heel, PA (?), 10⅝"L x 5"W, 19th C. • Robacker May 1989 price: **$65.00**

Bootjack, cast iron, openwork foot plate, very short, has large cutout diamond, small square, 2 round 'eyes' at bottom, 3 short peg feet, one at back end is shortest, American, 8¾"L, 19th C. **$30.00-$45.00**

Bootjack, cast iron, shaped like old pistol when in closed position; 2 halves hinge lengthwise; the barrel halves form bootjack jaws, the boldly cross-hatched grip forms the step-on rest. Elongated oval cartouch over trigger reads: "The American Bull Dog Boot Jack", named after (I'm sure), & prob. closely resembling, a real pistol of the time. American, 1860s-80s. Exact earliest date would be possible by determining when the pistol "American Bull Dog" was first introduced; said pistol was being sold at least as late as 1900. I suppose it is not unlikely that the bootjack may have been made by the pistol's maker. **$150.00-$200.00**

Bootjack, cast iron, with Pennsylvania German-style so-called "hex signs" & a heart, the jaws with slightly curved tips, American, 19th C. • The word Jack indicates that the device obviates the need for a living human or animal assistant, a human helper. Thus wagon jack & bootjack are related etymologically to spit jack, smoke jack, and bottle jack, all of which take the place of a person or dog used to rotate the spit by crank, gear or pulley. **$125.00-$150.00**

Bootjack, in odd insect form with 6 stubby legs, large head & heavy antennae curled at ends to form jaws, wings folded against length of wide body, known as a "cricket", this one polychromed in blue green, salmon, red, yellow & black, with all-white underside. The body touches floor at tail end, but progressively longer & longer legs raise head end about 10° above floor. You stand on the back with one foot, and use the "U" formed by antennae to pull off boot. No mark, American, 10⅛"L x 4⅛"W at widest point (at the 2 front legs), combination, partly by my family's experience with one. • *The Magazine ANTIQUES of Oct. 1937 has an interesting notice on the editor's page, quoted here in full:* "**Reflections on a Bootjack.** Years ago … on the December 1922 Cover, *ANTIQUES* published the picture of a cast-iron bootjack in the shape of an elongated beetlelike insect with scaly wings, bulging eyes, and a pair of spreading horns capable of seizing a recalcitrant boot heel with relentlessly conquering grip. The article portrayed was of no aesthetic value and very little monetary worth, yet its presentation in the Magazine started a flood of correspondence which, even after the interval of fifteen years, still yields an occasional trickle of laggard letters. Apparently what have come to be known as 'antique bugs' of the type described were cast by any number of iron founders of fifty to seventy-five years ago (ie. 1860s to 1890s), when men were still partial to boots.

"Mrs. A. W. Ferrin of Stowe, Vermont, writes to tell the (Editor) of finding such a bug, upon whose vitals is cast the device D. Kidder, Rumney, N.H. With so much information as a starting point, Mrs. Ferrin determined to pry into the geneology of her unlovely iron pet. Ultimately, from a surviving daughter of the maker, she learned that D. Kidder, born in 1838, was one of those Yankee geniuses who flourished in many sections of New England prior to the days of industrial concentration. According to a surviving daughter, Mrs. A. K. Blanchard, still a resident of Rumney, there seemed to be nothing in the field of mechanical engineering that he could not do or make. In all, he took out seventeen patents for household devices, most of which were in part made of iron. Kidder had barely passed his majority when he enlisted with the First Volunteers of New Hampshire for service in the Civil War. On returning from the conflict he settled down to his work and kept at it until his eighty-sixth year.

"Of rural manufacturing enterprises such as he conducted not a few are peacefully operating today, some of them on a more or less casual basis which gives the farm folk of the neighborhood remunerative employment during the winter months, but releases them to the fields when summer comes. Many persons believe that in some such unsystematic system lies the solution of distressing social and industrial problems. Perhaps they are right. Perhaps working folk are less in need of increased leisure than of more frequent shifts in the nature of their occupation." Homer Eaton Keyes, Editor. NOTE: I was not able to find a bootjack patent by Kidder, and the *Subject Index* which goes through 1873 failed to yield, serendipitously, any Kidder patents in other fields. A year-by-year search for his name, in individual issues of the *Official Gazette* would be necessary to research this further. • **Reproduction alert.** — This cricket bootjack is commonly found in reproduction. Most repros are painted black. An ad of John Wright, Wrightsville, PA, placed in 1978 in *Early American Life,* shows a 9''L cricket bootjack in cast iron (for $6.00) & cast brass (for $14.00).  **$35.00-$125.00**

Bootjack, "Naughty Nellie" also "Nelly". Bawdy, cast bronze, maker unknown, American, prob. 3rd quarter 19th C.  **$160.00-$185.00**

Bootjack, "Naughty Nellie", cast iron, busty woman in short slip or corset cover, her uplifted wide-apart legs form the jaws, according to one dealer ad mfd. by Screw Foundry Co., Alton, IL, 19th C. • **Reproduction alert.** — With old ones, the casting is smoother, denser, neater & the bootjack is worn. The reproductions usually have rough edges & a rather grayish iron. I found one unmarked repro "Naughty Nelly" in original box. It is rather poorly-cast iron painted black, cast with clothing

details — top of low boots, mid-thigh hem of step-ins, waist, and midway across bosom. The only mark is "LB26" on underside. The box has same stock number, plus "Mfd by Iron Art Co., RD No. 1, Phillipsburg, NJ" but no date. Looks perhaps 1960s.  **$120.00-$150.00**

Bootjack, "Naughty Nellie", cast iron, detailed casting includes hint of corset line & curly mop of hair on head, hands behind head, elbows out, legs up & out to form jaws, no marks, 9¼''L x 4½''W at elbows, 19th C. • Naughty Nellie or Naughty Lady bootjacks were also made completely naked.  **$120.00-$150.00**

Bootjack, unusual ladies' version, wood with old red paint, curvy jaws opening fits small court heel, American, 12''L, 19th C.  **$45.00-$55.00**

Bootjack, wood & iron, mechanical, dark stained wood, possibly oak, with forged iron and hammered sheet iron parts, the jaw pincers activated to grip the boot heel by stepping on the back of the jack with the other foot, very unusual, no marks, American, poss. PA (?), 16''L, maybe 3rd quarter 19th C.  **$65.00-$95.00**

Button hook, old square-head cut nail of forged iron, hammered, polished, twisted & chisel-cut with decorations on shaft, American, 4½''L, 18th C or early 19th C.  **$35.00-$55.00**

Button hook, steel shaft & hook, with decorative "Ivorine" or other celluloid ivory substitute handle, originally probably part of set for vanity table, with brushes, combs, mirror, etc., American, 7½''L, c.1910s.  **$12.00-$15.00**

Clothes brush, turned wooden handle painted red, natural fiber, American, 13''L, late 19th C.  **$90.00-$110.00**

Clothes hanger, bentwood shoulder with dowel pegged into shoulder and tacked with finishing nail, wire hook, I've seen several but found only one with maker's name, "Patented Phoenix Products Co.", Milwaukee, WI, 16¼''W, TOC. • Another one, 17½''W and ⅝ taller than Phoenix one, marked only with advertising: "Abbott-Hogan, Inc., Cleaners, Dyers, Orange, NJ". These came from Charlottesville, VA, yard sale, so you can probably find them anywhere.  **$5.00-$7.00**

Clothes hanger, cast iron, for trousers, mark is prob. clothing store not mfr, "Crow & Son, Hartford, Conn." Pat'd 1910.  **$40.00-$55.00**

Clothes hanger, coiled spiraled wire shoulders, 2 wooden clothespins threaded through bottom, American, TOC.  **$35.00-$55.00**

Clothes hanger, flat metal, accordian folding "lazy tongs" or "lazy elbow", to borrow term from hearth & early lighting, mfd by S. B. Kahnweiler & Co., NYC, NY, 16''L fully extended, early 20th C.  **$25.00-$35.00**

Clothes hanger, flat wood, with cord loop through hole in center, to hang on peg, broad shoulders with big round ends, from the Shaker community at Sabbathday Lake, ME, 16''L, 19th C. • The Shakers made many types of hangers cut from flat pieces of rather thin wood, all hung up with cords. Some have these nice round shoulder ends, others are just slats with the top edge rounded at the ends. Some have much more appeal than others, but a collection of several gains by having the simplest with the more shapely for comparison & contrast. In fact, the secret behind collecting, as opposed to accumulating, is **comparison & contrast.**  **$125.00-$185.00**

Clothes hanger, folding, sheet iron, "Buxton", prob. made for the luggage people, early 20th C.  **$7.00-$10.00**

Clothes hanger, folding wooden shoulders with wire hook, unfinished maple, no marks, ex-owner's pencilled name, "F. W. Shaw", 16½"W, late 19th or early 20th C.
**$7.00-$12.00**

Clothes hanger, folds & comes apart for traveling, stamped sheet metal, painted black, spring clips hold on the 2 shoulders, "The Tourist", mfd by The Beatty Stamping Co., Cleveland, OH, 17½"L, pat'd Jan. 3, 1905.
**$25.00-$35.00**

Clothes hanger, for suit or coat, bent heavy wire in simple shape, American (?), 17¼"W, TOC into early 1930s at least. • Some makers of wire clothes hangers (the type for dry cleaners I've tried to edit out) in the 1932-33 *Thomas' Register of American Manufacturers*, were: Parker Wire Goods Co., Worcester, MA; Washburn Co. Wire Goods, Worcester; Rupert Die Castings & Stamping, Kansas City, MO; Eastern Tool & Mfg. Co., Bloomfield, NJ; Troy Wire Goods, Troy, NY; Bromwell Wire goods, Cincinnati, OH; Keystone Wire Matting, Beaver Falls, PA; G. E. Ruhmann, Schulenburg, TX; Kaspar Wire Basket Works, Shiner, TX; & Milwaukee Wire Frame Co., WI.
**$15.00-$28.00**

Clothes hanger, from a trunk, as the long metal hook is very flat, shoulders of wood, no marks, 16⅞"W, TOC. • Trunk hangers have the least value, as they are pretty much useless without the context of the skinny pole in the trunk. In a way, they're like those hangers in motels & hotels, that can be used only by inserting on the permanent rings on the pole.
**$3.00-$5.00**

Clothes hanger, heavy gauge twisted wire, folds up, shoulders end in 2 hooks, no marks, American, 10 3/8"L when open, early 20th C.
**$20.00-$38.00**

Clothes hanger, long flat piece of shaped wood with rounded shoulder ends, hole in center for hanging cord, Church Family, Shaker community, Watervliet, NY, 10"L, 19th C.
**$170.00-$225.00**

Clothes hanger, telescoping type, for travelling, steel, with original very small snap-close leatherette case, American, small case is about size of dental floss container, but hanger opens up full size, pat'd 1913.
**$30.00-$45.00**

Clothes hanger, twisted wire, angle of the shoulders makes it look like a modernistic sculpture of an eagle with wings spread, no marks stamped in wire, American, 19½" tip to tip, TOC.
**$48.00-$70.00**

Clothes hanger, wire in shape of pullover sweater with long sleeves outstretched, child size, hanger loop at top, mfd by J. B. Timberlake & Sons, Inc., Jackson, MI, advertised early 1912.
**$30.00-$45.00**

Clothes hanger, wood & heavy wire, the 2 pieces of wood forming a sort of interior brace for the hanger, plus being a clamp for skirt waistband or trousers, the wire attached to it & extending out in 2 shoulder wings serving as levers to open the clamping pieces of wood, with hook at top, probably meant as part of a wardrobe or trunk system, as it couldn't be hung on a closet pole. On paper label, (showing skirt hanging on one, cloak on another): "The Belmar, Used in Connection with the Belmar Wardrobe System," mfd by Belmar Mfg. Co., Canton, PA, wooden part 9½"L; full length: 18", pat'd Nov. 2, 1897. (Company still making hangers in early 1930s.)
**$5.00-$8.00**

Clothes hangers, a novelty cartoon-character pair, cutout painted wood figures of Jiggs & Maggie, wire hooks, American, 1930s-40s. • Crossover interest from comix collectors.
**$30.00-$45.00**

Clothes hangers, pair made of orange stained wood, very unusual. At a quick glance they look like modern wooden suit hangers. But they were cut out — the shoulders and crossbar — of one piece of oak ¹⁵⁄₁₆" thick, the two slightly differ in outline. Both have holes drilled through neck with homemade heavy wire hook pushed through, bent for a small circumference closet pole, American, bought out of Staunton, VA collection, 6 ¼"H x 18⅛"L at bottom, prob. early 20th C. Price for each:
**$5.00-$12.00**

Hat stands, for closet use, available in sets or pairs, frequently charmingly painted & whimsically cutout wood, or metal & wood. Some are fairly plain. Some are figurals of animals, some flowers, some people. For example: colorful wooden & wire daisies, each with 2 leaves, on wooden plinths; or cutout and painted costumed bugs on wooden base with springy metal topped with large wooden balls; or turned wood columns with large convex tops; or satin ribbon-wrapped wooden stands, the tops slightly convex; or flat cutouts of flappers, gaily enameled with polkadots, the tops themselves shaped like cloche hats. American & European, usually about 12"H, but as much as 30"H, late 19th C (plain wood) into 1930s or 1940s. Pairs:
**$15.00-$50.00**

Shoe horn, also called a <u>shoeing horn</u> in the 17th & 18th Cs, wrought iron, with looped handle, American (?), 9"L, late 18th, early 19th C. • You can imagine Benjamin Franklin using this to put on those buckled shoes he's always depicted wearing!
**$85.00-$125.00**

Shoe horn, cast brass, handle in form of woman's leg with low top boot, American (?), 7½"L, late 19th C.
**$55.00-$75.00**

Shoe horn, colored celluloid, figural woman's leg (rather chunky — must be the cellulite, heh heh. Speaking of which, I always wondered why they don't call it celluheavy?). In high heel shoe, with rhinestone garter, c.1920s.
**$18.00-$22.00**

Shoe horn, enameled brass, in shades of turquoise blue shading to white, an eagle and shield stenciled in gold on top of enameling, "All America $3.50 and $4.00 Shoes", 4"L, TOC.
**$12.00-$15.00**

Shoe horn, lithographed hard cardboard, adv'g "Broadhurst-Young", Denver, CO, 1913.
**$7.00-$8.00**

Shoe horn, lithographed metal, very colorful, adv'g "Shinola" shoe polish, American, 1907.
**$25.00-$35.00**

Shoe horn, metal, adv'g "Father & Son Shoes", early 20th C.
**$5.00-$6.00**

Shoe horn, red plastic, figural "Slipper" with little court heel, decorated with scrolls & flowers, very pretty, early 20th C. • The only company in the 1932-33 *Thomas' Register of American Manufacturers*, listed as making plastic shoe horns was du Pont Viscoloid Co., Inc., Wilmington, DE. They made them of Celluloid, Pyralin & Lucite.
**$85.00-$120.00**

Shoe horn, simple steel curved shape with hangup hole, stamped adv'g for various companies, mainly shoe stores, including Dr. Scholl's, J. C. Penney, Penney's First Quality, Chicago Mail Order Co., etc., American, about 4½"L to 5½"L, c.1930s-50s (?). Shoe stores now give plastic ones..
**$2.00-$5.00**

Shoe horn, stamped & cutout brass, the handle flat and cut in the shape of a woman's leg in a boot, the formed horn is in the shape of a thigh in bloomers! Prob. European, 6''L, TOC. • Others of brass may have elongated narrower horns, and rounded legs, some with chasing and filework. • One handmade one is nickeled brass, almost 11''L, with fancy chisel cut & punched designs to indicate the lace on the bloomers.　**$65.00-$90.00**

Shoe horn, stamped steel, adv'g ''Chicago Mail Order Co.'', late 19th or early 20th C.　**$4.00-$5.00**

Shoe horn, whale bone, shell motif at top, fairly short, 5⅜''L, 19th C.　**$300.00-$400.00**

Shoe horn & button hook combined, folding, iron, pat'd 1915.　**$10.00-$15.00**

Shoe repair kit, for home use, wooden box, small cast iron lasts for children, ''Economical Cobbler'', American, early 20th C. • With the price of shoe repair going up exponentially, while the quality and imaginativeness of it goes down astronomically, this sounds like something whose time has come again! • A complete set would have lasts for men, women & children. Incomplete set: **$20.00-$30.00**

Shoe shine box, butt-jointed wood, painted black, long sides slant slightly outwards, footrest (which serves as carrying handle) is cut in shoe sole shape, heel part lower, room inside for brushes, rags & polish, American, 11''H x 12''L x 7''W, early 20th C (?).　**$25.00-$45.00**

Shoe shine box, cast unID metal, mounts to wall, apartment mailbox size, decorative front has pretty scallop shell at top, sunburst cast on front, hinged so it pulls down to reveal liquid bootblack, can of wax, shoe brush, ''Ideal Shine Cabinet'', A. C. Barler Mfg. Co., Chicago, IL, c.1890s.　**$25.00-$45.00**

Shoe shine box, metal & wood, ''Shoe Shine Street Box'', American Buttonhole Co., Philadelphia, PA, pat'd Dec. 12, 1871. • The very name of this one gives a hint at life in the 1870s. In the 1980s and probably as long as we wear polishable shoes, there will be an enterprising shoeshine person on the street. I used to patronize a very talented shoeshine musician in NYC, who played classical guitar between gigs (or shine shoes between gigs of playing), and gave a ragwhip wet shine as good as any in Chattanooga.　**$90.00-$115.00**

Shoe shine box, nicely formed wood, butt joints, 4 short turned legs, hinged padded lid opens to reveal screwed-on cast iron openwork footrest, awkward to reach under to get at brushes, polishes, etc., no marks, American, 13''H x 7''W, late 19th C.　**$75.00-$100.00**

Shoe shine box, oblong box with curved bent plywood ''roof'', finished in dark 'walnut'' brown color, opening at one end makes it look like small cat carrier, the carrying handle is a wooden footplate, with recessed or cutdown heel, screwed to top, in somewhat shappy condition, ''Slick Shoe Cabinet'', Slick-Shine Co., Newark, NJ, 14''L, early to late 1930s.　**$5.00-$10.00**

Shoe shine box, simple butt-jointed wood box, painted blue, with simple foot shape rest & handle, interesting because small stamped enameled iron ''Shoe shine license'' plate is tacked to one end, American, no city named, 1950 license tag.　**$15.00-$20.00**

Shoe shine box, simple butt-jointed, rather large, oblong lidless box divided into 4 compartments, entirely painted black, with shaped upright holding very well-shaped carved footrest with cutdown for heel, the piece so well carved it almost seems as if it were a manufactured part that

you could buy when building your own box. Best feature is on one side, the semi-script words ''Shoe Shine'' at a slightly jaywhoppered angle, created with faceted brass upholstery tacks. American, (found in Atlanta, GA), overall 15''H, box 7''H x 13½''L x 9½''W, c.1930s-40s.　**$75.00-$125.00**

Shoe shine box, wood, with 2 shelves, top has footrest in shape of shoe, with lowered cutdown part for heel, nice shaped sides, the unfortunate thing is the wood, like much of the wooden pieces in the Robacker Collection, has a dead refinished look, possibly due to Minwax® or its equivalent. This lowers value considerably in most cases, although I felt that there wasn't a shoe shine box collector (besides me & the losing & winning bidders) in the audience, poss. PA, though no visual clues to provenance, 15⅝''H x 14¾''L x 6⅝''W, 20th C. • Robacker May 1989 price:　**$60.00**

Shoe shine brush, for removing mud before applying polish, nickeled brass, beautifully turned wood handles, very stiff boar's bristles set in drum or roller, ''Alexander Feist'', W. Warszaw E., (Poland? or poss. the one in Illinois?), drum with brush is 4¾'' diameter, overall length is 14¾'', mid to 3rd quarter 19th C.　**$35.00-$45.00**

Shoe shine cabinet, cast iron with brass knob at top, meant to be mounted to wall, size of apartment house single mailbox, opens to reveal supplies, ''Barber's Shine Cabinet S195'', 16''H x 4¼''W, patent looks like Feb. 21, 1898, but this wasn't a Tuesday. • I haven't seen one of these, only read ads for them. One ad said 1898, another said 1893. It is possible that the 21 of February is the wrong day. In 1898, the closest Tuesday was the 22nd; in 1893 it was the 22nd. I can't check patent now; if you're interested, you can!　**$85.00-$120.00**

Shoe shine footrest, cast iron, figural horse with bobbed tail, one front leg raised, bolts or screws to wooden platform, no mark, American, 6½''H, late 19th C. Fairly common.　**$85.00-$110.00**

Shoe shine footrest, cast iron, in shape of dromedary with tasseled saddle & footrest at angle on hump, fairly common but nice looking. Unfortunately, the animal hasn't been made as popular as the horse. American, 8''H, TOC or a bit earlier.　**$45.00-$65.00**

Shoe trees, pair of homemade trees using old turned and red painted chair leg bottoms plus carved wood and metal hardware, American, 10¹⁵⁄₁₆''L, early (?) 20th C. • This is make-doing at its best, inventive, charming, useful.　**$20.00-$35.00**

Whisk broom, for clothes, natural broom, wire bound, reportedly PA German manufacture, 6½''L, early 20th C.　**$15.00-$17.00**

Whisk broom, handle is a painted sawdust & glue composition figural dog's head, American, early 20th C.　**$15.00-$20.00**

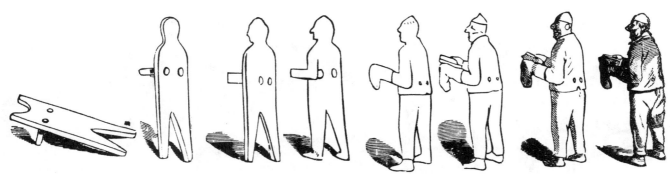

**IX-1.**

THE NATURAL HISTORY OF THE BOOT-BLACK, ACCORDING TO SOME NATURALISTS.

**Bootjack to bootblack.**
Metamorphosis cartoon that "tells the whole story...Perhaps a boot-black (one who earns a living by polishing shoes) might not like it, but then it is a great deal better to have had a humble origin, beginning low in the scale and working up, than it is to begin high and run down, as many a boy — and many a man too — has done." A cautionary tale in the "Boys' & Girls' Columns," in *American Agriculturist*, 6/1877.

**IX-2.**
**Bootjack.**
Cast iron, design of two hearts, a diamond, and various triangular interstices. 13 1/4"L, 19th C. (Similar ones are seen in a very useful article, "Bootjacks," by William Paley, which appeared in Spinning Wheel magazine, 9/1970. See Paley's figures 32, 38, 40 & 42). This one Ex-Earl F. & Ada F. Robacker Collection, autioned by Horst Auctioneers, 6/23-24/1989. Price realized: **$300.00**

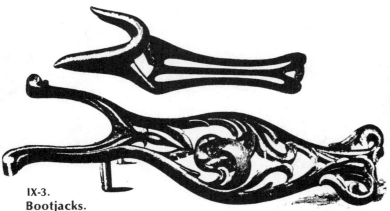

**IX-3.**
**Bootjacks.**
Japanned cast iron. Russell & Erwin Mfg. Co., 1865 catalog.
**$65.00-$125.00**

**IX-4.**
**Bootjacks.**
From an article called "Fashions in Boot-jacks," *American Agriculturist*, 4/1871. "One would suppose that a boot-jack was not susceptible of much improvement, and that a simple notched board, with a cleat to give it the proper elevation, would be all that was required. Yet boot-jacks have been improved, and have even been the subject of numerous patents. If one has to use an implement daily, he desires it to be made in as comely a form as possible; hence it is pleasant to have the crude appearance of the top picture, with its sharp angles, modified into the neatly-rouded implement next down. Those who travel much prefer carrying their own boot-jack to trusting to the uncertain resources of ordinary hotels. For the convenience of packing in the trunk, the folded implement, shown in the 3rd figure, has been contrived. Another folding style, shown in the 4th figure, has two stout pins, which, when in use, sufficiently elevates the end from the floor. When the parts are folded together, the pins fit into holes in the longer portion. All of the forms are easily made of wood, and numerous fancy paterns in iron may be had at the furnishing-stores. A bench for resting the foot while blacking, and which also serves as a box to hold the brushes, etc., is shown at bottom. Its legs are made in such a manner as to fold up and occupy but a small space."

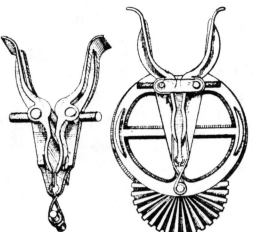

## IX-8.
## Bootjack.
*Cast iron bug bootjack that appeared in the 1874 Henry Arthur catalog of cobblers' tools, etc.; it was made by an unidentified foundry. Note the wrinkled neck and forehead and the pigmy-hippo-type feet with wrinkles. A reproduction design very like this was (perhaps still is) made by John Wright foundry in Wrightsville, PA, in the late 1970s.* **$35.00-$125.00**

## IX-5.
## Bootjack patent.
*Pat'd 10/21/1884, by Thomas M. Carpenter, Rockton, IL. Mechanical type, with "heel clamp levers" and "the pedal pivoted at its front end."* Official Gazette.

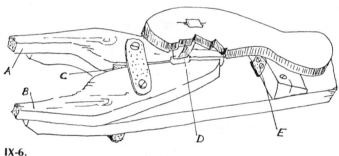

## IX-6.
## Bootjack.
*Mechanical homemade jack, with hinged footplate shown cutaway here to reveal the mechanism. "D" is a wedge that fits into a corresponding slot in the lower 2-part jaws "A" and "B", forcing them to close up and tighten around heel of boot. "C" is a piece of spring steel between the two halves, and it is supposed to spring the jaws back open as the foot which is pushed gas-pedal-fashion on the footplate rocks back in an ease-off-the-gas position. 16"L, 19th C., found in Pennsylvania. (Paley has a very similar one in his 1970 article, figure 13.)* **$65.00-$95.00**

## IX-9.
## Bootjack.
*This is a very similar one, with wrinkled legs & neck, but the back and folded wings are different. 10 1/2"L, 19th C. Photo courtesy Litchfield Auction Gallery, Litchfield, CT. Ex-Harold Corbin Collection, auctioned 1/1/1989. The price realized for a lot that included this beetle and a Naughty Nellie similar to the one in IX-13 was low — about half the estimate, or $140.00 for both.* **$85.00-$125.00**

## IX-10.
## Bootjack.
*Folding "American Bulldog Boot Jack," c.1880s-1900.* **$150.00-$200.00**

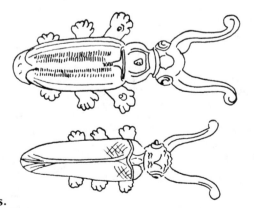

## IX-7.
## Bootjacks.
*Two "bug," "beetle," or "cricket" designs. Painted cast iron. Probably 3rd quarter 19th C. For more, see lengthy descriptions in price listings, p.168-169.* **$35.00-$125.00**

## IX-11.
## Bootjack.
*The famous "TRY ME" style in cast iron with lots of open cutout space around the letters on the footplate. 19th C.* **$65.00-$90.00**

**IX-12.**
**Bootjack.**
*Devil or imp, still, he's smiling and glad to help. 10 1/2"H, cast iron, 19th C.*            **$180.00-$235.00**

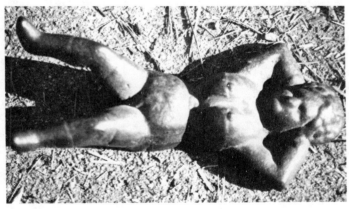

**IX-13.**
**Bootjack.**
*Cast iron "Naughty Nellie," no mark, 9 1/4"L x 4 1/2"W at elbows. Hint of corset line.*            **$100.00-$150.00**

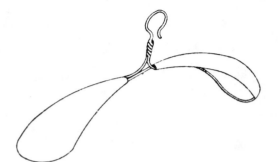

**IX-14.**
**Clothes hanger patent.**
*Pat'd 7/5/1887, by Frederick Taylor, Lowell, MA. "A wire frame provided with a suspending-hook and with shoulder pieces consisting of loops extended from front to back to form a broad bearing for garmets suspended thereon, and having the opening of said loop covered by sheet-metal pieces convex on their upper surfaces, and having their edges wrapped around the sides of said loops." Official Gazette.*

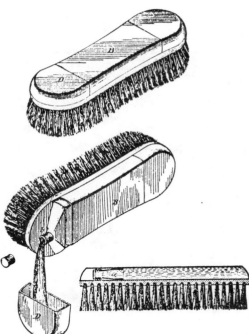

**IX-15.**
**Clothes brush patent.**
*"Combined clothes brush, flask, and drinking cup," pat'd 1/31/1893.*

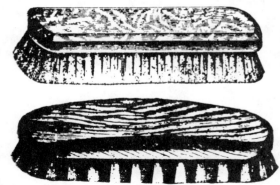

**IX-16.**
**Clothes brushes.**
*(T) Came in choice of 3 grades. Cheapest was 3-ply wood in mahogany finish. Next was one of varnished rosewood with black hog's bristles. Best was veneer oak in high figure, with "pure white horse hair" 1 1/4"L. (B) Slightly undercut edge to wooden back affords good fingerhold. Mixture of black & white bristles in outer row, rest was all black. A better grade was made with olivewood set with all black bristles. Both from Albert Pick, hotel supplier but not manufacturer, 1909 catalog. Similar brushes are found with advertising on the backs. The words are stenciled, stamped to look like pyreography, or pressed in under steam pressure. That type is more expensive.*            **$3.00-$7.00**

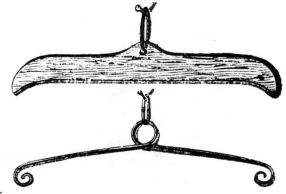

### IX-17.
### Clothes hangers.

*The Shakers are not mentioned in the 7/1876 <u>American Agriculturist</u> article by L. D. Snook, Yates County, NY, on "Hanging Up Coats & Vests." But the hanger seen at the top is very like the simple cutout flat wooden hangers with string loops that the Shakers are given credit for. Maybe Snook knew some brothers, or copied their ideas; anyone know? The article says, "If coats are hung up by the loop attached to the collar, they will, especially if heavy, and not frequently worn, become stretched out of shape, and when put on show an unpleasant distortion. To avoid this, careful persons use some kind of hanger, which will keep the back and shoulders in shape. A very common expedient is to use a portion of a barrel hoop, but it is not so suitable as the one shown at top, which is made from a piece of 3/4" board 5" wide. The length will be from 16" to 22", according to the size of the garment, it being an inch longer than the distance from the outside of one arm to the outside of the other, measured either across the chest or the back. A heavy wire, bent as in the bottom figure answers to hang up vests. Supports for both vests and coats, made of heavy copper wire, are sold by the street vendors in cities, but any one can make equally useful, if less showy ones, out of ordinary fence or bailing wire."*

### IX-19.
### Clothes hanger.

*One charm of old clothes hangers is their resemblance to flying birds. This illusion is enhanced by old ads and catalog shots presenting the hangers at angles. This is a "Favorite" skirt hanger, part of a "complete system for hanging clothes in closets or wardrobes, devised by the Chicago Form Co." The system "consists of a series of garment hangers, bars, and loops by which various articles of apparel, both for man woman, can be stowed away in the smallest possible space and without the slightest chance of becoming wrinkled." (Hah.) This skirt hanger "is so constructed that the arms carry the distended garment and the central clasp engages waistband. Arms can be bent to suit size and changed at will." <u>House Furnishings Review,</u> 8/1904.* **$10.00-$20.00**

### IX-18.
### Clothes hangers.

*"In these days of small apartments and smaller closets any one who can make two inches of room, where there was only one before, is a benefactory. Freeman Scott, Philadelphia, makes a specialty of the manufacture of suit and skirt hangers, that not only keep the clothes neat and shapely, but economizes space." <u>House Furnishings Review</u>, 2/1903.* These appear to have the vertical line of little hooks, from which to suspend additional hangers, that are found in closet-shops today. Although perhaps the twists are merely springy support to hold the half-circle shape. **$10.00-$20.00**

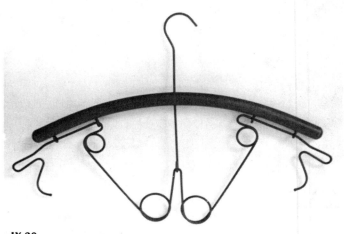

### IX-20.
### Clothes hanger.

*Coat & skirt hanger, bentwood rod, twisted spring steel wire. Partially mechanical—the wire's springiness allows the 'wings' to be pinched closer together, to fit within the waistband, or to have the tape loops hung over them; when released it straightens the band. No marks at all. 12 1/2"H overall x 18 5/8"W overall. Early 20th C. Compare with one top of next page, a similar hanger without the wooden piece.* **$25.00-$50.00**

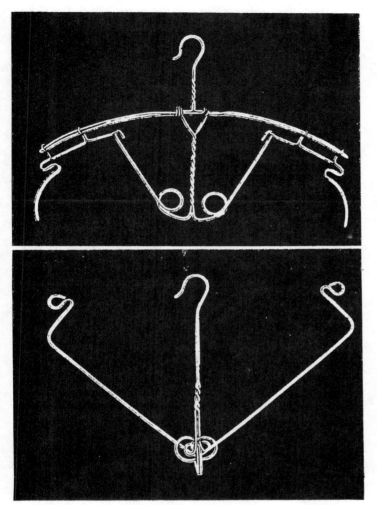

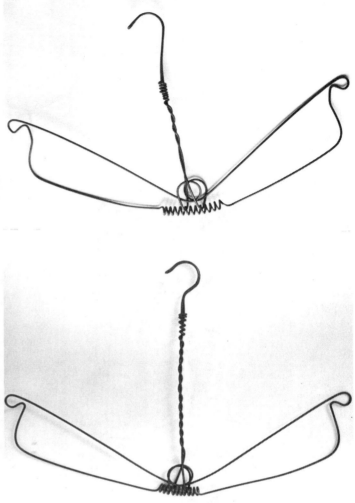

**IX-21.**
**Clothes hangers.**
*(T) "Vassar" ladies' suit hanger, for skirts and jackets — "entirely adjustable, and will allow the garments to hang in their natural form, retaining pleats and folds as when worn. Adjusting by the skirt's own weight to any size (waist) band, it leaves no mark nor causes any strain on the skirt." Meant to be good for travelers too because the hook folds down. Steel wire. Originally sold for $.10. (B) "Princess" ladies' skirt hanger, steel wire, adjusts automatically to skirt size. A very stylized bird form. Both mfd. by Pittsburg Wire Mfg. Co., Pittsburg, PA. Ad in House Furnishing Review, 8/1906.* **$25.00-$50.00**

**IX-23.**
**Clothes hangers.**
*Almost the same, and possibly they are different 'editions' of the same maker's skirt hanger. Both approximately 13 1/2" to 15"H x 18 1/4"W measured as the eagle flies. Maker unknown, but possibly Pittsburg Wire Mfg. Co., early 20th C.* **$25.00-$50.00**

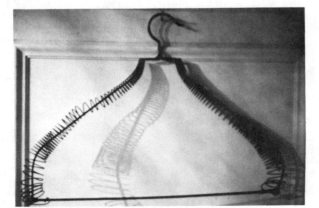

**IX-24.**
**Clothes hanger.**
*Simple, twisted spring steel wire jacket or coat hanger. 17 1/4"W. Probably early 20th C.* **$8.00-$15.00**

**IX-22.**
**Clothes hanger.**
*Twisted tinned steel wire, with springy graduated coil over shoulders. 15 1/2"W, late 19th or early 20th C.* **$25.00-$50.00**

**IX-25.**
**Clothes hanger & closet view.**
*Jacket or coat hanger similar to IX-24. Called the "Family" hanger, "very useful for hanging clothes in closet, clothes press or wardrobe." "Retinned No.9 Wire; 17"L; wires twisted to add strength to the hanger." Available with straight hook or offset hook. Norvell-Shapleigh Hardware, St. Louis, 1910 catalog.* **$8.00-$15.00**

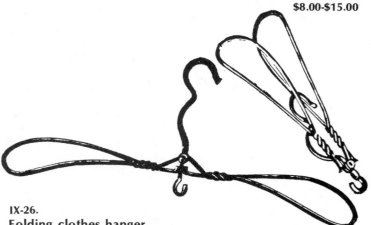

**IX-26.**
**Folding clothes hanger.**
*"Admirably adapted for use of tourists; very compact when folded; makes an excellent suit hanger when used with a trousers or skirt hanger suspended from hook," which can be seen mirroring the large hook. Nickel-plated polished steel No.9 wire. Norvell-Shapleigh Hardware, St. Louis, 1910 catalog.* **$10.00-$18.00**

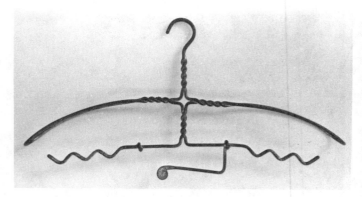

**IX-27.**
**Clothes hanger.**
*Woman's hanger, but I don't know what that lever-like hook at the very bottom does. 16 3/4"W x 8 1/4"H. The only mark appears on both sides of the small tab-like end of the bottom hook, and is "GO" or "6O" or "O9". Early 20th C. Right after I bought this, I was offered $100.00 for it, but that is too much.* **$30.00-$60.00**

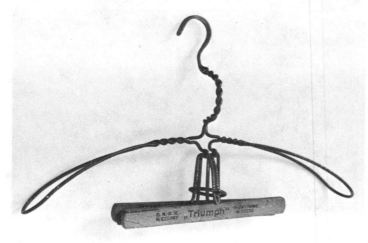

**IX-28.**
**Clothes hangers.**
*"Triumph" suit hanger, for a woman's, or possibly a man's suit. Twisted wire with slip ring to hold the two wooden parts together. Lined with red felt. 9"H x 15 3/4"W overall. Marked with German D.R.G.M. patent No. 220897, and British Patent No. 23252, which I can't date because the British patent system is quite different from ours. Prior to 1916, all patent applications were given a number; and awarded patents included the year and the serial number. In this case that might mean 1902, patent 3252 of that year. Beginning in 1916, British patents were numbered consecutively year after year, beginning with 100,000. The look of the hanger dates it to early 20th C.* **$30.00-$60.00**

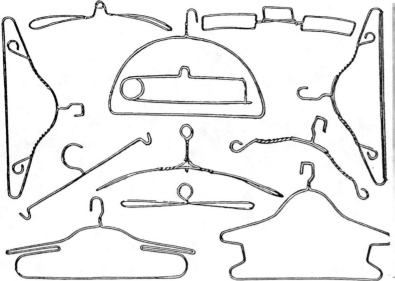

**IX-29.**
**Clothes hangers.**
*"Various styles of special garment hangers," approximately 12" to 20"W. All from the catalog of the Wire Goods Co., Worcester, MA, 1915.* **$5.00-$20.00**

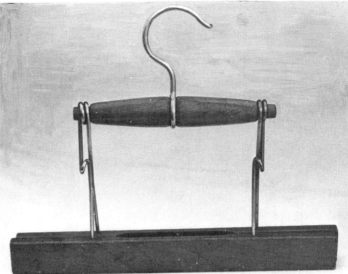

**IX-31.**
**Clothes hanger.**
*"One Hand" hanger, mfd. by Fox Craft. The patent# marked on it is probably 1,958,840, which, if a regular patent, would date it to 1934. But the word "trademark" is also stamped on the wood, and such a trademark patent number would be fairly recent. The hanger, appearing shiny and new in the picture, has signs of age. 7 1/8"H x 8 1/2"W.* **$5.00-$10.00**

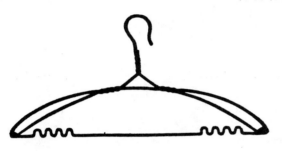

**IX-30.**
**Clothes hangers.**
*(T) Coat & trouser hangers with offset hook, heavily tinned steel no. 10 wire, 17"L. (M) Coat & skirt hanger, offset hook, no. 9 wire, 17"L; (B) "Tourist" folding coat & skirt hanger, no. 9 nickel-plated steel wire arms, 17"L. All from the 1927 "Androck" wares catalog of The Washburn Co., Worcester, MA & Rockford, IL.* **$5.00-$25.00**

**IX-32.**
**Coat & hat hooks.**
*Cast iron with japanned or bronzed finishes. Note acorn finials on center one, and swan necks on bottom one. Russell & Erwin Mfg. Co., New Britian, CT, 1865.* **$5.00-$12.00**

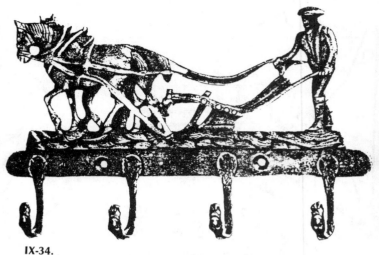

**IX-34.**
**Hat & coat rack,**
*also sold as a fireplace tool set rack. Cast brass, "The Ploughman," referring to a poem by 18th-19th C Scottish poet Robert Burns. 6"H x 10"L, available with 3 or 4 hooks. Pearson-Page, 1925.*
**$35.00-$55.00**

**IX-33.**
**Wardrobe hooks,**
*or hat & coat hooks. All cast brass. They are what were called in the trade "novelty" or "art" items, and are probably not reproductions, although the company specialized in repros. The names of many designs ("The Robert," "The Falstaff," "The Dun Cow," etc.) offered by the company can be traced; others are obscure, at least to an American unfamiliar with British lore. Some seem to be related to literature, some to architecture, some to churches, some to shires, counties, or villages. Clockwise from top: "The Durham," 8"H x 3"W. It represents a leonine sun figure. "Lincoln Imp," refering to a grotesque carving of a one-legged, long-eared figure in the Angel Choir (loft) of Lincoln Cathedral. It is 6 1/2"H x 2"W. Note that the tip of the hook also has a little impish face. "The Helston," 4 3/4"H x 2 1/2"W. The intricate heart's connection to the market town of Helston, in Cornwall, England, is unknown to me. "The Merton," 4 3/4"H x 3"W. Perhaps this is a reference to the zodiac (here a sign for Leo), a notable feature in Merton College, Oxford University. "The Collins," 5 1/2"H x 4 1/2"W. There are many entries for "Collins" in the Encyclopaedia Britannica, the connection with angel is unknown. All from the Pearson-Page Co. Ltd catalog, 1925. Birmingham, England.*
**$15.00-$50.00**

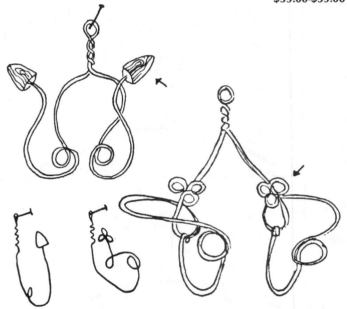

**IX-35.**
**Shoe racks.**
*At least, I'm sure the top one is. I saw it at an antique show the day before getting a letter from collector Sue Beckman of California, with a drawing and photos of something quite similar which she had. The top drawing is mine: it represents twisted wire with half-egg smooth wooden tips, like those found on shoe trees. About 7"H. Beckman's drawing, shown below, is twisted wire, 6 1/2"H. Two side sketches, extrapolated from photos by me, show approximate projection from the wall. Early 20th or late 19th C.*
**$20.00-$40.00**

**IX-36.**
**Shoe-blacking stand.**
*"Well blacked shoes are a necessity, but the operation of blacking them is irksome, and the apparatus used is a nuisance in the eyes of the housekeeper. Hence the blacking and brushes are banished to some out of the way place, to which the one who would use them must follow them. The house-furnishing stores keep neat blacking stands, made like the one shown in the engraving. They are made of black walnut, and when closed no one would suspect their use. Upon lifting the lid we find a place for the brushes, one for the blacking, and a stand upon which to rest the foot while performing the polishing. Probably the majority of our readers do not find it necessary to black the boots in the house, but a stand of this kind, even roughly made, would be found a great convenience in the shed or other place. It would keep the brushes and blacking together, and free from dust, and prove a comfort in affording a foot rest of the proper height. A person trying to black his boots with his foot in an inconveniently elevated position, shows himself in an attitude, the awkwardness of which is as amusing to others as it is uncomfortable to himself."* American Agriculturist, 2/1870.

**IX-38.**
**Shoe shining cabinet interior.**
*This is the actual interior of the cabinet shown bottom left. It has an Art Nouveau cast iron footrest with flowers & heart. This particular one was found with the carpet cover in poor condition; my mother hooked a cover that shows a ladybug. Collection of Robert D. & Mary Mac Franklin.* **$70.00-$125.00**

**IX-37.**
**Shoe shining cabinet.**
*Wood with high legs, cast iron footrest, carpet top. 16"H x 14" x 11". From Albert Pick catalog, 1909.* **$50.00-$100.00**

**IX-39.**
**Shoe polish tins.**
*(T) "Medal de Honor Exposition Centennial" polish, 3" diameter, lithographed tin. (B) "Eagle" brand, mfd. by The American Shoe Polish Co., Chicago. 2 1/4" diameter, lithographed tin with eagle with pennant reading "patent" in beak. Three choices — for russet, box calf or patent leather shoes. Albert Pick catalog, 1909.* **$3.00-$10.00**

**IX-40.**
**Shoe shining cabinet.**
*Oak, oblong hexagon with arched legs, cast iron footrest, hinged lid. 15 1/2"H x 17" x 15", carpet top. Albert Pick catalog, 1909.*
**$50.00-$100.00**

**IX-42.**
**Shoe shine box.**
*Homemade, butt-jointed wood. Partially painted in white (perhaps whitewash), with numeral "10" painted carelessly on one end, "V" on other. Elegantly shaped carved footrest with arch that provides handgrip. Carrying strap tacked on — it is leather cut from something, with short length of zipper left at one end. 10 7/8"H x 11"L x 7 1/8"W. Possibly dates to WWII. Found in Virginia.*
**$50.00-$70.00**

**IX-41.**
**Shoe shine box.**
*Wood, left natural except for cutout snake, which is painted green. Rubber on footrest. Rather deep bin on each side for rags & brushes; narrow dowel on side facing camera, forming rack for cans of shoe polish. 15"H x 16 1/2"L x 12 7/8"W, c.1930s-50s. Found in Virginia.*
**$125.00-$175.00**

**IX-43.**
**Shoe shine boxes.**
*Both homemade of wood. (L) Made of orange crate or similar crudely-cut wood, finger jointed at corners. Painted mustard yellow, scratch-carved with word "SHOE" on one side, "SHINE" on other. Plus the letters C I A F E N L or perhaps F I A FGENL (??). Shaped footrest made up of three pieces of wood. Slant front opening. 9 3/4"H x 11 3/4"L x 6 1/2"W. (R) Butt-jointed wood with leather belt hinges. Crosswise shaped three-quarter footrest. Painted a dull metallic gold. 6 1/4" x 12 1/4"L x 7"W. Both found in Richmond, Virginia area. Both probably from Depression era.* **$40.00-$60.00**

**IX-44.**
**Shoe shine box.**
*Homemade, of an elegant simplicity rivalling Japanese arts. Reddish stained wood of two thicknesses, simple cleat forms the footrest on slanted handleboard. 9 1/2"H x 12 1/2"L x 6 7/8"W. Probably 1930s-40s. Found in Virginia.* **$65.00-$100.00**

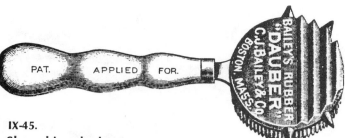

**IX-45.**
**Shoe shine dauber.**
*Brush for applying shoe blacking to "a low Shoe or Gaiter Boot without blacking your hose or the cloth top." Dauber made of hard rubber, and has corrugated back and pointed pieces for picking out dried mud, etc., before polishing. Mfd. by C.J. Bailey & Co., Boston, MA. Ad in* Century, *6/1888.* **$5.00-$10.00**

**IX-46.**
**Shoe shine dauber.**
*"T.M.C.", mfd. by Thompson Mfg. Co., Lansingburgh, NY. Bristles set in nickel head with sheet metal handle. Ad in* Century, *2/1891.* **$5.00-$10.00**

**IX-47.**
**Shoe shining bracket.**
*"Cleanem Shoe Shiner," a convenience that everyone will appreciate. Nickel-plated steel. From 1936 Washburn catalog. The fellow looks like a lounge lizard, but he is heeding the advice of an ad for shoe-polishing from the 1909 Albert Pick catalog: "The neat man is given credit of being prosperous. The man thought prosperous is the one that has the following. Hang out your sign of prosperity."* **$3.00-$7.00**

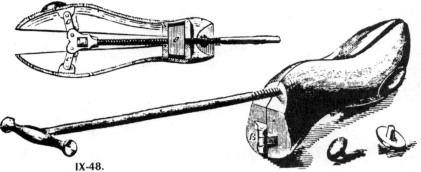

**IX-48.**
**Shoe stretcher.**
*This illustration is from a patent application by N.C. Stiles, of West Meriden, CT, as described in Scientific American, 10/15/1859. The two halves are cast iron and hollow, and connected by a hinge. Two levers shown on the underside view, are connected by a "rolling joint to the screw" of the long handle. "Local stretching may be given to different parts (as for bunions) by inserting the large headed pins into holes prepared for them near the ball and toe of the last." I've seen something very like this, only made of wood.*
**$25.00-$35.00**

# LEADAM'S SHOE TREES

For your feet's sake — for your shoes' sake — know what Leadam Shoe Trees **ARE** and the **GOOD** they do. Acquire the shoe tree habit and prolong the life of your footwear — take away that "vicious" curl at the toe — hold the sole of the shoe flat — drive wrinkles out of the uppers — avoid ill effects of wet and make your shoe a luxurious home for your foot.

WITHOUT TREES

WITH TREES

All progressive shoe dealers **SELL** Leadam Shoe Trees for men and women. Name on every pair.

If you cannot be supplied in your town, send **$1** direct. State size of shoe. **A Leadam Fountain Pen Free!**—Write us!

**Lionel O. Leadam**
**229 CENTRAL AVE., NEWARK, N. J.**

**IX-49.**
**Shoe tree.**
*Mechanical shoe tree, of wood & unidentified metal, mfd. by Lionel O. Leadam, Newark, NJ. Ad from Harper's 12/1904.*
**$5.00-$10.00**

**IX-50.**
**Shoe trees or Pinocchio's feet?**
*Pair of homemade trees, of carved wood, metal hardware, and red-painted chair legs. 20th C., possibly from 19th C., chair. 10 15/16"H, found in Pennsylvania.* **$20.00-$35.00**

# X. BATHING:

## BATHE, LAVE, BRUSH & SHAVE

Surely not! you say. People don't collect bathroom stuff! Fortunately, they do. This chapter has only a few selections, but I think I've touched on most subject areas. The large fixtures like bathtubs, wash basins or lavatories, and toilets (or commodes, as some people say), are mainly bought for creating restored bathrooms in old houses. As such, they aren't really collected. A row of kitchen chairs might be displayed in any room, but not a row of bathtubs. As far as I know, there are only a few people who collect, and thereby salvage, fancy cast iron bathtub feet, but that is an interesting area related to the salvaging of the smaller more portable parts of old stoves.

I remember in the 1950s and 60s finding lots of china chamber pots and gaily decorated pitcher and basin sets in antique shops. Many of them were from Europe. In those days, my mother and I attended Schmidt auctions in Ypsilanti, Michigan, almost every month, and there were always long makeshift tables set up in the back with platoons of pottery pots and porcelain pitchers. In the last decade or so, at least in the East, decorated tin (sometimes called tôle) toilette sets, each consisting of a water can, basin and slop jar, have been showing up in quantity at sales and shows. Although American companies made both the china and the tin ones, most of either type found for sale in America today are European. Perhaps the most popular ones today are decorated and/or plain enameled steel toilette sets.

The **Futurewatches** for this chapter are placed on figural rubber hot water bottles, small beauty appliances (electric and otherwise), and toilet seat sets. The first is particularly good for variety and span of manufacture (they are still made today), but on the downside, old rubber, particularly rubber that's been immersed in, or filled with, very hot water many times, tends to be partially decayed. Old rubber bathtub toys, not in this book, are a related field with similar shortcomings as a collectible. Most old rubber pieces past a certain age (say 1945 or 1950) have sagged permanently. I suspect that some collector somewhere has come up with a method for partial restoration — perhaps by slowly filling the hollow piece with some kind of air-reactive plastic foam (like wall insulation) or something to stabilize the sag and perhaps remind the rubber of the original shape in which it was molded. I've heard that old rubber toys and perhaps rubber hot water bottles can be filled with polyester fiber fill, and the rubber treated with neat's foot oil to protect against further drying.

The second upcoming category includes non-mechanical, mechanical, and gas-powered and electric implements and gadgets meant to maintain or restore beauty or health. Some of the things, particularly the strange ones from the 1870s and 80s which were galvanic batteries that were strapped on to various parts of the body, especially around the waist, and which were supposed to send revivifying electrical currents through the offending part, are collected by people who collect old patent medicines and quack medical devices.

From a more modern age, a very handsome collection of electric hair dryers could be made, along with various hair curlers, bobby pins, etc. Massagers made of hard rubber, wood, and/or metal would also be a great category. Some look like rolling pins from a strange bakery. Small beauty devices (including some that existed perhaps only in patent papers and maybe never made) include contraptions that you would strap to your jaw at bedtime and adjust to create the dimple of your choice (it had a small hernia pad-like presser that pushed into the cheek or chin, night after night), to steel finger-traps that reshaped fingertips and/or nails into an ideal rounded shape. Shades of Chinese foot binding!

About the third category, enough is written under the entry "Toilet seats" — near the end of the chapter. But mark my words!

**TOC** = turn of century (about 1900). <u>HFR</u> = House Furnishing Review

Baby bath, gray graniteware, oval with high sides, 14"L, TOC. **$135.00-$160.00**

Bathtub, porcelainized cast iron, long & deep, rolled edges, 4 ornate lion's-paw feet, no maker visible (probably on bottom), American, 28" deep x 5 feet L, 1890s. • Many variations of these exist; the most famous founder was J. L. Mott, of NYC. Many variations in the feet. Not all are lion's paws, some are fanciful scrolls or acanthus leaves. Most of this type of tub have been painted on the outside, and the porcelainized finish inside is chipped. They can be restored. • Another variation has a pieced oak rim. I always liked the contrast of sitting in that deep pool of hot water and being able to touch the cooler rim of iron. • Range is for unrestored to fully restored & re-enameled, with old brass fixtures. A re-enameling job is reportedly about $1000.00 for a tub. **$50.00-$2000.00**

Bathtub, so-called <u>zinc</u> (galvanized iron. See zinc under a washboard entry in the Laundry chapter) varnished oak rim, nice fat comfy shape, very light weight so if you find one, you won't have to hire a crane to get it up to your restored bathroom, "Kohler", WI, 4½ feet L, late 19th C. **$135.00-$175.00**

**"The Inspirational Bathtub."** — Here's part of a short piece, by Nora McNeil, that appeared in *American Cookery*, Aug./Sept. 1939. "If there is one type of advertisement that fills a need in me — that is, by way of wish fulfillment — it is the full-page, highly colored picture of the Luxurious Bath. I used to say, 'If I ever have a choice of just one room to myself, or if heaven turns out to be a chance to live peaceably alone in one room, let it by all means be the bath.' At that time my heavenly bathroom was done up in angelic white porcelain with bright nickel-plated fixtures and possibly a terrazzo floor. ... But time — and advertising — have changed all that. I have been increasingly 'educated up' to the higher realms of bathing, to the inspirational bathtub with decorations luscious as a stage set. It is difficult to determine whether the influence of these sometimes gorgeously Oriental — sometimes delicately pastel — tones and overtones has been deleterious or beneficial. On the one side, they have created in me covetousness, greed and envy, discontent with my humble lot. On the other, they have ennobled my conception of bathing. ... In a mood of depression, of morbid reaction to the tragicomdy of living (caused perhaps by some pinprick of pettiness like not liking your lunch or having on an unbecoming hat) you idly turn to the advertising pages of — well, almost any physically full-grown magazine. You do this because you are too dismally dull to read seriously. You are in doleful dumps indeed, when suddenly — your eyes are filled and soul uplifted by an ecstatic color print of the World's Most Beautiful Bathroom, a Great American Poem in Plumbing. ... There in the glowing sea-green bathtub, a foaming ultramarine bath rises into view. ... The faucets are fascinating little gargoyles, or sea horses, in silver or old-gold handicraft (or delicately wrought iron, if you like. No, better leave that for masculine baths). ... It is to be assumed that no one is waiting impatiently outside the door. This particular world is all yours. There is a wardrobe behind the ombre orchid panels. ... You are mistress here, surrounded by shapes and colors made solely for the enhancement of your loveliness ... alas, how few of us have the face or figure really to fit into the picture — of these godlike bathing places!''

Chamber pot, also vulgarly called a thundermug, white enamelware with cobalt rim & handles, child's size, TOC. **$12.00-$15.00**

Chamber pot, white enamelware, with strap handle, a sanitary product not in great demand today by collectors. Even less desirable are white enamel urinals, which cannot even be used as planters. American or European, last quarter (?) 19th C. • *The Vanishing American Outhouse: A History of Country Plumbing*, by Ronald S. Barlow, an amazingly entertaining & informative paperback book on outhouses was published in early 1989. It has everything from privy post cards, shown in color, to folklore on these smallest of outbuildings. It's highly recommended as Americana, and can be ordered for $15.95, plus $2.00 postage & handling (price subject to change with increase in postage), from Windmill Publishing, 2147 Windmill View Road, El Cajon, CA 92020. **$45.00-$55.00**

Chamber pots, ceramic, a collection of 29 of them from the early to late 19th C, mainly English, a few American and Canadian, was offered for sale in Jan. 1989. According to the ad they included an ''unusual crockery'' one made in America about 1840 that has a fitted snap-on tin lid. Other makers were listed: Soho, Ionic, Myott Son & Co., Ludgate Middleport Burleigh, Crown Devon, Falcon, Old Hall, Brantford, etc., from c.1813 to Art Nouveau period. • The asking price included shipping & packing for all 29: **$1230.00**

Electric foot massager, chrome base with green enameled metal body, white plastic movable foot part, ''Dr. Scholl's'', 3½''H x 6'' x 6'', c.1940s (?). **$25.00-$35.00**

Electric hair dryer, in original box, enameled metal with wooden handle fitting into base, looks robot like, ''Eskimo'', United Electrical Mfg. Co., Adrian, MI, 1930s. **$20.00-$25.00**

Electric hair dryer, metal, detachable from stand, electric, Knapp-Monarch, c.1940s. **$10.00-$15.00**

Electric vaporizer—See Vaporizer.

Fixtures for the bathroom, a set with wash basin (or sink) with pedestal base, large rectangular top with half round basin, toilet or commode & tank, all made of boldly, even extravagantly, sponge patterned ''flow blue'' stoneware

pottery! Royal Doulton, English, early 20th C. Note: Although a chandelier is a ''lighting fixture'', in bathroom parlance, a fixture can be the commode or sink or tub, as well as the faucets, wall-mounted racks, etc. • This fabulous set was shown by Bill Saks in his regular column on ''English Ceramics'' in Antique Trader Weekly, Aug. 23, 1989, in response to a reader's query. Saks provided the date, as well as the information that Doulton ''made a living ... producing a full line of telephone insulators along with sewer pipes'' as well as the figurines we think of as associated with the name. Saks decided he wasn't bold enough to place a valuation on the set, not being confident that ''many people would be interested in buying a toilet seat.'' Bathroom collectors are growing in numbers; ceramic collectors have been active for centuries. The twain shall meet — it's only a matter of when. If this set is ''unique'' in that no other exists in flow blue, the price could be in the thousands. If it is unique only because blue decoration was applied by hand to no pattern, but is one of a number of sets of basins and toilets decorated with ''Flow Blue'', then the value might be in the high hundreds or low thousands. • Wide price range pure speculation: **$900.00-$3000.00**

Hair curler & comb, 2 parts, nickeled iron rod with screw threads on end, attachable nickeled short toothed comb, longish turned wooden handle, to be used as a ''Bang fluffer and curler''. The directions read ''Heat the rod quite hot and insert it in the comb giving it a few turns to fasten it. Then pick up a lock of hair with the comb and by turning the comb wind the hair around it. This will produce the beautiful fluffy Bang now so popular and which will remain in curl a long time, even in hot weather. ... The handsomest and most practical curling implement in the market.'' ''Bijou Pompadour'', no maker's name given, American, ''pat. appld. for'' prob. 1890s. • Instructions helped too, in case you wanted a ''Mikado or Russia Bang. The bangs should be cut in rows shortest on the top and allowed to fall over the forehead in something the shape of a horse-shoe, being cut quite high on the temples, and left long between the eyes.'' **$8.00-$15.00**

Hot water bottle, copper, pat'd 1912. **$25.00-$30.00**

Hot water bottle, light greenish blue molded rubber in shape of pig dressed in morning suit, hands in pockets, pants striped, boutonniere in lapel, traces of black and white paint on eyes, a little red in nostrils, very charming, ''Noah's Ark'', English, 13''H, c.1920s-30s, Reg. #883164 (?). • Noah's Ark rubber products are quite desirable. **$35.00-$60.00**

Hot water bottle, molded rubber, Jayne Mansfield, c.1950s. **$55.00-$60.00**

Hot water bottle, red rubber figural teddy bear, in uniform, American, c.1940s. • **The Final Bounce.** — During WWII (and probably WWI?), rubber was a vital material needed for the war machine, and drives to collect rubber (toys, tires & doubtlessly hot water bottles) coincided with metal drives. My personal experience with a war drive was giving up my moon man rubber ball, molded with features in relief, to a rubber drive in Memphis early in WWII. **$55.00-$65.00**

Hot water bottle, rubber, shaped like a pilgrim bottle, round with the part for the water like a fat doughnut around center joined disc which forms a depression for an aching ear, could be folded in half & buttoned; as a half-round it could be placed at foot of bed for warming feet, "Bailey's Good Samaritan", mfd by C. J. Bailey & Co., Boston, MA, face size 5" diameter, 1 qt. 8"D, 2 qts. 10"D, 3 qts. 11"D, TOC. **$6.00-$8.00**

Hot water bottle, rubber, shaped like cat, Japan, 20th C. **$25.00-$35.00**

Hot water bottle, rubber with embossed nursery rhymes, American, 8½" x 4½", 1930s-40s. • Rubber hot water bottles were made long before this one. In *Thomas' Register* from 1905-06, at least one manufacturer was listed, viz., Hardman Rubber Co. of Belleville, NJ. There is no clue if they made figural ones. • Makers of rubber hot water bottles in the early 1930s were: Seamless Rubber Co., New Haven, CT; Universal Hospital Supply, Chicago; Tyer Rubber Co., Andover, MA; Davidson Rubber Co., Boston; Robert Pierce Rubber Co., Trenton, NJ; Parker, Stearns & Co., Brooklyn; United States Rubber Co., NYC; B. F. Goodrich Rubber Co., Akron, OH; Miller Rubber Products, Akron; Faultless Rubber Co., Ashland, OH; Sun Rubber Co., Barberton, OH, who made "toy" hot water bottles, probably referring to figurals; Pretty-Scheffer Rubber Co., Carrollton, OH; K. & W. Rubber Corp., Delaware, OH; and Davol Rubber Co., Providence, RI. A number of other companies made them of aluminum, or of unspecified materials. **$25.00-$40.00**

Hot water bottle, white rubber, embossed piggy in clothes & ditty "This Little Piggie went to Market", American, 9"L, 20th C. **$35.00-$45.00**

Lamp shades, for a pair of wall-mounted bathroom lights, common truncated cone shape, but with uncommon & colorful decoration on the treated paper: one has a shapely young woman wearing a teddy, standing on typical highish scale of the period, with bathtub in background & towel rack. Her hands are up in surprise or dismay. The other is a man wearing plaid bathrobe, shaving at sink & whistling (music notes), American, 7"H x 5" diameter at bottom, c.1930s. **$4.00-$10.00**

Paper dispenser, for advertiser called "toilet paper" (but what we call paper towels). Embossed stamped tin cabinet with pronounced cylindrical part at bottom for the paper towels in it, knob on side, at bottom, directions "turn knob to right & pull the sheet", "Hoyt's Toilet Paper", Scott Paper Co., Ltd., Philadelphia, PA, pat'd Dec. 22, 1885. • This also came in a nickeled finish with a mirror. **$10.00-$12.00**

Razor blade bank, off-white glazed modernistic donkey, with long slot in top for used razor blades, this one an advertising & political piece that was made at the same time as an elephant-shaped one, marked "Free with Listerine Shaving Cream Offer", American, 1936-37. • Other figural types include a square ceramic frog (also Listerine); at least 2 painted wooden ones meant to look like barbers; and a simple 2 part ceramic one with closeup image of man shaving, made by the California Cleminsons (and/or Cleminson Brothers). An all purpose ceramic one — "Samsonchina", came only in jade green, and is a sort of rack for the safety razor and a box of blades, with a slot for used blades. It's 3⅝"L x 2⅜"W, and was made in the late 1920s by S. D. Baker Corp, NYC. • Added value. — A

Democrat with its Republican counterpart, would bring more than twice as much as one alone. For a single: **$30.00-$42.00**

Shaving stand, floor standing, nickeled brass, adjustable beveled oval mirror, talcum powder tins on little shelf, American (?), 53"H, TOC. **$85.00-$150.00**

Shaving stand, floor standing, with round beveled mirror & swingout shelf, ornate cast iron, finished black, 52"H, 1890s. **$150.00-$185.00**

Shaving stand, tabletop, mirror, with brush holder, cast brass, TOC. **$45.00-$75.00**

Shaving stand, tabletop, not floor standing, ornate cast iron, bronzed frame with tilting mirror, 1890s. **$45.00-$75.00**

Shower head, in original box, molded plastic caricature of Richard Nixon's face, harge open grinning mouth — the shower nozzle comes out where his tongue would be, "flesh" color plastic, dark hair, to be mounted in place of existing shower head. I'm trying to imagine for whom this was the perfect gift. Gerald? Ronald? mfd by (or for?) Banning Enterprises, Baltimore, NY, 9"H, no date, prob. a Watergate item, prior to 1973. **$25.00-$40.00**

Sink, heavy porcelainized cast iron, thick pedestal, rectangular bowl has truncated corners, brass mixer faucets, no chips, American, sink 24"L x 20"W, TOC. • It has only been in the last few years that old bathroom fixtures, especially claw foot tubs and pedestal sinks, have gained a good share of the market. You used to find such sinks thrown out (and maybe chipped the first time in 80 years), on the sidewalk. Now restorers sell them for lots of money. Especially nifty, though comparatively useless in a one sink bathroom, are tiny corner sinks. • Added value. — Shapely pedestals, extra wide size, marble tops, and brass & porcelain faucets greatly increase value. **$500.00-$750.00**

Sink, or lavatory, round, with round pedestal base, porcelainized cast iron, faucets missing, 26"W x 20"D, TOC. **$200.00-$300.00**

**Up to Date Bathroom.** — "Though the house was not large it had, like all houses on Floral Heights, an altogether royal bathroom of porcelain and glazed tile and metal sleek as silver. The towel-rack was a rod of clear glass set in nickel. The tub was long enough for a Prussian Guard, and above the set bowl was a sensational exhibit of tooth-brush holder, shaving-brush holder, soap-dish, sponge-dish, and medicine-cabinet, so glittering and so ingenious that they resembled an electrical instrument-board. But the Babbitt whose god was Modern Appliances was not pleased. The air of the bathroom was thick with the smell of a heathen toothpaste. Verona been at it again! 'Stead of sticking to Lilidol, like I've *repeatedly* asked her, she's gone and gotten some confounded stinkum stuff that makes you sick!' ... He hunted through the medicine-cabinet for a packet of new razor-blades (reflecting, as invariably, 'Be cheaper to buy one of these dinguses and strop your own blades.') and when he discovered the packet, behind the round box of bicarbonate of soda, he thought ill of his wife for putting it there and very well of himself for not saying 'Damn.' But he did say it, immediately afterward, when with wet and soap-slippery fingers he tried to remove the horrible little envelope and crisp clinging oiled paper from the new blade.

"Then there was the problem, oft-pondered, never solved, of what to do with the old blade, which might imperil the fingers of his young. As usual, he tossed it on top of the medicine-cabinet, with a mental note that some day he must remove the fifty or sixty other blades that were also temporarily, piled up there." Sinclair Lewis, *Babbitt*, 1922.

Sink, pedestal type, with nickeled brass faucets, porcelain drain with overflow, central hot & cold mixer, heavy porcelain, 26''X x 22''D, TOC. • The square-based pedestals used to turn up frequently on NYC streets on Wednesday nights, when garbage pickups were scheduled. When you live in one room, you can't save 'em. I used to live in 16 rooms, and used several of the bases as plant stands. **$450.00-$600.00**

Sink, wall-mounted, porcelain, with very slender supportive leg that looks like a table leg, 26''W x 18½''D, TOC. • These sinks have a plump splashback, and were being sold by Scherer's complete with faucets and porcelain overflow drain, for: **$150.00-$185.00**

Soap & cup holder, wall-mounted, nickel plated brass, American, 8''H, c.1910 to 1920. **$45.00-$55.00**

Soap dish, brown & cream flint glaze "Bennington" type pottery, with drain holes in dish, one drain hole on short side, oval shape (some are rectangular), American or English, 19th C. **$65.00-$85.00**

Soap dish, brown glazed "Bennington" type pottery, all one piece, perforated dish level for soap, water drips through to bottom & can be poured off (and probably saved) with drain hole at one end, American, 2¼''H x 7''L x 5''W, 19th C. **$95.00-$110.00**

Soap dish, brown glazed pottery, with pierced set-in soap "tray", prob. American, 3'' x 4¾'', 19th C. **$85.00-$120.00**

Soap dish, carved burl, reach the soap through cutdown edge in front, beautifully bleached & smoothed by soap, American (?), early 19th C. **$220.00-$250.00**

Soap dish, cast iron, "Seargent's" or "Sargent's", poss. Chelsea, MA, 1858. **$40.00-$60.00**

Soap dish, cast iron, could be wall hung or set on sink ledge, nifty oblong holder with slanted slotted & ridged place for soap, 2 very short legs in front, 2 longer ones in back, 3 hanging holes in backplate, marked only "No. 8", American, 5¼'' x 3¾'', mid to 3rd quarter 19th C. **$25.00-$35.00**

Soap dish, gray graniteware, metal stamped before enameling with petal pattern, "Extra Agate Nickel Steel Ware," mfd by Lalance & Grosjean, Woodhaven, NY, late 19th C. • Very unusual. Probably used in kitchen rather than bathroom. Has sort of built-in wide hanger in front ... possibly for washrag or towel. **$75.00-$100.00**

Soap dish, molded rubber, it floats, shape of Donald Duck, Disney licensed, mfd by Sun Rubber, Barberton, OH, 1930s or early 40s. **$28.00-$38.00**

Soap dish, or soap scoop, carved pine, with handle, for early soft soap, nice bleaching from lye in soap; wood feels very satiny, American, early 19th C. **$125.00-$140.00**

Soap dish, painted cast iron Black Americana "Mammy", the oval "wicker" clothes basket on her head is a separate piece & forms the soap dish, American, 5''H, TOC. **$150.00-$200.00**

Soap dish, white china decorated in blue flowers, with perforated strainer tray, TOC. **$20.00-$32.00**

Soap dish, purple slag glass, late 19th C. **$45.00-$50.00**

Soap dish, turned wood, pedestal base, shallow bowl with approximately ⅙ of the rim neatly & partially cut down to make place to scoop out soap. Some possibility this bowl was for something else, & after the rim suffered a crack or big chip it was cut away & adapted to use for soap. Earl Robacker said this was from the Ephrata Cloister, Ephrata, PA. 3¼''H x 5 ⅛'' diameter at top, 19th C. • Robacker May 1989 price auction: **$225.00**

Soap dish, wall hung, blue enamelware, TOC. **$30.00-$45.00**

Soap dish, wall hung, enamelware in medium blue with brown & white agate veining, blue is in big round blobs. It's gorgeous, called "Duchess" by manufacturer, but "Turtle", "Tortoise" or "Chickenwire" by collectors, according to Vogelzang and Welch. Mfd by Vollrath Co., Sheboygan, WI, TOC. **$75.00-$115.00**

Soap dish, wall hung, gray graniteware, late 19th C. **$25.00-$45.00**

Soap holder, wall hung, twisted wire, lacy openwork oblong holder with wire twisted to make hanging holes on "backplate", American, 4½''L, TOC. **$20.00-$35.00**

Soap dish, wall mounted, nickel plated brass, very simple scallop shell shape with cutouts, no marks, American, 4½''W, TOC. • **Reproduction alert.** — This kind of accessory is being reproduced by firms that cater to restoration buffs. *Old House Journal* and *Preservation News* carry ads. . **$22.00-$25.00**

Soap dish, wall mounted, stamped nickeled brass, beaded edge, dish fluted, mfd by H. & H. Mfg. Co., NYC, NY, c.1907. **$12.00-$20.00**

Soap dish, or soap holder, wall mounted, cast brass, like slotted scallop shell, back plate has 2 holes for screwing to wall, possibly mfd by H. & H. Mfg. Co., or one of a number of other makers, American, 4½''L, early 20th C. • **Reproduction alert.** — And, you ask, how can I tell what's a repro? You have to look and look and look at old brass, many times polished. The reproductions never have nickel on them, instead they are lacquered (which lasts about a year). The old ones may have remnants of nickeling left. Tiny networks of multiple scratches going every direction, larger scratches, signs of polishing, dents or dings, and the color may be pinker or browner than new brass. **$12.00-$15.00**

Soap holder, wall mounted, nickeled brass, "Silver & Co.", Brooklyn, NY, TOC. **$12.00-$18.00**

Soap holder, wall mounted, sheet iron, fluted backplate, 3 connected sections — cup or tumbler holder flanked by dish for "toilet" or hand soap, also one for laundry soap, each meant to have grille for drain, Silver & Co., 11''L, c.1890. **$15.00-$25.00**

Soap holder combination, with tooth glass & toothbrush holder, brass, TOC. • These are often found still nickel-plated. Originally, sometimes, you had your choice; some people liked polishing more than others did. **$22.00-$35.00**

Soap & sponge holder, hung over tub edge, nickeled brass & copper, no mark, American, approx. 7''W, c.1910-1915. • Often these are found stripped of the nickel, revealing that the perforated soap dish part is usually copper, the wires are brass. They are being reproduced for restorers of old homes. **$40.00-$60.00**

Sponge basket, nickeled brass with perforations and heavy wire to hang over tub's rim, very fat and generously endowed, prob. American, c.1900-1915. **$15.00-$20.00**

Toilet chair, painted wood chair, cabriole legs, the hinged seat replaces the toilet seat, the space between the legs and the shaped back all filled in with painted caning, a nightmare for cockroach haters, but very fashionable with the extremely wealthy in the 1920s, "Zundel Sanitary Toilet Chair", by Killzun, Inc., Chicago, IL, fits down neatly over standard toilet, just slightly bigger than toilet, 1920s. • Hoity-Toity. — Whereas the Victorians made their toilet bowls into works of art of molded, glazed and fancily-decorated pottery, with polished oak seats, 40 years later the pure of mind & spirit decided to cover the whole thing and make it look like somebody left a chair in the bawthroom. The first one I saw, in situ, I burst out laughing. It seemed so absurd. **$15.00-$25.00**

Toilet paper holder, brass, cutouts, crested backplate, wooden roller, "J. L. Mott Ironworks", NYC, NY, TOC. **$40.00-$50.00**

Toilet paper holder, ornate nickeled brass, cutout side plates, scrolled backplate, wooden rod, 9" across, TOC. **$35.00-$45.00**

Toilet seats, yep, collectible. If not now, soon. After all, people were paying upwards of $30.00 for authentic turn-of-century golden oak toilet seats as far back as the early 1970s. Now in the 1990s, you can look for high tacky ones from the 1960s and 70s, reflective of the more popular visual images, color schemes and "simulations" (of marble, tortoise shell, caning, bamboo, etc.) of the time. The seats are either made of cushioned soft plastic, hard molded plastic with something embedded in the lid, or wood composition material printed with designs and given a baked-on gloss finish. American mostly, full range maybe 1950 to 1990. • **Futurewatch for Fauncy Schmauncy Toilet Seats.** — Among those advertised in, for example, 1973 issues of House & Gardens, and House Beautiful: "The Alumnus Johnny Seat", advertised as the "ultimate seat in the field of higher learning", with "your college or university's insignia and colors decoratively inserted on our exclusive foam insert and protectively plastic coated. Molded hardwood composition seats fit all bowls. Seats come in decorator colors: antique white, gold, avocado, light or dark blue, pink, black, woodgrain or red ... with matching hinges." $13.95 originally. "Crushed Velvet"... "something new in toilet seats. 21 striking colors of molded wood-baked enamel. Available with 12 luxurious velvet inset color combinations. Send swatch of material and we'll blend the closest combination." Also "World Replica ... Vivid reproduction of antique map with subtle tones blended together. fits any room decor — a marvelous conversation piece." (When?) All of these in the "Sitting Pretty" line of Window World cost only $9.99. Another winner is the "Fluffy Cushioned Toilet Seat...like floating on AIR. Sooo Soft! Not a thin foam padded seat, our base cushion alone is 1½" thick. Our top is heavily cushioned, too. Available in black or brown alligator, tortoise shell and solid wet-look patent colors of white, black, yellow, lime, avocado, pastel or hot pink, soft, medium or deep blue, metallic gold, brown, antique gold, orange or red." Only $17.49. (No further comment, but read it again. Ed.) Also look for those charming ones with "ancient coins" embedded in clear plastic lids & seats, and who knows what other delights! • In the Fall/Winter 1975 Sear's catalog are several $7.39 "Fun 'n Fancy" silkscreened seats with rather modest decorations

on the top of the lid, & larger designs inside, ie., "Fancy" on top & "Fun" inside. These include: "Throne", black linecuts on white background of small regal throne on lid, old toilets & plumbing pipes underneath; "Frog", with marsh flowers on top, perky frog & daisy on "yellow green", no joke underneath; "Dragon" with castle on top, friendly dragon underneath; "Eagle" with modest blue insignia on top, eagle & shield surrounded by scrolls & flowers (?!?); "Tavern Sign" with signpost on top, a ye olde rustic wood sign on underside; and "Poodle", a pink bow & dog. • Much earlier, "The alluring charm of ... lovely pastel shades and richly lustrous sea-pearl tints" were available in Church Sani-seats..."Toilet Seats For Better Bathrooms", c.1930. I bet you can't wait to get started! And I bet that guy who "did" lunchboxes, and is now doing cereal boxes, will read this and start doing collectible toilet seats. **$1.00-$15.00**

Toilette set, painted tin, 3 pieces, viz. a basin, water can and waste can. Basin or bowl has stepped foot, waste can has high bell-shaped domed lid, both have 2 gilded cast iron Egyptian motif ring handles, with Nefertiti-type head and headdress, triangular ring. Water can has crooked spout and high domed lid, also swinging strap handle & braced strap handle on side, all painted decoratively with dark blue borders, cream or ivory background with dark rose pink, black & gold *Japonisme* designs of butterflies, fans & bamboo swatches scattered around, also called Eastlake Style. Probably mfd by Heinz & Munschauer, Buffalo, NY, but could be European. Basin about 7½"H x 15" diameter, cans both about 18"H, c.1880s. **$250.00-$350.00**

Toothbrush holder, Fuller Brush, 20th C. **$9.00-$12.00**

Toothbrush holder, bisque china, "Three Little Pigs", with a flute, a trowel, and a fiddle, 4"H, 20th C. **$60.00-$70.00**

Toothbrush holder, ceramic in Tea Leaf design, mfd by Anthony Shaw, Staffordshire, England, last quarter 19th C. **$75.00-$90.00**

Toothbrush holder, ceramic, Lone Ranger figural, American, 1939. **$85.00-$100.00**

Toothbrush holder, ceramic, Moon Mullins, Japan, 5¼"H, 20th C. **$50.00-$55.00**

Toothbrush holder, ironstone, "Wedgwood & Co.", English, 20th C. **$20.00-$28.00**

Toothbrush holder, like a miniature coat rack, with engraved cast metal base with drip basin, vertical center shaft with 4 hooks at the top, ending with ball finial, advertised by, & possibly made by, Florence Mfg. Co., who made toothbrushes, Florence, MA, c.1889. **$12.00-$15.00**

Toothbrush holder, molded ceramic, glazed in rose & blue, early 20th C. **$115.00-$125.00**

Toothbrush holder, or rack, wall mounted, nickeled brass, scrolly shaped backplate with 2 holes for screwing to wall, labeled A, B, C, D, E, F for 6 toothbrushes, Forsyth Mfg. Co., Buffalo, NY, c.1905. **$12.00-$18.00**

Toothbrush holder, stoneware, bamboo style, with Tea Leaf decoration, mfd by Alfred Meakin, Staffordshire, England, late 19th or early 20th C. **$125.00-$165.00**

Toothbrush holder, wall mounted, machined & cast brass, nickel plated, a sort of arm that sticks out, elbow bent, with a catch basin concave disc at lower end of upright part, & a convex disc at top with hole slots for the toothbrushes, mfd by H. & H. Mfg. Co., NYC, NY, c.1904. • The same holder, only with beaded edges to both discs, was advertised just three years later. **$15.00-$28.00**

Toothbrush holder, wall mounted, opaque green 'Jadite' glass, no mark, prob. OH, c.1930s. • "Jadite" is actually Jeannette Glass Co.'s trade name for an opaque green glass. Anchor Hocking used **"Jadeite"**; Fenton Glass Co. used "Jade"; McKee used "Jade Green". Actually, I don't know who made this piece. **$25.00-$35.00**

Tumbler holder, brass wire, mounts to wall, American, c.1905-1915. **$10.00-$15.00**

Tumbler holder, machined & cast brass, mounts to wall, arm sticks out from wall, holds upright low-edge cup into which the glass tumbler is set, mfd by H. & H. Mfg. Co., c.1904. **$12.00-$18.00**

Tumbler holder, very unusual openwork nickeled brass, works like a tapered cuff bracelet, the middle part screwed as backplate to wall, the arms hold cup securely, very elegant, trademark is an artist's palette with S. M. Co. inside, mfd by Searls Mfg. Co., Newark, NJ, c.1908-09. **$12.00-$20.00**

Vaporizer, cobalt enamelware, 3 piece, for vaporizing into air some nostril-opening substances, TOC. **$125.00-$155.00**

Vaporizer, electric, aluminum cylinder, white wood handle, "Moderne Monarch Co.", St. Louis, MO, 1934 patent #1975939. **$22.00-$30.00**

Water can, for filling wash basins, looks sort of like a watering can for gardens, except spout is different angle, and it has a lid & is used to fill wash basin or bowl, (usually came in set with matching bowl), pieced tin, mustard grain painting, strap handles, crooked spout pieced at elbow & "wrist", American (?), 10⅜"H, c.1870s to 1890s. • These came in so-called Lavatory Sets, Toilet Sets, or Toilette Sets, which might include a great variety of wares, water can, pitcher and basin, shaving mug, chamber pot, slop jar, sponge holder bowl, brush vase, drinking cup, footed brush box, dentifrice box, cosmetic box and footed soap dish. • **German vocabulary** — Wasserkanne: water can. **$60.00-$80.00**

Water can, painted tin, green with gold & red bands, wooden knob on lid, 10¼"H, c.1870s-80s. **$125.00-$140.00**

Water can, yellow enamelware with black trim and handle, probably part of toilette set, marked "O F Co." or "O & F Co.", English, 8"H, qt. size, c.1900-1920s. **$50.00-$65.00**

**X-1.**
**Bathroom interior.**
*This and the next two pictures are from an article about "modern bathrooms" in The Metal Worker, 3/15/1890. The magazine took them from a catalog put out by Leonard D. Hosford, NYC, of bathroom designs. Above is a bathroom in Brooklyn. Under the window is a porcelainized bathtub with stiz bath & bidet attachment. Then a large bathtub with "shampoo cock" over it. Then a lavatory (sink) with nickeled legs. Next the "closet of the syphon kind with (wood) panelled cistern" above, and a wooden seat. Note fancy modeling of the molded china toilet. The room is tiled, and pipes are exposed to aid in cleaning. $450.00 was the estimated cost of installing such a bathroom, plus $200.00 for tiling!*

**X-2.**
**Bathroom interior.**

*This one is from a NYC bathroom, in a 10' x 4' room. At left, with the pull-around rubber curtains is a shower, called a "needle bath". Next a sitz bath. Above it note the warm air register with chains to pull to open or close. Next a "syphon" toilet, a porcelain sink under leaded window, with a mirror and a shelf. At far end of right wall is a "solid white earthen slop sink resting on plated brass legs", which may have been for a mop or for cleaning the bathroom. Finally, a sunken porcelainized bathtub within a marble rim, waiting for an accident to happen. The room looks huge here, but the scale is all off — they claim the tiling goes up six feet on the walls! Note lights over sitz & towels, and painting above tub.*

**X-3.**
**Bathroom interior.**

*This bathroom is from a house at 453 Fifth Avenue, NYC, and very compact. The article in* The Metal Worker *states that "the cost of a really fine bathroom varies from a couple of hundred dollars...to as many thousands as one chooses to pay. The merely useful with incidental ornamental features cannot well go beyond $500, but when art steps in the limit to the game is wiped out, and one can play as high as his pocket-book will go. Many of the most beautiful works of art, both in fresco and oil paintings are in bathrooms, and costly statuary in bronze and marble is frequently added."*

**X-4.**
**Bathroom interior.**

*Actually, this is probably a corner of a bedroom, showing a folding bathtub opened up and the hot water and cold water cisterns or tanks in view. The water comes from below, in the kitchen, where there is a force pump causing the water to rise to the chamber above. From catalog of The Mosely Folding Bathtub Co., Chicago, 1896.*

This illustrates a modern bathroom equipped with "Standard" ware costing approximately $145.00. The pleasure of shower-bathing is a revelation to those not familiar with its delights. The "Standard" Portable Shower shown in this illustration, costs but $15.00 complete, and enables you to equip your bathroom with a perfect Shower, as efficient as the more expensive permanent fixture. Our new book "For Beauty's Sake" tells all about this and is free.

**X-5.**
**Bathroom interior.**
*This "modern" bathroom, with portable shower ring above the footed tub, is from a Standard Sanitary Mfg. Co. (Pittsburg) ad in* Harper's Magazine, *8/1903. The toilet is seen to the far left, in its own little room.*

"Standard"
PLUMBING FIXTURES

In a Bathroom Five Feet Square.
Standard Sanitary Mfg. Co.
Pittsburgh

**X-6.**
**Bathroom interior.**
*"Standard" had the most wonderful ads over a couple of decades. They must have been very expensive, and many are in color, showing how color could be used in the bathroom. The first decade, in particular, of this century, saw a great new focus on bathroom design. This ad, from a 1923* American Magazine, *depicts a room five feet square — about the size of many NYC bathrooms now.*

**X-7.**
**Bathroom interior.**
*Another "Standard" interior, very much upscale, with a maid to assist the lady of the house in her toilette. (I laugh to think of a maid trying to fit into my bathroom to work on my hair. Hah!) Notice in particular the bathroom scale at the back, a c.1905 Chatillon "clock-face" scale, very rare, which would be worth hundreds of dollars.* Ladies' Home Journal, *7/1919.*

**X-8.**
**Child's bathtub.**
*An ad for Pears' Soap in* Century, *6/1887, gives an accurate view of the kind of pieced sheet metal portable tub used for bathing children. It was probably painted, both inside and out, and required thorough drying after use. It is perfectly shaped for sitting, with the legs straight out.* **$40.00-$75.00**

NELSON B. MOULTON, DORCHESTER, MASS.

**X-10.**
**Child's bathtub.**
*This ad in* Century, *5/1893, is one of a series showing real children, always named in the ad. This is Nelson B. Moulton of Dorcester, MA. The ad is for Mellin's Baby Food, mfd. by Doliber-Goodale Co., Boston. The tub is a painted round sheet iron tub with cast iron brackets for the side handles. The bands are a decorative carry-over from the hoops on coopered tubs of a similar shape.* **$30.00-$65.00**

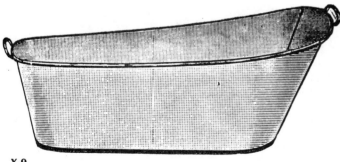

**X-9.**
**Child's bathtub.**
*This one, though found in a 1920 catalog, is of a type probably a hundred years old even then. It is pieced sheet metal with fixed handles, and was painted white. Note supportive higher end. It came in three sizes: 28"L, 30 1/2" and 33"L. Central Stamping Co., NYC.* **$30.00-$65.00**

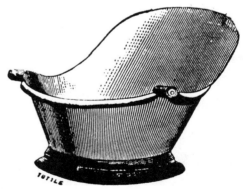

**X-11.**
**Hip bath.**
*Also from the 1920 Central Stamping catalog is what is also called a "sitz" bath, and it was meant for bathing the bottom and immersing the abdominal parts in soothing hot water. This was offered with green paint, and was 27". Note the handle grips (which may have been turned wood), and the rolled rim.* **$40.00-$85.00**

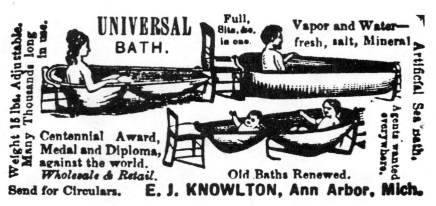

UNIVERSAL BATH.

Full, Sits, &c. in one.

Vapor and Water— fresh, salt, Mineral

Weight 15 lbs. Adjustable. Many Thousands long in use.

Artificial Sea Bath. Agents wanted everywhere.

Centennial Award, Medal and Diploma, against the world.
*Wholesale & Retail.*

Old Baths Renewed.

Send for Circulars. E. J. KNOWLTON, Ann Arbor, Mich.

### X-12.
### Portable bath.

*I believe these "Universal" bathtubs were rubberized cloth, and were meant to be stowed away between uses, or perhaps even taken on trips. Many tiny ads (this is blown up considerably) appeared in the 1880s in* Harper's *and* Century. *The value would be low, but the curiosity value is high.*

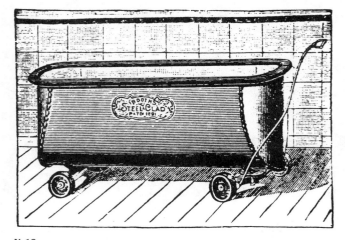

### X-13.
### Portable bath.

*Another type is this "Steel Clad" bath on wheels, actually meant for hospitals "and the sick room", but useful I'm sure in other circumstances. Those of you who have been to Brimfield, MA, to the huge flea markets there, have seen many people dragging little red wagons behind for their possessions. It is considered much "cooler" than dragging a folding shopping cart, which is what I use. Couldn't we set them all back with one of these tubs!* Steel Clad Bath Co., NYC. Century, *12/1895.* **$40.00-$60.00**

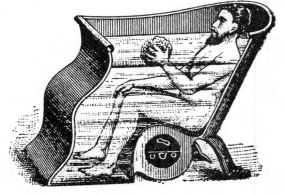

### X-15.
### German bathtubs.

*"The German engravings show tubs that if only mounted with American casters could be moved with ease. Under the seat is a heating stove. A pattern could be obtained for such a tub by taking a sheet of paper against the wall, having a person sit up close to the paper, then marking about him. The ordinary bath, in which one sits flat with feet extended, is neither a convenient nor comfortable resting place, for it is only in fancy that we can sit flat on a floor without discomfort. Furniture-makers provide us with chairs to sit on in the day time and beds to lie on at night, but the manufacturers of bathtubs make them so that we can neither sit nor lie in comfort."* The Metal Worker, *1/25/1890.*
**$100.00-$200.00**

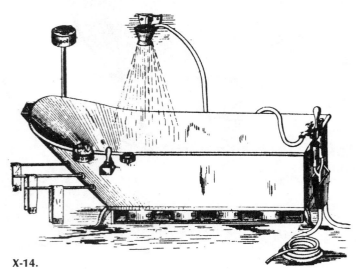

### X-14.
### Portable bath-tub patent.

*Pat'd 6/16/1885 by Horace R. Allen, Indianpolis. This tub is served by a "showerer", a flexible drainpipe, a water pump & pipes, and even fold-out rods for towels.*

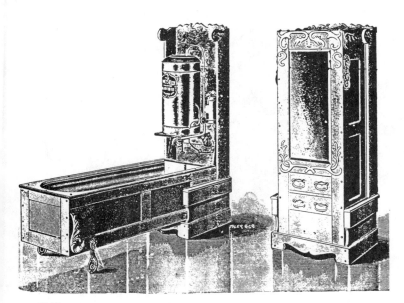

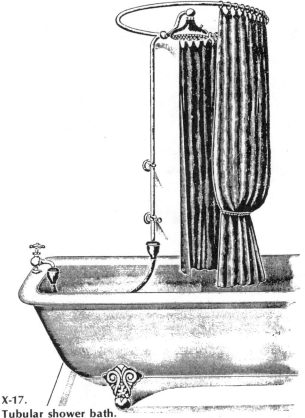

### X-16.
### Foldaway bathtub.
*"Saves the expenses of a bathroom" claims the maker of this and 11 other folding tubs. This one is the "Armour", made of ash wood, finished "either Antique, XVI Century or Natural." The mirror is beveled, the drawers are "imitation". The tub is 5'6" lond, 22"W and 17" deep, and it could be ordered with a kerosene, gas or gasoline heater, with enameled interior, and with faucet; also a more expensive version could be had with a tinned copper lining. In the catalog are reprinted wonderful letters from users. One from S.P.R. Triscott, Monhegan Island, ME, states the tub "is a thing of beauty and a joy forever." Has anyone ever seen one? Mosely Folding Bathtub Co., 1896.* **$100.00-$200.00**

### X-17.
### Tubular shower bath.
*The catalog picture here shows a shower attachment which is fixed to the wall above the tub and hung with rubber curtains. The rubber hose between the tub's faucet and the shower pipe is actually five feet long! S. Sternau & Co., Brooklyn, 1900.*

### X-18.
### Shower bath spray.
*Everyone at the turn of the century was interested in showers it seems. This one, also from S. Sternau, is almost identical to the shower attachments we can buy today for fitting to a tub faucet, except that the hose length is definitely more generous. The spray head is nickeled brass.* **$2.00-$5.00**

### X-19.
### Bronchitis kettle.
One form of vaporizer meant for putting soothing medicated hot steam or mist into the air. Pieced and stamped tin, with detachable spout fitted with a spatulate nozzle with holes. It came in 3, 4 and 6 pint sizes. H. Rogers, Wolverhampton, England, 1914. **$20.00-$35.00**

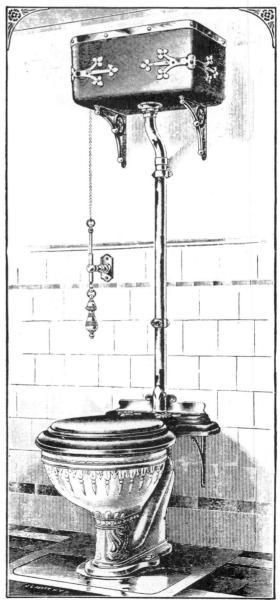

### X-21.
### Chamber pails.
(L) A commode pail of galvanized sheet metal, with wire bail handle, close-fitting lid, and a rounded wooden detachable seat. It held 10 7/8 quarts. (R) A chamber pail, without a seat, finished either in white paint or imitation oak graining. It came in a 10 and 12 quart size. Central Stamping Co., 1920. **$10.00-$20.00**

### X-20.
### Advertising broadside.
Humorous giveaway advertising was commonly printed on flimsy paper. Often the subject of the broadside was not connected to the company employing them. Here, the "joke" is the pronunciation of Covert — the company making harness chains and ropes. Covert Mfg. Co., West Troy, NY, c.1870s. **$12.00-$20.00**

### X-22.
### "Syphon-Jet Water-Closet."
This highly decorative toilet with water tank above and pull chain (note the neat bracket on the wall) is the "Primo" style. "The bowl contains a large body of water, and there are no mechanical parts liable to get out of order. When the pull is drawn the Syphon is started and contents of Bowl are almost noiselessly ejected." The J.L. Mott Iron Works of NYC placed the ad and called it "imported". They did cast and enamel their own cast iron bathroom fixtures. _Century_, 5/1892. The value lies mainly in the decorative bowl. **$200.00-$300.00**

Copyright 1892, by The J. L. Mott Iron Works.

**X-23.**
**Electric hair dryer.**
*Hamilton Beach Junior No. 3. Held in the hand or set in the stand at any angle. Switch gave either hot or cold "blasts" of air. Nickeled or finished in "boudoir old ivory". D.J. Barry wholesale catalog, 1924.*

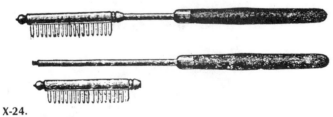

**X-24.**
**Bang fluffer and curler.**
*This is the Bijou Pompadour curling iron, with detachable comb so that the rod could be heated by itself and the comb only "indirectly" heated. Nickeled brass. From a c.1880 flyer, which itself is worth about $10.00.* **$10.00-$15.00**

**X-25.**
**"Electric" massage roller.**
*The word "electric" was used frequently in connection with health and beauty aids, because it implied a certain galvanic, immediate, startlingly good result. Some items actually had some kind of battery in them, others did not, or claimed a galvanic reaction by the mixing of metals within. This one, available in gold or silver finish, with turned wood handle, required "no charging. Will last forever." The Dr. John Wilson Gibbs' roller was meant both for the "reduction of corpulency" and the "building up of (muscle) tissues." The ad, from McClure's, 3/1899, quotes a newspaper writer as saying it could "take a pound a day off a patient, or put it on."* **$5.00-$10.00**

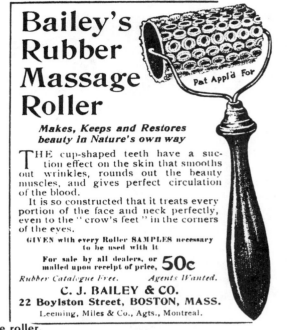

**Bailey's Rubber Massage Roller**

*Makes, Keeps and Restores beauty in Nature's own way*

THE cup-shaped teeth have a suction effect on the skin that smooths out wrinkles, rounds out the beauty muscles, and gives perfect circulation of the blood.

It is so constructed that it treats every portion of the face and neck perfectly, even to the "crow's feet" in the corners of the eyes.

GIVEN with every Roller SAMPLES necessary to be used with it

For sale by all dealers, or mailed upon receipt of price, **50c**

*Rubber Catalogue Free.* *Agents Wanted.*

**C. J. BAILEY & CO.**
**22 Boylston Street, BOSTON, MASS.**
Leeming, Miles & Co., Agts., Montreal.

**X-26.**
**Massage roller.**
*The roller here is rubber and has "cup-shaped teeth (that) have a suction effect on the skin that smooths out wrinkles, rounds out the beauty muscles, and gives perfect circulation." C.J. Bailey & Co., Boston. Ad in* Ladies' Home Journal, *9/1902.* **$5.00-$10.00**

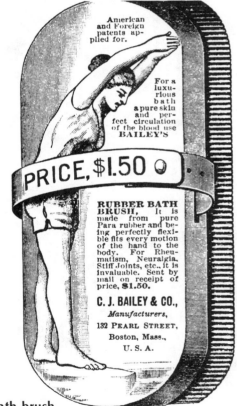

American and Foreign patents applied for.

For a luxurious bath a pure skin and perfect circulation of the blood use BAILEY'S

**PRICE, $1.50**

**RUBBER BATH BRUSH.** It is made from pure Para rubber and being perfectly flexible fits every motion of the hand to the body. For Rheumatism, Neuralgia, Stiff Joints, etc., it is invaluable. Sent by mail on receipt of price, $1.50.

**C. J. BAILEY & CO.,**
*Manufacturers,*
**132 PEARL STREET,**
Boston, Mass.,
U. S. A.

**X-27.**
**Flesh & bath brush.**
*Again here is something that works on the theory that scrubbing the surface hard and thereby increasing circulation would carry away fat cells. Two types of ads were used: this one, with a well-drawn bathing beauty, and the text of the ad printed on the back of the rubber brush, and a later one which shows the back of the brush as it really appears — with a much simplified embossed image of the woman, and the words "Bailey's Rubber Bath and Flesh Brush Gives Perfect Circulation on The Blood and Purifies the Skin." 5' x 3".* Century, *11/1887.* **$10.00-$15.00**

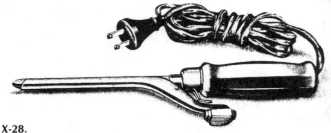

### X-28.
### Electric curling iron.
*General Electric Hotpoint. Chrome-plated with "cool, insulated tusk-ivory finish handle." The other styles had detachable cord, and wood handles. 1935-36 catalog.* **$8.00-$15.00**

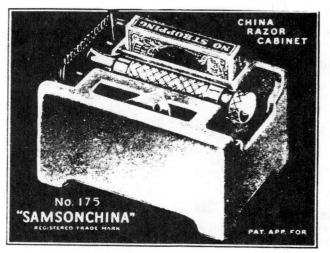

### X-31.
### Razor cabinet.
*Jade green china holder that "provides parking space for a Safety Razor and a package of New Blades." "Used blades are deposited like pennies in a bank for future disposal. 3 5/8" x 2 3/4". "Samsonchina", S.D. Baker Corp., NYC. Ad from House & Gardens, 12/1927.* **$5.00-$10.00**

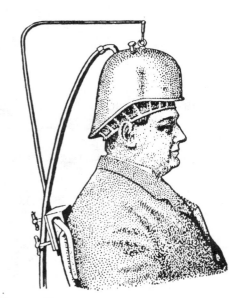

### X-29.
### Hair-growing appliance.
*"The Evans Vacuum Cap provides the scientific means of applying to the scalp the common sense principles of physical culture." This ad claims that stagnant blood causes the hair to fall out, and this electric sucking cap would cause it to grow back. The appliance clamped to a chair. Dating up to 1905, the cap fitted neatly into a faddish fitness movement of the time, exemplified by Bernarr McFadden, which put the pursuit of "physical culture" on par with the 10 Commandments.* **$15.00-$30.00**

### X-32.
### Shaving brush.
*"Drip-Cup Lather Brush", pat'd 2/15/1887. The dripping water and soap "collects in the handle-cup, where it remains during the process of lathering the face. The water flows out of the drip-cup when the Brush is returned to the Shaving Mug." The cup could be had with a britannia metal or nickel-plated handle, and the brush with "white" or "badger" bristles. Manning, Bowman & Co., Meriden, CT, c.1892.* **$7.00-$10.00**

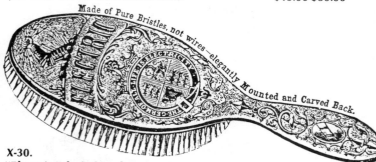

### X-30.
### "Electric" hair brush.
*A bristle brush set in an embossed "new odorless composition (back) resembling ebony — a combination of substances producing a permanent electro-magnetic current which acts immediately upon the hair glands and follicles. This power can always be tested by a silver compass which accompanies each Brush." In five minutes it was claimed to cure "nervous headache, bilious headache, neuralgia, dandruff, and falling hair." At the time of the Harper's Weekly ad, 10/22/1881, it was claimed that over 3-million had been sold. Have you ever seen one? Dr. George A. Scott, NYC.* **$18.00- $30.00**

**X-33.**
### Soap & toothbrush dishes.
*(L) Tinned steel wire, with rack for three brushes. Wallhung. 4 3/4"L x 3 1/4"W. Dish is 1" deep. (R) Footed one, same measurements. Wire Goods Co., Worcester, MA, 1915. This company either took over, or evolved from the much earlier Sherwood wire goods company of the same place.* **$10.00-$20.00**

**X-36.**
### Soap dishes.
*All sink or countertop. All are nickeled brass with cast feet. Top (L & R) have reticulated (perforated) cup with separate china dishes. Oval 6" x 4 3/4"; oblong 5 1/4"L x 4"W. Bottom one 6"L x 4 3/4"W. Sternau, 1900.* **$10.00-$22.00**

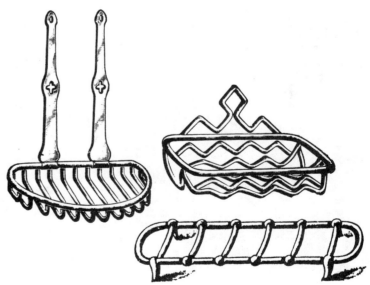

**X-34.**
### Comb & brush tray.
*Nickeled wire bent in zigzags. Looks very like their soap dish of the same design — only the size is a clue: 9 3/8"L x 4 3/4"W. 1" deep. Sternau, 1900.* **$6.00-$12.00**

**X-37.**
### Soap dish.
*Galvanized sheet iron, removable drainer with holes. Size not known, but looks as if it were to hook over back of rounded edge of sink, so probably quite large. John Van Co., Cincinnati, 1914.* **$10.00-$22.00**

**X-35.**
### Soap dish.
*Nickeled brass. Has a removable slotted metal drainer inside. Hinged cover. 5"L x 3 1/2"W. Sternau, 1900.* **$10.00-$18.00**

**X-38.**
### Soap dishes.
*All nickeled brass welded wires. (L) Wallhung or adjustable, with sheet metal hangers that could be kept vertical, or bent to fit curve of sink back or tub edge. 5"L x 3"W with 9"L hangers. 1" deep to zigzag one is so constructed as to "absolutely prevent soap from slipping through". It's 6"L x 3-1/2"W x 1-1/4" deep. Overall 3-1/2"H. The rack with widely-spaced wires below is toothbrush rack. Sternau, 1900.* **$10.00-$22.00**

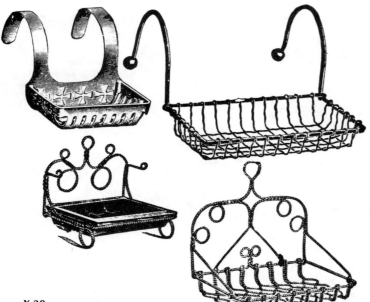

### X-39.
### Soap dishes.
*Top two from the Albert Pick 1909 catalog are the "adjustable" kind, meant to be bent to fit edge of tub or sink. Top (L) is "self-draining. Nickeled stamped & reticulated brass. 5"L x 3 1/2"W. Bottom two are from the Paine, Diehl & Co. 1888 catalog, and date back much further that the catalog in which they are found, probably to the early 1870s. They are tinned iron wire, and the (L) one has two projections on which to lay a toothbrush. (R) is "Hayward's Patent Adjustable", originally mfd. by Sherwood's wire goods company in Worcester, MA. Bottom two worth the most.*
**$10.00-$30.00**

### X-41.
### Sponge baskets or holders.
*All nickeled brass. (T) Combination with soap dish below, for tub edge. Mackie-Lovejoy Mfg. Co., Chicago. Top (R) is simple but graceful wire, oval, 9"L x 6"W. Below that is a sponge or soap holder for mounting on the wall. It's oval and has a hook underneath for towel or washcloth. 5-1/4" x 3-3/4". (B) Another combination — "both self-draining." Soap cup oval 3-1/4" x 5"; sponge holder is 5-1/2" x 6-1/2". Last three are from Albert Pick catalog, 1909.*
**$12.00-$30.00**

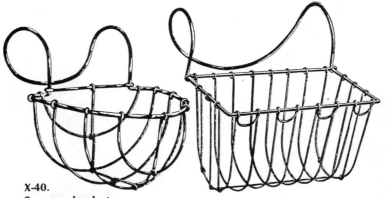

### X-40.
### Sponge baskets.
*People didn't seem to have used washcloths, but rather natural sponges, which were bulky and plump and had to be drained after the bath. These nickeled brass wire baskets hung over the edge of the tub. (L) 7" x 4 1/2" x 4 1/2". (R) 8" x 5" x 5". These are beginning to be seen at flea markets, now that more people are interested in them. Price is quite low for the simple type.*
**$10.00-$15.00**

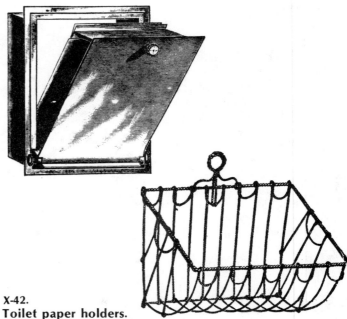

### X-42.
### Toilet paper holders.
*(L) One to be set into wall, called a "recess" holder. Approx. 7"H x 5"W. Probably meant for sheet paper. Sternau catalog, 1900. (R) Tinned twisted wire, originally made by Sherwood, this found in Paine, Diehl catalog, 1888. It was called in their catalog a "closet paper rack", and you could get it 8"W or 10"W, for either sheet paper or rolls. It is large enough for use, now, for just about anything. Twisted wire goods are very popular collectibles.*
**$12.00-$30.00**

No. 1.

No. 00.

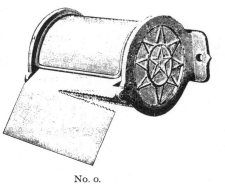

No. o.

| | | | |
|---|---|---|---|
| No. 1, Family, Bronzed, to be Used with Perforated Paper, | - - - | per dozen, | $ 2 00 |
| 00, Union, " " " Factory or Economy Paper, | - | " | 7 50 |
| 0, " " " " . " " | - - - | " | 10 00 |

## TOILET PAPER.

| | | |
|---|---|---|
| Factory not Perforated, | doz. | $2 00 |
| Economy, " " | rolls, | 2 50 |
| Perforated, Best Quality, | | 3 00 |

Chicago manilla tissue, wire loop, full 700 count......per case of 100 packages, $4 50
Less than case lots........ per doz., 60

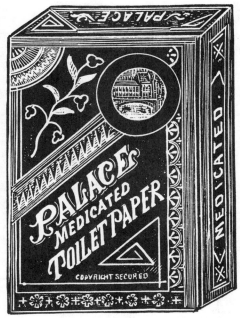

Palace, wire loop, full 1,000 count, per case of 100 packages............................. $8 65
Less than case lots...............per doz., 1 20

Standard wire loop, full 800 count, per case of 100 packages............. $5 85
Less than case lots......per doz., 75

**Toilet paper & w.c. fixtures.**
*A composite catalog page, made up from pictures from several mail order catalogs from 1885 to 1890, showing a few more graphic examples of paper wraps, and handsome rollers. Page courtesy of Ronald S. Barlow.*

*There are several clubs and publications for collectors of ephemera — ephemera being printed paper that's expected to have a very short life, for example tickets, bus transfers, trade catalogs, can labels, etc. The organizations are: Ephemera Society of America, POB 37, Schoharie, NY 12157; PAC - Association of Paper & Advertising Collectors, POB 500, Columbia, PA 17552; and Paper Collectors' Marketplace, POB 127, Scandinavia, WI 54977. Please use SASE. A fuller list is on pages 627-628, 3rd edition 300 Years of Kitchen Collectibles.*

No. 3. Hotel fixture, nickel....per doz., $6 00
" " " bronze.... " 3 00
Less 15 per cent.

**X-43.**
**Toilet paper holders.**
*Top two are both mfd. by Sternau, 1900. They are fancy cutout sheet brass, nickel plated, and furnished with a wooden roller. They "will hold rolls of paper 5"W and 4" diameter." Bottom two are from the Albert Pick catalog, 1909, but the one on the right looks very like the Sternau line. The one on the left is still found today in bus station bathrooms and out of the way rest stops. While it was claimed to be the "reguatlion style" fixture, it would "hold any size roll of toilet paper made." (R) was called in the catalog a "massive roll" holder. Original prices were about $2.00 a piece for the top ones; 20¢ and 70¢ each for the bottom ones.*
**$3.00-$22.00**

**X-44.**
**Toilet paper rolls.**
*Don't laugh! I actually started a small collection years ago of the wrapping for toilet paper, wanting only the commercial brands. They have simple, bold printing that looks like woodblock prints. I only found them in commericial settings, where extra rolls were set out in view. These are all taken from 1909 Albert Pick catalog. the wrappers appear to merely encircle the roll, and were not tucked into the top & bottom as they are today. This is a **futurewatch:** If no-one collects them before this, I'm sure that the sight of these wrappers will make them a potential ephemera collectible.*
**.50¢-$1.00**

**X-45.**
**Toilet paper rolls.**
*Ah...more appealing now? There are three with classic Art Nouveau designs to the wrappers, and three figurals. Note that while the "Lenox" has 2000 sheets, the "Mascot", with the great sulky picture, has only 1000. "Lion" and "Mascot" were pat'd June 18, 1889. In this catalog there were many other brands. The sheet size is between 4 1/2" x 5" and 4 3/4" x 5 1/2", or even larger. "Fair quality manila perforated tissue" was used for some (shades of Eastern Europe), and the best was made of "extra grade pure tissue." Some of them even claimed that the weight in ounces given was "honest weight." Albert Pick, 1909.* **$2.00-$6.00**

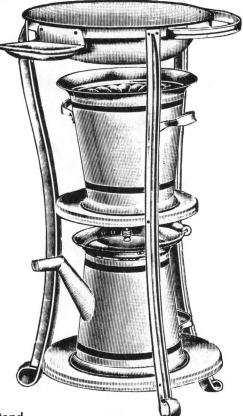

### X-47.
### Toilet stand.
*Stamped & pieced sheet metal, all white, with towel rack at right, enameled attached soap dish and loose basin, and japanned slop jar and water can. The stands varied form 30 1/2"H x 13 7/8" diameter to 30 1/2"H x 17 3/8" diameter. All the slop jars, water cans and soap dishes were the same — 10 1/2"H x 10" diameter; 10 5/8"H x 10" diameter; and 6 1/4" x 4". The basin varied from 14 1/2" diameter to 18" diameter, between 3 3/8" x 4". The basin varied from 14 1/2" diameter to 18" diameter, between 3 3/8" and 4 1/2" deep. D.J. Barry & Co., hotel suppliers, 1924.* **$90.00-$175.00**

### X-46.
### Toilet set.
*Almost a complete bathroom on a stand. A fancy japanned iron stand, surmounted by a cast cherub, with adjustable oval mirror, rack for toothbrush and comb, a wash basin, below it the slop pail for used water, below that the water can for carrying fresh water, and to the left a tumbler in a holder and to the right a soap holder. The short curved arm above the tumbler may have been for a little towel. This came in "assorted colors", some with a fancy band decorating the vessels, some finished in faux walnut or oak. 61 1/2" x 17 1/2" diameter at base. Lalance & Grosjean, NYC, 1890.* **$100.00-$250.00**

### X-48.
### Toilette sets.
*In Matthai-Ingram's "Greystone" graniteware. Above is the "Garland" style, with a 12-1/2"H water can, a 16-3/4" foot tub, and a 12"H slop jar. Below is a set the name of which was not given. Catalog c.1890. Value range for sets:* **$90.00-$200.00**

**X-49.**
**Toilet stand.**
*Simple one with colorful japanned water pitcher in a Japonism design. Could be had in "assorted colors", with bowls 12" or 14" diameter. Central Stamping Co., 1920.* **$90.00-$200.00**

**X-50.**
**Tooth polishers.**
*"For Father, Mother, Sister, Brother and Friends young and old." Comprises a metal holder with a bone, horn or celluloid handle, and ridged felt inserts. Horsey Mfg. Co., Utica, NY. Ad in* Century, *12/1888.* **$4.00-$10.00**

Pitcher and Bowl.

No. 870 Slop Jar.

No. 809 Chamber. Diameter, 9 Inches.

No. 890 Brush Vase.

No. 855 Drinking Cup.

No. 865 Brush Box, With Drainer Bars. each

No. 880 Soap Dish, With Drainer Plate.

No. 885 Sponge Holder. With Drainer Plate.

No. 895 Cosmetic Box. Nickel Plate, each, $4.00

No. 875 Dentifrice Box.

**X-52.**
**Toilette set.**
*A complete set for which you needed a table or shelves for all these things. Pitcher and bowl; slop jar for waste water; chamber pot with lid and fancy cast handle; brush vase for a toothbrush; drinking cup; a brush box, with drainer bars inside and a lid, for toothbrush; a soap dish with drainer and lid; a sponge holder with drainer; a cosmetic box (probably for powder); and a dentifrice box for tooth powder. All Manning & Bowman's "patent mottled pearl agateware" with nickel-plated white metal mountings and protection bands. Porcelainized white inside. The pitcher held 10 pints; the bowl was 18" diameter. A complete set with a brush box, not a vase, was $71.50. c.1892 catalog. Price range for set:* **$400.00-$800.00**

**X-51.**
**Tooth powder can.**
*The famous "Dr. Lyon's Perfect" powder, "used by people of refinement for over a quarter of a century, at the time of this ad, in* Century, *throughout 1891. Condition is key to value, as with all tins.* **$5.00-$25.00**

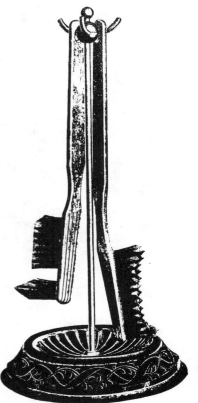

**X-53.**
**Toothbrush holder & toothbrushes.**
*Bronzed or japanned cast iron dished base with "hall tree" vertical rack for four brushes. Considered good because "the water drips from the head, keeping the brush sweet and clean." (L) the "Prophylactic" brush with a pointed tuft at the end; and (R) the "Dental Plate" brush. Mfd. by Florence Mfg. Co., Florence, AL. Ad in Century, 12/1888.* **$5.00-$15.00**

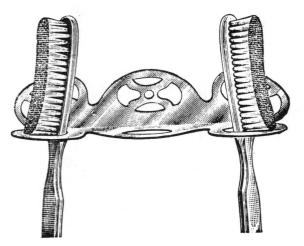

**X-54.**
**Toothbrush holder.**
*Nickeled brass, to be mounted to wall. Holds three brushes. 4 1/2"L. Norvell-Shapleigh Hardware catalog, St. Louis, 1910.* **$5.00-$10.00**

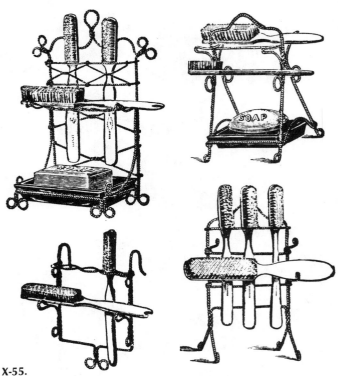

**X-55.**
**Toothbrush, soap & nail brush racks.**
*All Hayward's Patent Adjustable, made by Sherwood. All tinned iron wire. The wallhung one top left might be most valuable. It also has a glass soap dish, as does the one top right. The charm is in the wire, which is highly collectible. Paine, Diehl catalog, 1888.* **$20.00-$45.00**

**X-56.**
**Tumbler & toothbrush holders.**
*All nickeled brass. (L) for three brushes and with etched glass tumbler; (R) top for five brushes. (R) bottom with reticulated tumbler cup and rack for six brushes. It's 4 1/2"H overall, the cup is 2 7/8" diameter. Mackie-Lovejoy Mfg. Co., 1904 ad; and Albert Pick catalog, 1909.* **$5.00-$25.00**

**X-57.**
## Combination fixture.
*For tumbler, toothbrushes, and with tilting soap dish. All reticulated brass nickel-plated. Buhl Sons Co., Detroit, ad in* Hardware News, *4/1912.* **$20.00-$45.00**

**X-59.**
## Wash basins.
*Actually called "wash hand basins". Cast iron. Top is what the stove foundry who made them called the "medium"; it came in three sizes: 3 1/4"H x 8 1/2"; 3 1/2"H x 9 1/2"; and 3 3/4"H x 10" diameter. They could be had plain, tinned or porcelainized. The other called "deep", came in five sizes: 3 3/4"H x 9 1/2"; 4 1/4"H x 10 3/4"; 4 5/8"H x 11 3/4"; 5"H x 12 3/4"; and 5 3/8"H x 13 1/2", plain or tinned. Both from Leibrandt & McDowell Stove Works and Hollow-Ware Foundries, Baltimore & Philadelphia, 1861 catalog. Today some of us think there are too many choices — in everything from cereal to cars. But diversity is a requisite for a capitalist economy. Divide (confuse) & conquer (sell).* **$95.00-$150.00**

**X-58.**
## Tumbler holders.
*All wall-mounted, all nickeled brass. Upper right one has towel hook underneath. The bottom left one has a spun brass cup 3 3/16" diameter, and cast brass base & stem. It's Norvell-Shapleigh Hardware, 1910; the others are all Albert Pick, 1909.* **$5.00-$12.00**

**X-60.**
### Suction and force pump ad.
*If that man only knew what was right above him! This ad for Coles' Double Acting Suction and Force Pump, "intended for Wells, Cisterns, Factories, Railroad Stations, and all places requiring the conducting or elevation of water. They will pump Hot or Cold Water, ... in sizes to throw from 20 gallons to 9 barrels per minute." For sale at E.A. Marshall, Agent for Coles, in New York City. Ad from* History of Prominent Mercantile and Manufacturing Firms in the U.S., *by David Bigelow. Published in Boston, 1857.*

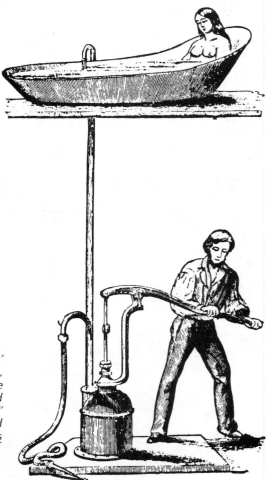

# SELECTED BIBLIOGRAPHY
## RELATED TO HOUSEKEEPING

I have put the eighty some titles here into general groups to help you find what you want. While there are a number of books related to the bathroom, for example, there are none related to the closet. I have one category called ''Object History & Identification'' for those books dealing with narrow subject areas such as sadirons, sewing machines and washboards. Other subjects await treatment in a book. The background material that will give you a better understanding of the context for the objects you collect is found in the ''Social History of Cleanliness and/or Housekeeping'' section. ''Representative Periodicals'' has a few magazines that in the past, and often in the present, have articles of interest. Most ladies' magazines, however, are not listed. Remember ''Woman's Day'' and others from the grocery checkout in the 1950s? A stack would be worth volumes today for research into mid-20th century housekeeping mores and techniques.

I have a few, but there are many more, foreign books, in English and other languages. For the most part, these have been unavailable, even unknown, here. I would be interested in knowing about books from Canada, all of Europe, Australia, New Zealand, Africa and South America relating to housework, in any language. Also please let me know about books which have been published privately.

Many of the books listed here are still in print; others are rather easily obtained through dealers who specialize in books on antiques. Some books are very hard to find; your library may be able to help you. I do not have a book-selling service at this time, and cannot assist in book searches.

### Bathroom

Frazier, Gregory & Beverly Frazier. *The Bath Book.* San Francisco, CA: Troubador Press, 1973 Some history, plus soap recipes & how-tos.

Lambton, Lucinda. *Temples of Convenience.* NYC: St. Martin's Press, 1978. About toilets — a.k.a. commodes, thrones, latrines, water closets, necessaries, johns, cans and conveniences.

Palmer, Ray. *The Water Closet.* Newton Abbot, England: David & Charles, 1973.

Pudney, John. *The Smallest Room. A Discreet Survey Through the Ages — with an Annexe.* Michael Joseph, © 1954, revised 1959. History, with amusing anecdotes, euphemisms, etc.

Scott, G.R. *The Story of Baths and Bathing.* London: T. Werner Laurie, 1939.

Wright, Lawrence. *Clean and Decent. The Unruffled History of the Bathroom and the Water Closet.* London: Routledge and Kegan Paul, 1960.

### Representative Periodicals

*American Agriculturist.* Monthly. NYC: Orange Judd & Co., 1840s-1880s.

*House Furnishing Review.* NYC: c.1890-1930. Trade journal for buyers in hardware stores & housefurnishings departments.

*Ladies' Home Journal.* Monthly. Philadelphia: Curtis Publishing Co., 1887-1920 consulted.

*Scientific American.* Weekly. NYC: Munn & Co., c.1850s-on, consulted. Nineteenth century issues almost always have something on a household improvement. A book called *Wrinkles & Recipes, Compiled from Scientific American,* was published by the magazine in 1875.

### Housekeeping How-to & Receipts

*America's Housekeeping Book,* compiled by New York Herald Tribune Home Institute, under the direction of Eloise Davison. NYC: Charles Scribner's Sons, 1941. Big, covers everything in a methodical way.

Balderston, Miss. *Housekeeping Workbook. How To Do It. House Care and Cleaning.* Chicago & Philadelphia: J.B. Lippincott Co., n.d. [c.1920s-1930s]. Quick, one-sentence guides to everything from repairing electric wires to cleaning aluminum.

Cornelius, Mrs. M.H. *The Young Housekeeper's Friend.* Boston: Taggard & Thompson, 1868.

Jewry, Mary, editor & compiler. *Warne's Model Cookery & Housekeeping Book. People's Edition.* London: Frederick Warne & Co., 1868.

Leslie, Miss Eliza. *The Housebook; or, a Manual of Domestic Economy.* Philadelphia: Carey & Hart, 1840.

Willich, Antony Florian M. *The Domestic Encyclopedia; or a Dictionary of Facts and Useful Knowledge...Chiefly Applicable to Rural and Domestic Economy.* 3 volumes. Philadelphia: W.Y. Birch & A. Small, 1803-1804. Additions brought it up to 5 volumes by 1821 edition.

### Object History & Identification

Adamson, Gareth. *Machines at Home.* London: Lutterworth Press, 1969. Includes sociology.

Andere, Mary. *Old Needlework Boxes and Tools: Their Story and How To Collect Them.* Newton Abbot, England: David & Charles; 1971.

*Antique American Sewing Machines, A Value Guide.* 3400 Park Blvd., Oakland, CA 94610: Singer Dealer Museum, 1992.

Barlow, Ronald S. *A Price Guide to Victorian Houseware, Hardware and Kitchenware.* 2147 Windmill View Rd, El Cajon, CA, 92020: Windmill Publishing Co., 1991.

Berney, Esther S. *A Collector's Guide to Pressing Irons and Trivets.* NYC: Crown Publishers, Inc., 1977. Irons, trivets, electric irons, toy irons, laundry stoves, etc.

Bremseth, Hattie. *Washboards. An Identification and Value Guide. Book I and Book II.* Grand Meadow, MN, 55936: Author, 1980; 1981

Burgess, Fred W. *Chats on Household Curios.* NYC: F.A. Stokes Co., 1914.

Cooper, Grace Rogers. *The Invention of the Sewing Machine. Bulletin 254.* Washington, DC: Smithsonian Institution, 1968.

Corley, Thomas Anthony Buchanan. *Domestic Electrical Appliances.* London: Jonathon Cape, 1966.

Cripps, Ann, editor. *The Countryman Book of Rescuing the Past. Articles from The Countryman* magazine. Newton Abbot, England: David & Charles, 1973. Rural trades, domestic life, includes laundry.

de Haan, David. *Antique Household Gadgets and Appliances 1860-1930.* Poole, England: Blandford Press, 1977.

*Dover Stamping Co. 1869. Tinware, Tin Toys, Tinned Iron Wares, Tinners Material, Enameled Stove Hollow Ware, Tinners' Tools and Machines.* Illustrated Catalog and Historical Introduction. American Historical Catalog Collection. Princeton, NJ: The Pyne Press, 1971. Includes tinware for toilette.

Franklin, Linda Campbell. *300 Years of Kitchen Collectibles.* Second edition. Florence, AL: Books Americana, 1984.

Fredgant, Don. *Electrical Collectibles.* San Luis Obispo, CA: Padre Productions, 1981.

Glissman, A.H. *Evolution of the Sad-Iron.* Oceanside, CA: Author, 1970.

Gilbert, Keith Reginald. *Sewing Machines.* Science Museum. London: Her Majesty's Stationery Office, 1970.

Gordon, Bob. *Early Electrical Appliances.* Aylesbury, Bucks, England: Shire Publications Ltd., 1984. 32 pages booklet overview.

Groves, Sylvia. *The History of Needlework Tools and Accessories.* NYC: Arco, 1973.

Hankenson, Dick. *Trivets, Books 1 & 2.* Maple Plain, MN: Author, 1963; 1965 [?]

Harrison, Molly. *Home Inventions.* London: Usborne Publications, 1975.

Head, Carol. *Old Sewing Machines.* Aylesbury, Bucks, England: Shire Publications Ltd., 1986.

Herzberg, Rudolph. *The Sewing Machine: Its History, Construction, and Application.* Tr. from German by U. Green. London: E & F.N. Spon, 1864.

Horowitz, Estelle & Ruth Mann. *Victorian Brass Needlecases.* 3379 Stewart Ave., Los Angeles, CA 90066: Author, 1990.

Houart, Victor. *Sewing Accessories. An Illustrated History.* London: Souvenir Press, 1984.

Hutchinson, E. Lillian. *The Housefurnishings Department. Kitchenware & Laundry Equipment.* (Department Store Merchandise Manuals series). NYC: Ronald Press Co., 1918. Lots of manufacturing background; good descriptions of tools and equipment, with selling points.

Jewell, Brian. *Smoothing Irons. A Historical and Collector's Guide.* Tunbridge Wells, Kent, England; and Des Moines, IA: Midas Books; and Wallace-Homestead Book Co., 1977. Sadirons, smoothing irons, goffering irons.

Jewell, Brian. *Sewing Machines.* Tunbridge Wells, Kent, England: Midas Books, 197-?

Johnson, Eleanor. *Needlework Tools.* Aylesbury, Bucks, England: Shire Publications Ltd., 1978.

Kelly, Rob Roy & James Ellwood. *A Collector's Guide to Trivets & Stands.* P.O. Box 1110, Lima, OH 45802: Golden Era Publications, 1990.

Lancaster, Maud. *Electric Cooking, Heating & Cleaning.* NYC: D. Van Nostrand, 1914.

Lasansky, Jeannette. *To Cut, Piece, & Solder. Work of the Rural Pennsylvania Tinsmith 1778-1908.* Lewisbury, PA: Oral Traditions, 1982.

Leoni. *Macchine per Cucire. (Sewing Machines)* Milan, Italy: BE-MA Editrice, 1987. Small format, gorgeous pictures, bi-lingual (Italian & English).

Lewton, Frederick L. *The Servant in the House. A Brief History of the Sewing Machine.* From the *Smithsonian Report.* Washington, DC: 1930.

Lifshey, Earl. *The Housewares Story: A History of the American Housewares Industry.* Chicago, IL: National Housewares Manufacturers Association, 1973. Incredibly useful, well-illustrated trade-sponsored history.

Lincoln, E.S. & Paul Smith. *The Electrical Home. A Standard Ready Reference Book.* NYC: Electric Home Publishing, 1936.

Longman, Elanor D. & Sophy Loch. *Pins and Pincushions.* London; NYC: Longmans, Green, 1911.

Lundquist, Myrtle. *The Book of a Thousand Thimbles.* Des Moines, IA: Wallace-Homestead, 1970.

Macdonald, Anne L. *Feminine Ingenuity: Women and Invention in America.* NYC: Ballantine Books, 1992. Author of *No Idle Hands* and patent holder herself for a knitting device, this chronicles 200 years of female inventors in many fields.

*L.H. Mace & Co. 1883. Woodenware, Meat Safes, Toys, Refrigerators, Children's Carriages and House Furnishing Goods.* Illustrated Catalog and Historical Introduction. American Historical Catalog Collection. Princeton, NJ: The Pyne Press, 1971. Woodenwares, many kitchen, many toys, some laundry, etc.

Matthai-Ingram Co. *Illustrated Catalogue of Sheet Metal Goods. Catalog 41.* Baltimore: c.1890.

Matter & Matter. *Collector's Guide to Toy Sewing Machines.* P.O. Box 1110, Lima, OH 45802: Golden Era Publications, 199-?

Mitchell, James R., editor. *Antique Metalware. Brass, Bronze, Copper, Tin, Wrought & Cast Iron.* NYC: Universe Books, c.1976. Anthology of metal-related articles from *The Magazine ANTIQUES,* 1922-1976.

*Official Gazette.* Washington, DC: U.S. Patent Office, 1873-. Also illustrated patent records prior to the *Gazette.*

Palla, Laura. *I Ferri Da Stiro. (Flat-Irons)* Milan, Italy: BE-MA Editrice, 1987. Small format, gorgeous pictures, bi-lingual (Italian & English).

Peet, Louise Jenison & Lenore E. Sater. *Household Equipment.* NYC: John Wiley & Sons, 1934; 1940.

Pinto, Edward H. *Treen & Other Wooden Bygones.* London: Bell & Hyman, 1969. Reprinted in 1979.

Politzer, Judy & Frank. *Tuesday's Children: Collecting Little Irons and Trivets.* San Francisco: Stone Press, 1977.

Politzer, Judy & Frank. *Early Tuesday Morning — More Little Irons and Trivets.* San Francisco: Stone Press, 197-?.

Quennell, M. & C.H.B. Quennell. *A History of Everyday Things in England. Part 3: The Rise of Industrialism, 1733-1851.* London: Batsford, 3rd ed., 1945. Includes chapter on sanitation and bathrooms. 1851 saw opening of world-shaking Crystal Palace Exhibition in London.

Revi, Albert Christian, editor. *Spinning Wheel's Collectible Iron, Tin, Copper & Brass.* Pasadena, CA: Castle Books, 1974. Anthologized articles from late, lamented magazine.

Rihn, Gerald J. *Antique Irons. A Pictorial History of Irons.* Glenshaw, PA: Author, 1972. Irons and trivets

Rogers, Gay Ann. *An Illustrated History of Needlework Tools.* London: John Murray, 1983.

Russell, Loris S. *Handy Things to Have Around the House: Oldtime Domestic Appliances of Canada & the United States.* NYC: McGraw-Hill Ryerson Ltd., 1979. Tools for fireplace, cooking, lighting, textiles, clothing & housecleaning.

Sambrook, Pamela. *Laundry Bygones.* Aylesbury, Bucks, England: Shire Publications Ltd., 1983

Seymour, John. *The National Trust Book of Forgotten Household Crafts.* London: Dorling Kindersley, 1987. Much on laundering & housecleaning, and also the bathroom.

Sparke, Penny. *Electrical Appliances. Twentieth-century Design.* First published in Great Britain. NYC: E.P. Dutton, 1987.

*Subject-Matter Index of Patents for Inventions. Issued by the U.S. Patent Office, 1790 to 1873, Inclusive.* 3 volumes. NYC: Arno Press, 1976.

Thompson, Frances. *Mountain Relics: Vanishing Artifacts as Collectibles.* Cranbury, NJ: A.S. Barnes & Co., Inc., 1976. Arranged by a week of housekeeping, each day's chores handled separately.

Toller, Jane. *Turned Woodware for Collectors. Treen & Other Objects.* Cranbury, NJ: A.S. Barnes, 1975.

Whiting, Gertrude. *Old-Time Tools and Toys of Needlework.* NYC: Dover, 1971. Reprint of 1928 edition.

Zalkin, Estelle. *Zalkin's Handbook of Thimbles & Sewing Implements.* Willow Grove, PA: Warman Publishing CO., 1988

## Sociology of Cleanliness, Housekeeping & Women's Work

Baker, Elizabeth F. *Technology and Women's Work.* NYC: Columbia University Press, 1964.

Beer, William R. *Househusbands. Men and Housework in American Families.* South Hadley, MA: Bergin & Garvey Publishers, 1983. Results of studies and interviews, includes questionnaire used by Beer.

Bode, Carl, editor. *Midcentury America. Life in the 1850s.* Carbondale, IL: Southern Illinois University Press, 1972. Popular culture of the time between pioneer days and full steam industrialization.

Bradley, Rose. *The English Housewife in the Seventeenth and Eighteenth Centuries.* London: Edward Arnold, 1912.

Byers, Anthony. *Centinary of Service: A History of Electricity in the Home.* London: Electricity Council, 1981.

Cowan, Ruth Schwartz. *More Work for Mother. The Ironies of Household Technology from the Open Hearth to the Microwave.* NYC: Basic Books Co., Inc., 1983. Pre-industrial to late 20th C housework vis a vis technological change and ''progress''.

Davidson, Caroline. *A Woman's Work Is Never Done. A Social History of Housework in the British Isles 1650-1950.* London: Chatto and Windus, 1982.

Ehrenreich, Barbara & Dirdre English. *For Her Own Good. 150 Years of the Experts' Advice to Women.* Garden City, NY; then London: Anchor Press/Doubleday; Pluto Press, 1978; 1979. Chapter ''Microbes and the Manufacture of Housework'' on domestic science, new tasks, germs.

Faulkner, Wendy & Erik Arnold, editors. *Smothered by Invention: Technology in Women's Lives.* London: Pluto Press, 1985. One section is on housework technologies & how women work just as hard or harder, even with better tools, in order to fulfill increased expectations.

Giedion, Siegfried. *Mechanization Takes Command. A Contribution to Anonymous History.* NYC: Oxford University Press, 1948. How human lives are affected by machines. One section is entitled ''Mechanization Encounters the Household''.

Gilbreath, Lilian. *The Home-Maker and Her Job.* NYC: D. Appleton, 1927.

Gilman, Charlotte Perkins. *The Home: Its Work and Influence.* Reprint. Urbana, IL: University of Illinois Press, 1972 (© 1903). Pioneering feminist.

Green, Harvey. With the assistance of Mary-Ellen Perry. *The Light of the Home. An Intimate View of the Lives of Women in Victorian America.* NYC: Pantheon Books, 1983. Illustrated with artifacts from Margaret Woodbury Strong Museum; accompanied exhibit of household tools, etc., in social context.

Hardyment, Christina. *From Mangle to Microwave. The Mechanization of Household Work.* Cambridge, England; and NYC: Polity Press; and Basil Blackwell Inc., 1988. Servants, sewing machines, laundry, housecleaning, bathroom, kitchen gadgets, etc.

Hayden, Dolores. *The Grand Domestic Revolution: A History of Feminist Designs for American Homes, Neighborhoods, and Cities.* Cambridge, MA & London: The MIT Press, 1981. New ''woman's places'', from communal kitchens to women's hotels to sharing housework with husbands.

Katzman, David M. *Seven Days a Week. Women and Domestic Service in Industrializing America.* NYC: Oxford University Press, 1978. Study of domestic servants.

McBride, Theresa M. *The Domestic Revolution. The Modernization of Household Service in England and France 1820-1920.* London: Croom Helm, 1980 (© 1976).

McLaughlin, Terence. *Dirt. A Social History as Seen Through the Uses and Abuses of Dirt.* NYC: Stein & Day Publishers, 1971.

Meinhardt, Lela & Paul Meinhardt. *Cinderella's Housework Dialectics. Housework as the Root of Human Creation.* 277 Hillside Ave., Nutley, NJ, 07110: Incunabula Press, 1977. Feminism, mysticism, archaeology, by two people living in commune.

Mussey, Barrows, editor. *Yankee Life by Those Who Lived It.* NYC: Alfred Knopf, 1947. Excerpts from journals, autobiographies, letters, etc.

Oakley, Ann. *The Sociology of Housework.* London: Martin Robertson, 1974.

Plunkett, Mrs. H.M. *Women, Plumbers and Doctors, or Household Sanitation.* NYC: D. Appleton, 1897

Reynolds, Reginald. *Cleanliness and Godliness or The Further Metamorphosis. A Discussion of the Problems of Sanitation raised by Sir John Harington, together with Reflections upon Further Progress recorded since that Excellent Knight, by his Invention of the Metamorphosed AJAX Father of Conveniences... with numerous digressions upon all aspects of cleanliness.* Garden City, NY: Doubleday & Co., 1946. Informative & amusing narrative packed with social history.

Strasser, Susan. *Never Done. A History of American Housework.* NYC: Pantheon Books, 1982. So-called labor-savers, effect of advertising, the ''servant question'', and the science of housekeeping.

*Utne Reader. The best of the alternative press.* Articles: ''The second shift,'' Arlie Hochschild; ''Must men fear women's work?'', Mary Stewart Van Leeuwen; ''Domestic chores weren't always women's work,'' Debbie Taylor; ''Change the family; change the world,'' Susan Moller Okin; ''Sloppy housekeepers unite,'' Ann Lovejoy; ''How to love housework,'' Thich Nhat Hanh; ''Beginner's guide to housework,'' Dave Barry; ''Rediscovering a partnership society,'' Raine Eisler. Also cartoons. Pittsfield, MA: Utne Reader, March/April 1990. Articles mainly reprinted from other publications.

Wallance, Don. *Shaping America's Products.* NYC: Reinhold, 1956. Industrial design.

Wiebe, Robert H. *The Search for Order.* NYC: Hill & Wang, 1967.

Yarwood, Doreen. *Five Hundred Years of Technology in the Home.* London: B.T. Batsford Ltd., 1983.

# INDEX

# An Identification and Value Guide
# 300 Years of
# KITCHEN COLLECTIBLES
# Third Edition
## by Linda Campbell Franklin

**$22<sup>95</sup>**

plus $3.00 shipping

The collectors will find this 3rd Edition has doubled in size and information over the 2nd edition.

- 7000 plus fully described price listings
- 1800 plus illustrations and photos
    showing over 5000 items
- 111 old-fashioned recipes

Containing Sections on:

**Preparing, Measuring, Holding and Handling, Cooking, Preserving, Kitchen Furnishing, Electric Gadgets, Appliances, etc.**